T3-BIE-824

The super catalog of car parts and accessories

The super catalog of car parts and accessories

by John Hirsch

WP

Workman Publishing
Company, New York

Workman Publishing Company
231 East 51st Street
New York, New York 10022

Printed in the United States of America

Hardcover ISBN: 0-911104-32-1

Paperback ISBN: 0-911104-33-x

Cover: Paul Hanson

If you know of a parts source or car club that should be included in a future edition of this book, won't you please let us know by writing to the author at R. R. 1, Box 6, Berme Road, Kerhonkson, New York 12446. All suggestions resulting in new entries will be acknowledged in print.

First printing: April 1974

This book is dedicated to:

All the auto enthusiasts, particularly car club members, who generously responded to my requests for information. Capt. Ralph S. Stevens, Jr. and Dr. Henry J. Kelley were most helpful of all.

All the fine mechanics I have known, most especially the late Walter L. "Sonny" Lewis, Jr.

And to those who helped in the considerable correspondence, record-keeping and typing which this book entailed— Ronnie Bruh, Kathy Clinton and Amy Hirsch.

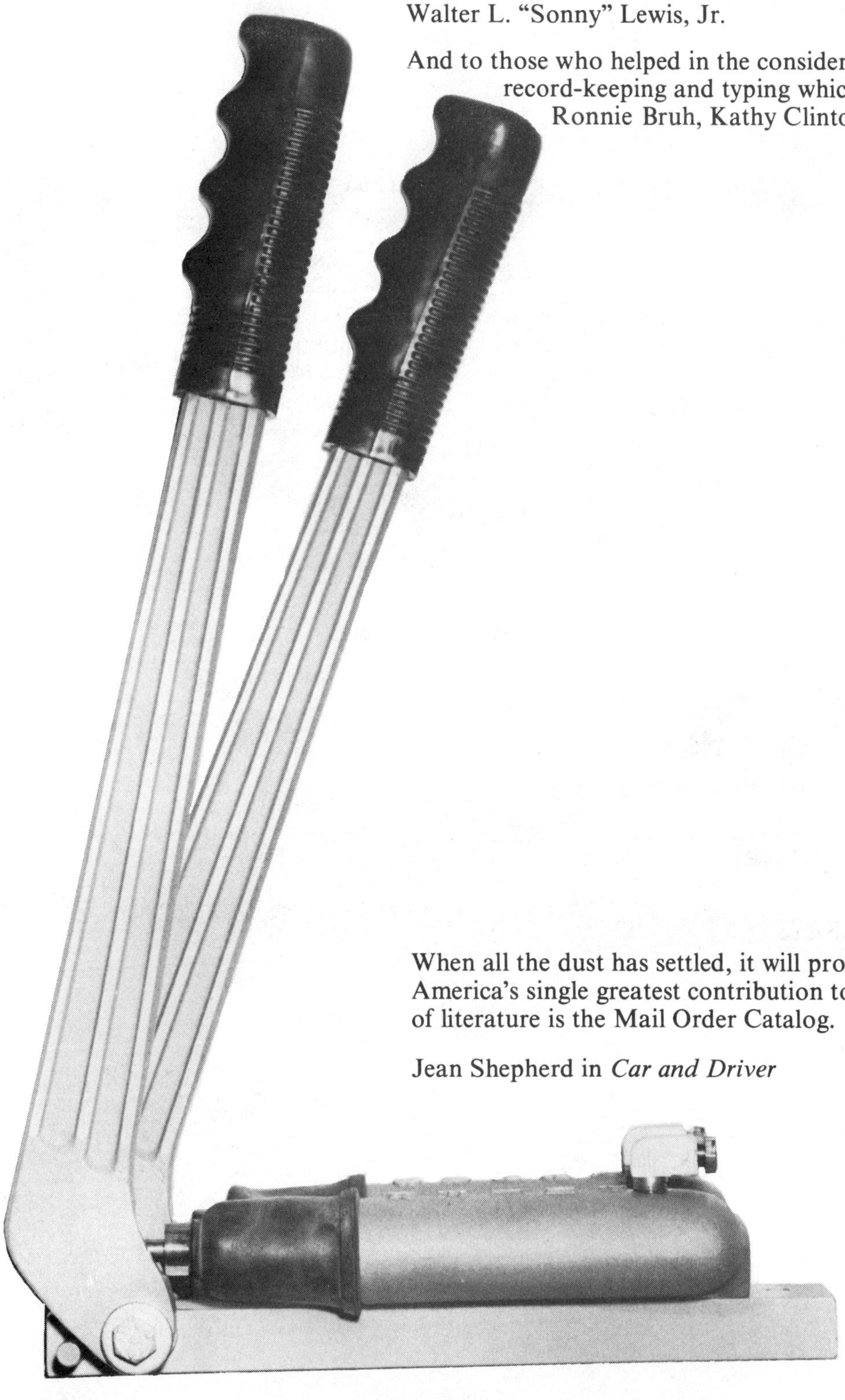

When all the dust has settled, it will probably turn out that America's single greatest contribution to the world's stockpile of literature is the Mail Order Catalog.

Jean Shepherd in *Car and Driver*

CARTER

Contents

AUTO METER
REV-CONTROL
MODEL 452
GRD.
-METER+
DIST.
PRI.
OFF-TIME
ADJUST
DECREASE
AUTO METER PROD. INC ELGIN, ILL.

11

Introduction

World War II was hardly over when the first MG-TCs were imported and the cult of the sports car took wing. Buicks had portholes. Deuce roadsters still had metal bodies and flathead engines in those days. Incredible classics like J Duesenbergs and Marmon V-16s could be turned up mouldering away in some country barn and purchased for less than a fortune. People laughed at Volkswagens with their queerly-sloping fronts and little split windows. Mickey Thompson and Don Garlits were crew-cut youngsters, more talented than most but still classified as "crazy hot rodders" by their conservative elders.

During the postwar era and on into the early fifties, the sports car movement mushroomed. At least there were enough of them around so that their owners occasionally encountered each other on the streets and waved to signal their common contempt for Detroit iron. Hot rods and street rods became more numerous also, and a young man named Bob Petersen, who had been just barely meeting his printing bills with a new magazine daringly called *Hot Rod*—still a semi-outlaw term—suddenly began to prosper. By the end of the decade, automotive specialty shops were already springing up in little towns all over California.

If we could look at the automotive world today through the perspective of that exciting era when the outlines of our national mania for cars were so firmly shaped, it is not the magnitude or diversity of the movement that would astonish us, but rather its eclecticism. For today we have dune buggies and plushed-up vans, custom cars which are both more raunchy and more sophisticated than their "frenched and decked" forbears, special-interest cars which have taken the place of unavailable classics, antiques, sports cars, semi-custom Detroit cars which go and handle right off the showroom floor, utility vehicles—pickup trucks and four-wheel drives—which are much modified and used solely for pleasure, small foreign sedans at the drag strips, fiberglass replicas of classics; and there are always options which can transform the mildest little-old-lady car into a rip-snorting performer, capable of giving Ralph Nader the d.t.'s.

Perhaps it is this very diversity of choice, this combination of plushness and performance, backyard ingenuity and engineering sophistication, outlandish styling and everyday practicality, which has broken down those barriers which were once so much a mark of the car enthusiast *virgo intacta.*

Jaguar rear ends are now a popular item on Ford pickup trucks, but Ford parts can also be found on Jaguars. Sports cars are being hot-rodded and hot rods made to handle. Sleek Lamborghinis and wacky Fad Ts stand side-by-side in the same garage while the editor of a popular rodder's magazine confesses his ambition of finding a nice Bentley, vintage '55 or so, lowering it all around, fitting mag wheels and fat tires, hood louvres, a V-8 engine with Turbo-Hydro.

Volkswagens are tricked out with fiberglass parts to look like old Ford V-8s—or mini Rolls-Royces. DeSotos with gigantic tailfins and rococo pushbutton shifters are coming on strong as collector's items. People who used to drive Ramblers and Falcons are now busily at work building street rods out of old delivery vans or racing around in goosed up plastic creations cleverly disguised as Datsuns and VWs. They are jazzing up classics with 19 coats of metalflake lacquer and roll and tuck upholstery à la George Barris.

Cars are becoming more blatant and a lot funnier. We have learned to recognize the excesses of the past and to revel in them. Some will inevitably see this as a weakening of the old standards, the pristine definitions of "what is a sports car?" and so on. Others will find, in this blurring of thoroughbred lines, a rebirth rather than a mongrelization. A redefinition of the pleasure vehicle as one which brings frank and unashamed joy.

By now you know where my sympathies lie. Sure, cars are hazardous, dirty and expensive. They pollute the atmosphere, cause untold accidents, and cost a good bit of the national income to maintain. And maybe they are substitutes for sexual and/or aggressive impulses as certain psychologists assert. And perhaps they have no future as mass transportation. So much the better. Let them be pure pleasure objects, free from the encumbrances of harnesses, buzzers, and Tom Swiftian emission-control devices. Let them be individual and idiosyncratic; fine gadgets upon which to lavish all our neuroses. Let them be swift and graceful and untamed.

This book is aimed at the confirmed enthusiast who knows what he wants, but isn't sure where to get it. The sources listed range from giant mail-order houses, such as J.C. Whitney and Honest Charley, to the many individuals who have turned their hobbies into part-time businesses in order to stay ahead of the game.

The emphasis is on U.S. suppliers, who are most readily accessible, though many foreign sources offering unique or scarce items are included.

The book also covers auto clubs which offer parts-locating services and technical advice, or carry advertisements in their newsletters.

I have tried to exclude products of dubious value without eliminating those which appeal to some tastes and not to others. There are no magic engine rejuvenators or amazing battery additives listed within these pages, but readers are likely to encounter at least a few items which seem juvenile or tasteless. My only excuse is that I had fun writing about the more esoteric examples of automobiliana and I hope that most will enjoy reading about them.

Although I have attempted to make the book as complete and useful as possible, there is obviously no way a single individual could test even a small fraction of the items covered. All I can honestly say is that no one paid to be included.

Each entry in the book is a result of direct correspondence. There are no old lists reprinted or obsolete addresses listed as current at the time of publication. Those who failed to answer queries were not listed, without exception.

The Super Catalog of Car Parts and Accessories is designed to please catalog freaks as well as car lovers, and I make no apologies for its unabashed materialism. In an age when the most popular works are no longer the Bible and Shakespeare, but the Sears-Roebuck catalog and the S & H Green Stamp book, who is there to cavil at the car enthusiast and his preoccupations?

How to use this book

All listings are alphabetical. If you are interested in parts for a particular brand of car, or accessories and services within a certain category, you will find a detailed breakdown in the index at the back of the book.

Prices are for information and comparison only. Since shipping charges and applicable taxes are not included, it is wise to get a price quote directly from the supplier before you order. In any case, prices current at the time this book was published will probably be higher by the time your order goes in. This is known as inflation.

Lest there be any confusion, neither the publisher nor the author of this book is in the parts supply businesss *Send your order or query to the source listed, not to us.*

Since many suppliers print their catalogs only once or twice a year and sometimes run out, there is occasionally a long delay before a catalog is received. The only answer is to be patient or take your business somewhere else.

Many manufacturers will not ship merchandise until a personal check has cleared the bank. For swifter service, send a bank check or money order. For payment to suppliers outside the U.S., an international money order, which is available at any post office, will bring the fastest shipment.

To avoid confusion about which part you want, it is wise to state the make, model, year, chassis number, and—if applicable—the engine number of your car when you send in an order.

Although commercial suppliers and car clubs listed in this book often have a great deal of technical expertise at hand, they have neither the time nor the clerical help to answer extensive queries. Most will answer short and pertinent questions, especially those which relate to the use of a product, if you include a self-addressed stamped envelope and leave room in your letter for a handwritten reply to be penciled in. When corresponding with suppliers outside the U.S. and Canada, an international reply coupon should be forwarded along with your self-addressed envelope.

A & A Fiberglass, Inc.
1534 Nabell Avenue
Atlanta, Georgia 30344

Makers of that legendary kit to transform the homely old Beetle to an elegant Rolls-Royce. Price for the complete kit is $695.00. A rally sport kit for Vegas, consisting of front bumper, front panel, front spoiler with dual air ducts for brake cooling, bolt-on hood scoop, rear spoiler, and Trans-Am type stone guards, lists for $239.50. A "Boss" Pinto kit, with front and rear spoilers, hood scoop, and stone guards, is $112.50. Some other fiberglass body parts of interest are spoilers for the Datsun 240Z; universal air foils and spoilers; Continental-style trunk lids for recent Cougars, Torinos, Montegos, Thunderbirds and Pinto sedans; VW chopper kits; hood scoops of all types; Corvette flares; Stingray-type replacement hoods for the Camaro, Chevelle, and Chevy II; and fiberglass replacement parts for the 1948-53 Anglia, 1955-57 Chev, Camaro, Challenger, Chevelle, Chevy II, 'Cuda, Dart/Demon, Duster/Scamp, GTO, Hornet, Comet/Maverick, Mustang, Pinto, and Vega. Some items for these cars have been discontinued from stock and are now available on a custom basis only. Custom-made items include body parts for 1937-42 Willys. Free information.

VW Beetle transformed with an A & A Fiberglass, Inc. kit

A & W Chrysler Performance Products
11801 East Slauson
Building E
Santa Fe Springs
California 90670

Mopar racing equipment. Full-competition oiling system for small-block Chrysler engines. High performance pump shafts, adjustable rocker arms, roller tip rockers, hard chrome rocker shafts, rocker shaft plugs to prevent oil pressure loss during engine tear down, cam sprocket washers, 340 engine gear drive, double roller timing chains, pre-oiling tool to obtain oil pressure before engine is started, taper bore ring compressors, high performance con rods and bolts, overlength head bolts, fully-degreed balancers, aluminum crankshaft and alternator pulleys, fuel "Y" block kits, lifter valley oil baffles, flex hones for Chrysler engines, engine cleaning brush kit, main bolt kits for Mopar engines. Free literature.

R. C. Abarta
18950 Ansley Place
Saratoga, California 95070

Buys and sells auto literature of all types and quantities. Send a stamped, self-addressed envelope with query.

Roger Abbott
1199 South El Molino
Pasadena, California 91106

Packard items include collected Packard service letters for all 1933 and '34 Packards (104 pages) at $6.50 (photo-offset reproduction with many illustrations), Packard pedal arm seals for clutch and brake arms at $3.85 a pair, booklet of basic mechanical and electrical information on 1923-32 Packard 8 (except Model 900), which is a 16-page reprint of the Factory-issued workshop letters, at $3.00, and gearshift boots for 1940-54 at $2.75. Custom runningboard side moldings for any car made of stainless steel. Free information.

Abingdon Spares Ltd.
1329 Highland Avenue
Needham, Massachusetts 02192

New mechanical and body parts, wooden coachwork and upholstery items for MG TC, TD, and TF. TC and early TD head gaskets are $13.55; TC oil pans go for $64.00; and reconditioned radiator cores for the TC-TD are $95.00. Some other prices are: oil pumps, $44.00; clutch discs, $20.50; clutch pressure plates, $24.95; TC front end kingpin set, $14.00; major carb overhaul kit, $14.00; cowl rubber, $4.00; TC map reading light, $5.40; TF fuel pump, $22.50; wiring harnesses, $37.20; 19″ wire wheels, $47.00; TD-TF master cylinders, $23.50; polished aluminum valve covers, $25.95; TD-TF anti-sway bars, $29.50; leather upholstery seat kits, $175.00; TD-TF carpet sets, $52.00; combination oil pressure/water temperature gauges, $25.00 exchange; floor boards, $16.60; TC-TD walnut veneer dash panel, $22.50; TD muffler and tail pipe, $27.50; and TF grille slat set, $36.00. Catalog, $.50.

AC Cars Ltd.
High Street
Thames Ditton
Surrey
England

Mr. D. Taylor, the store's manager, advises that parts catalogs and price lists are out of print, but certain parts for older ACs are still available. Prices and parts will be quoted upon application.

ACF Industries, Inc.
Carter Carburetor Division
2840 North Spring Avenue
St. Louis, Missouri 63107

Carter carbs include the well-known Dune Buggy Deuce, the Thermo-Quad and the AFB matched dual quad sets. Carter also makes carb rebuild kits, high capacity filters, fuel line adaptors, combined "Electromech" electrical and mechanical fuel pump systems, and Strip-Kits containing rods, jets, needles and seats for the trackside mechanic. Free literature.

Acme Fabricating Co.
Corvette Corner
2409 17th Street
San Francisco, California 94110

Fiberglass body panels for Corvettes and other sports cars. The Corvette line is rather complete and goes back to the seminal 1953-55 Vettes. Panels are represented to be at least the quality of factory stock. Lighter than stock panels for competition cars can also be furnished. A complete front end shell less hood for 1956-57 models goes for $223.33, while the same component for 1968-71 Vettes is $233.33. Also available are one-quarter, half, and three-quarter front end panels, hoods, fenders, inner panels, rear shells in one-quarter, half and three-quarter varieties as well as full shells, trunk lids, door skins and fastback roofs. Custom parts, available for many Corvette models, include flared fenders to accommodate wide wheels, spoilers, two varieties of custom fronts for 1958-62 models, called the "X-7 Shark" and "The Elegance," and a modified front end with fixed headlights (rather than disappearing ones) for 1968-72 models called "The Potrero." For the Lotus Elan, Acme offers front end parts and fiberglass bumpers. There is also a rather attractive Sprite/Midget custom front with a racing car look, flared VW fenders for big wheels, Jaguar XK-E replacement front ends with or without ducting (the "with" version costs $437.33), and various Corvette tops. Catalog, $1.00.

Active Antenna Co.
P.O. Box 18967
Raleigh, North Carolina 27609

The miniature electronic antennas offered by this Company feature electronic integration of antenna elements and amplifiers. This allows an optimum signal-to-noise ratio. The Alpha-3 model ($26.00) is incorporated in a fender-mounted rearview mirror, while the Beta-3 antenna ($22.50) is a stainless steel whip only 15.75" long. The antennas are for negative ground systems only. An extension cable kit is optional. Free literature.

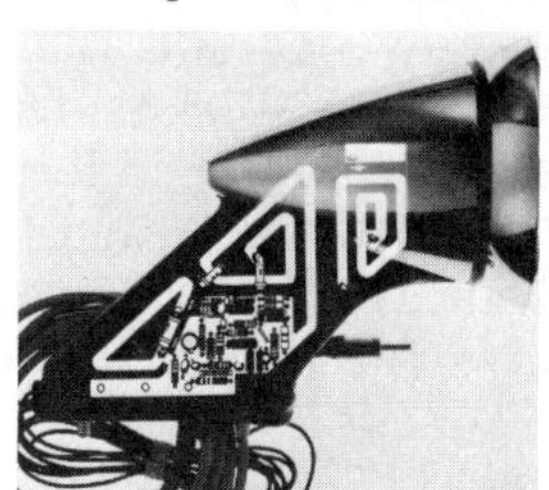

The Alpha-3 antenna from Active Antenna Co.

Adams & Oliver Ltd.
Ramsey Road
Warboy
Huntingdonshire
England

Complete service and spare parts for 1925-65 Rolls-Royce and Bentley. Some new parts manufactured by Adams & Oliver for these cars include radiator caps and mascots, replacement fiberglass fender and rocker panels for standard postwar Rolls and Bentley, exhaust systems, and special tools. The company will also do repairs or complete restorations, supply all the literature available on these cars, or sell the cars themselves to overseas buyers. Another service to overseas visitors is a long term leasing and repurchase plan. Adams and Oliver will further inspect cars for purchase, insurance evaluation, and probate. Write for further information.

Addco
40 Watertower Road
Lake Park, Florida 33403

Anti-sway bars for most domestic cars and Alfa Romeo, Austin, Mini-Minor, Austin-Healey, Sunbeam, smaller BMWs, Datsun, Fiat 850 and 124, Capri, Cortina, MGA and later MGs, Mazda, Opel, Porsche 911 and 914, Renault 10, Toyota, Triumph, VW, and Volvo. Prices range from approximately $30.00 to $45.00. Free literature; booklet on handling, $1.00.

ADEC, Inc.
P.O. Box 3738
Danville, Virginia 24541

Training is offered in Formula Ford, Touring, GT and Baby Grand cars at the ADEC school of motor racing. Courses are held at Virginia International Raceway near Danville. There is a two-day master drivers course, three-day novice racing course, and three-day advanced racing course. Tuition is $150.00 a day if the school car is used, and $120.00 a day if the student uses his own car. Those who wish to go around the track in their own cars and receive a critique can do so for $50.00 a day. Free information.

Advance Adapters
12120 Woodruff Avenue
Downey, California 90241

Makes kits to adapt most automatic and manual transmissions to the transfer cases of popular 4WD vehicles. Prices range from $125.00 to $295.00. Also makes engine to transmission adapters for Jeeps and Scouts taking Chev, Ford, Chevy II and Vega engines. Other off-road accessories in stock are conversion kits for installing Saginaw steering boxes in Jeeps, Bronco constant velocity driveshaft replacement parts ($49.50), Jeep V-6 scattershields, Jeep floating axle kits, Jeep cable clutch linkage control assemblies, Toyota Land Cruiser engine conversion kits, Toyota heavy-duty clutches, Toyota mechanical transfer case shifters, Heco hydraulic steering stabilizers, Cutlas free-wheeling hubs, roll bars, Gabriel and Delco shocks, tow bars, custom steering wheels, Stewart-Warner instruments, alloy wheels, Jeep V-6 intake manifolds, transmission coolers, Warn and Superwinch electric winches, shifter repair kits ($1.80), gaskets, tune-up kits, and many other small mechanical components. Fiberglass body parts in stock are fender extenders for Land Cruiser, Bronco, Jeep CJ and Jeepster; dashboards to fit the Jeep CJ-5 and M38 A-1; and Jeep floorboard covers and firewalls. Advance Adapters carries headers specially designed for engine conversions. Free catalog.

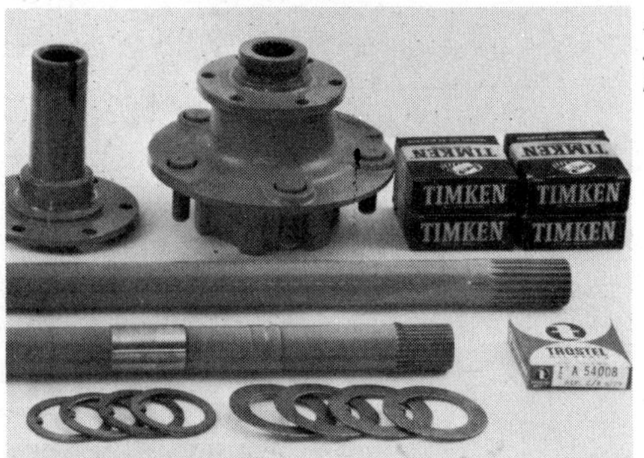

Advance Adapters' Jeep floating axle kit

Advanced Four Wheel Drive
2354 East Huntington Drive
Duarte, California 91010

Accessories for popular 4WD vehicles. Toyota carpeting $39.95, overdrive $375.00, headers $90.00, V-8 conversion Toyota headers $115.00, Offy dual carb manifold for Toyota to '67 is $89.50 and valve cover $39.95. Husky overdrive for Jeep, $234.95. Bronco and Blazer roll bars with padding, $49.95. Toyota V-8 conversion kits, $155.00 and up. Other items include Gabriel shocks, Filtron air cleaners, Holley and Rochester carbs, Muncie 4-speed adapters, Hurst shifters, Heco steering stabilizers, Warn electric winches, tow bars, auxiliary gas tanks, cage roll bars, Flex-a-Lite fans. Free price list. Write for availability of catalog.

Advance Fiberglass
P.O. Box 762
421 East Broadway
Haverhill, Massachusetts 01830

Fiberglass bodies and repro parts. Bodies include '23 T-Bucket ($120.00), '23 T-Tourer ($175.00), '27 T-Roadster ($160.00), '32 Austin-Bantam Roadster ($125.00), and C-J2 Jeep. Parts are for '55 and '57 Chev, '28-'29 Ford coupe (front and rear fenders), early and late Corvettes (flares), and some general hot-rodding parts such as short pick-up beds with lids, rod fenders (6″, 9″, 12″ wide) and fiberglass bucket seats. All fiberglass items have outer layer of smooth white or colored gel coat. Dune buggy type bodies for street use are available in styles known as Rough Rider III (4 seater), Rough Rider SW (fits unshortened VW chassis), Pioneer SW Pick-Up and Special Sport T. Prices are $325.00 to $380.00. "Glowble" flake finish is $20.00 extra. Also has $50.00 kit, with any body, which includes windshield frame, headlights, fasteners and instruction booklet. Other items include hood scoops, VW fiberglass parts and Baja bug kits, VW accessories, fiberglass materials, and special order Deuce Roadster bodies. Free literature and price lists.

Aero Tec Laboratories
1100 Blanch Avenue
Norwood, New Jersey 07648

Safety fuel cells approved for racing by SCCA, USAC, FIA, IMSA and NASCAR. Sports cell, for use with gasoline only and not intended for fast refueling, $149.95 for 8 gallon size to $239.95 for 22 gallon size. Super cell, for various fuels and fast-refilling, $259.95 for 8 gallon, $319.95 for 22 gallon. NASCAR style with ball check valves is $329.95 for 22 gallon size. Accessories include remote fill kit for $54.95; hook-up kit for $14.95; fuel level gauge, foam baffling, flex hose, fuel lines and fittings, vent check valve. Also on-board fire extinguisher systems. Free literature.

Ageavant Racecars
13234 Sherman Way, No. 12
North Hollywood
California 91605

Designers and constructors of Formula and sports racing cars of all classes. Sells CABCO rod ends and bearings, and racing fuel cells. Repairs monocoque and tube chassis, and fiberglass bodies. Will construct any special racing part to specifications. Free information.

Airborne Sales Company
8501 Stellar Drive
Culver City, California 90230

If you're the type of person who goes wild in a surplus parts store and grooves on all the crazy jet engine gauges and electrohydraulic thingamajigs, Airborne Sales has the perfect catalog for you. Seriously now, if you can figure out what it is, and dream up a way to adapt it for your purposes, you may have a bargain. Among the more mundane but useful items listed are utility pumps, compasses, metric wrench sets, tap and die sets, intercom systems that can be rigged up for use in a camper, all sorts of small electric motors and hydraulic pumps, hand winches, fire extinguishers, screw and nut drivers, files, stainless steel tanks, hardware assortments, electric and capstan winches, snatch blocks, needle valves, air check valves, solenoids, inverters, squirrel cage fans, inspection lights, switches and relays, welding supplies, magnets, stopwatches, 8-day panel clocks, and generators that could be used to rube up an arc welder. And then, if you're looking for something a little further out, there are lavatory doors taken out of old B-29s (only $10.95!), aero medical test kits designed for testing urine samples for radioactivity, and . . . Oh well, that's enough. Catalog, $.35.

Airflow Club of America
(Chrysler and De Soto Airflow)
8554 Boyson Street
Downey, California 90242

Club activities comprise regional spring meets, an annual national meet in late summer, the monthly Airflow newsletter with advertising free to members, and technical advice available through Club experts. License plate badges are available for $2.00 each. It is not necessary to own an Airflow to join the Club. Yearly dues: $7.50.

1.

Somewhere West of Laramie. The gutty roadsters of the teens and twenties—the Mercer, Stutz, Kissel, and Jordan—gave rise to a more civilized roadster and convertible, designed to appeal to the rich young men of the prohibition era. In terms of modern performance standards, most of these early American sports cars cannot measure up. In sheer excitement, however, they remain unsurpassed and unsurpassable.

1. *1913 Mercer Raceabout, Series J.* This was the famous Mercer, the finest American example, many enthusiasts claim, of the totally functional sports car with no compromises or concessions.

2. *1929 Du Pont Speedster.* The Du Pont was fast and eminently roadable. Though never as successful as the Stutz or Auburn, in terms of sales, it is a much desired rarity among collectors today.

2.

3. 1911 Mercer. Sitting bolt upright in a bucket seat, feeling every irregularity in the road through cartwheel suspension and trucklike steering, the Mercer owner was king in a thrilling new world of speed.

4. 1922 Templar. There were quite a few serious competitors to the Mercer and Stutz during the early 1920s. The Templar, never produced in any quantity, still has its coterie of hard-bitten enthusiasts.

5. *1933 Auburn.* There are those who say that the Auburn was all show and no go. But Auburns in any guise never caused any traffic jams.

6. *1927 Stutz Black Hawk.* The boat-tailed Black Hawk is ranked with the later Bearcat as the epitome of Stutz production.

7.

7. 1935 Duesenberg SSJ. The Duesenberg was the perfect Jay Gatsby car, a vehicle as fabulous as it was rare. Today any Duesenberg J-series is worth a cool $80,000 minimum, and tomorrow, who knows?

8. 1937 Cord Convertible Coupe. The Cord flowered in the late depression era, a legend in it's all too brief production life.

Air Lift Co.
P.O. Box 449
Lansing, Michigan 48902

Air Lift Springs are butyl rubber bags which fit inside of coil springs and can be inflated directly or by remote dashboard control. Springs are available for almost all domestic cars and small trucks. They can be used as overload springs, or as heavy-duty off-road suspension units. Air Lift sets are priced at approximately $40.00 to $45.00. Free information.

Air Lift Co. springs

Airtex Automotive Division
Fairfield, Illinois 62837

Makers of water pumps and fuel pumps for domestic and foreign cars, including a number of off-beat makes and models. Catalogs list pumps for everything from Rolls-Royce Silver Shadows to the late lamented Henry J. Consult catalog at wholesale parts house.

Wm. D. Albright
16581 Arrow Boulevard
Fontana, California 92335

Mr. Albright is interested in some of the more unusual cars of the postwar years. He is just completing restoration of a Muntz-Jet and is willing to correspond with others who own or contemplate restoring a Muntz. Another interest is the Volvo P-1900, of which there were only 20 imported into the U.S. Anyone owning this model Volvo or knowing of one which has not been registered with Mr. Albright's Volvo P-1900 Register, is invited to write him. Still another unusual vehicle in the Albright collection (which also includes 12 Hudsons) is a 1960 Shamrock Convertible, made in Ireland.

Alexander Engineering
Haddenham
Buckinghamshire
England

Known for its "Alexpress" conversion kits for many British cars, this firm also carries many hard parts for British and Continental cars, along with some goodies for amost any car. Alexpress kits include two Stromberg CD carbs fitted to a suitable intake manifold and assembled with all necessary linkages and hoses. Each kit also includes a pair of non-restrictive air cleaners. Kits are available for most BMC cars, Opels, British Fords, and Rootes products. Parts available for many British and Continental cars include thermostats, fan belts, gasket sets, air filters, and valve springs. Among the items with universal application are Springalex steering wheels, Alexander instruments and Speedview mirrors. A few unique items are wipers to fit headlights, radio suppressor kits and the Alexander Adjustalamp, which has a long goose neck and would be most suitable for interior illumination on rally cars. Free literature.

ALF Enterprises
P.O. Box 1815
Los Gatos, California 95030

Makes front and rear bumper guards and front "bras" for Alfa Romeo Spiders. Free literature.

Alfa Romeo Association
(Alfa Romeo)
2115 El Camino Real
Redwood City, California 94063

Active West Coast organization which sponsors competitive and social events along with publishing a monthly newsletter, *Overhead Cams.* Also technical advice and demonstrations. Membership open to Alfa owners or recent owners only. Membership dues cover the national Alfa-Romeo Club also. Yearly dues: $12.50.

Alfa Romeo Inc.
215 Douglas Street South
El Segundo, California 90245

Western Alfa Romeo distributors.

Alfa Romeo Inc.
250 Sylvan Avenue
Englewood Cliffs
New Jersey 07632

Eastern Alfa Romeo distributors.

Alfa Romeo Owner's Club
(Alfa Romeo)
c/o Viscount Villiers
Pembroke
Manor Crescent
Haslemere
Surrey
England

Club activities include monthly meetings held at The Steering Wheel, Curzon Street, London, and by area branches all over Great Britain and in Dublin. There are also sprints, gymkhanas, weekend tours and a monthly glossy magazine. Services consist of technical advice, parts location, a stock of spares for older Alfas held by the Club and workshop manuals at reduced prices. Yearly dues: $9.60.

Alfa Romeo Owners Club
P.O. Box 331
Northbrook, Illinois 60062

The AROC sponsors a variety of activities and publishes a monthly newsletter, called *Alfa Owner,* which carries a classified section and technical advice. Particular questions are answered by the Club's technical editor. Another good source of information suggested by Club president Ken Askew is Mr. Aldo Bozzi of Alfa-Romeo, Inc. in Englewood Cliffs, New Jersey. Yearly dues: $10.00, pro-rated to $5.00 after July 1.

Alfa Romeo Section
of the V.S.C.C.
(Pre-1941 Alfa-Romeos)
c/o Mr. and Mrs. A. Cherrett
The Old Forge
Quarr
Buckhorn Weston
Near Gillingham
Dorset
England

Among the club services offered are technical and historical information, a spares registry, cooperation on the manufacture of repro parts, the maintenance of parts stocklists, and copying owner's handbooks. There is a bi-monthly newsletter and an annual roster. Yearly dues: $1.80 in addition to the V.S.C.C. subscription cost.

Allard Motor Co., Ltd.
51 Upper Richmond Road
Putney, London S.W. 15
England

As the nearest British counterpart to Honest Charley, Inc., Allard carries a wide variety of hop-up equipment, suspension parts, wheels, rally equipment, and general goodies. Can supply new or reconditioned British Ford engines including the Lotus Twin-Cam, and modification kits for Cortina, Anglia, and Lotus engines. Sells the Shorrock Rotary Vane Supercharger which can be fitted to most British car engines plus Renault and VW. Has Tecalemit fuel injection unit for 4-cylinder engines. Among other items for sale are Salisbury limited slip differentials for the Anglia, Cortina, Corsair, and Capri; lightweight aluminum body panels for Mark II Cortinas;

oil cooler kits for BMC, Ford, Triumph, Rootes Group and Vauxhall cars; competition exhausts for British Fords; complete close-ratio gearboxes for Anglia, Cortina, and Corsair; Peco straight through mufflers; high-ratio steering boxes for Escorts and Mark II Cortinas; front wheel disc brake conversion units for various Anglias and Cortinas; mag wheels; anti-roll bars; suspension lowering kits for numerous British cars plus Opel and Fiat; shock absorbers and special heavy-duty springs and struts or complete rally or racing suspension kits for British cars; sump shields and

Wade Supercharger on the Mark III Cortina 2000 SOHC engine from Allard Motor Co., Ltd.

long-range fuel tanks along with roll bars, headlamp stone guards, and other rally equipment for British Fords; Cibie headlights; Kenlowe engine cooling fans for most British cars; vinyl roof coverings; workshop manuals; the Golde Continental sun roof for many cars including Aston, Alfa, Bentley, BMW, Lancia, Riley, Saab, and other European cars; and complete British Ford conversions for racing or rally use. Write for availability of catalog.

Allard Owners Club Ltd.
(Allard)
51 Upper Richmond Road
Putney, London S.W. 15
England

Open to Allard owners around the world, this Club has many members in the U.S. Publications include a monthly newsletter, and road tests and history sheets as requested by members. Club holds regular monthly meetings, an annual dinner and concours, film shows, etc. All activities are in London area. There is a spare parts register for members, and a few items, such as radiator grilles, have been remanufactured at the instigation of the Club. Yearly dues: approximately $4.80 (£2).

Allard Owners Club U.S.A.
(Allard)
33 Underwood Road
Montville, New Jersey 07045

It is estimated that there are less than 100 Allards left in the U.S., and 25 of them are owned by Club members. There is an irregular newsletter, and technical information plus parts location services. Yearly dues: $7.00.

All Car Equipe
Main Road
West Kingsdown
Sevenoaks
Kent TN 15
England

Performance engine and chassis components for many British cars. Modified cylinder heads are available in three stages for British Ford, BMC, Viva and Imp engines. Also has exhaust and intake systems, modified cams, S.U. carb kits, rally suspension components, Spax shock absorbers, steel and alloy wheels, Weber carb kits, fiberglass body panels, zinc-treated steel door sills, Smiths instruments, Fiamm air horns, leather-rimmed steering wheels, front-end spoilers, Corbeau rally seats, roll bars, oil cooler kits, Britax full harness seat belts, Cibie lamps, Kangol helmets, and sump guards. Many prices are below identical or

	equivalent equipment from American suppliers. Cars covered include most late model Austins, Minis, Spridgets, Anglias, Cortinas, Capris, Escorts, Hillmans, Spitfires, some Vauxhalls, Lotuses, Triumph GT-6s, MGs, Jaguars and Austin-Healeys. Free parts and price list.
Alondra, Inc. 826 West Hyde Park Boulevard Inglewood, California 90302	Makers of Filt-O-Reg fuel pressure regulators and View-All in-line gas filters. Service parts in stock. Free literature.
Martin Alperstein Box 412 Glenham, New York 12527	Mercedes-Benz mechanical parts for cars 1955-65 and much Mercedes literature. Spare parts lists for most postwar Mercedes, factory workshop manuals, owners' handbooks, and Mercedes magazines. Send a stamped, self-addressed envelope for list.
Alvis Owner Club **(Alvis)** c/o E. W. Wimble 82 Dorling Drive Ewell Surrey England	Organized into five sections covering Great Britain, this Club nevertheless reports a large overseas contingent including a strong American section. The larger sections of the Club run an "Alvis Day" each year, while a National Alvis Day is held at Crystal Palace. A publication entitled *The Bulletin* is sent to members monthly and contains parts advertisements as well as technical and historical articles. There is a membership list issued from time to time, a spares registrar for both pre- and postwar cars, a technical advice service, a full set of instruction manuals available on loan, and a film and photograph library. Annual dues: $6.00, pro-rated for those who join later in the year.
Alvis Owners Club **(Alvis)** 109 Portland Road Kingston upon Thames Surrey England	Regular Club activities include concours and driving tests, Regional Alvis Days, and a Club Sprint every September. The primary publication of the Club is the monthly *Alvis Owners Club Bulletin.* Also offers technical advice, some spare parts, repro parts, and instruction manuals on loan. Yearly dues: $6.00.
AMBAC Industries Inc. **American Bosch** **Marketing Division** 3664 Main Springfield Massachusetts 01107	Original equipment and replacement electrical components for most cars. Voltage regulators, starter motors, electric windshield wiper components, and windshield washer systems are covered in various Bosch catalogs. Consult catalogs at wholesale supply house.
AMCO 7425 Fulton Avenue North Hollywood California 91605	AMCO foreign and sports car accessories include leather and walnut shift knobs, bumper guards, custom consoles, arm rests, tops and side curtains, car carpets, rubber floor mats, tinted plexiglass sun visors, gearshift pattern plates, wind wings, tonneau covers, pickup bed covers for mini-pickups, reupholstery kits, side panel kits, luggage racks, and ski racks. A console for Datsun 510 sedans and wagons, with three trays and two rocker switches, sells for $17.30. An ashtray/lighter combination, fitting most 12-volt sports cars, is $12.20. Replacement carpet kits range in price from about $25.00 to $50.00. Bumper guards are priced from $18.35 to $30.55 for front or rear, depending upon the model. AMCO accessories are available direct, or through many other accessory dealers. Catalog, $1.00.

Amerace Brands Division **Amerace Esna Corporation** Ace Road Butler, New Jersey 07405	Accessory stop and turn signals, amber and red reflectors, "lollipop" reflector markers, European-style emergency warning triangles, heater hose, fuel line tubing, and windshield washer and wiper tubing. Free information.
American Auto Parts Co. 1830 Locust Kansas City; Missouri 64108	Hard parts for military and civlian jeeps, 4WD Jeep trucks and station wagons. Exchange price for rebuilt flathead military and civilian Jeep blocks, with pistons, pins, rings, crank, con rods, rod and main bearings, timing gears and valves, is $195.00. Other hard parts available include cylinder heads, cranks, piston sets, valve gear, oil pumps, oil pans, oil filters, intake and exhaust manifolds, flywheel and ring gear, engine mounts, clutch components, fuel tanks, fuel pumps, rebuilt carbs, choke and throttle controls, exhaust system parts, radiators, water pumps, fan assemblies, generators, starters, distributors, regulators, coils, ignition wiring kits, lights, switches, battery hardware, instruments for 24-volt and conventional systems, gears and transmission parts, transfer cases, prop shafts, front and rear end components, steering gear, wheel bearings and seals, brake parts, shocks, most body parts, and windshield wiper components. Accessories available are Viking electric winches, winches with power takeoff, heavy-duty clutch kits, front seat replacement cushions, rear seats, can carriers, spare tire covers, rear fender seat pads for CJ models ($18.95), Bestop tops, roll bars, trailer hitches, and Heco steering stabilizers. Jeep service manuals and free-wheeling hubs are always in stock. Dualmatic overdrive units are available for M38 and CJ Jeeps. Free literature.
American Brakeblok Division **of Abex Corporation** 900 West Maple Road Troy, Michigan 48084	Brake system components including industrial friction materials, disc brake pistons, and brake linings for rebuilders. Publishes informative literature on brake drums, and disc and drum brake service. Free literature.
American Honda **Motor Co., Inc.** 100 West Alondra Boulevard Gardena, California 90247	Honda car distributor.
American Motors Corporation Automotive Customer Relations Section 14250 Plymouth Road Detroit, Michigan 48232	AMC has been publishing some unique literature on older products in limited editions. The *American Motors Family Album,* with detailed information on Rambler, Jeffery, Nash LaFayette, Hudson, Essex and Terraplane cars, is a 146-page soft cover book, with many photos, which sells for $2.00. Also, technical service manuals for the 1936-38 Nash and LaFayette, and the 1941-48 Nash, have been reprinted in the past and may still be available. For details on current publications, write to John A. Conde, Assistant Director of Public Relations. Also available are service manuals for current vehicles.
American Racing Equipment 355 Valley Drive Crocker Industrial Park Brisbane, California 94005	Mag wheels in various sizes and styles. Models available are the Spirit (13″x5½″ to 15″x10″); Torq-Thrust 70 (14″x7″ to 15″x8½″); 200S (14″x7″ to 15″x10″); Libre (for popular small

	cars, sizes 13″x5″ to 14″x5½″); Le Mans (for Porsche 914, late VW or Alfa); Silverstone II (for Toyotas with 13″ tires); TT-P (for 911, 912 and 914/6 Porsches only, size 15″x7″); G.T.D.M. (for Funny Cars in size 15″x4″ with zero offset); 250 Drag Wheel (for Pro-Stocks and Altereds in size 16″x 13″); 12 Spoke D.M. (15″x3½″, 17″x2¼″ and 18″x2¼″ with zero offset); and Trans-Am (15″x8″ and 15″x10″ with zero or ¼″ positive offset). Genuine magnesium wheels, for off-road and competition use, are available on special order. Accessory items include wheel maintenance kits, splash guards, chrome dust caps, chrome valve stems, mag wheel lug nuts and locks, and competition tire gauges. Free information.
Amilcar Register (Amilcar) c/o Mrs. E. Drake Rockbourne Near Fordingbridge Hampshire SP6 3NL England	Principal activity is an annual September weekend rally of Amilcar/Salmson owners held alternately in France and England. There are also a few social meetings and a newsletter published about four times a year. Technical advice and a spare parts pool are other services offered. Yearly dues: approximately $1.20 (50 pence); initial membership fee, approximately $12.00 (£5).
Andeck Automotive 4566 Spring Road Cleveland, Ohio 44131	Andeck, which is a division of Mr. Gasket Company, specializes in accessories for sub-compact and foreign cars. Their line of components includes VW speed shifters; solid walnut dash trim for many small cars; bucket seats to fit the VW seat track; foam padded roll bars; universal clutch stops; intake and exhaust gaskets; headers for Datsuns, Toyotas, Pintos, Vegas and VWs; front and rear anti-swaybars for many mini cars plus the Datsun 240Z; Datsun 240Z and 510 heavy duty springs; Toyota, Vega and Pinto springs; shocks for most Datsuns and Toyotas; Vega traction bars; Pinto lift kits. Also the following VW items: power pulleys, timing discs, chrome generator and belt cover kits, finned valve covers, air cleaners, skid plates, wiring harnesses, big bore piston and liner assemblies, case savers for replacing stripped-out threads, high volume oil pumps and extra capacity sump pans, remote oil filter adapter kits, full-flow oil coolers, windage trays, quick-change push rod tubes, high-ratio rocker arm assemblies, chrome-moly push rods, rocker arm stud repair kits, heavy-duty valvetrain components, flywheel gland nuts, electric and mechanical fuel pumps, solid motor mounts, VW sedan engine brace kits, extracter exhaust systems for most VWs and Porsches, VW intake manifolds, front end lowering kits, tow bars, quick steering kits, "flop-stop" anti-flip kits, and many cosmetic items. For dune buggies, Andeck carries windshields, tops and side curtains, carpet kits, nerf bars, and chrome tubular bumpers. Free catalog.
Bob Anderson P.O. Box 7 Houtzdale, Pennsylvania 16651	Lincoln Zephyr and Continental parts, 1936-48. Send a stamped, self-addressed envelope with query.
The Anderson Company 1075 Grant Gary, Indiana 46404	Windshield wipers, washers, washer anti-freeze and allied products. Consult catalog at wholesale supply house.

Anderson Industries, Inc.
Route 1, Box 15C, Ridge Road
Hanover, Maryland 21076

Fiberglass body parts in light grey gloss gelcoat finish, available in two grades: an all-purpose street weight and a lighter racing weight. Parts are available for 1967-72 Camaro, 1962-72 Chevy II, 1937 and 1955-57 Chev, 1948-53 Anglia, 1948-53 Austin, 1937-42 Willys, 1949-52 Henry J, 1971-72 Vega, 1970-72 Duster, 1970-72 Gremlin/Hornet, 1958-67 Corvette, 1968-69 Plymouth, 1964-66 Mustang, 1923-40 Ford. Also various models of bucket seats and hood scoops. Ford 1923-25 roadster body with opening door is $150.00, 36″ pickup bed $75.00, fiberglass top $80.00. For '55 Chev, one piece front end at $180.00, hood $70.00, front fender $70.00, trunk lid $70.00. For Anglia 1948-53, one piece front end for $160.00, two doors $190.00, firewall $35.00, rear fenders $60.00, trunk lid $35.00; or body with integral roof panel, trunklid and rear fenders for $500.00. Catalog $1.00.

Andrews Auto Restoration Center
4921 Folsom Boulevard
Sacramento, California 95819

Complete auto restorations including woodwork, sandblasting, plating, upholstery, painting, and fabrication of parts. Mr. Andrews' particular specialty is 1923-41 Packards, for which he has many parts on hand. Classic T-birds, which Mr. Andrews himself collects, are another area of specialization. This is a large operation with eight full-time workers, and complete repro bodies can be fabricated. In addition, the Company will transport vehicles to and from their shop in trailers kept for this purpose, and will inspect cars for a fee. Write for further information.

Andy Hotton Associates
510 Savage Road
Belleville, Michigan 48111

Company offers conversions on new Lincoln Continentals. Their formal sedan has a one foot longer wheelbase than standard, while their formal limousine and brougham have a wheelbase which is two feet longer than normal. They can also supply a Lincoln Continental 9-passenger station wagon and a Continental convertible. Once you have specified the general type of car you would like, the options you can select are practically unlimited. If you happen to be the hereditary ruler of a small Arabian country where new oil wells are being drilled every day, you may opt for rear compartment air-conditioning, a partition with a power-operated divider window, a custom console with a TV set on top, a built-in bar (discreetly known as "Beverage Service"), a vinyl roof with opera window, leather-trimmed jump seats, European style road and fog lights, a sun roof, and perhaps a front grille and rear deck lid emulating the original Continental and known as the "Mark" style. Should you desire something special, like extra seats for the members of your harem, or a "throne" in the rear, the company will undoubtedly be amenable to negotiation. Free literature.

Anes Electronics, Inc.
4112 Del Rey Avenue
Venice, California 90291

Auto burglar alarms and accessories. Bell alarm kits to prevent tampering with doors, hood and trunk; motion detector for wheel and tire protection also guards against hit and run bashers; car horn alarm system; many 6- and 12-volt accessories. RV alarm system (solid state or electro-mechanical) can be ordered with fire alarm sensor, siren, bell or horn alarm, and many accessories. Free literature.

Ansen Automotive Engineering
13715 South Western Avenue
Gardena, California 90249

Alloy wheels, traction bars, bellhousings, engine and chassis components, and racing accessories. The Ansen Sprint wheels are available in sizes from 13″x5½″ to 15″x14″, and truck wheels are available in sizes up to 16.5″x9¾″. Special wheels are made for Sprint and Midget cars, large recreational vehicles, and off-road trucks. Wheel accessories include hub caps, lug nuts, wheel locks, wheel spacers, lug nut wrenches, and wheel adapters for VW. Race-related accessories include safety bellhousings for most domestic cars, aluminized fire suits and breather hoods, competition lap belts and shoulder harnesses, motor mounts and frame adapters for popular engine conversions, adjustable crossmembers, dropped drag links, Hartford friction shocks, clutch slave cylinder units, universal brake and clutch swing pedals, traction bars for most domestic cars, adjustable lowering kits, coil spring lifters, split wishbone brackets, heavy-duty Ford steering arms, locking differential gears, rear end lift kits, hydraulic throttle kits, forged racing pistons and rods, valve train components, aircraft quality engine hardware, pneumatic pressure oil systems, water and oil filler necks, wire looms and dividers, carb adapter kits, Flex-A-Lite fans, speed shift kits for cars and pickup trucks, shift boots and wooden gearshift knobs, custom steering wheels (including 9″ deep-dish dragster steering wheel) and insignia T-shirts and jewelry. Catalog, $1.00; wheel catalog, $.50.

Antique & Classic Car Club of Canada (Veteran and Vintage Cars)
c/o J.R.A. Turner
430, Heath Street East
Toronto, 17
Ontario
Canada

Holds three big national events: a summer tour, a concours in September, and a convention and model car show in March. Also sponsors a variety of social events and monthly lectures. The Club magazine *The Reflector* is published quarterly, and there is an advertising and news supplement *The Reflector Beam* published eight times a year.
There is also a Club roster and a library of technical information for member's use. Yearly dues: $10.00.

Antique and Classics, Inc.
5483 Shimerville Road
Clarence, New York 14031

If you are an impecunious admirer of the Bugatti Type 35 Grand Prix cars, you may be interested in a Bugatti Replicar to fit the ubiquitious VW chassis. The basic kit, at $795.00, includes a two-piece fiberglass body with molded-in louvers; aluminum finish radiator shell; medallion and mesh for shell; cycle fenders; side bottom pans; chrome 6V or 12V headlights; large Motometer for radiator shell; engine-turned dash overlay; Brooklands style plexiglass windscreen; pre-marked plywood for cutting dash, seats, and bulkhead; welded steel body supports; and gas tank. The body is finished in white gelcoat, ready for sanding and painting. Accessories include extra windscreen, wood rim steering wheel and horn assembly, 8-spoke steel 15″ Bugatti-type wheels ($40.00 each), and Naugahyde seat covers ($70.00). Free literature.

Antique Auto Items
South 1607 McCabe Road
Spokane, Washington 99216

New and used small parts for cars vintage 1915-50. Specialties are ignition parts, wiper blades and arms, pedal pads, taillights, dash instruments and other accessories. Send a stamped, self-addressed envelope with queries.

Antique Automobile Club of America (Antique and Classic Automobiles) 501 West Governor Road Hershey, Pennsylvania 17033	This substantial and well-established organization covers all pre-1917 automobiles and runs many meets with competitive events and prizes awarded. There are more than 150 regions and 70 chapters all over the U.S. National meets in spring and fall are held in various areas of the country. The annual meeting is at Philadelphia in February. The AACA sponsors the Glidden Tours in alternate years. There are also tours to Europe, from time to time, on a charter basis. Club publication is the bi-monthly glossy magazine *Antique Automobile,* which carries many classified advertisements. AACA emblems and other items of jewelry are available, as are back issues of the magazine. Ownership of a car is not necessary for joining the AACA; however, each applicant must be recommended by a member in good standing. Members will receive notices of all events, membership rosters, and issues of the Club magazine. Yearly dues: $6.50. Life memberships: $100.00. Wives or husbands of active members can join for $2.00 a year.
Antique Auto Parts 9113 East Garvey Avenue Rosemead, California 91770	Ford parts, 1920 to the present. Has complete rubber goods, top irons and woods, Ford disc brake conversions, speed equipment, aluminum timing gears, custom wiring and ignition parts. Write for information.
Antique Auto Sheet Metal R.R. No. 1, Box 326-D Brookville, Ohio 45309	Body parts for Fords, 1928-32. Rear body panels below trunk lid, rumble seat and trunk compartment inner panels, engine splash pans, running boards (pair with mat and zinc installed are $39.00 for 1928, '29, '31; $65.00 for 1930 with splash shield), seat frames, radiator splash aprons, body channels, curtain pans, window channels (1928-31 door window glass channels, $5.00 a pair), body patch panels, door bottom patch panels, sun visors. For 1932 5-window coupe and roadster: rumble seat riser ($15.00), rumble seat stops ($4.00 a pair, or $6.50 with rubber bumpers), rumble seat hinge set ($16.50). Send a stamped, self-addressed envelope for parts and price list.
Antique Motorcar Center, Inc. 15 Hinckley Road Hyannis, Massachusetts 02601	Sells antique, classic, and special-interest automobiles. Has complete restoration facilities. Also manufactures repro parts for GM cars of the 1930s and '40s. Has some NOS parts for same cars. Send a stamped, self-addressed envelope with queries.
Antique Motor News & Atlantic Auto Advertiser 5406 Village Road, Suite 6 Long Beach, California 90808	Vintage and contemporary cars with a strong West Coast orientation. Monthly magazine. Subscription rate: $4.00 a year.
Antique Popcorn Wagons, Inc. 12201 South Indiana Avenue Chicago, Illinois 60628	Replica popcorn wagons and pullcarts. Model 50 pullcart with all steel welded construction, painted wire wheels, mahogany window frames, and red and yellow enamel finish, hand striped and lettered, is $2,195.00. Those who are contemplating going into business will be interested in knowing that the popping cabinet will fill up to 350 standard size containers an hour, and that a peanut storage compartment is included. Model 100, a motorized version of an antique popcorn wagon, has three red and white

canvas awnings, a red enamel finish with solid brass trim, and wooden wagon wheels. The electric engine resembles the original steam model. Options include concession equipment, air conditioning, a space heater, and oversized kettles to service a high-volume business. The model 100 is $10,875.00. Free literature.

Antique Studebaker Club, Inc. (Studebaker)
P.O. Box 142
Monrovia, California 91016

Devoted to Studebakers 1942 and earlier. Publishes bimonthly magazine *Antique Studebaker Review* and a roster with parts and service directory, once each year in January. Has access to large private library of Studebaker literature and provides members with technical data and research information at reproduction cost. Maintains file of parts and service suppliers and offers free classified advertising to Club members. It is not necessary to own an antique Studebaker in order to join the Club. Yearly dues: $6.00.

Antique Truck Club of America (Antique Trucks)
8-19 115th Street
College Point, New York 11356

As a requirement for membership, you must swear never to make any "keep-on-truckin' " jokes, and must have an interest in antique commercial vehicles or the history of the trucking industry. There are monthly meetings and occasional truck-ins in the metropolitan New York area. The monthly Club publication is an impressive document entitled *Double Clutch*. There is also an annual roster of members and their cars. Technical advice and library services furnished on request. Yearly dues: $5.00; members' wives, $1.00.

Apco Mossberg Co.
Lamb Street
Attleboro, Massachusetts 02703

Socket wrenches, lug wrenches for cars and trucks, Budd-type rim wrenches, universal drain plug wrenches. Free literature.

Apogee Enterprises
Box 266
Sheboygan, Wisconsin 53081

Apogee calls their catalog *The Whole Light Catalogue* since it contains quartz iodine and conventional lamps for every application. Among lights listed are those from Carello, Hella, Lucas, Miller, Marchal, and Per-Lux. Another manufacturer represented is Aras, makers of louvered driving and fog lights as well as switches, horn buttons, fuse holders, electrical connector strips and relays. There is much interesting information on lighting in the catalog. Catalog, $1.50.

Apollo Welding and Fabricating Co.
4922 Delemere
Royal Oak, Michigan 48073

Makes "Trick Titanium" components for drag racing cars. Items available include strut bar kit ($72.00); K-frame bolts and washers ($55.00 per set of four); chopped front spindles ($185.00 per set); titanium steering knuckles for Vega, Gremlin, Colt, Hornet and Pinto ($135.00); foot pedal kit with bearings and shaft ($150.00); and hood pin kit ($12.00). Also has cylinder head studs, water pump studs, head bolt washers and valve spring retainers. Custom fabricating of any part in titanium, magnesium, or aluminum. Free information.

Howard and Shelby Applegate
1410 Stallion Lane
West Chester
Pennsylvania 19380

Automotive literature, photos, owner's manuals, stock certificates, annual reports, brochures, and related memorabilia. Lists of items on many marques, $.10 each.

Appliance Industries
23920 South Vermont Avenue
Harbor City, California 90710

Magnesium, aluminum and steel wheels to fit most domestic and foreign cars. Styles include slotted, smooth center, wire, and unpolished spoke designs. Also has wheel adapters for VW 4- and 5-bolt wheels. Manufactures complete line of headers for domestic cars. Free literature.

Applied Power Industries, Inc.
P.O. Box 3100
Milwaukee, Wisconsin 53218

Manufacturers of hydraulic jacks, presses, and body and frame straighteners. Other products include transmission jacks, jack safety stands, engine stands, mobile cranes, bumper and scissor jacks and static wheel balancers. Consult catalog at wholesale parts house.

Archer Brothers
19745 Meekland Avenue
Hayward, California 94541

Mostly for Jeeps, including the War II variety. Archer Brothers carries an extensive line of hard parts for Jeep Universals, along with heavy-duty springs, tie-rods, bell cranks, shocks, clutches and clutch linkages, and brakes (the 11″ variety). For military Jeeps they can supply spare tire mounts, a driver's side helper spring, tire supports, and other goodies. For all Jeeps there are various chrome and steel wheels along with the very reasonably priced Thompson brand of off-road tires. Gates and Desert Dog tires are also available. There are Husky and Bestop tops, and Bestop doors, top boots and door pockets. Also rear seats for most 4WD vehicles and rear fender seat pads for Jeeps. Other standard items include Husky pickup truck tonneau covers; Bestop swing-away tire and G.I. Can carriers; Husky front mount spare tire carriers; Stewart Warner gauges; Warn, Selectro and Easylok free-wheeling front hubs; Offy 4-barrel manifolds for the Jeep V-6; Ramsey, Superwinch and Warn winches; Motor Guard oil filters (the filtering element is that magic stuff, T.P., a roll of which is available at the nearest supermarket); and Filtron foam-element air cleaners. Chrome rock guards for the vulnerable under-door portion of Jeep Universals sell for $17.64. Rubber body access hole plugs are $2.50. A padded dash for the CJ-5 is $17.20. Chrome hood latch kits for CJ-3B and CJ-5 are $2.81 apiece (two are needed to latch both sides). Heavy-duty tow bars for Jeep Universals are $32.50. G.I. jerry can holders with chain and lock are $6.60. Roll bars for the Jeep, Toyota L.C. and Scout cost $37.50. For the Bronco they are $60.00 and Blazer/Jimmy roll bars go for $65.00. Two types of locking differentials are offered. The "Hy-Torq" clutchless type ranges in price from $245.50 for one-ton models down to $179.33 for the quarter-ton variety. Spicer limited-slips for passenger cars and most light trucks (equipped with Spicer design axles) are $129.19 for the rear-axle model, $112.18 for the front. Those who are building their Jeeps from the ground up, or converting a military model, will be interested in a rebuilt OHV or flathead 4-cylinder engine, complete T-90 transmissions with extended input shafts available for engine swaps, and entire bodies in fiberglass (CJ-2A, 3A and MB) or steel (CJ-5). There are also rubber or plastic fender extenders for Jeeps and a fiberglass model for the Bronco. You can add a final fillip to your faithful four-banger with Husky overdrive, a hand throttle control cable, a lever-

	operated hydraulic lock for holding brakes on hills, and the appropriate front hub lock nut socket for your toolbox. Free catalog.
Arias Racing Pistons 13420 South Normandie Avenue Gardena, California 90249	Forged racing pistons and piston rings for American V-8 engines. Catalog, $1.00.
Arly's Street Rods & Components 209 Lakeview Way Redwood City California 94062	Dash panels for T-Buckets ($59.95 in walnut, oak, birch or mahogany), Jag disc brake conversion kits for Ford and Chev spindles, aluminum tie bars for Jag rear end installations ($21.95), and custom polishing of alloy wheels and engine goodies. Company will also custom make aluminum gas tanks and fenders, do Jag rear end installations (approximate price $285.00 including Koni traction stabilizers), and do other custom chassis and frame construction to customer's specifications. Catalog, $1.00.
Armstrong Siddeley Car Club (Armstrong-Siddeley and Predecessor Vehicles) c/o I. L. Barnett 29b Oakes Road Carlingford 2118 New South Wales Australia	A lot of enthusiastic Siddeley owners down under. There are branches of this Club in Sydney, Newcastle, Melbourne, Adelaide and Canberra. The Club is also affiliated with the Armstrong Siddeley Car Club of New Zealand (c/o Mr. Les Death, P.O. Box 126, Cambridge, New Zealand). The Club sponsors many activities, including an Annual Federal Rally at Easter, and an International Rally for 1975. Club newsletter is the monthly *Southern Sphinx,* and technical services plus parts sales are offered to members. Yearly dues are $8.50 single or $10.00 family membership.
Armstrong-Siddeley Owners' Club (Armstrong-Siddeley) c/o John D. Hubbuck 90 Alumhurst Road Bournemouth Hampshire England	Club covers the late-lamented British makes of Siddeley Deasy, Deasy, Armstrong Whitworth, Wolseley Siddeley, and Stoneleigh, as well as Armstrong-Siddeleys of course. The more than 500 members live all over the world. Club activities include a quarterly glossy magazine, *Sphinx,* a monthly newsletter, called *Preselector,* a library of literature, with books available on loan or via photocopy, and the largest stock of Armstrong-Siddeley spare parts in the world. Parts for most models can be supplied. Drawings, specifications and technical advice are readily available. The Club has three national meetings a year in Britain. Yearly membership: U.K. or Europe approximately $5.40 (£2.25); $7.80 (£3.25) for overseas membership. For applications between January 1st and April 30th the dues are pro-rated. Life membership is also available.
Arnolt Corporation P.O. Box 540 Warsaw, Indiana 46580	Formerly known as makers of the exemplary Arnolt-Bristol sports cars, the company now specializes in Solex carbs and parts. They have carb rebuild kits for rarer European makes such as Allard, Auto-Union, Borgward, DAF, Facellia, Goliath, Frazer-Nash, Isetta, Lancia, Land Rover, Lloyd, Moretti, NSU, Morgan, Panhard, Singer, Standard, Wolseley, and the Siata Mitzi. Free literature.

The Beetle in Many Guises. German in origin, the VW has been adopted throughout the world and appears in as many guises, or disguises, as Lon Chaney at his theatrical best. Here are just a few of the innumerable VW variations.

1. VW on Skis. Produced by the South African Department of Transport, a VW Snowmobile for use in Antarctica.

2. VW "Schwimmer". Volkswagen produced an amphibious "Schwimmwagen" for use during World War II, but even an ordinary VW can take to the water at times. This "Yellow Submarine," a 1958 Bug, is making a choppy crossing from the Isle of Man to St. Bees, in the Irish Sea.

3. VW Planter. The secret life of plants may be an urge to speed along the highways and watch the telephone poles grow closer to each other.

4. *Are You Privy?* Nein, dumkopf. I said the *Schmidt* house.

5. *Wooden You Like a VW?* Homemade VW made of oak will never rust, but termites could be a problem.

4.

5.

Association of Healey Owners (Healey Cars excluding Austin-Healeys) c/o Mrs. Diana Hunter Gayfield Dunley Whitchurch Hampshire England	Cars covered by this club include the Warwick-built "Big" Healeys of 1946-54. Most of these have Riley engines and bodies by Tickford and Abbot. There was also the famed Healey Silverstone, the American Nash Healey, and the rare Alvis-engined Healey. Three national meetings are held in Great Britain and a gazette is published quarterly. There is also a comprehensive spare parts service, a register of all known Healey cars, and technical advice upon request. Yearly dues: Great Britain £2: U.S. approximately $2.40.
Aston-Martin/Lagonda, Inc. 650 Clark Avenue King of Prussia Pennsylvania 19406	U.S. distributors.
Aston-Martin Owners Club, Ltd. (Aston-Martin) c/o R. J. Stokes 22, The Mall East Sheen London, S.W. 14 England	This is the parent organization whose U.S. affiliates are listed below. Publications include a monthly news sheet, a quarterly magazine and a membership register. Many events are held throughout the year. Basic yearly dues: $15.00; entrance fee $4.50. Prospective U.S. members should contact their regional affiliates.
Aston-Martin Owners Club Ltd. (Aston-Martin) U.S.A. East: c/o Charles L. Turner 195 Mt. Paran Road N.W. Atlanta, Georgia 30327 U.S.A. West: c/o Richard F. Green 7440 Armillo Road Dublin, California 94566	Club features are monthly newsletters, quarterly magazines, register of all known cars. Various club badges may be purchased, but must be returned if membership lapses. Those who don't own Astons must be proposed by a Club member. Yearly dues: $15.00; entrance fee, $4.50. Family membership, $18.00.
Atkinson Auto Parts Co. 720 Huron Avenue Port Huron, Michigan 48060	NOS mechanical parts for most cars 1932-56. No body parts except some rocker panels for 1948-62 models. Most chassis parts and glass channels, window regulators, some door locks, striker plates, trunk handles and hinges, door lock springs, etc. When ordering, the year, exact model number, engine bore, and size must be specified for proper identification. Send a stamped, self-addressed envelope with query. Lists for each car by year and model are being prepared and will be sent to those on mailing list.
Atlanta Imported Auto Parts 5383 Buford Highway Doraville, Georgia 30340	New and used replacement parts, primarily for British cars. Transmissions are a specialty. No catalog.
Atlantic British Parts Ltd. Box 109 Burnt Hills, New York 12027 Valley Center, California 92082	Hard parts for all popular models of the Land Rover at prices which are stated to be below those of the official distributor. Since parts availability on Land Rovers has been a problem in the U.S., Atlantic should be a winner. Proprietor William Post Hubert advises that some accessories, such as mirrors, gauges, wheels and winches, are also on hand. Those

inquiring about parts or requesting a catalog should state the year, model, and serial number of their Land Rovers. Catalog free from either location.

Auburn-Cord-Duesenberg Club
c/o Fred O. Benson
Rt. 2, Hathaway Road
Harbor Springs
Michigan 49740

Regular Club activities include a national meet at Auburn, Indiana every Labor Day weekend and regional meets on the West and East Coasts in the spring and fall. A newsletter is published ten times a year and there is an annual membership directory. Although there is no formal program for parts location or remanufacture, advertisements are included in the newsletter and many members send out lists of parts for sale. Yearly dues: $13.00.

Auburn-Cord-Duesenberg Co.
Box 15520
Tulsa, Oklahoma 74115

As most A-C-D owners know, there are still quite a few NOS parts in the bins at Auburn-Cord-Duesenberg Company and restoration services are available. Under the leadership of president Glenn Pray, the Company has been manufacturing repro cars in recent years. The Glenn Pray Cord and Auburn Speedster 866 have both been in limited production, although currently only the Auburn model is available. The appointments are first class all the way and the price is somewhere around the 20-grand level. If you are a potential buyer, Mr. Pray will be glad to provide more details.

Austin Seven Club, Southend-on-Sea (Austin Seven)
c/o Miss D. DeRitter
49, Parklands
Rochford
Essex
England

Holding meetings on the last Thursday of each month, and sponsoring the Oxbridge to Rayleigh Road Safety Run for veteran and vintage vehicles, the Club also publishes *Crank Case,* and offers spare parts and technical advice to members. All members must own an Austin Seven, vintage 1923-39. Yearly dues: approximately $2.40 (£1); entry fee about $3.60 (£1.50).

Austin Seven Clubs Association (Austin Seven)
c/o John Ward
North House
Ousterne Lane
Fillongley
Warwickshire
England

This Association coordinates numerous Austin Seven Clubs in England, Scotland, Australia, and New Zealand. These include the 750 Motor Clubs, Swallow Register, Van Register, and Big Seven Register. Mr. Ian Dunford, Honorable Secretary of the Association, sends details on his own Club, the Bristol Austin Seven Club. Along with sponsoring numerous tours and rallies, the Club can supply virtually all spare parts, and maintains a spares directory, membership roster, and a library. There is also a newsletter and the magazine *A7CA*. Yearly dues: $2.00. Mr. Dunford can supply a list of clubs affiliated with the Association. Send an International reply coupon.

Austin-Healey Club Pacific Center (Austin-Healey)
3623 Westview Drive
San Jose, California 95122

Club for owners of big Healeys. Sponsors some events such as rallys and tours. Has stock of used parts available to members. Publishes monthly newsletter *Healey Highlights* with classified section. Also patches, jackets, pins, decals available to members. Healey History Chart sent to new members. Yearly dues: $15.00.

Autobooks
2900 R Magnolia Boulevard
Burbank, California 91503

KGM, Intereurope, and other service manuals. Free list.

40

Autodynamics, Inc.
2 Barnard Street
Marblehead
Massachusetts 01945

A dazzling array of products from dune buggies to Formula racing cars to electric commuter vehicles for urban transport. Now that "dune buggy" has become a dirty word, Autodynamics likes to stress the sports-car-like aspects of its fiberglass kit car, the Deserter GT. The Deserter has an 84″ chassis—midway between the uncut VW chassis and the 80″ version which is customary on dune buggies. The Deserter basic buggy kit is $700.00, while the deluxe kit with much more hardware is $1,100.00. A GT gullwing coupe version is $1,500.00 and there are many accessories available so that only the bare VW running gear is necessary to build a very complete car.
An even more sophisticated dune buggy offshoot is the Deserter GS with a tubular space frame designed to accommodate a VW, Porsche or Corvair engine. It is termed an "autocross" car and the ground clearance is easily adjustable from normal street height to a ground-hugging racing configuration. The standard kit, which includes such things as rear Koni shocks and a master cylinder, is $1,650.00, while the deluxe kit goes for $2,000.00. Among the many available accessories are roll bars, front spoilers, wiring harnesses, and a heater kit to be used with either VW or Porsche engines.

The Deserter GT VW-based kit car from Autodynamics, Inc.

For those who are out for laughs rather than trophies, Autodynamics sells the Maxi-T, a fiberglass body which looks like Jack Benny's old Maxwell restyled by George Barris. It fits an unshortened VW chassis and the basic price is $456.00. An essential builder's kit costs an additional $125.00 and the deluxe accessory package goes for $469.00. To go along with their fiberglass bodies, Autodynamics has become a prime East Coast source of VW accessory parts. They carry the complete line of Pacer, Bugpack, Deano Dyno-Soar and S & S products, along with Crown accessories for the VW and Corvair. They also list Zenith and Holley carbs, Bosch distributors, various manifolds, a full line of Filtron air cleaners (models for the stock VW carb, Bug Spray and Zenith 32NDIX go for $14.95, those for Weber 48 IDAs are $22.50), oil coolers, VDO instruments, Koni shocks, nerf bars and fiberglass custom parts including fenders for Transporters. Autodynamics' wide steel wheels in 4-lug or 5-lug VW varieties are $24.00 each in sizes up to 6″ wide and $30.00 to 10″ wide. While these prices are higher than the competition out on the West Coast, Easterners will find that shipping more than makes up the difference. Now we take a quantum jump to the Autodynamics competition products. They sell Caldwell

D-13 Formula Vee cars utilizing new engines from VW plus rebuilt gearboxes and drivetrain parts for $4,000.00 complete. Kits are $1,700.00. A Caldwell D-9B Formula Ford, factory-prepared and ready to race with a 105 minimum dyno horsepower engine goes for $7,550.00. For this price you get such things as four extra wheels, four gear sets with your choice of ratios, an Autodynamics trailer, and even a sorting out session at the Lime Rock (Connecticut) track with a technician/driver from the Autodynamics racing team. A race ready car without the extras costs $6,500. Autodynamics is also the Northeastern distributor for all Lola racing cars. Prices and specs on request. Along with race cars, a selection of racing hardware is carried. Scarce items such as aircraft quality cushioned tubing clamps, grade eight hex cap screws, an assortment of jamb nuts, lock nuts and hardened washers, safety wire, quick release pins, Loc-Tite products, spherical bearings and rod ends, Monocoque wheels for many cars, and stainless steel covered teflon brake lines with pressure fittings in anodized aluminum alloy or stainless, are offered. Hewland racing gearboxes and Hewland parts are offered with a gearbox workshop manual going for $4.00.

Finally there's the Autodynamics electric vehicle, a diminutive but appealing 4-passenger urban car which runs on 14 6-volt golf cart batteries. It is called the Concept I and offers a top speed of slightly over 60 mph, a payload of 600 pounds, a cruising range of about 85 miles, and a recharge time (from total discharge) of only 4 hours. The makers claim that the economy of operation would be comparable to a gasoline-powered vehicle getting 60 miles to the gallon. One drawback may be the acceleration—roughly comparable to that of an out-of-tune Citroen 2-CV—but urban commuters may not notice. There is also a van version of the Concept I which is equally appealing, has a 1,000-pound payload, and accelerates even more slowly.

The Concept I is currently available "by special order for use in materials, component and systems development." Production versions are scheduled for the near future while prices are as yet unspecified.

Catalog $2.00; literature on the Concept I is free.

The Autodynamics electric commuter vehicle

Auto Enthusiasts, Inc.
21 Juniper Road
Lynnfield, Massachusetts 01940

Custom rear seats for the 350SL and 450SL Mercedes, otherwise unavailable in the U.S., are $195.00. Installation requires no tools and the seats are upholstered in vinyl to match the original (you must send your upholstery code number). A third seat for the Volvo 145 wagon, similar to the factory option, which is not available in the U.S., costs $150.00. The seat can be upholstered in black, blue or brown and faces the rear. A unique import handled by Auto Enthusiasts is the Motor Wrist Watch from England. The dial face is available in just about any logo you can think of (except Mickey Mouse and Spiro Agnew), and the price is $24.95. Free literature.

Auto Enthusiasts International
Box 2379
Dearborn, Michigan 48123

This unique group is a non-profit club of auto literature collectors. They publish a bi-monthly bulletin which contains an illustrated article on some aspect of automotive history. The literature department lists for sale catalogs, manuals, and advertisements on American cars and some trucks from 1900 through the 1950s. These are original items, many one-of-a-kind, which are usually sold on consignment from members. For those who wish to deal directly, there is a classified advertisement section in the bulletin, and each member is entitled to one free advertisement a year. Auto Enthusiasts also maintains a warehouse, with more recent literature and Club reprints, in Detroit. Each year a rare classic or antique auto catalog is sent to members as a free premium. Past reprints have included 1926 Kissel, 1927 Stearns-Knight, 1932 Ford V-8, 1938 Packard Custom Body Catalog, 1929 Gardner, Cunningham (the original American car, not the Briggs Cunningham Cunninghams), Duesenberg, Cord L-29, Stutz, and others. All reprints are still available. Auto Enthusiasts International was founded in 1948. Yearly dues: $6.50; pro-rated for those who join late in the year.

Auto Haus
1953 Newport Boulevard
Costa Mesa, California 92627

VW, dune buggy and off-road accessory supplier. Lines carried include Fire Fly sand buggy poles; Deist safety restraints; VW and Porsche hard parts; Rayjay turbocharger kits for the VW; Drager tire pressure gauges; Andeck headers; S&S headers; VW and Porsche racing headers; Neal hydraulic linkages; Almico steering brakes; Judson electric magnetos; Ja-Mar hydraulic brake system locks; Holley carbs and parts; Offy manifolds and oil pans for Jeep V-6, Toyota, Pinto, Vega, Datsun, Corvair and Gremlin; Webster ring and pinion gears; EMPI high-performance oil pumps with filter; DDS dual port manifolds; dual Weber linkage assemblies; VW close ratio gears; DDS gland nuts and washers; Gasgacinch products; Par-A-Bolic velocity stacks; carb-to-air-cleaner elbows and boxes for Zenith, Holley and Solex VW carbs; Cyclopac air filters; Donaldson air cleaner accessories; Filtron elements; Deves racing piston rings for VW and Porsche; VW big bore kits; VW self-tapping case studs and case inserts; socket wrench sets; VW special tools; VW valve cover breathers; heavy-duty front torsion bars; Crower camshafts and valve train gear; Engle cams; VW fiberglass body parts; tow bars and skid plates for Baja Bugs and dune buggies; VW solid motor mounts; DDS performance pulleys; VW quick-change push rod tubes; volumetric air intake screens; Duramax fan housing plugs; flip top gas fillers; nerf bars; VW wheel adapter kits; Aras driving lights; VW taillight and turn signal assemblies; Cibie and KC HiLites lighting equipment; Rapid Cool oil and transmission coolers; Auto Haus chassis components including rear axle stiffeners, rear shock mounts, front axle supports, and transmission straps. Also carries VW roll bars and roll bar padding, Baja Bug front and rear bumper cages, sand rail frames in kit form or completely welded (single, dual, or 4-seat units), stainless steel gas tanks, Mickey Thompson and Hurst speed shifters, Porsche and VW "Bras", universal bicycle racks, Beetle and Fastback consoles, Add-a-Dash walnut dash panels for Porsche and VW, VW and dune buggy quick steering kits, Transporter side scoops, padded rear shelves for VW—available with Craig speakers, VW overload shocks, Koni and Bilstein shocks, Racimex and VDO dash instruments, Auto Meter instruments, Scientific workshop manuals, Autopress, Drake, H.P., Clymer and Bentley manuals. Free information. Consult catalog at speed shop or accessory dealer.

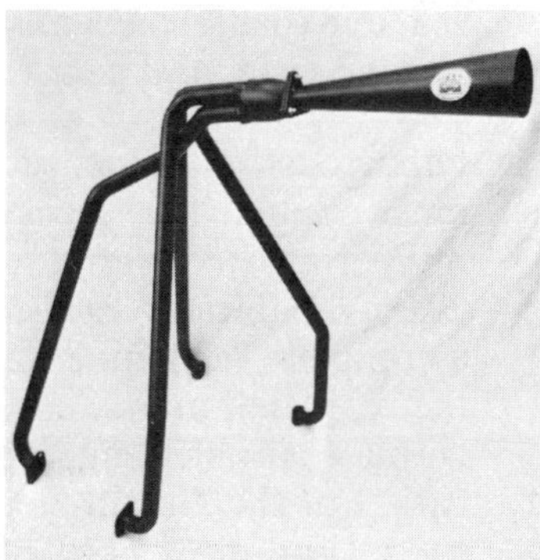

The "Tee-Pee" buggy header from Auto Haus

Autokit Industries
P.O. Box 1073
Alameda, California 94501

Autokit's Invader GT 4A is a racy, hatchback design with gull-wing doors, a louvered rear window, and recessed headlights behind plexiglass covers. The car is designed to fit a full-length Volkswagen chassis and can take VW, Porsche or Corvair engines. The basic kit, which includes a one-piece unitized body, molded fiberglass dash, weather-tight inner panel, adjustable bucket seats, and a mounting and hardware kit, sells for $695.00 f.o.b. San Rafael, California. The Deluxe kit adds plexiglass gull-wing doors, door hinges and fasteners, and tailored naugahyde upholstery for a total of $895.00. The Super $1195.00 kit includes steel-front bumpers, pre-fitted and trimmed doors and hatchback, installed rear window, gastank mounting kit, and spare tire carrier. Free literature.

Automags
24248 Crenshaw
Torrance, California 90505

Original sales catalogs for many American cars, and both English and American car magazines. This is the place to find old *Road & Tracks,* issues of the late lamented *Sports Car Graphic,* and the *Horseless Carriage Club Gazette* from 1953 to the present. Free lists.

Auto Marine Instruments Corporation
6101 Grosse Point Road
Niles, Illinois 60648

Tune-up instruments for the professional or backyard mechanic include power timing lights, tach/dwell meters, alternator/generator/regulator testers, compression and vacuum testers, exhaust gas analyzers, and complete tune-up kits. Free literature.

Exhaust gas analyzer from Auto Marine Instruments Corporation

---

Automark
641 Vermont Street
Palatine, Illinois 60067

Tire gauges, ignition coils, oil filter wrenches, spark plug gap gauges, electronic fuel shut-off anti-theft devices, car thermometers, fuel line tubing, auto compasses, wide-angle rear view mirrors and pocket calculators for travelers and performance enthusiasts. These small calculators, working on the slide rule principle, can be used to figure such things as trip expenses, gas mileage, weight/power ratios, elapsed time, and gear ratios. Free literature.

AutoMat Co. Inc.
223 Park Avenue
Hicksville, New York 11802

Offers custom carpet sets and Naugahyde seat covers for most popular foreign cars. Carpeting comes in nylon hi-pile or deep twist versions, and in numerous colors. Carpets also available for 1949-present American cars at $49.95 for a complete set. Some foreign car kits include carpeting for the rear shelf area. Seat covers, made of thick Naugahyde with a foam backing, cost $45.00 to $60.00 for most sports cars. For the Austin-Healey, Triumph TR-series and Porsche there are jump seat kits for $32.00. Jaguar XK 140 & 150 jump seat kits are priced at $15.00. Kits are also available for front and rear seats of the Mini-Minor, Fiat 850 coupe, Ford Cortina/Anglia, Saab, VW and Volvo. Colors are red, black, medium blue, MG-TD green, Alfa grey, and Jaguar biscuit. Matching leatherette material for door panels (54″ wide) is $4.50 per yard. Free literature and samples.

Auto-Matic Products Co.
1918 South Michigan Avenue
Chicago, Illinois 60616

Auto burglar alarms. Manufacturers of Auto-Matic Alarm Model OC-9 and Auto-Guard Model SK-0A3. Model OC-9 is a complete system with contact switches in all doors, hood and trunk compartment. There is a master control lockswitch and siren under the hood. When alarm is set with key, an attempt to tamper with door, hood or trunk lid will set off siren which continues to blow until turned off with key. Cost per unit is $56.70, going down to $44.00 for 12 units or more. Installation may be done by distributor, but unit is supplied with complete instructions and all parts for home installation. Model SK-0A3, also a complete system which sounds siren, is $38.00 per unit or $19.00 in quantities of 12 or more. Free literature.

Auto Meter Products 22 South State Street Elgin, Illinois 60120	Electric speedometers and tachometers, and mechanical pressure gauges. Also makes a rev limiter unit to be used in conjunction with competition model tachometer. Free literature.
Automobilhistoriska Klubben (Vintage and Veteran Cars) c/o Sven Harnstrom Tekniska Museet, 115 27 Stockholm Sweden	For those who expect to travel in Scandinavia, or have an interest in things Swedish, this club sponsors rallies and meetings, publishes a quarterly magazine and a newsletter, maintains a spares registry and library, and keeps tabs on local parts and equipment suppliers. Yearly dues: $15.00. There is also an entry fee and applications must be countersigned by two current members.
Automod Atlanta 120 Copeland Road N.E. Atlanta, Georgia 30342	Foreign car accessories and performance products. Sells all sorts of goodies plus anti-sway bars, electronic ignition systems, dash instruments, spoilers and spooks, rally equipment, ski racks, and wind wings. Catalog $1.00.
Automotive Cooling Products Route 2, Box 12 Grand Rapids Minnesota 55744	Cooling system hard parts for most popular domestic and foreign cars. Also carries heavy-duty transmission coolers, stainless steel flex fans with five and seven blades, increased-capacity radiators for tow cars and recreational vehicles, replacement heater cores, and air conditioning condensers available on an exchange basis. Does business both on a wholesale and retail basis. Free literature.
Automotive Design and Development, Ltd. Willments Shipyard Hazel Road Woolston Southampton England	Makers of the Nova kit car based on the VW chassis and VW or Porsche 4-cyl engine. The basic kit for this aerodynamic coupe comes with wheels, tires, seats, carpets, steering wheel, windscreen, windows, lights, locks, switches, windscreen wiper, and the exhaust system. A VW engine conversion of 2.2 liters displacement can also be supplied. Top speed claimed for the most highly modified version is 135 mph, with a 0-60 time of 6 seconds. The body work comes already finished in lime green, blue or red. Price of the kit is about $1,875.00. Free information.
Automotive Development 501 West Maple, Unit V Orange, California 92668	Sells complete Formula Ford engines at $1,795.00, plus individual parts for Cortina and uprated engines. Also has Webster gearboxes and parts, Teledyne racing batteries, A/D headers for Formula Ford, and much small racing hardware. Body components available include nose sections for the Titan Mk. 6B, Brabham BT-21, Winkelmann WDF-2 and Merlyn Mark II, plus a belly pan and engine cover for the latter. Free information.
Automotive Historical Society of Sweden (Pre-1939 Cars) c/o Kurt Kramer Box 244 S-14200 Trangsund Sweden	The Society organizes two rallies each spring, one for cars of the 1930s, and one for cars from 1946-56. In addition, they are the organizers of two swap meets, in the spring and fall, which are the largest in Sweden. The general Club magazine is *Motorhistoriskt Magasin,* with ten issues a year. Another publication, *46/56—aktuellt,* covers the section of the Club for cars 1946-56. The latter comes out five to six times a year. There are also three membership rosters: one of members, one of cars, and a third covering motorcycles owned by Club members. Yearly dues: approximately $10.00 (50 Swedish crowns).

Automotive Machine Specialties
2120 East Howell Avenue
Unit 506
Anaheim, California 92805

Strictly VW machine work. Valve job (heads off) $12.00; counterbore heads for larger barrels (a pair) $10.00; spark plug inserts installed $4.50 each; resurface clutch face $7.00; drill flywheel for 8 dowels $5.00; cases bored for oversize cylinders $8.00; machine cases for stroker cranks $18.00. Many other services listed plus custom head work available on request. Heliarc welding available for heads and cases. Free price list.

Automotive Obsolete
c/o Duane Steele
1023 East 4th Street
Santa Ana, California 92701

Sells Ford repro parts. Send a stamped, self-addressed envelope with query.

Automotive Specialties Division of Electrodyne
2316 Jefferson Davis Highway
Alexandria, Virginia 22301

Parts and accessories for Porsche and some other foreign cars. Porsche items include 914 center seats, front end protectors ("bras"), stone shields for 911 and 914, front adjustable sway bars for 911/914, trailer hitches, tow bars, front spoilers, fender flares and other fiberglass parts for 911 and 914, a complete line of workshop manuals, Marchal and Hella lights, Racemark steering wheels, headers and mufflers, Abarth exhausts, Bosch replacement parts, many hard parts for Porsche models 356 to present, metric tools and Ferodo brake parts. Also has some accessories for 240Z, Audi, BMW and Capri. Free catalog.

Autopower Corporation
3163 Adams Avenue
San Diego, California 92116

Bolt-in roll bars for most American cars, 4WD vehicles, sports cars, and many small foreign sedans. Prices range from $69.50 all the way up to $165.00 for some SCCA-approved racer's models for American cars. Free literature.

Autopress, Ltd.
Bennett Road
Brighton
Sussex, BN2 5JG
England

Service manuals (Autobook series) for English and some continental cars.

Auto Specialties Manufacturing Co.
Graves Street
St. Joseph, Michigan 48085

Lifting and hydraulic body repair equipment. Ausco makes hydraulic jacks, one-end lifters, transmission jacks, dual wheel dollies, cranes, bumper jacks, tripod jacks, scissor jacks, jack safety stands, lug wrenches, hydraulic presses, and hydraulic body straightening kits. Free literature to wholesalers.

Autotronics, Inc.
P.O. Box 31433
Dallas, Texas 75231

Ever been zapped by radar while winging it down the turnpike? Well here's the ultimate anti-zapper for self-defense in the technological age.

The Snooper is a long-range radar detector to monitor the fuzz who are monitoring you. It is a compact, solid-state device which mounts on the windshield or dash and can be permanently wired in or powered by a plug which fits the cigarette lighter receptacle. It is available for 12-volt systems only.

You and I don't need the Snooper, being law-abiding types, but it could be just the gift for Cousin Harvey who flies his

Lamborghini a couple of feet above the road. And it's guaranteed for one year against everything but the possibility that next year's fuzzwagon will come equipped with an anti-anti-zapper and pick Harvey off like a low-flying duck.
The cost of the unit is $59.95, and extra baseplates are available for switching it from car to car. Free literature.

Autoweek
13920 Mt. McClellan
Reno, Nevada 89506

Autoweek is a newspaper primarily concerned with race reports. But there is much more of interest within its pages each week. There are feature articles on special-interest autos, new developments in race and road cars, and trends in the field. Many advertisements for race cars and goodies appear in the classified section each week. And there used to be a fine gossip column edited by Claudia Hosepian, until she switched over to the PR-advertising part of the business and left us all cold. Come on, Claudia. Yearly subscription: $12.00.

Auto World
701 North Keyser Avenue
Scranton, Pennsylvania 18508

Sports car and racing accessories from famed Oscar Kovaleski, president of the Polish Racing Drivers of America. The big Auto World catalog lists racing club rule books, hood locks, Nomex clothing, racing number sets, Nomex driving boots and gauntlet gloves, Bell and Pro-Tec helmets, shields and visors, safety belts, bucket seats, Aero-Tec fuel cells, AutoPower bolt-in roll bars, Heuer timers, rally tables and computers, stopwatch holders and data boards, Momo steering wheels, steering wheel covers, AMCO accessories, many types of quartz halogen lights, light switches and relays, fiberglass hardtops for popular sports cars, Talbot mirrors, NASA air scoops, Pinto and Vega spoilers, stripe kits, Datsun performance parts from BRE, Corvette and VW fiberglass body parts, car covers, Koni shocks, Armstrong lever shocks, swaybars for imported and domestic cars plus vans and off-road vehicles, header systems, Abarth and Stebro free-flow exhaust systems, Auto-Mech carb tune-up kits, race car trailers, performance manifolds for popular subcompact cars, Rajay turbocharger kits, Weber carbs and manifold kits for sportscars, Conelec fuel pumps, Stelling and Helling air filters, tune-up accessories, Z-F limited slip differentials for the VW ($370.00), many tune-up accessories, Monza-type gas filler caps, Smiths instruments, Sun tachs, foreign and American tune-up parts, SK tool sets, Repco and Raybestos disc brake pads, engine oil coolers, lubricants by Castrol, Loctite kits, H.P. and Fram oil filters, Minilite wheels, American Racing Equipment wheels, Goodyear racing tires, many auto books and technical manuals, plus those smaller accessories which every racer needs for his kit—race tape, cable ties, safety wire and safety wire pliers, pit trouble lights, spun aluminum headlight covers, lap timing sheets and scoring sheets, race car inspection forms, Teflon tape, and a universal pit signalling board. For those who are into car models and radio-controlled miniature racing cars, Auto World has a special catalog which is the largest in the field. Regular catalog, $1.00.

The Regal Rolls. From its inception, the Rolls-Royce was aimed at those with the wealth and discrimination to insist upon the best conservative engineering, the most meticulous craftsmanship, and sumptuous custom coachwork by masters of the craft. Even at this late date, when the parent aircraft company has foundered and most of the great coachbuilders exist only in memory, there are still fabulous Rolls-Royces, with built-in service bars or harem accommodations, designed for American billionaires or the rulers of oil-rich Arabian sheikdoms.

1. Rolls-Royce Sedanaca de Ville by H.J. Mulliner. The epitome of the "razor edge" Rolls, with "damn the chauffeur" Sedanaca coachwork, this Mulliner Silver Wraith is at the apex of British luxury car design.

2. 1948 Rolls-Royce Sedanaca de Ville by Saoutchick. Some examples of the Rolls-Royce were also supplied to Continental coachbuilders. This example, with canework siding, lushly curving fenders, and a trochoidal porthole window is in the Rubensesque French mode.

3. Rolls-Royce Sport Touring. Though unidentified, this Rolls is undoubtedly also by Saoutchick, the most flamboyant of the French designers. Saoutchick reveled in fat slathers of glittering chrome, elaborate fender skirts, and graceful, swooping fender lines.

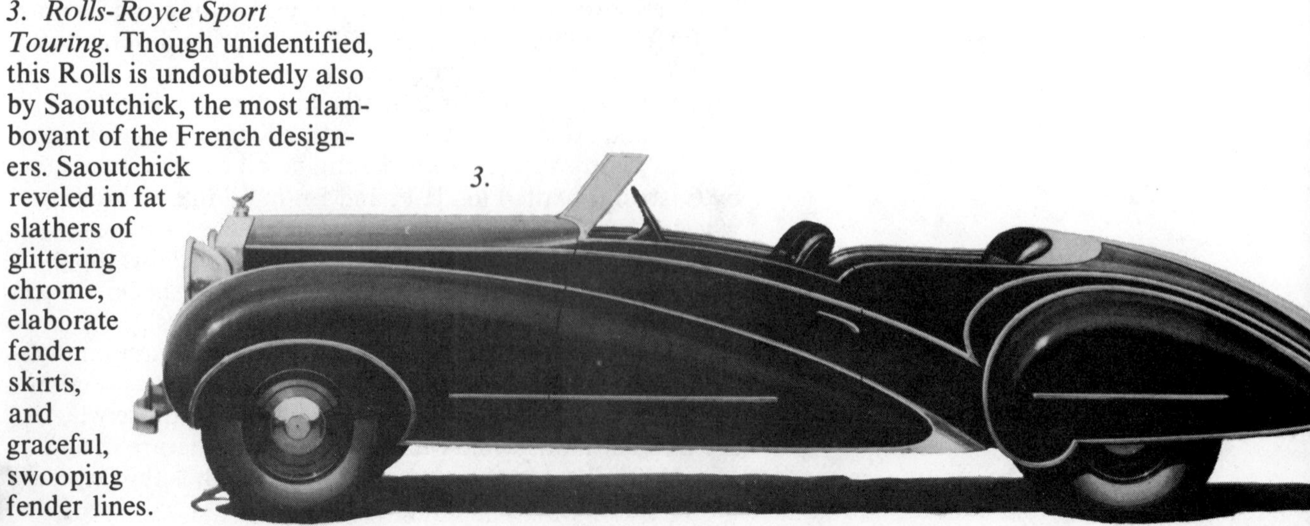

4. Rolls-Royce Limousine by Hooper. Hooper, along with Mulliner, was well thought of at the Rolls factory and turned out innumerable limousines and sedans on the Rolls chassis.

5. Rolls-Royce Silver Wraith by Hooper. A later development in Rolls coachwork was the softening and partial integration of the fender line, along with deepening of the trunk, forming a somewhat awkward, humpy line. Although the design was practical and allowed more luggage space, Rolls-Royces in this mode by Hooper and James Young are generally considered less desirable than those in the razor edge style.

6. Rolls-Royce Corniche Convertible. The semi-custom Corniche (at $35,000 or so) is now the top of the Rolls-Royce line. Although a hint of elegance remains in the side molding and shortened version of the traditional grille, the overall design is very much in the neatly packaged modern manner of Mercedes and certain Italian designs. The basic form is an elongated box, strengthened by moldings and by the distinct front fender line.

Avanti Motor Corporation
765 South Lafayette Boulevard
South Bend, Indiana 46623

Remember the Raymond Loewy-designed Studebaker Avanti, that company's entry in the T-Bird-type "personal car" sweepstakes? There are no more Studebakers, but there is an Avanti, thanks to the dedication of one Nate Altman, a former Studebaker-Packard dealer who doesn't give up easily.

Altman and his partner, Leo Newman, bought the Avanti body dies, made a deal with General Motors for power-train components, and have been happily making Avanti IIs ever since.

The fiberglass body is still produced by the same company which made them for Studebaker, while Altman and his approximately 100-man crew spend about six weeks putting each car together and making sure that the finished product meets their high standards.

The Avanti II comes with 400 cu. in. Chevrolet engine, a Turbo-Hydro or 4-speed manual transmission, power disc front brakes, built-in rollbar, front hydraulic bumpers, complete instrumentation, and many other standard features which are usually optional on Detroit cars. The price is $8,645.00.

Among the many options are an electric sunroof ($695.00), electric windows ($100.00), air-conditioning ($425.00), Borrani wire wheels with knock-off hubs ($795.00), a burglar alarm ($60.00) and much else. Since the Avanti is essentially a custom-built car, you can have just about any interior upholstery and paint you want and then talk to Altman about other options. He'll listen.

While the Avanti II is not cheap, it's a highly-refined automobile offering the sort of personalized fitments and attention to customer desires which can hardly be found anywhere else. About 300 Avanti IIs are produced each year—half of them sold from the factory and the other half through affiliated dealers. Free literature.

Avanti Owners Association International, Inc.
(Avanti and Avanti II)
3900 Church Road
Mitchellville, Maryland 20716

The Avanti Owners Association, with fourteen local chapters at last count, holds both national and regional meetings. The club's bi-monthly magazine, *Avantopics,* includes both technical information and members' advertisements. The club maintains a library of technical and historical information, and publishes a membership roster. Also available are club jewelry and jacket patches. Yearly dues: $7.50.

B&B Motors Ltd.
150 Lakehill Road
Burnt Hills, New York 12027

Racing accessories in the B&B parts bins include Racemark fire extinguishing systems, Rupert belts and harnesses, Bell helmets, Heuer timers, roll bars for sports and foreign cars (an Alfa Guilietta model is $99.50), side stripes, front and rear roll bars, Koni shocks, Stebro free-flow exhaust systems, Conelec electric fuel pumps, Carello and Cibie driving lights, Semperit tires, the well-regarded Scheel rally seats, Racemark and B&B competition seats, custom car covers, Bursch header systems, American Racing Equipment alloy wheels, Drake shop manuals, Maserati air horns, VDO instruments, Goodyear rain suits and helmet bags, Ferodo disc brake pads, cocoa floor mats, enamel badges, Rapid Cool oil and transmission coolers, and AMCO accessories. For the Porsche 914, B&B offers a center seat ($17.95), front spoiler ($59.95) and stone shield ($29.95). Other Porsche items are power pulleys for all engines, adjustable push rod tubes, mechanics service covers designed to fit around the Porsche engine compartment ($24.95), metric nut and bolt emergency kits ($4.95), and 911 front spoilers and fiberglass rear panels. Catalog, $1.00.

B & J Racing Transmissions
38 West Henderson
Porterville, California 93257

Makes a two-speed underdrive transmission for drag racing and funny cars. Also has optional reverser. Transmission with shift kit costs $860.00. A 3-speed racing transmission is $1,400.00 or $1,780.00 with reverser. A new product is an underdrive 4-speed transmission, with various optional ratios, which sells for $2,650.00 complete with reverser. A dry sump lube system is a $75.00 option. Free information.

B & K Instruments, Inc.
5111 West 164th Street
Cleveland, Ohio 44142

Sound level meters and allied equipment. Mostly intended for the professional, but could be of interest to car clubs and those who are thinking of starting their own road testing mags. Also sound, vibration, and data analysis instrumentation. Free catalogs.

Jim Babb Radiators
Route No. 1, Box 2128
Colfax, California 95713

Brass radiators for Fords 1909-32. All standard brass radiators are $225.00, while some are available in black finish at a reduction in cost. Built-in transmission oil coolers and/or provision for pressurized cooling systems are available as extra cost options on all models. Custom built radiators also available. Other products include polished brass pressure caps ($4.95), brass transmission coolers, and brass polish. Free literature.

Balance Technology, Inc.
41 Enterprise Drive
Ann Arbor, Michigan 48103

Manufactures cradle balancers, vertical balancers, portable balancing instruments, electronic vibration monitors and portable vibration analysis instruments. Free information.

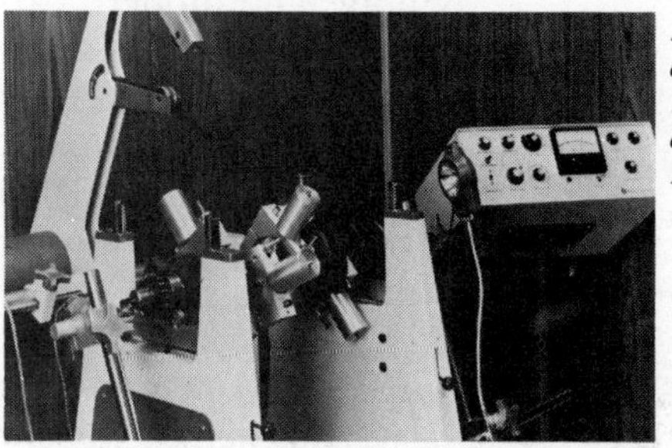

Automotive balancer model D500LR from Balance Technology, Inc.

Ballard's Antique Costumes
317 Wayside Drive
Plainfield, Indiana 46168

Also shop at 959 North Oxford
Indianapolis, Indiana 46201

The place to get a duster and goggles to go with your Mercer Raceabout and maybe a bustle skirt and parasol for milady. Write for information.

D. Barrett
4514 Whitney Drive
El Monte, California 91731

Mr. Barrett is a Berkeley enthusiast and has quite a few parts for sale, mostly used. He also offers photo-reproduced service manuals and information sheets. Send a stamped, self-addressed envelope with queries.

Bayless Racing, Inc. 1488 Hester Street Memphis, Tennessee 38116	Hard parts and accessories for all Fiats. In stock are Abarth exhausts, Fiat 128 front and rear spoilers, Fiat 124 spoilers, seat covers and floor mats for most Fiats, velocity stacks for 124 and 128, custom steering wheels, roll bars, competition brake pads, sway bars, skid pans for Fiat 124 and 128, and Abarth and Campagnolo wheels. Performance items include Weber carbs and Abarth manifolds for Fiat 124 (manifold and dual Weber IDF 44s with velocity stacks are $325.00); Abarth cooling fans and oil sumps; Fiat 850 oil pumps ($31.00); cams; competition pistons with rings ($110.00); heavy-duty main bearings and connecting rods; Abarth double valve springs; close-ratio gear sets ($225.00); racing springs and shocks; safety harnesses; and oil systems. Can supply new and used O.E.M. parts for all Fiat and Fiat Abarth cars. Free list of accessories and prices.
Frank L. Beall 2830 South Maple Sioux City, Iowa 51106	Parts for Jeep and Mighty Mite. Surplus Jeep parts for M38A1 and MB-GPW include tops, canvas doors and side curtains, deep mud type muffler ($2.50 each), capstan winch driveshaft, ($20.00 each), Spicer or Rzeppa front axles (long $28.50, short $27.50), and other parts as available. Free lists.
Bear Manufacturing Co. 2830-5th Street Rock Island, Illinois 61201	Power equipment for professional mechanics. Bear makes wheel alignment and balancing equipment, tire-out-of-roundness detectors, body and frame straightening equipment, brake repair devices, and engine dynamometers. The Company also runs a school for professional mechanics. Free information to jobbers and garages.
Earle Beaver 6141 Vanderbilt Dallas, Texas 75214	Sells auto bud vases made from imported German cut crystal. Set of two vases complete with brackets and screws is $30.00. Write for further information.
Paul Beck Barneys Farm Happisburgh Norwich Norfolk England	Mr. Beck's unique stock consists of some hard-to-obtain raw materials, plus many small parts of general use on vintage and modern cars. A cast aluminum fish tail, secured with a set screw, is about $7.20 for the small size and $10.50 for the large size. Gasket materials, including graphited asbestos and felt, are available in various thicknesses and sizes. Other materials and small mechanical parts include copper tubing, nylon tubing, solderless terminals, grease nipples, brass cup greasers, winkley oilers (whatever they are), brass drain plugs, hood latches, flush floor lifting rings, silk rope pulls, lift-the-dot fasteners, turnbuckle fasteners, snap fasteners, carpet fasteners, flexible window sheet made of a resistant synthetic called "Vybak," toggle fasteners, aluminum strip with rubber insert or without, aluminum sheet, spiked brass strip, rubber matting, door handles, leather hood straps, and other items. Gas filler caps available include Monza and Aston types. Mr. Beck will send his parts list overseas by first class or air post for $1.00. For particular queries send an International Reply Coupon.
Bee Line Engineering 117 West Street Jonesville, Michigan 49250	Headers for domestic cars, 4WD vehicles and pickup trucks, dragsters and street roadsters. Also makes traction bars in bolt-on styles for many American cars. Free literature.

Beettle Auto Haus
8709 Highway 99
Vancouver, Washington 98665

Makers of the Beettle Dune Buggy (basic body, $179.00 to $225.00 depending on model) and Tow'd body ($139.95). For the Tow'd, an assembled rail frame goes for $349.95 with an exchange front axle and rear suspension. Many accessories are available. Other featured items are Baja Bug kits, steering brakes, roll bars, skid plates, extractor exhausts, bucket seats, convertible tops, fiberglass hardtops, VW performance items, Century steel and chrome wheels, fender flares for the VW and some 4WD cars, hood scoops, spoilers for the VW and most Datsuns, and heavy-duty VW suspension components. Free literature.

Bell Auto Parts
3663 East Gage Avenue
Bell, California 90201

Billing itself as "Racing's General Store," Bell handles performance parts and racing accessories from the following suppliers: Accel, American Safety, Ansen, Bell Toptex, Bendix, Cal Custom, Carter, Cragar, Crower, Develco, Edelbrock, EELCO, Engle, Filt-O-Reg, Flex-A-Lite, Iskenderian, JE, Jahns, Gabriel, Grant, Hedman, Holley, Hooker, Hurst, Hurst-Airheart, Lakewood, M/T, Mallory, Milodon, Moon, Offenhauser, P&S, Paulson, Ross, Savage, Segal, Simpson, Stewart-Warner, Sun, Thermo-Chem, Trans-Dapt, Velvetouch, Worth, and Weiand. Bucket seats for VW sedans are $29.95, and for vans $69.95. Indy speed shifters for most popular 3-speed transmissions sell for $35.00. A Pure Air standard race hood, made of aluminized, flame-resistant material, with external breathers, is $44.00. Catalog, $1.00.

Bell Star Helmet in sizes 6 3/8-7 7/8 by Bell Auto Parts

The Bendix Corporation
Motor Components Division
Elmira, New York 14903

Makers of Zenith and Stromberg carbs; drum brake components for domestic cars; brake system components for VW, Toyota, Datsun, and Opel; ignition parts for domestic and many foreign cars; disc brake components; and starter drive units. Catalogs and Brake System Service Manual available to jobbers.

Bennett Garfield Publications
2119 Route 110
Farmingdale, New York 11735

Publishers of the annual *Tire Guide* with listings of wheel and tire sizes for passenger cars and light trucks (including imports), along with tire size conversion information. The book sells for $3.00. Other publications about tires are *Tire-Fax,* with price lists of major tire companies ($12.00 for yearly subscription), *Who Makes It? And Where?,* with tire codes and the addresses of all manufacturers ($1.00), and *TBA All-Purpose Percentage Book* with tables to compute tread and battery adjustments—designed for the professional. Free information.

Robert Bentley, Inc.
872 Massachusetts Avenue
Cambridge, Massachusetts 02139

Service manuals. Free literature.

Bentley Drivers Club (Bentley)
c/o Miss B. M. Gunstone
A.C.I.S.
76a, High Street
Long Crendon
Buckinghamshire
England

The main Club events of this very active organization are a race meeting at Silverstone in August, the Kensington Garden Concours in June, a sprint meeting, and a driving test competition. The Club publishes the *B.D.C. Spares Advertiser* and *Club Notes* monthly. Bentley literature, an optional spares scheme, and Club jewelry and ties are also offered. Yearly dues: $11.75.

Berens Associates
6046 Claremont Avenue
Oakland, California 94618

Warehouse distributor for off-road accessories and Toyota Land Cruiser items. Carries the following lines: Warn, Ramsey, Bestop, Hone, Powerwinch, Gates, Mico, Husky, Cutlas, Flex-A-Lite, Appliance Wheels, Offenhauser, Per-Lux, Heco, Tiltometer, Barden, Whitco, Hayden, Valley, and others. Free catalog of Toyota Land Cruiser accessories available from retailers who carry the Berens line.

Gene Berg
784 North Lemon Avenue
Orange, California 92667

Gene Berg, famous for the modified VWs he has put together, sells both standard VW performance parts and special items he has devised. Berg specials include magnesium or aluminum oil sumps, 4″ deep drag sumps, flow-tested and blueprinted oil pumps, carb installation kits with metric hardware, and tools such as a special crankshaft gear puller ($23.95), and flycutter for boring cases and heads for big-bore cylinders ($99.95). Also has Kolbenschmidt, Mahle and EMPI pistons; Deves and ATE rings; dowels and drill jigs for 1961 and later cranks; 6- and 12-volt lightened flywheels; starter shaft adapters; heavy-duty clutch parts; Glyco bearings; Okrasa crankshafts; counterweighted stroker cranks; Porsche 912 rods and converted Buick and Chevy rods; Thermo-Chem coolers; remote oil filter system hardware; Sig Erson and Engle cams; valves and valve train gear; swivel-foot valve adjusting screws ($17.65 for set of eight); polished aluminum pulleys; dual carb linkage; Weber, Solex and Holley carbs along with a great variety of jets, venturis, and other carb hardware; single and dual carb manifolds; headers of all types; solid transmission mounts and rear engine supports; traction bars; close-ratio gears; beefed-up transaxle parts including Berg's shim kit to remove side trust from large spider gears ($13.50); Wito shocks; Racimex dash instruments; and VW workshop and technical manuals. Catalog $.50. Catalog of instructions on all Berg parts, $1.00.

C. E. Berry
41 Musket Trail
Simsbury, Connecticut 06070

Car books, magazines and miscellaneous literature, primarily for vehicles from 1950 to the present. Mr. Berry is also archivist for the Road-Race Lincoln Register and deals in parts and literature for 1952-55 Lincolns, all models. Send a stamped, self-addressed envelope with query.

Bieber Enterprises, Inc.
R.D. 1
Pipersville, Pennsylvania 18947

The Bieber Shifter is a unique cam-operated model designed to work with Muncie 4-speed boxes. Instead of one shift lever, there are three. Two are side-by-side levers which diverge at the top to form a "Y." Pull back on the left-hand lever and you will find yourself upshifting like now. A swift tug on the right-hand lever and you are back in a lower gear. The straight line action is provided by a programmed cam and is just the thing for drag racers looking to pick up as much as a tenth of a second on their E.T. A third lever controls reverse gear and makes the shifter suitable for the street also. Price of the Bieber Shifter is now $100.00 and it is guaranteed for the life of the original owner. Free literature.

In-line four-speed shifter for Muncie transmissions from Bieber Enterprises, Inc.

Zigmont Billus 52 Harrison Avenue Glens Falls, New York 12801	Automotive connecting rod and main bearing rebabbitting and boring. Send a stamped, self-addressed envelope with queries.
Bioya Engineering 224 South O'Neil Street Joliet, Illinois 60436	Can supply *all* parts for Austin/Morris Mini-Minor. Also some accessories. Send query for price of parts you need.
Bird Automotive P.O. Box 793 Fremont, Nebraska 68025	Street Roadster frames, and fiberglass body parts. The standard Roadster kit, which includes a 'glass 1923 "T" style body, grille shell, jig-welded Roadster frame, and kit instructions, sells for $249.95. The Deluxe Roadster kit, which has all of the above plus an 11 gallon fuel tank, Metalflake body and matching fenders, and set of vinyl covered polyfoam seats, costs $399.95. Components also available individually. Free information. Roadster plans, $2.00.
Keith Black Racing Engines 11120 Scott Avenue South Gate, California 90280	Complete 426 Chrysler Hemi racing engines, 426 blocks, and all individual engine performance components. Keith Black also has parts for small block Chrysler engines and small and big block Chevrolets. Other products include superchargers, blower drives, racing clutches, fuel injector accessories, modified Enderle fuel injection units, and precision tools. Complete unblown fuel or gas 426 engines are priced from $5,525.00. Superchargers are $495.00 in aluminum and $595.00 in magnesium. Enderle fuel injection units with port kit and pump are $497.00. Catalog, $1.50.

Blackhawk Manufacturing Co. Box 2870 Milwaukee, Wisconsin 53227	Body repair tools, lifting equipment, hydraulic presses, and jacks. Manufactures Porto-Power hydraulic ram systems for body and frame straightening, mobile cranes, engine stands, transmission jacks, air lifts and jack safety stands, wheel balancers, headlight alignment systems, vehicle vibrators to locate sources of rattles, and Korek air-hydraulic body repair equipment. Consult catalog at wholesalers.
BMW Automobile Club of America (BMW) P.O. Box 401 Hollywood, California 90028	Club activities include monthly meetings, a one-day Bob Bondurant School high-performance driving class (usually in April), and an Oktoberfest get-together. Meetings are in Los Angeles. A monthly newsletter with technical advice and a classified section is called *The Whispering Bomb.* Members also receive various emblems, a pennant, and a car badge. For the future, it is planned that members will also receive a national club newsletter and BMW journal, the latter translated from the German. Although the Club is mainly devoted to current 4-cylinder and 6-cylinder BMWs, there are some members with older models and at least one resident expert on the 2-cylinder BMW minicars. Yearly dues: $12.00 for local members; $7.50 for those who live outside the Los Angeles region. The first year's dues are pro-rated upon the month of joining. There is a $5.00 initiation fee.
BMW Car Club of America (BMW) P.O. Box 96 Boston, Massachusetts 02199	Local chapters of the BMWCCA run their own activities, while the National has a yearly Oktoberfest, hosted by one of the chapters. Chapters are: Boston Chapter, Box 450, Bedford, Massachusetts 01730; New York Chapter, Box 312, Bayside, New York 11361; New Jersey Chapter, Box 293, Summit, New Jersey 07901; National Capital Chapter, Box 2413, Hyattsville, Maryland 20784; Buckeye Central, Box 53, Worthington, Ohio 43085; Tidewater Chapter, Box 62145, Virginia Beach, Virginia 23462; Greater Dayton Chapter, 5470 Access Road, Dayton, Ohio 45431; Windy City BMW, Box 689, Lake Forest, Illinois 60045; St. Louis Chapter, 3218 Utah Place, St. Louis, Missouri 63116. The Club's monthly newsletter is *Blau Mit Weis Roundel,* which includes technical articles, an "At Your Service" column on accessory sources and BMW-related products, and want-advertisements free to members. Yearly dues: $5.00; initiation fee $5.00.
BMW 507 Owners' Club (BMW 507) 2815 Philmont Avenue Huntingdon Valley Pennsylvania 19006	Pretty much a one-man operation of dedicated 507 owner Barry McMillan. Principal activity is an annual meeting on Memorial Day weekend, usually near Philadelphia. There is also an irregular report to members, all of whom must be either current or past owners of a 507. Technical inquiries, the import of parts from Germany, and the remanufacture of some smaller parts no longer available are functions handled by Mr. McMillan. Yearly dues: none.
BMW 507 Owners Register (BMW 507) c/o John M. Kessler 3223 Kenmore Road Richmond, Virginia 23225	Register of 134 BMW 507s, and their owners, world-wide, available to 507 owners from Mr. Kessler. Since there were more than 248 507s built, some owners have been delinquent in sending in information. Among presumed 507 owners who had not yet responded at last report were King Hassan II, King Constantine, and Elvis Presley.

Bob's Antique Auto Parts 121 North Third Street Box 1856 Rockford, Illinois 61110	Comprehensive list of hard parts and accessories for Model T and Model A. Used "T" right or left axle housing, $7.50; axle shaft, $16.95; standard ratio ring and pinion gear, $32.95; lined accessory brake shoes for two wheels, $10.50; used front radius rod, $5.00; Ford solid brass hub cap with script or block letters, $14.95 for set of four; black or tan spare tire cover with script, $9.95; used cylinder block, $25; gullwing radiator caps in brass or chrome, $6.95; new spring shackles, front or rear, $4.95 for 16-piece set. For Model A: rear wheel grease seal, $1.15; 4.50"x21" Armstrong or Firestone tire, $23.95; used front axle, $12.50; complete spindle bolt set, $8.95; exhaust pipe, muffler and tail pipe assembly, $9.95; front spring, $18.95; rear spring, $29.95; engine gasket set, $5.75; heavy-duty radiator, $49.95; exhaust cut-out, $11.85. Many other parts and comprehensive listing of Ford literature. Also exterior paint and engine enamel. Free catalog.
Bob's Auto Body 88 Elinor Avenue Akron, Ohio 44305	Parts for classic 1955-57 T-Bird. Quarter panel sections are $75.00 each; rear wheelhouse extensions, $25.00 each; 1955-56 dash covers, $35.00 each. Also carpeting, seat covers, other interior and body parts. Send a stamped, self-addressed envelope for parts and price list.
John Bokeeno The Arms, Apt. J-302 Collegeville, Pennsylvania 19426	Parts for Willys 1952-55. Both body and mechanical parts, new and used. Also service and parts manuals. New parts are listed on computer printout. Send a stamped, self-addressed envelope for list.
Bolt-on-Parts, Inc. 15551 West Dixie Highway North Miami Beach Florida 33162	Mail-order distributor for BRE Interpart, Koni, DA Oil, Superior Industries, Midland Wheels, Essence Wheels, Minilite Wheels and Urushibara & Co. Write for availability of catalog
Bob Bondurant School of High Performance Driving, Inc. Ontario Motor Speedway Ontario, California 91764	Has four high performance driving courses. A one-half day skid control course is $65.00. Full day advanced highway driving course is $125.00. A 2-day high performance course with some fundamental racing techniques is $250.00. A variant of this course extends one more day and gives the student actual experience in precision and slalom driving; the cost is $375.00. The all-out 5-day competition road racing course for $895.00 gives student eligibility for IMSA license and helps obtain an SCCA log book and 50 percent waiver of driving school requirements. Courses are given at Ontario Motor Speedway. Cars are provided for the 5-day competition course. Otherwise student must supply his own vehicle or rent one from the school for $25.00 a day. Free information.
Terry and Barry Bone Mount Place North Chailey Lewes Sussex England	Repro and used parts for all MGs 1927-49. Have most mechanical and some body parts for OHC models from 1929-35. New parts for later model MGs include most rubber items, body parts, windshield wiper components, seats, shock absorbers, and insignia plates. Handle instruction and workshop manuals for all models. Free information.

The Book, Sports Car & Racing Equipment
Box 500
230 East 5th Street
St. Paul, Minnesota 55101

Racing accessories, competition preparation, and sports car goodies. Small hardware items include metric fasteners; SAE grade 5 and grade 8 nuts, bolts, and washers; Aeroquip Teflon hose; Woodruff Keys; wiring terminals; cable ties; toggle switches; rivets; Bosch ignition parts for most foreign cars; and accelerator springs. Among the competition accessories available are Fypro and Nomex clothing, Bell helmets, race goggles, Velvetouch metallic brake linings and competition sway bars for sports cars and small sedans, carb rampipes, Aero Tec fuel cells, front and rear spoilers, roll bars, on-board fire extinguishing systems, Varley batteries, racing numbers and pit signal boards, SCCA publications, and Repco disc brake pads. Competition preparation services include engine machine work on any car, Magnafluxing and Heliarc welding. Other products include Stewart-Warner dash instruments, SSP

Engine cylinder-head work—part of the competition preparation services offered by The Book, Sports Car & Racing Equipment

transistorized ignition systems, Koni shocks, Firestone racing tires, wheels by Chassis Engineering and American Racing Equipment, oil coolers for popular sports and foreign cars, Cibie lights, Heuer timers and AMCO accessories. Company also distributes Pinto and Vega performance parts, Blaupunkt radios and Stebro exhaust systems. Catalog, $2.00.

Booth-Arons Racing Enterprises
3861 West 12 Mile
Berkley, Michigan 48072

Specializes in small and big block Chevrolet performance parts. Also supplies complete Chev racing engines: 427 aluminum head model ($3,200.00); 454 E.T. aluminum head model ($3,080.00); Super Stock 454 engine, developing 450 h.p., built to N.H.R.A. specs ($2,850.00); 427 Super Stock engine ($2,700.00); 396 Super Stock ($2,600.00); 327 Modified/Pro Stock engine ($3,200.00); Super Stock 350 engine ($2,600.00); and Modified 302 engine ($3,200.00). Engine components available include bare blocks, short blocks, reworked heads, crankshaft assemblies, steel and aluminum con rods, pistons, rings, cams, and valvetrain gear. Driveline and chassis items listed are rear axle gears, 12-bolt Positraction, Borg-Warner T-10 and Super T-10 close-ratio transmissions, Chrysler racing transmissions, Turbo-Hydro 400 manual shift transmissions, modified torque converters for Turbo-Hydros, axle shafts, Chev Borg & Beck clutch assemblies, specially calibrated rear leaf springs and front coil springs for Chevy II and Camaro, metallic brake linings for Chevy II and Camaro, chrome valve covers, Chev windage trays, deep oil pans, harmonic balancers, oil pumps with long pickups, and traction bar wedges for Lakewood type bars. Company will also rework Quadra-Jet and Holley carbs and Chev distributors. Has facilities for building race cars from the ground up. Catalog, $1.00.

Borg-Warner, Automotive Parts Division
11045 Gage Avenue
Franklin Park, Illinois 60131

Among the many replacement parts B-W can supply are clutch components, driveline parts, U-joints, driveshaft center support assemblies, timing chains and sprockets, water pumps, starter drive units (including drives for a number of imported cars), ignition components for domestic and foreign cars, U.S. and foreign carb rebuild kits, electrical cables and hardware, PCV valves, starters and alternators for domestic cars and foreign vehicles using Lucas systems, Lucas and domestic distributors, fuel pumps, manual transmission gears including transmission parts for some older cars, and tune-up kits for Bosch and Ducellier systems. Borg-Warner also makes tune-up tools and performance ignition and carb parts under the "Power Brute" name. Consult catalogs at automotive parts house.

Borrani Wire Wheel Service
328 Lincoln Boulevard
Venice, California 90291

Sales and service of Borrani wire wheels. Includes truing, respoking, rechroming and rebuilding. Also custom manufactures wire wheels up to 10″ wide on special order. Sells rebuilt wire wheels and parts for wire wheels. Can perform any service needed on any wire wheel. Send a stamped, self-addressed envelope with queries.

Boyce Engineering
5622 North Western Avenue
Chicago, Illinois 60625

Stock car chassis and wide wheels. Roll cage kits are available for the Chevelle, Monte Carlo, Mustang and Torino at prices from $302.40 to $510.00. A complete Chevelle-Monte Carlo cage chassis kit, which consists of the cage kit installed on a new frame with steering and suspension components, is $1,287.00. A Camaro, Firebird or Mustang sub-frame assembly with cage but without front frame section sells for $1,275.00. Complete Camaro-Firebird chassis kit is $1,650. For do-it-yourselfers there are components such as roll cage tubing, square tubing, rectangular tubing, heavy-wall tubing, strip stock and aluminum sheet, to suit a wide variety of needs. Services available include tube bending, saw cutting, notching, forming and welding. Other products are wide wheels called "Trailblazer," "Dune Buggy" and "Truck and Camper," in widths from 6″ to 14″ and diameters of 13″ to 16.5″. Racing wheels, known as the "Sprint," "Super Modified," "Stock Car Special" and "Grand National," come in widths up to 15″ and are constructed from steel. Also available are coil springs, adjusters and adjuster parts. Free literature.

Bradford Auto Supply
Fairground Road
Bradford, Vermont 05033

Model A and Model B Ford new repro and used parts. Chrome plated windshield frame for 1932 Roadster and phaeton, $75.00. Trunk rack painted black with four stainless steel moldings, complete and ready to bolt to frame, $150.00. Also top irons, top bows, 1930-31 Roadster subframe cross members, wooden floor boards, hood hooks and taillight doors, front seats for Model A, and complete restorations on Model A and B. Free price list.

Bradley Automotive
10 West 38th Street
Minneapolis, Minnesota 55409

The attractive Bradley GT kit car, for the VW chassis and standard Beetle running gear, sells for $1,495.00 for the basic body kit which includes headlight covers and housings, windshield frame/hardtop unit (designed to accept Corvette windshield), rear deck and engine cover, tinted plexiglass gull-wing doors, fiberglass bucket seats (not upholstered), and various hardware and trim items. The Super GT kit is $2,395.00, including kits for fuel tank, wiring, lighting, instruments, upholstery, windshield, heater/defroster and fresh air vent. Additional items included are license plate frames, custom steering wheel, interior mirror, chrome fender mirrors, and windshield wiper arms and blades. Individual components of Super kit are also sold separately. Other options are roll bar ($119.00), and air conditioning kit ($495.00). The Bradley GT body is available in a choice of over 50 impregnated colors including Metalflake. Brochure and poster, $1.00. Metalflake color charts, $2.00; upholstery samples, $1.00; and illustrated assembly manual, $7.00. These prices are deductible from kit cost when ordering.

Breco Wheel Works
16756 Bennett Road
North Royalton, Ohio 44133

Restoration of Model T type wheels. Prices are $3.85 a spoke replacement, $14.00 a felloe replacement (½ section), and $4.95 for complete sanding of a wheel. Services include dismantling, inspection, heat treating, sandblasting, installation, tightening, reassembly, centering, and balancing. All wheels other than Model T are restored on a labor plus material basis. Kiln dried hickory and white oak are used. Minimum time is 14 weeks. Metal wheel parts, such as rims, hubs, and drums, must be shipped regardless of condition before restoration can proceed. Also available are do-it-yourself spokes. Write for further information.

Bremen Sport Equipment, Inc.
P.O. Box 221, U.S. 6 East
Bremen, Indiana 46506

Manufactures Maxi-Taxi and Citation dune buggies. The Citation in its basic kit form is $368.50, or $419.50 with Metalflake body. At slight additional cost a "T-hood" version can be supplied. The latter resembles a Lotus Seven rather than Henry's first love and is available in 4 solid and 20 Metalflake colors. For another $55.00 or so, the kit can be supplied in its No. 2 version, which has a windshield and chromed headlights. The gamut of optional equipment includes a hardtop, front and rear seats, carpeting, bumpers, a skid plate, and other useful appendages. The top also comes in a version with port hole windows. The Maxi-Taxi carries a basic kit price of $628.00, or $848.00 as the Maxi-Taxi II version with pre-hung doors. It utilizes the stock VW chassis (unlike the Citation, on which the chassis must be cut a bit more than 14″), and has the vintage custom look. The Maxi-Taxi, in either version, comes as a "B" kit

The Maxi-Taxi buggy by Bremen Sport Equipment, Inc.

with many accessories standard. There is also a list of options which includes VDO instruments, a dual exhaust system, front and rear seats, running board covers, and—for the final touch—polished aluminum lanterns ($85.00). Bremen Sport also makes fiberglass VW Beetle body parts and many accessories for universal dune buggy application. Free literature.

The Brentwood Company
P.O. Box 727
Brentwood, Tennessee 37027

Will custom make extruded or molded rubber items for any car. While it is usually impractical to have single items custom-made, as few as 25 copies of a molded item, or a few hundred feet of extruded goods, can be economically feasible. Car clubs take note. Free information.

Jerry L. Brewster
Route 2
Bastrop, Louisiana 71220

Although stocking many parts for 1953-72 Corvettes, Mr. Brewster's particular specialty is early Corvette sales brochures and owners' manuals. Electrical wiring diagrams for 1953-55 6-cylinder, 1955-57 V-8, 1958-60 Corvette, and 1961-62 'Vette are $1.00 each. Free literature list.

Bristol Cars
Filton
Bristol BS99 7AR
England

The spares manager, Mr. S. E. Gibbens, advises that most mechanical parts for all Bristol cars and engines can be supplied from stock. Body panels are available for the Bristol 401 on out. Prices will be quoted including carriage and packing charges by any method of despatch required.

Bristol Owners Club (Bristol and Bristol-engined Cars)
c/o R.J.T. Hewitt
5 St. Leonard's Court
East Sheen
London, S.W. 14
England

Club activities consist of an annual concours plus Northern and Southern "Affiliation Exercises" which consist of tours following a published route with members joining or leaving anywhere along the way. Many Club sections hold monthly get-togethers. The principal Club publication, the quarterly *Bulletin,* is supplemented with irregular newsletters. An annual membership roster is issued in June. Technical advice, spare parts location and library services can be provided. Film shows are held in various parts of Great Britain. Yearly dues: $7.00.

British Book Centre, Inc.
996 Lexington Avenue
New York, New York 10021

Will obtain any British book in print, except those published in U.S. editions, on special import basis. Titles in stock include Interauto technical books and a series of tuning guides for British cars and VWs. Also carries the Automotive Workshop series of books published by Interauto. Titles in stock are shipped FOB Elmsford, New York. Free catalog.

British Leyland Special Tuning Department
Abingdon-on-Thames
Berkshire
England

600 Willow Tree Road
Leonia, New Jersey 07605

If you took your Sprite or MG out to the local track and found people passing you as easily as the Road Runner zips by the Coyote, then it must be that you were missing some essential performance parts that everyone else has obtained from some secret source. The secret is out, and the British Leyland Competition Department will send you parts lists and tuning data on all Triumphs and Spitfires, the Mini-Cooper "S," Spridget, MGB, and Dunlop racing tires. Among the parts which British Leyland can supply are Spitfire close ratio gears ($185.00), overdrive kits ($395.35), camber compensators ($29.95), no-spin differentials with ratios of 4.1 or 4.55 ($203.50), cams, headers, velocity stacks, Koni shocks, competition brake pads, and oil cooler kits. For some cars there are also alloy body panels and perspex windows. Free literature.

Design, Italian Style. The pacesetters in postwar auto design were the Italian coachbuilders, such as Pinin Farina, Vignale, Ghia, Touring, and other relatively small independent designers who could work directly from their drawing boards and produce a completed car within months. Todays Mustang, Vega, and Pinto still show the seminal influence of these early designs.

1. Ferrari 166 "Inter" by Touring. The first Ferrari V-12 to come into the U.S. in any numbers was the very clean 166, available both as a roadster and coupe. Touring was a coachbuilder known for lightweight construction and successful use of the "stressed skin" concept.

2. 1953 Alfa-Romeo by Castagna. Alfa was a popular chassis which served as a basis for much design competition. This example was clean and traditional.

3. 1953 Alfa-Romeo by Ghia. Ghia began a heavier, squared-off style which was to influence the design of many American and European cars of the 1960s.

4. 1953 Alfa-Romeo by Vignale. Vignale was almost as commercially successful as Pinin Farina and had a hand in the styling of many American cars, though few ever appeared in production. This Alfa is in the mainstream of Vignale designs.

5. 1961 Ferrari California. Perhaps the most successful Ferrari design in the U.S. was this "California" model by Scagliotti. It set the pace for speed and style, influencing many later designs.

4.

5.

British Motor Car Distributors
1200 Van Ness Avenue
San Francisco
California 94109

Service manuals for BMC cars.

John Britten Garages, Ltd.
Barnet Road
Arkley
Barnet
Hertfordshire
England

Another version of the "classic" British kit car is the Arkley SS designed to fit a Sprite or Midget of any year from 1958 to the present. The general look of the car is definitely Lotus Seven complemented with wide alloy wheels. Basic cost of the Arkley SS is about $2,900.00 with wheels and tires, plus all other essentials, fully assembled and ready to go. The basic Arkley body shell is available at about $265.00, with all sorts of accessories offered. The Arkley SS is about 70 pounds lighter than a standard Spridget, but the larger diameter tires raise the overall gearing so that acceleration is similar. Among the disadvantages of the Arkley are the lack of a luggage compartment and somewhat inferior aerodynamics which hinder gas mileage when compared to a stock Spridget. Advantages are better handling and the unusual styling. Free information.

BRM Limited
7614 Rae Lane
Gurnee, Illinois 60031

Distributes racing accessories including ATL Fuel Cells, Accusplit 1 digital split action stop watches, Aeroquip brakeline kits, competition headlight ducts with screening, on-board fire extinguishing systems, helmets and accessories, master kill switches, Nomex clothing, silicone brake fluid, tachometers, roll bars, mag wheels, Spridget goodies (Sprite and Midget) and Formula Ford items. Write for availability of catalog.

Brooks Racing Components, Inc.
15161 Golden West Circle
Westminster, California 92683

Pistons, rods and rings for Ford, Chev and Mopar engines. Free literature.

Brown Bearing and Supply Co.
789 Jersey Avenue
P.O. Box 246
New Brunswick
New Jersey 08903

1444 South Pennsylvania Avenue
Morrisville, Pennsylvania 19067

Looking for a timing chain for your Kissell Kar or Graham-Paige? Chances are that Brown has it. They supply timing chains for all autos, not to mention planes, boats and trucks. As authorized distributors for an impressive roster of chain, gear and bearing suppliers, Brown carries all sorts of gears, bearings, pulleys, belts, bushings, hose, idlers, "O" rings, pillow blocks, rod ends, retaining rings, oil seals, and even leather parts. They do supply literature, but it is best to write them and state your needs, enclosing the customary stamped, self-addressed envelope. Free literature.

Brown Mold Design
108 Janet Avenue
Streamwood, Illinois 60103

Makes fiberglass repro bodies. Basic Deuce Roadster body is $650.00 with opening doors and deck lid, cowl vent, dash, firewall, and floor. Body plus front and rear fenders, radiator shell, splash pan, running boards, gas tank cover, and frame horn covers is $995.00. Options include filled cowl vent, dash with flat instrument surface ($21.00 extra), and rear fenders 2″ wider than stock at $46.00 each. Other bodies available are 1923 Model T ($120.00 basic price),

1923 T radiator shell, $25.00; T body with 14″ or 18″ pickup bed, $165.00; T pickup bed with tailgate, $45.00; 1948 Fiat coupe body and nose (with or without doors), $350.00; and race car nose, $42.00. Free literature.

A.J. Buck
Kimberly Bungalow
Swan Street
Sible Hedingham
Essex
England

Mr. Buck, who is the Postwar Spares Registrar and Technical Advisor to the Alvis Owner Club, specializes in mechanical work on these cars. He carries both new and used spares in stock, and can do complete engine rebuilds when required. Send international reply coupon with queries.

Buffalo Motor Car
25 Myrtle
Buffalo, New York 14204

Specializing in Model A and T and Ford V-8 parts, including tires, sheet metal, accessories, mechanical parts, seat springs, motometers, horns, whistles, rebuilt engines, mufflers, chassis parts, generators, and starters. Also many other parts for all cars 1900-50. Is East Coast distributor for Model A fiberglass, steel-reinforced, 1930 Roadster body priced at $1,500.00. Also has Chevrolet literature of the 1930s in stock and deals in some antique motorcycles and bicycles. Free information.

Bugatti Owners' Club (Bugatti)
c/o Sir Anthony Stamer, Bt.
Cedar Court
9 The Fair Mile
Henley-on-Thames
Oxfordshire RG9 2JT
England

The Club owns Prescott Hillclimb and organizes five annual events there (including two national events counting toward the R. A. C. Hillclimb Championship). Also, holds several annual touring and social events, publishes *Bugantics* magazine and a newsletter (both quarterly). Other services include maintenance of a Bugatti register, technical advice, and a spare parts organization which produces and stocks many otherwise unobtainable Bugatti spares (available to members only). Yearly dues: $12.50 single; $16.50 husband/wife membership. Life membership is $250.00.

Bug-Formance
944 West El Camino
Sunnyvale, California 94087

Carries large line of dune buggies, off-road equipment, VW performance equipment and accessories from most popular manufacturers, VW replacement parts and technical manuals, metric tools, Datsun and Toyota parts and accessories, and complete machine shop services. Send a stamped, self-addressed envelope with queries.

Bug Inn
530 Cottman Avenue
Cheltenham
Pennsylvania 19012

Warehouse distributor for minicar performance parts and accessories. Among brands featured are EMPI, SCAT, Deano-Dyno-Soars, S&S Headers, Andeck, Appliance Wheels, Arron Instruments, Calseco Upholstery, Sig Erson Cams, Per-Spec Wheels, Radatron Instruments, Superior Industries, Segal Products, and more. Also complete machine shop and head services. Has two retail stores in Cheltenham and Bethlehem, Pennsylvania. Write for literature.

Bug-Power Unlimited
712 Broadway
Massapequa, New York 11758

Complete VW engines, engine components, interior accessories, and body parts. A 75 h.p., 1385 cc VW engine with single port heads and Weber carburetion (including clutch and exhaust system) is $600.00 on an exchange basis. Other engines available include a 135 h.p. street engine ($1,060.00), 1600 cc Super Vee engine ($1,095.00), and a 2180 cc racing engine developing from 165-230 h.p. ($2,250.00). Individual engine goodies are high-lift cams, headers, big-bore kits, stroker cranks, Whitfield cranks, plenum chamber manifolds, Mallory and Bosch distributors, Weber carbs, close-ratio gear kits, heavy-duty clutches, oil filter and cooler kits, power pulleys, and solid engine mounts. To make your VW handle as well as it goes, there are sway bars, rear air shocks, Koni shocks, alloy wheels, and quick steering kits. Other items in stock include Hurst and DDS shifters, custom steering wheels, VDO gauges, fiberglass flared fenders and scoops, nerf bars, and many dress-up components. Company also sells VW hard parts and shop tools. Free information.

The Buick Collector's Club of America (Buick)
4730 Centre Avenue
Pittsburgh, Pennsylvania 15213

Although on inactive status since 1966, this club, with 1,200 members still on the roster, is slated for the resumption of activities again. The *deus ex machina* is Sid Aberman, BCCA member Number One. Prospective members will receive a membership card and the last-issued club bulletin (1966) for $1.00. Also some one-page news bulletins will be published until the regular newsletter resumes. When the BCCA goes back to full active status, an annual meeting, a technical and parts service to members, and perhaps a club directory or yearbook will be offered. Mr. Aberman can supply more information to those interested.

Buick Motor Division Opel Sales
General Motors
Flint, Michigan 48550

Opel distribution in U.S.

Buick Motor Division Service Publications Department
General Motors Corporation
Flint, Michigan 48550

Service manuals.

Bullnose Morris Club (Bullnose and Flatnose Morris)
48 Peters Road
Ashtead
Surrey
England

The cars of interest to Club members are all 4-cylinder Morris vehicles, with the exception of Morris Minors, manufactured before January 1, 1931. The Bullnose Morris was the Model T of England, and many are still in existence. The Club sponsors three major rallys, known as the Spring, Northern and Oxford. There is a bi-monthly newsletter and a magazine each Christmas. The Club's spares registrar holds stocks of the most vital spare parts and will coordinate the production of other needed items. Technical advice is available. Entry fee: $4.80; yearly dues, $4.80.

Jack Bunton
North 6802C Jefferson
Spokane, Washington 99208

Regrinds camshafts and sells sandblasting equipment. Free information.

Burchill Antique Auto Parts
4150 24th Avenue
Port Huron, Michigan 48060

Parts for 1914-54 Chrysler product cars, 1911-54 GM cars, and 1909-48 Fords. Also sandblasting and repair services with shop facilities to handle engine, chassis and body work. Catalogs available include 1909-27 Model T, $1.00; 1928-31 Model A, $1.00; 1932-48 Ford, $2.00; special listing of non-Ford parts, $2.00; wiring diagram and electrical data for any American car 1915-37, $2.75; mechanical data and adjustment specs for any American car 1933-48, $2.75; body supply catalog including sample materials, $2.00; and book list free.

B.X. and L. Industries, Inc.
17905 Sky Park Boulevard
Suite K
Irvine, California 92707

Makes Brake-A-Thief hydraulic brake lock theft prevention system for most U.S. and foreign cars. Price is about $49.95 plus a few dollars for installation kit. Free literature.

Hydraulic brake lock from B. X. and L. Industries, Inc.

C & D Engineering
P.O. Box 202
Warner Robins, Georgia 31093

Makes components for brake systems including Teflon/stainless-steel fittings, Aeroquip type brake hoses in various sizes, and line support clamps. Sells aircraft quality bolts, nuts, and miscellaneous fasteners such as the Dzus variety. Also has automatic bleed valves for brakes at $5.25 a set of four. Free literature.

Cadillac-La Salle Club, Inc.
(Cadillac and La Salle)
c/o R.E. VanGelderen
1611 North Kent Street
Suite 200
Arlington, Virginia 22209

The officially-recognized Cadillacs are those more than 25 years old, while La Salles from 1927 to 1940 receive the imprimatur. However, ownership of a Cadillac or La Salle is not a membership requirement and non-recognized Cadillacs are made welcome at meets. The monthly club newsletter is called *Self-Starter* and includes a classified section covering parts, accessories, literature and cars for sale. At last report a glossy magazine was being planned. The CLC publishes an annual directory which includes a list of previously unavailable parts that have been remanufactured. There are six CLC regions, with both regional and national meets. Yearly dues: $9.00 per family.

Cadillac Motorbooks
P.O. Box 2892-D
Pasadena, California 91105

Reprints original showroom literature on classic Cadillacs and a few other cars. Has reprints on 1936-38 La Salles, 1933 Packard Eight, 1932 Lincoln Twelve, Marmon Sixteen and Duesenberg. Free literature.

Cadillac Motor Car Division
Service Publications
Department
General Motors Corporation
Detroit, Michigan 48232

Service manuals.

Cadillac Parts P.O. Box 66 Albertson, New York 11507	New 1937-48 Cadillac (V-8 only) and La Salle parts. Fuel pumps, $28.00; oil pumps, $35.00; hydraulic lifters (plungers and body), $100.00; regulator $18.00; distributor cap and spark plug wire set, $10.00; 10 mm A.C. spark plugs, $1.00 each; exhaust valves, $3.50; intake valves, $4.50 each; starter motor with solenoid, $85.00; engine rebuild gasket set, $28.00; camshaft, $45.00; set of eight pistons with rings, $100.00. Many other mechanical parts. Send a stamped, self-addressed envelope with query.
CAE Racing Equipment 6580 Federal Lemon Grove, California 92045	Chassis components, body parts, and transmissions for Sprint and Modified cars. Complete front suspensions and suspension components for track cars and drag racing. Models include spring over, longitudinal spring, and dropped axle assemblies. Also Airheart disc brake components, weight jacker spring mounts, birdcage kits to accept Airheart and Halibrand spot calipers, rear radius rods, knock-off front hubs, and individual racing suspension components. Transmission and driveline components include clutch drive or direct drive in and out boxes, in and out box components, ball joint housings, driveline assemblies, drag boxes for single or double disc clutches, 3″ Championship axle assemblies, Championship and Grand National quick-change rear ends, transaxle-type center section assemblies for rear-engine cars, hub uprights, half axles for upright hubs, Ross and Schroeder steering units, lightweight Sprint Car radiators, and racing headers for Sprint and Super-Modified Chev, Ford, and Buick engines. Complete in and out boxes sell at prices ranging from about $195.00 to $215.00. Front suspensions are priced from approximately $112.00 to $295.00. Also available are fiberglass bodies and body components for Sprint and Super-Modified cars. A complete Spring Car body is $207.20, while a Super-Modified body goes for $179.85. Also sells accessories such as racing buckets, seat belts, aluminum fuel tanks, race car grilles, filler caps and necks, Sprint Car steering wheels, Simpson race clothing and face masks. Catalog, $1.00.
Cal Automotive 8044 Lankershim Boulevard North Hollywood California 91605	Fiberglass body parts for modern and early cars. A 1926 Model T coupe body with doors, wood and fenders is priced at $500.00. Model A Roadster body is $300.00 with wood. Complete VW body lists at $468.00. Repro parts also available for Mustang (complete 1965 body, $682.50), GTO, Fairlane, Comet, Falcon, Barracuda, Chevelle, Impala, 1941 Willys, 1932 Austin Bantam, 1948-51 Anglia, 1948 Fiat, and various models of Henry's T and A. Also available are T roadster and pickup chassis ($575.00), roadster or pickup frame for old type rear spring, fiberglass bucket seats (upholstered Shelby racing seat is $50.00), T and Deuce radiator shells, replica Ford steering wheels, and windshield posts for 1923-27 T roadster. Catalog, $1.00.
Cal Custom 23011 South Wilmington Carson, California 90745	Cal Custom chrome accessories include air cleaners, velocity stacks, carb scoops, valve covers, oil filler caps, battery terminal clamps, water necks, oil breather caps, dipstick handles, cooling fans, wire looms, fuel pump block-off plates, alternator covers, gas line kits for Holley carbs, fuel block kits, rear axle covers, mag wheel centers, lug nuts, splash

guards, hub caps, shift handles, hood latch kits, hood pins, exhaust pipe extensions, and spotlights. Also carries head gaskets, PCV valves, silicon ignition wire sets, hoses and hose clamps, brass hose fittings, small engine hardware, waterproof distributor and coil covers, Holley carb performance parts, Chev valley oil baffles, valvetrain components, timing gear and chain sets, competition components for Borg-Warner T-10 and Muncie transmissions, aerosol touch-up paints and metal flaking kits, striping and design kits, wheel locks, wooden shift knobs, VW cosmetic and performance components, universal aluminum hood scoops, electric door kits, electric trunk locking and opening kits, exhaust cut-outs, traction bars for standard and sub-compact cars, GM rear coil spring lift kits, leaf spring lift kits, engine safety chains, shock extensions, Mopar pinion snubbers, and Pinto and Vega chassis components. Under the Hanson-Hawk name there is a complete line of dash instruments, tune-up tools, and professional diagnostic equipment. Free information. Consult catalog at speed equipment dealers.

Calgary Austin-Healey Club (Austin-Healey)
M.P.O. Box 2293
Calgary
Alberta
Canada TZP 2M6

Holds many competitive and social events throughout the year. Publishes a monthly Club journal and has a spare parts registrar. Club members must own a "big Healey" (100-4, 100-6 or 3000), or intend to purchase one in the near future. For local members, there are suppliers who offer Club discounts. Yearly dues: $10.00 for local members; $5.00 for out-of-town members.

Canadian Classic MG Club (MG and Jaguar)
P.O. Box 8775
Postal Station H
Vancouver
British Columbia
Canada

This very active Club sponsors or participates in numerous events including tours, concours and hill climbs. Their monthly bulletin is entitled *Classical Gas.* Technical advice and help with restoration is available through the membership. Sorry—no information on yearly dues.

Candy's Speed Products
Box 15244
Santa Ana, California 92705

Candy's thing is "Footz," which are swiveling-end feet for replacing VW valve adjusting screws. They reduce wear and maintain proper valve lash more closely. Also sells block savers, to restore stripped threads, in metric sizes, oversize bearing pins to fit a re-drilled block hole, intake and exhaust valve guides for stock or racing VW engines, head savers and tools to restore stripped spark plug threads, valve guide remover and installer kits for VW and Porsche, lightweight valve spring retainers and positive shut-off fuel valves. Free literature.

W. A. Cannon
175 May Avenue
Monrovia, California 91016

Mr. Cannon, publications editor for the Antique Studebaker Club, is also a machinist who will hand make Studebaker parts. More than 150 parts can be made from patterns in stock, or custom-made parts can be ordered with a four to five week delivery time. Some prices are: headlight bar emblem drilled for 7/16″ diameter rods, $8.50; Commander emblem, $7.50; spark, throttle and light levers for steering wheel hub of 1928-32 models, $4.50 each; rumble seat step plate in cast aluminum, $10.00 each; Studebaker wheel ornament, $2.00; reproduction of centennial medal, $6.00. Send a stamped, self-addressed envelope with query.

Cannon Industries, Inc.
9067 Washington Boulevard
R1
Culver City, California 90230

Accessories for imports and mini cars. Front and rear fiberglass spoilers are available for the Vega, Pinto, and a number of sports cars and small foreign sedans. There are headers for most small cars and also free-flow exhaust systems. Cannon is a distributor for Offy induction systems, Weber carbs and linkage kits, Judson magnetos, Hurst shifters for VW and Toyota, Heuer timers, AMCO accessories, and Cibie driving lights. Other products include campers for small trucks; a compact portable refrigerator ($89.95); headers for Datsun and Toyota pickups; side pipes for mini pickups; upholstery, headlining and door panel kits for Datsun, Toyota, and Luv pickups; tonneau covers and carpeting for small trucks; Craig sound equipment; fiberglass hardtops for a number of sports cars; a vinyl top kit custom-designed for VWs and available in a universal kit for many other imports; seat covers; bucket seats; car covers; rear scoops and license plate panels for Porsche 911; ski racks and bike racks; street and competition roll bars; anti-sway bars; disc brake pads; and Scientific workshop manuals. Free catalog.

Capri Car Club
(Capri)
557 Newark Court
Aurora, Colorado 80010

The C.C.C. and its chapters publish a quarterly newsletter *Capri Capers,* hold social meetings and sponsor various rallys, gymkhanas, autocrosses, technical sessions and other events. As the national club grows, bi-annual national meetings are planned. There is no technical advisor to Club members as yet, but technical tips appear in the Club newsletter. Capri owners can also receive *Capri Scene,* a quarterly publication sent out free through dealers. Those not receiving the publication, but who are eligible, should write to *Capri Scene,* The American Road, Dearborn, Michigan 48121. Yearly dues: $5.00; initiation fee $2.50. Chapters may charge additional dues not exceeding $5.00.

Carbooks, Inc.
2628 Atlantic Avenue
Brooklyn, New York 11207

Service manuals and car repair books. Free information.

Car Corporation
12263 Market Street
Livonia, Michigan 48170

Cosmetics, hatchback tents and turbo-superchargers. Pinto tent is $59.95, Ventura model is $59.50. Dress-up items for Chevy Luv consist of woodgrain applique for sides, black or white vinyl roof finish molding, red or white beltline accent, and red or white rocker panel accent. For El Camino a rocker panel kit in white or black is $18.95 and a sail panel kit in the same colors is $25.95. For the Vega there is a hatchback spear kit and a woodgrain kit for the wagon model. There are tape stripes in silver or black for the Maverick and a woodgrain kit for the Pinto. Also available are mag and wire spoke wheel covers at $35.00 a set to fit most 13″ wheels. A complete turbocharger kit with all parts and instructions is available for the Pinto, Vega and Capri. Package fits under the hood with no sheet metal changes necessary. System allows for retention of stock carb and air cleaner. Price is $445.00. Free literature.

The Car Mat Company Ltd.
16 Colville Road
London, W. 11
England

Custom made car carpets, mohair floor rugs, ribbed rubber mats, coconut fiber mats, and rubber link mats are specialties of the Car Mat Company. Also available are a full line of Conway seat covers, in various grades and designs, to fit most British and Continental cars. Along with stretch nylon and Bedford Cord, seat covers are available in ocelot, leopard, worsted, and velvet designs. To keep you comfy on the cold British (or American) evenings, there are fur fabric footmuffs, steering wheel covers, and wedge cushions for back support. Free catalog.

Carousel Racing, Inc.
6120 Brooklyn Boulevard
Suite 102
Brooklyn Center
Minnesota 55429

Specializes in performance parts for all Porsches. For Porsche 914 sells front spoiler, plastic (Butyrate) stone shield, adjustable front sway bar, tow bar, trailer hitch, Aeroquip braided steel brake lines, various performance chassis parts, racing exhaust systems ($125.00), Richie Ginther racing windscreen ($248.40) and front and rear fiberglass hoods ($140.00 each.) For Porsche 911 sells front spoiler, fiberglass rear panel, tow bar, trailer hitch, suspension parts and Koni shocks. Also has Carrera 911RS front and rear spoilers and camshaft. Other items available are Mahle racing pistons, cylinder Big Bore kits, and some parts for Porsche 356. Carousel is the exclusive dealer for Accusplit 1 digital split-action stopwatches. Free literature.

Dennis Carpenter
9835 Pinewood Lane
Charlotte
North Carolina 28213

1932-40 Ford V-8 dash knobs, window crank knobs, radio face plates, small body parts, window channels, antennas, clutch and brake pedal pads and small rubber items, choke and throttle rods, Columbia Overdrive parts, convertible straps and snaps, quarter panels, and other parts which are exact repros of original. Also rebuilt distributors, carbs and new fuel pumps. Knobs vary in price from about $3.00 to $5.50 each. A kit to convert 1933-34 spare tire cover assembly to incorporate an antenna is $10.00. Distributors are $9.50 exchange. Carb for 1932-33 is $25.00 exchange, for 1934-37, $17.50 exchange, and for 1938-48 the exchange price is $15.00. New fuel pumps with glass settlement bowl are $10.00. White oak header bows for 1933-34 roadster and phaeton are $25.00; for 1935-36 header bows the price is $40.00. Free price list.

Cars & Parts
P.O. Box 299
Sesser, Illinois 62884

One of the primary media for advertising cars and parts for sale or wanted in the U.S., this magazine includes interesting historical articles and information on car club activities in each issue. It is a monthly glossy magazine chock-full of advertisements and pictures. Yearly subscription: $5.00.

Carter Carburetor Division
AFC Industries, Inc.
2840 North Spring Avenue
St. Louis, Missouri 63107

Carter carbs and fuel pumps, which are original equipment on many American cars, are also available in performance versions for aftermarket installation. There are both 4-barrel and 2-barrel carbs as well as electrical or mechanical fuel pumps. An interesting kit sold by the company contains a wide assortment of rods, jets, needles and seats for various carb models. The kits are $10.50 for most applications and $11.50 for press-in-jet models. Free information.

Cartune Ltd.
147 Stanwell Road
Ashford
Middlesex
England

All the better British Beetles go to Cartune for facelifting and health treatments. They offer complete machine shop services plus Big Bore kits, SPG roller cranks, Performance cams, oil coolers, carb conversions, exhaust systems, wide steel wheels, Cibie lights, Bosch electrical equipment, Hella horns, Hermes front spoilers, and a good many other accessories including fiberglass panels. Some items are manufactured on the premises. Free catalog.

Casler Performance Products
1031-D West Brooks Street
Ontario, California 91762

Headers for most standard American cars plus VW and dune buggies. Dune buggy headers come in a high rise model. Also available are mufflers for headers and ram-flow intake manifolds for VW to fit Zenith, Holley and Carter carbs. Casler sells side mount pipes with glasspack mufflers for any car or truck. Side mounts cost $112.50 to $127.50 with muffler depending upon the size and whether black or chrome finish is desired. Catalog, $.50.

C.C.L. Enterprises, Inc.
147 Pearl Street
South Braintree
Massachusetts 02184

C.C.L.'s Super Sprint free flow exhaust systems are made for Alfa Romeo, Audi, BMC cars, BMW, Fiat, Capri, Opel, Peugeot, Porsche, Renault, Triumph, VW, and Volvo. Prices range from $59.50 for a VW system up to $169.50 for a Jaguar XJ6 system less head pipe. Company also makes leather covered, aluminum-spoked steering wheels for $55.00. Free catalog.

Dick Cepek, Inc.
9201 California Avenue
South Gate
California 90280

Off-road tires and accessories. Mr. Cepek has become the reigning expert in off-road rubber and has many varieties of Armstrong and other tires for sand, snow and even swamp use. To go along with the tires he has both mag and steel wheels in many wide sizes. He also offers package deals such as four Armstrong Norseman tubeless tires and 9″ wide one-piece steel wheels for $196.95 a set of four. Among the off-road goodies in stock are fender extenders for 4WD vehicles plus VW buses, quartz lights, compasses and altimeters, heavy duty roof top racks for Jeeps, Toyotas and the like, portable bead breaking irons ($8.95), steering stabilizers, the well known Enginair pump for inflating tires in the boonies, the versatile Hi-Lift jack, government surplus tool boxes and other G.I. items, Baja California guide books and maps, outside spare tire and jerry can carriers, and much camping equipment. There are flat rates for shipping tires to various parts of the country which range from $12.00 in the California area to $40.00 for Alaska and Hawaii—these prices are for shipping up to five tires, tubes, and wheels. Free catalog.

Armstrong Norseman tires from Dick Cepek, Inc. on the car Drino Miller drove to victory in the 1970 Mint 400 and Baja 1000

Challenger Equipment
687 East Edna Place
Covina, California 91723

Carries a wide variety of suspension systems and individual components including AA/Gas Supercharged chassis with rectangular tube frame and full roll cage; BB/Altered Funny Car chassis; threaded tube and rod end kits for 1928-48 Fords; radius rods; shackle kits; tie rod ends; rod end plugs; ladder bars; coil spring kits; tube axles; shackle perch kits; U-bolt kits; leaf springs; sub-frame kits for Chevy II, Mustang and Falcon; front axle kits for Chev, Chevy II and Corvette; adjustable competition coil shocks; tube motor mounts for Chev V-8 and 1951-58 Chrysler; adapters for any late model open-drive into early Ford Chassis with stock transverse spring; tie rods and drag links; Watts sway bar kits ($49.95); shackle mounted shock adapter plates; universal crossmembers ($38.50); steering arms for Ford, Chev and Econoline spindles; polished valley covers for 1951-58 Chrysler Hemi; welded radius rods; Funny Car type radius rods; driveline couplers; spherical rod ends; radius rod mounts; kingpins; shock mounting kits for tube axle installations with rectangular or boxed tube frames; transverse front end axle kits for T roadsters, early Fords and competition cars; wheelie bars ($79.95 a pair); T roadster frames; torsion bar assemblies; grade-8 nuts and bolts; front engine mounts to adapt small or large block Chevrolet engines to early Ford and Merc chassis; shock absorber bracket kits; competition lift bars; rectangular frame Roadster kits; and disc brake kits for all bolt patterns and wheels. Catalog, $1.50.

Tony Chamings Products Ltd.
Department HC1
Hawkhurst Service Station
Horns Road
Hawkhurst
Kent
England

Carries a complete line of suspension components for Mini-Minors. Makes the Hi-Lo Mark II adjustable height suspension kit for Minis. Free information.

Chassis Engineering Co.
705 West 13th Street
National City
California 92050

Chassis Engineering Co. has available a sports-racing car designed for SCCA road racing in classes B, C, and D, and for the FIA Group 6 Sports/Prototype class. The Quasar SR-70 has an aluminum semi-monocoque chassis and polyester-reinforced fiberglass body. The engine bay will accommodate various 4-, 6-, or 8-cylinder engines, and the rear bulkhead is designed for the Hewland 4-, 5- or 6-speed transaxle. An introductory package containing photos, sample drawings, and the prices of all parts, kits, or the complete car is $3.00. Company also sells fiberglass body parts for the following race cars: Brabham BT-21 and BT-29; Le Grand Mk. 3 and Mk. 6; Lotus 18 and 41; Merlyn Mk. II; Porsche 911, 914 and 908; Tecno; Wasp; and Winklemann. Other fiberglass components include NASA scoops, oil cooler ducts, and a Corvair engine cooling shroud. Fiberglass seats, available as a bare shell or with upholstery, include high back, Trans-Am, Sprint Car and Formula models. Other products include monocoque aluminum racing wheels, with disc or flat centers, in diameters from 10″ to 16″ and widths from 2″ to 18″. Monocoque wheels can also be anodized in a variety of colors. Wheels sized 13″x5½″ are $105.50 apiece, while prices climb to $255.00 for wheels sized 15″x18″. Monocoque knock-off wheels are available for cars originally equipped with pin drive knock-offs. Wheels are adapted by using an external crusher plate priced from $30.00 per wheel. Two other versions of the monocoque wheel are wheels with disc brake caliper clearance hubs, and wheels with lightening holes machined in for an approximate weight saving of quarter of a pound per wheel. Other products include Quasar racing batteries, fiberglass battery boxes, kit engine stands ($29.95), grade 8 hardware, Dunlop racing tires, foreign car headers, ear plugs, velocity stacks, pillow blocks, quick-fill fuel caps, air density gauges, and helmet bags. Catalog, $2.00.

Chenowth Racing Products
943 Vernon Way
El Cajon, California 92020

Off-road racing frames and chassis components, plus accessories for VW and Corvair. Chenowth Company does custom mandrel bending, and sells roll bars for VW and Jeeps, Corvair frame kits and chassis, VW frame kits and chassis components, Corvair headers, Corvair manifolds, VW headers, custom gas tanks in many shapes and sizes, and wheels in sizes from 13″x7″ to 16″x10″. Other products include VW solid motor mounts; front end supports; remote air filter housings; intake manifolds for Bug, Variant and 411; rack and pinion steering units ($137.50, or $179.95 for cars with A frame type suspension); chrome moly axle tubes; VW axle retainers; steering shaft U-joints; carb and exhaust flanges of many types; header collectors and reducers for all sizes of tubing; megaphone pipes; hydraulic cutting brakes ($69.95); and hydraulic throttle and clutch kits for VW and Corvair. Catalog, $1.00.

Chet Herbert Racing Cams
1933 South Manchester
Anaheim, California 92802

Solid, hydraulic or roller tappet cams. The roller tappets are available for the Chevy 327 and 427, Ford 427, Chrysler 1951-58 and Olds 1949-63. Various grinds are offered. Solid and hydraulic cams are available for almost any engine. If you don't see what you want on Chet Herbert's list, send details on the engine, year, make, size, solid or hydraulic, and grind you want, and Chet will supply a reground cam. He will also select a grind for you if you specify rpm range, type of carb, transmission, rear end gear ratio and weight of car. Free literature.

Chicago Truckin' Accessories
P.O. Box 294
Algonquin, Illinois 60102

Offers custom van interior kits, which include diamond quilted panels for the side, top, all doors, fender wells and sun visors, plus a shag carpet, dual stereo speakers and a spare exterior tire mount with cover. Kit price is $495.00, with all items available individually. Other van goodies available are port holes ($34.95), white translucent roof vents ($14.95), and a sliding sun roof ($85.00). Similar upholstery kits are available for mini-trucks at a price of $248.00. Other items available include swiveling seat pedestals, Hi-Rider bucket seats with or without arm rests, pickup cab steps, luggage rail and ladder kits, powered roof vents (12-volt or 110-volt), Velvetouch brake linings, anti-sway bars for some vans and pickups, custom-made

	wooden bumpers (prices start from $18.00), plug-in spotlights, fender splash guards, Hooker headers, Ansen and Cragar alloy wheels, Edelbrock high-rise manifolds, Holley carbs, Aris driving and fog lights, and Arrow dash gauges. "Keep on Truckin' " decals are out of stock, but "Just Passin' Through" appliques featuring Mr. Natural can be had for only $6.95. Catalog $1.00.
Chilton Book Co. 401 Walnut Street Philadelphia Pennsylvania 19106	Service manuals and annual books. Also U.S. and foreign car and truck repair manuals. Free literature.
Chinetti-Garthwaite Imports, Inc. 1215 County Line Road Rosemont Pennsylvania 19010	Ferrari distributors.
Christie Electric Corporation P.O. Box 60020 Los Angeles California 90060	Battery charging, testing, and servicing equipment for the professional mechanic. Catalog free to jobbers.
Chroma House Restmor Way Hackbridge Surrey England	Has a large line of die-cast alloy wheels in 10″, 12″, 13″, and 14″ sizes. Also metric wheel accessories. The standard wheel in size 13″x5½″ goes for about $30.00. Free information.
Chrome Crankshafts 3727 New Getwell Road Memphis, Tennessee 38118	Manufactures and repairs high performance crankshafts used in racing cars. Company has facilities for hard chroming, welding, magnafluxing, straightening, heat treating, and sand blasting crankshafts. Complete price sheets available upon request.
Chronosport, Inc. Rowayton, Connecticut 06853	Company makes a relatively inexpensive chronograph designed for timing yachting events, but suitable for lap times. Price is $79.95. Free literature.
Chrysler Motors Corporation Performance Parts Services P.O. Box 1081 Warren, Michigan 48090	Those interested in parts for fairly recent Chrysler Corporation cars may want to write for a parts catalog. Catalogs are generally a single year type, containing parts information on all Chrysler-built vehicles for that year. Prices vary between $5.00 and $10.00. Free price list.
Chrysler-Plymouth Division Service Department Chrysler Motors Corporation P.O. Box 1658 Detroit, Michigan 48231	Service manuals.
Chrysler Restorers Club (Chrysler) 426 Orchard Lane Manheim, Pennsylvania 17545	Club has annual meeting and three other meetings each year. Also has quarterly newsletter. Furnishes information on restorations and will help to locate needed parts. Yearly dues: $3.00

The Silver Brutes. Although Mercedes has manufactured many modest sedans and diesel-engined taxis, their early reputation was built upon grandiose roadsters and convertibles of unparalleled barbaric splendor, as well as periodic, all-conquering sorties in racing competition. A remarkable percentage of the pre-war Mercedes in America are believed (by their owners, at least) to once have been the personal property of Eva Braun or Hermann Goering. And it was undoubtedly some preposterously ostentatious custom Mercedes that served as a prototype for the block-long town car that was flaunted by Walt Disney's Scrooge McDuck.

1. 1928 Mercedes SSK. The protracted hood punctuated with snaky chrome tubing, indicating that a supercharger was fitted, was the symbol of the SSK Mercedes. The factory body, shown here, represented the essence of Teutonic splendor—a Wagnerian conveyance to Valhalla.

2. 1928 Mercedes SSK. This custom body, by an unidentified coachbuilder, has sacrificed the tautness of the factory design for a closer-coupled look and the padded comfort of a tailored top with landau bars.

3. 1938 Mercedes 540K. The 540K was the last of the classic Mercedes sports cars and a far cry from the "people's car" that Hitler had commissioned Dr. Porsche to design. It was every bit as flamboyant as its predecessors, and the "K" still stood for "Kompressor," meaning that there was a wailing supercharger beneath the hood.

4. 1954 2.5 Liter Grand Prix Mercedes. When Mercedes made an overwhelming assault on the Grand Prix circuit in the mid-fifties, they introduced wind-tunnel streamlining to the previously open-wheeled formula. Although the streamlined cars were faster on some circuits, Fangio and Moss preferred the open-wheel design, which was more controllable and less subject to fender dinging.

5. 1955 Mercedes-Benz Monoposto. This is the open-wheeled Grand Prix car that Moss and Fangio drove to clockwork victories under the supervision of rotund team manager Neubauer.

6. 1955 Mercedes-Benz 300-SLR. The sports-racing 300-SLR was as successful as its Grand Prix counterparts and came in both open and coupe versions. Stirling Moss drove one in the long road races, such as Mexico and the Mille Miglia, with outstanding success. In many ways the 300-SLR served as a prototype for the production "Gull Wing" 300-SL Mercedes of the late fifties and early sixties.

Chrysler 300 Club
(Chrysler 300-series)
8736 S.E. 58th Avenue
Portland, Oregon 97206

Dedicated to the Letter Series Chrysler 300 (1955-65) and the 1970 Chrysler 300-H by Hurst. Three chapters in Washington, Oregon and California. Quarterly newsletter, decals, jacket patches, license plate frames. Technical advice and parts location for members. Yearly dues: $7.50.

Brian Chuchua's
Four Wheel Drive Center
P.O. Box 301
Fullerton, California 92632

What Vic Hickey is to Blazers and Stroppe is to Broncos, Brian Chuchua is to Jeeps. Along with hard parts for all Jeep models from the Military MB's to the latest CJ-5s and Jeepsters, Chuchua carries a comprehensive list of accessories. The line includes high-compression cylinder heads for Jeep flatheads, various manifolds from Chuchua and Edelbrock, Holley carbs, complete AMC 401 V-8 engines (at $1,200.00 apiece), Hurst motor mounts and frame adapters for engine swapping, Cyclone headers, Flex-A-Lite fans, remote oil filter kits, Trans-Dapt conversion kits to convert a variety of engines and transmissions (including the 400 series Turbo Hydro automatic transmission) to Jeeps and Scouts, Thomas adjustable rocker arms for Jeep and Buick V-6 at $59.75, Warn and Rancho overdrives, Hayden oil coolers for engine or automatic transmission of many pickups, vans and 4WDs, Spicer NoSpin differentials, auxiliary and saddle gas tanks for Jeeps and Scouts (left or right 7-gallon tanks for CJ-5 are $41.75), fiberglass body panels for Jeeps and Jeepsters, rubber Jeep Universal fender extenders at $21.95, Jeepster fiberglass extenders and Bronco extenders for $39.95 a pair, Meyers and Kelly full and half cabs for CJ-5, CJ-6 Jeepsters and M-38A-1, Kayline convertible tops for Jeep Universals and Jeepster Commandos, Whitco and Kayline tops for Broncos and Scouts, Whitco convertible pickup caps, hood and deck pins plus hood locks, Sun Tachs, steering wheels, floor mats, seat covers, rear fender seat pads with and without roll bar cutouts, heavy-duty bell cranks for MBs and most CJs, a special tie-rod to keep toe-in distance constant on CJs (price, $8.95), Heco steering stabilizers, Velvetouch Metalik brakes, bead breakers, tire sealant, the Mark II Jackall 4-ton capacity high-lift jack ($29.95), steel wheels in widths from 7″ to 10″ for Jeep, Scout, Bronco and Toyota, Ansen Sprint mag wheels, heavy-gauge metal fender extenders for Jeeps with extra wide tires or dual wheels ($24.95 a pair), Per-Lux and Cibie lights, and Halda rally instruments. The Chuchua catalog contains a comparison between Cibie and aircraft landing lights which convincingly makes a case for buying the Cibies. Other rally equipment includes a selection of gears and cables for the Haldas—items which can be tough to find; safety belts; crash helmets; the Gemini helmet which contains a 2-way radio ($165.00); the Filt-Air helmet, face shield, 12-volt filter and hoses for off-road racers who are tired of eating dust ($276.00 for the whole megilla); roll bars and roll bar padding, fiberglass Buggy Whips to hold a red flag and light 8′ or 9′ in the air for maximum visibility on sand dunes, and Hadley or Maserati air horns.

Off-roaders will appreciate Chuchua's bumper-mounted tool racks, custom-made for most 4WDs and pickups, which hold the Jackall high-lift jack, a shovel and axe. All are available for $53.00 without tools and $82.50 with. Other items of interest are various outside tire and spare G.I. gas can carriers; Ramsey, Warn and Superwinch winches; Kelly and Warn selective front hubs, and a variety of parts for Broncos including roll bars, skid plates, under-hood tool boxes ($23.50), headers for 6s or V-8s, air lift and adjustable shocks, luggage racks, and Mitchell dual exhausts. For Blazers Chuchua lists an extensive line of Vic Hickey accessories. There are also Almico steering brakes, hill holders and anti-theft brake locks which fit most cars, Weathershield ignition covers for waterproofing distributors and coils, Gabriel racing shocks, G-Lox gun racks which fit the inside trunk lid on sedans or various places inside the cab on pickups, tow hooks and dual battery isolators. Chuchua carries a complete line of Jeep service manuals. Catalog $1.00.

Circle Tire Company
111 Worcester Road
Route 9
Natick, Massachusetts 01760

The name of this company is somewhat misleading since it services BMW automobiles exclusively and claims to have the largest stock of used and rebuilt BMW mechanical parts anywhere. Parts for virtually all BMWs manufactured since 1967 are at hand. Free information.

Circolo Veneto Automotoveicoli d'Epoca (Vintage and Veteran Cars)
via Beata Giovanna 95
36061 Bassano del Grappa
Vicenza
Italy

There are six or seven vintage car meets per year operated under Club auspices, and a bi-monthly publication, *Circolo Veneto Auto-Motoveicoli d'Epoca,* is sent to members. Assistance in parts location and restoration, as well as a technical library consulting service, is offered by the Club. The cost of membership includes registration with the Automotoclub Storico Italiano. Yearly dues: $28.00.

Citroen Car Club (Citroen)
21, The Paddocks
Leatherhead Road
Great Bookham
Surrey
England

Everyone knows that Citroens are the most logically-designed cars in the world, right? In that case, why not join the Citroen Car Club of Great Britain and feel superior to those who haven't learned the truth yet. The Club promotes sporting and social events, publishes an exemplary monthly magazine *Citroenian,* and can supply workshop manuals, car badges, and similar items. Only Citroen owners are eligible for full membership; others can become associates. Yearly dues are $7.20, pro-rated for those joining late.

Citroen Cars Corporation
40 Van Nostrand Avenue
Englewood, New Jersey 07631

U.S. distributors for Citroen.

Classic American Auto Club of Great Britain (Vintage and Veteran Cars)
c/o Harry C. G. Shell
Old Laundry Cottage
Copthall
Hunsdon
Hertfordshire
England

Principal Club events are a fall scenic tour and a main meet in late August. Club members are dedicated to the preservation of pre-1942 American automobiles, with the Lincoln Continental to 1948. Along with publishing a bi-monthly bulletin, *Hood & Fender,* the Club will aid in spare parts location (some parts are kept in stock) and will photostat instruction manuals and catalogs in its collection. Yearly dues: $3.60.

Classic Automotive Reproductions
Box 12531
Lake Park, Florida 33403

Metal scale models of classic cars. Scale is approximately 1/18″ to 1/24″ and available models include various Duesenbergs, Packards, Model As, 1932 Chevrolets, Bugattis, Alfa Romeos, Bentleys and Mercedes. Scale models are also mounted on desk sets and display bases, or split in half to make wall plaques and bookends. Prices for scale models are $30.00 to $50.00. Bookends are $14.00 a set and two wall plaques are available for the same price. Free literature.

Models of familiar cars of yesteryear available from Classic Automotive Reproductions

---

Classic Batteries
P.O. Box 134
Plymouth Meeting
Pennsylvania 19462

Offers many types of batteries which are shipped dry charged. Also battery accessories including cables, ground straps, and battery hold-downs. Company also does business as "Harnesses Unlimited" (see separate listing). Free price lists.

The Classic Car Club of America (Classic Cars)
P.O. Box 443
Madison, New Jersey 07940

This is *the* club which pretty much determines which cars are classics and which are not. The C.C.C.A. runs the Grand Classic, a concours competition held at six locations throughout the country. Other events are an annual CARavan tour in the summer and the members meeting in January at Buck Hill Falls, Pennsylvania. Publications include the *Classic Car Bulletin,* a newsletter issued ten times a year, and *The Classic Car,* a superbly-designed quarterly glossy. The C.C.C.A. has twenty-two regional affiliates, many of which have their own publications. Many of the regions have projects for the remanufacture of small parts or accessories for classic cars. Such things as cylinder head nuts, top material, repro owners' manuals, hubcaps, and fire wall plates are offered by the regions in the C.C.C.A. bulletin. There are two types of members, active and associate. An associate member is the spouse of an active member and receives no publications her (or him) self. Yearly dues: active members, $15.00; associate members, $3.00; lifetime active members, $500.00.

Classic Car Investments, Inc.
1624 Atlanta Road
Marietta, Georgia 30060

Owned by Charles L. Turner, Eastern U.S. chairman for the Aston-Martin Owners Club Ltd. Aston dealer, and specializes in Aston parts and restoration. Send a stamped, self-addressed envelope with query.

The Classic Corvette Club (Corvette)
c/o Mr. John Hutchins
9417 North Rich Road
Alma, Michigan 48801

Covers Corvettes from 1953 to 1955. Ownership not a prerequisite but recommended. Club activities include at least two national meets a year, usually centered in the Great Lakes area, and a quarterly newsletter which includes sections on parts wanted, repro parts available, and a list of fellow members. Yearly dues: $5.00.

Classic Jaguar Association (SS, Jaguar Mark IV & V, XK-120)
c/o Herbert G. de Bruyn
3023 165th Place, N.E.
Bellevue, Washington 98004

Services of the CJA include the *News and Technical Bulletin* with unlimited want ad service to members, and a very active parts procurement service. Parts can be obtained from England through agents in that country, and members may receive discounts through selected dealers. The CJA offers advice to members on any sort of technical problem in the repair or restoration of a Classic Jag. A list of technical publications and accessories available and a list of back issues of the *News and Technical Bulletin* are available for $.50 apiece. Social events are primarily regional meets in various areas of the country. Yearly dues: $10.00. In addition, all new members in North America are required to purchase a bumper badge at $5.75.

The Classic MG Club (MG)
1307 Ridgecrest Road
Orlando, Florida 32806

Monthly meetings, club events such as rallies and gymkhanas, a monthly newsletter *The Octagon,* a Club library, and aid in parts location are some of the benefits of this Club devoted to T-series MGs. It is affiliated with the New England MG T registry. Yearly dues: $5.00.

Classic Motorbooks
3106 West Lake Street
Minneapolis, Minnesota 55416

Probably most extensive catalog of current automobile literature available anywhere. Along with general-interest auto books and workshop manuals, the Classic Motorbooks catalog lists literature by make of car from Abarth to Wolverine. You can find listings for such cars as the Isotta-Fraschini, Locomobile, Maybach, McFarlan, Miller, and many others. Other listings are for military vehicles, model cars, trucks and buses, tractors, steam engines, racing and rally books, and restoration manuals. Subscriptions are accepted for many of the better American and British motoring magazines. Free literature.

Classic Parts Center
961 San Mateo Avenue
San Bruno, California 94066

If you are too old to fool around with Model As and too young to really appreciate the VW, you can always buy a 1955-57 Thunderbird and own your own version of an underground classic. The Classic Parts Center will supply all the goodies you need to keep your T-Bird in pristine condition. Along with mechanical parts they handle upholstery and carpets, convertible tops, body parts and paint touch-up kits. Complete metal rear body sections ('55, '56 and '57) are $395.00, while front body sections go for $550.00. Seat cover sets sell for $85.00, and rayon carpets in a variety of colors are $38.50. Some used parts are also available including 1955-56 front brake drums ($19.50), rear brake drums ($12.50), rebuilt power brake boosters ($49.50 exchange), steering wheels ($25.00), cylinder block assemblies ($75.00), and rear spring assemblies ($15.00). Free literature.

Classic Thunderbird Parts Club (Thunderbird)
1115 West Collins Avenue
Orange, California 92667

Members receive a brochure illustrating and identifying all parts of classic Thunderbirds and then get a comprehensive catalog of new Thunderbird parts available. The catalog is published bi-monthly and includes most mechanical and sheet metal parts that were standard on classic T-Birds. Yearly membership: $15.00 for first year; $10.00 for renewals. Members receive discounts on all parts.

The Classic Thunderbird Trader
3930 Cobblestone
Dallas, Texas 75229

Classic T-Birds, as if you didn't know, are two seaters made in '55, '56 and '57. This newsletter-sized monthly publication is solely devoted to advertisements for these cars and parts. Subscribers advertise free. Subscription rate: $4.00 a year.

Classique Car Exchange Inc.
P.O. Box 176
Hewlett, New York 11557

Automotive memorabilia. Correspondence between Mr. Bell and Mr. Apperson of Apperson Brothers Auto Company (1902) is $5.00; *Ford Ideals,* signed "Henry Ford" on flyleaf is $150.00; eight letters written between 1930 and 1932 by Fred S. Duesenberg to Dave Lorraine are $375.00. Many other authentic items in all price ranges. Also sells antique and classic vehicles, such as Rolls and Model A. Free memorabilia and car listings.

Classi-Tique Products
Box 444
Springfield
Pennsylvania 19064

Grease and oil specially compounded for classic cars. Free folder giving detailed information on products and applications.

The Clausen Company
1055 King George Road
Fords, New Jersey 08863

Products for leather restoration. Complete procedure calls for application of Solvent-Cleaner, treatment with sandpaper, application of Rejuvenator Oil with a brush, on large and deep cracks the use of Crack Filler applied with a putty knife and more sanding, and the final application of Leatherique with a fine hair brush. Everything needed is supplied in a kit which comes in three sizes at $11.50, $19.50 and $33.50. For a custom color match, which also is adjusted for leather sheen, the cost is $3.00 additional and a sample must be sent. All products are also available individually. Free literature.

Clifford 6 = 8 Research
774 Newton Way
Costa Mesa, California 92627

This is the home of performance equipment for inline 6 engines, plus some factory stock parts for Hudsons and other cars of fond memory. Among performance items are headers for 6-cylinder GM, Ford, Hudson, Mopar and American Motors cars, foreign car headers (the brand name is Vipar), header collectors and gaskets, side mount exhaust systems, Weber carbs with intake manifolds to adapt them, Weber hard parts and jets, ram-flow quad intake manifolds as well as tri-ram and dual-quad manifolds, and carb linkage kits. To go along with the Webers, Clifford carries the Moon air density gauge and tune kit. Hard parts for Hudsons are available to fit 202, 232, 262 and 308 cu. in. engines. There are cams, engine bearings, carb repair kits, clutch parts, crankshafts in both stock and stroker models, distributor/ignition parts (1948-56), engine mounts, fuel pumps, gaskets, engine seals, timing chain gears, high-compression cylinder heads (1951-56 engines), intake manifolds, pistons, limited-slip differentials (for 1952-54 type 44 Spicer units), traction bars, stock and modified Hydramatic transmissions, U-joints, valve train components, Algon fuel injection systems, shop manuals, T-shirts and decals. Clifford has special catalogs available covering their head and crank service for street cars, drag racing, and oval track cars. Hudson catalog, $1.00; fuel system and header catalog, $1.00. Write for availability of other catalogs including extensive new catalog of hard parts for sixes.

Climax Headers 5636 Shull Street Bell Gardens, California 90201	Headers for domestic cars, trucks and vans, VWs, and dune buggies. Also header mufflers, flange kits, formed collectors, gaskets, and mandrel bends. Free information.
B.H. Clinkard Pump Farm Assington Essex England	Stocks spare parts for 1932-39 Alvis vehicles and does mechanical repair and overhaul work on these cars. Send International Reply Coupon with queries.
Clover Products 1645 Callens Road Ventura, California 93003	Company is run by Vic Hickey, who sells Blazer components under his own name. Clover handles accessories for the Bronco, Ford van and pickup, Courier, and International Harvester Scout II. Bronco items include Hickey's new Side-winder winch ($469.50); regular electric winches; hydraulic steering stabilizers; snatch blocks; rear tire carriers and can holders for Bronco and Econoline; Air Lifts; tow hooks; winch extension cables; front end guards and rear step bumpers for the Ford pickup; pickup transfer case skid plates; pickup and Bronco power steering assemblies; foam steering wheels; front hub seal kits; Bronco roll bars and wheel well cut-outs; pickup roll bars and motorcycle racks; headers; front disc brake conversion kits; automatic transmission oil coolers; Bronco front and rear dual shock mount kits; heavy-duty tire chains; pickup and van tow hitches; van roof racks; Bronco middle front seats; Courier grille guards and rear step bumpers; headers, roll bars and 18.5 gallon replacement gas tanks for the Courier; anti-sway bars for Bronco, pickup, Econoline and Courier; Hurst shifters; Gabriel shocks; quartz-iodine driving lights; Bronco sun screens; translucent roof vents; Citizens Band receivers and stereo tape decks; Courier and Ranchero truck bed tarps; Bronco convertible tops; folding steps; assist grips; free-wheeling hubs; Velvetouch metallic brake linings; alloy wheels; hydraulic bumper jacks; dual battery selector switches; and fire extinguishers. For the Scout II, accessories available are roll bars, dual exhaust systems, steering stabilizers, directional stability and shimmy damper kits, front end guards, driving lights, consoles, front and rear spring shackle kits, skid plates, tow hooks, spare tire and jerry can carriers, heavy-duty shock kits, 15″x8″ steel wheels, convertible tops, 32 gallon replacement gas tanks, and sun screens. Once you have your Bronco or Scout all fitted out with Clover accessories, Hickey will sell you Baja maps and guide books and wish you happy traveling. Catalog, $1.00.
Cloyes Gear and Products 17214 Roseland Road Cleveland, Ohio 44112	Timing chains for a great many foreign cars including Berkeley, Bond, Daimler, Hotchkiss-Gregoire, Invicta, Lagonda, Maserati, Tatra, and other exotic makes. Also has timing gear sets for domestic models. Free information.
Club Automoviles Clasicos (Classic Cars) c/o Nicolas Dellepiane Libertador 16121 San Isidro Pcia Buenos Aires Argentina	Along with organizing rallys and salons, this Club publishes a quarterly magazine, *Rueda Rudge,* and provides spare parts and technical advice to members. Yearly dues: approximately $18.00 (360 pesos); initiation fee, $50.00 (1,000 pesos).

Club Charentais de Voitures Anciennes (Vintage Cars) 35, Avenue Guiton 17 La Rochelle France	This group of vintage car enthusiasts meets the first Friday of each month, and would welcome American car fanciers who speak French. Yearly dues: $8.00.
Club Columbiano de Automoviles Antiques y Clasicos (Antique and Classic Vehicles) c/o Antonio Durana Samper Apartado Aereo 45-99 Bogota Colombia	Those who are interested in early car club activities will be glad to know of this flourishing Club with about 100 members and 110 vintage and veteran cars. Publications (in Spanish) include Club bulletins and a brochure giving the Club purposes and bylaws. There are frequent meetings, rallys, and tours, and the Club maintains a small library. Members would be interested in corresponding with their American counterparts. This information was supplied by Sr. Hernan Tobar, Club founder. Yearly dues: $8.00.
Club de Automoviles Clasicos y Veteranos (Vintage and Veteran Cars) E. Rodriguez de la Viña c/o Montalban, 13 Madrid 14 Spain	The Club holds meetings each Saturday and holds many events for pre-1939 cars and some later models. Publications include the magazine, *Automovile Antiquario,* periodical circulars, and, in February, a list of spare parts sold at the fair of Joyas y Chatarras (Jewels and Scraps). Members also can receive mechanical help during rallys, take advantage of the Club's library, and hoist a few at the Club bar. Mr. Rodriguez de la Viña can also supply information on the Union Espanola de Clubs de Automoviles Antiguos, which is the Federation of Spanish Vintage Car Clubs. Prospective members must be sponsored by current ones and approved by the board of directors. Entry fees and yearly dues vary according to the category of membership.
Club de Automoviles Sports de la Argentina (Sports Cars) c/o Ernesto Dillon 11 de Septiembre 2234 Buenos Aires Argentina	Devoted to vintage and modern sports cars, the Club organizes rallys and provides advice to Latin American sports car owners. The only Club publication is an annual report. Yearly dues: approximately $3.00 (60 pesos); initiation fee, $5.00 (100 pesos).
Club des Amateurs d'Anciennes Renault (Pre-War Renault) c/o Maurice Broual 53 Champs Elysees Paris 8e France	Organizes two annual rallies: Le Rallye Anglo-Normand in May and the Rallye du Val de Loire in July. Also organizes various commemorative meetings. Club services include technical advice and the loan of library materials. Yearly dues: approximately $10.00.
Club Elite of North America (Lotus Elite) P.O. Box 351 Clarksville, Tennessee 37040	Activities of this 100-plus member Club include an annual register of Elite owners, a monthly newsletter with technical information and some advertisements (the newsletter is simply called *Club Elite*), and an annual meet. The Club also sells some parts from time to time and has close ties with Lotus parts supplier William Hutton (he is the moving spirit behind the Club), who is listed elsewhere in this book. Yearly dues: $10.00.

Clube Português de Automóveis Antigos (Vintage and Veteran Cars)
c/o Jose Tavares
Rua Anselmo Braancamp 215
Porto
Portugal

Along with organizing rallys, meetings, and weekend tours, the Club has a magazine *Boletim do Clube Português de Automóveis Antigos* which is printed four times a year. There is also a technical committee, Club library, and some spare parts available. Yearly dues: overseas members approximately $10.00.

Club Mexicano de Automoviles Antiguos (Vintage and Veteran Cars)
c/o Alberto Lenz
Lorenzo Barcelata 23
Mexico, D.F.
Mexico

Regular Club activities consist of monthly social and competitive events, a newsletter, and the glossy bi-monthly magazine *Caminos de Ayer*. There is also a membership roster and some library services. This Club is open only to owners of antique cars. Yearly dues: $20.00.

Clyno Register (Clyno)
c/o J.J. Salt
Chimley Corner
High Street
West Lavington
Devizes
Wiltshire
England

I really can't tell you what a Clyno is, but there was both a Clyno car and motorcycle, and the club has 40 members—presumably all staunch enthusiasts for the marque. The *Clyno Gazette* is sent out very irregularly according to Mr. Salt who edits it. The Register does offer technical advice and library services, but, when it comes to spare parts, they're still searching. Yearly dues: approximately $1.20.

The Cobra Club (Cobra)
833 Lakeshore Road
Grosse Pointe Shores
Michigan 48236

Bruce W. Jodar sends along the following information which should be of interest to Cobra owners and potential owners. The first 75 Cobras imported (Nos. CSX 2000 to CSX 2075) were equipped with 260 cu. in. Ford engines and the first 125 had worm and sector steering. Also the first 75 had Lucas electrics with a generator. After these, all cars came with reinforced suspension, strengthened drive train, 289 cu. in. Fords, rack and pinion steering, and Stewart-Warner electrics with an alternator. The 427 Cobras (CSX 3000-3358) had either 427 cu. in. Fords or 428 cu. in. Ford engines. The 427 had cross-bolted mains and can be distinguished by a row of bolts visible on the block just above the oil pan/block junction. The 427/428 Cobras were completely redesigned with only a few body panels interchangeable. They had coil springing and fender flares along with Halibrand pin-drive wheels. Options included side exhaust systems, hood scoops and fender flares. Nos. CSX 3022-3047 were built as street/competition cars with an additional flare on the rear fenders as well as full competition specifications. The two biggest problems for current Cobra owners are overheating and lower ball joint wear. The former can be licked with auxiliary electric fans, shrouding, a larger radiator, and asbestos cloth insulating the cockpit. The ball joints should be replaced with units drilled for a grease fitting.

The Cobra Club offers regional meetings many times a year with varied activities, technical advice and parts-locating services, a monthly newsletter with a classified section (the newsletter is called *Snake Bits*), a World Registry of Cobras, various emblems, posters and badges, and members are working now on a definitive *Cobra Manual.* Yearly dues: $10.00.

Cobra Owners Club of America, Inc. (Cobra)
4737 Buffalo Avenue
Sherman Oaks
California 91403

Owners of any Shelby-prepared automobiles are eligible for membership. Club activities include monthly meetings, participation in rallys, slaloms, concours events, etc., and a bi-monthly newsletter. Also available are Club jackets, patches, decals and T-shirts. Parts location, discounts, and technical advice are available through the Club. Yearly dues: $15.00 for those within 150 miles of Los Angeles. Members outside the area pay $10.00 annually.

Cobra Performance, Ltd.
110 2nd Avenue South
Building C-6
Pacheco, California 94553

Parts and accessories for the Cobra roadster. Sole distributor in U.S. About 90 percent of original parts currently available. Send a stamped, self-addressed envelope with query.

Coburn Improvements
Banbury
Oxfordshire
England

This British version of Pete Brock's BRE or More Opel offers everything for the racing or rally Vauxhall. Included are Blydenstein carb conversions (using Weber carbs), modified intake manifolds, big valve cylinder heads and modified heads for most models, headers, limited slip differential assemblies, heavy-duty clutch parts, high pressure oil pumps, hard rubber engine mounts, waterproof spark plug covers, high-output alternators, heavy-duty rear axle casings, front and rear sway bars, adjustable shocks, Koni spring shocks, auxiliary air springs, increased capacity road springs, camber compensators (known as negative camber wishbones in British parlance), alloy wheels, heavy-duty brake pads and linings, oversized hub and brake assemblies, master cut-out switches, dash instruments, auxiliary fuel tanks, bucket and reclining rally seats, electric fuel pumps, door pockets, leather rim steering wheels, hood and trunk locks, fiberglass body panels, plexiglass side and rear windows, anti-lift wiper arms and blades, chrome rocker covers, fly-off hand brake assemblies, rally car intercoms, Britax full harness seat belts, roll bars, rally tripmeters, halogen headlamp conversions, Cibie lights and brackets, gas tank skid plates, flexible brake tubing protection springs, rear axle hanger links, strengthened and welded front axle beams, skid plates for sump and front suspension lower arms, windscreen washer units, and engine oil coolers. Free literature.

Cole-Hersee Co.
20 Old Colony Avenue
Boston, Massachusetts 02127

Electrical hard parts and associated hardware for most cars and industrial vehicles. Items available include switches, connectors, sockets, relays, fuse holders, senders, solenoids, and protective and wiring devices. Consult catalog at wholesale parts house.

Coleman-Taylor
466-468 Union Avenue
Memphis, Tennessee 38103

Makers of racing automatic transmissions. Also rebuild and install auto transmissions. Retail and wholesale. Write for information.

Cole's Power Models
P.O. Box 788
Ventura, California 93001

Model engineering supplies. Cole's offers engineering drawings, castings and materials for making models of many gas and steam engines of historical interest. They also offer raw materials and fittings including pressure gauges, safety valves, whistles, water injectors, copper tubes, brass and mild steel rod, sheet metal, machine screws, miniature wrenches, special taps and dies, jeweler's files, brazing supplies, small vises, drill presses, and lubricants. There is much literature on machine shop practices, steam boilers, steam engine history, and modern steam cars. The Company catalog also contains a directory of steam railways and museums throughout the U.S. Catalog, $1.50.

Competition Engineering
2095 N. Lake Avenue
Altadena, California 91001

Hairy performance components for VWs and Porsches. Porsche items on the menu include Weber, Zenith and Solex carbs; Weber to Porsche manifolds; dual carb linkage assemblies; velocity stacks; Bosch electrics; crankcase extension sumps; full-flow filter adapters; S.P.G. roller bearing cranks; racing pistons; 2500cc super bore kits for the 911, and 1700cc Big Bore kits for all 4-cylinder Porsches except the 914; Norris cams and tappets; and Porsche service manuals. Among the VW items are drag racing heads, rear motor supports for racing conditions, and Norris cams. Machine shop services include flywheel re-conditioning, the repair of damaged or cracked Porsche heads, and racing valve jobs. Catalog, $1.00

Competition Equipment Company
600 North Linden Avenue
Oak Park, Illinois 60302

Sells racing accessories including fire extinguishers; lightweight black plastic outside mirrors for weight watchers ($8.50 a pair); master kill switches ($9.95); sealed toggle switches which are waterproof, shockproof and dustproof; Rupert competition seatbelts and harnesses; roll bar padding kits ($7.95); anti-backlash shift-linkage joints; crash helmets and face shields; Repco ignition components and disc brake pads; Bayco racing fan belts; Phoenix on-board fire extinguishing systems; grade-8 cap screws and lock nuts; quick-lock and link-lock fasteners; tie-down belts; and nylon lock ties and clamps. Free literature.

Competition Heads
27554 Wick Road
Romulus, Michigan 48174

Porting and polishing for American engines plus VWs. Also cylinder head valve seat work, flow work, milling, special welding, intake manifold mods, valve guide work, spring seat machining, valve seal machining, screw-in studs installed, cylinder head assembly, canted plug machine work. Price of porting and polishing runs from about $145.00 to $225.00 on most V-8 engines without pro-exhaust. Catalog, $1.00.

Competition Limited
23840 Leland
Dearborn, Michigan 48124

Run by well-known rallyist Gene Henderson, the Company offers a complete line of rally equipment. Listings include Halda instruments and parts, "Tunaverter" receiver for time signals ($29.50 for model receiving WWV and CHU), Curta calculators, Stevens rally indicator, Heuer timers, Marchal and Cibie lights, Grimes navigation and cockpit lights, Repco disc brake pads, Impact seat belts, Koni shocks, Maserati air horns, VDO tachs, Stewart-Warner electric fuel pumps, all models of Recaro seats (prices from $165.00 to $265.00), Superwinch electric winches, Jac-Lift hoists, and "POR Jacks" which are hydraulic model high lift jacks ($32.95 for 1½-ton model). Free literature.

The Complete Automobilist Ltd.
39 Main Street
Paston
Peterborough PE6 9NX
England

Manufactures accessories for vintage and veteran cars, particularly British cars. In stock are a range of sidelamps, rear lamps and reflectors to fit anything from a 30/98 Vauxhall to a stately Edwardian horseless carriage. Also has lamp brackets, dash lamps, license plate lights, light bulbs, spotlights, mirrors, Klaxon horns, wiper blades and motors, headlight lenses and stone guards, "Brooklands" screens, hood straps and latches, grab handles, running board step plates and mats, gas can brackets, repro gas cans, dash instruments, filler caps, Hartford shocks and parts, jointing and shim materials, silk pulls, parcel nets, upholstery and headliner materials, exterior and interior handles, door locks and catches, Smiths Easy Starters, bulb horns and reeds, badge bars, acetylene lamp burners, fishtail exhausts ($15.98 for combined Brooklands type silencer and fishtail pipe in cast aluminum), Boyce Motometers, Edwardian double twist brass bulb horns ($74.68), fuse and junction boxes, horn and starter buttons, switches, terminals, control rod ball joints, pipe fittings, fuel taps, grease fittings, oilers, lift-the-dot and Tenax fasteners, keyhole covers, cowl vents, Rolls-Royce hood ornaments, Boa Constrictor horns, leather crash helmets, brass pressure pumps, and many small fittings appropriate to older cars. Catalog, $.50.

Conelec
Cass City, Michigan 48726

Specializes in electronic, solid-state fuel pumps for 6- and 12-volt cars. Free literature.

Con-Ferr, Inc.
300 North Victory Boulevard
Burbank, California 91502

Known as the supermarket of 4WD accessories, Con-Ferr carries roll bars, auxiliary gas tanks, skid plates, outside tire mounts, bucket and bench seats, storage consoles, trailer hitches, heavy-duty bumpers and bumper guards, tow bars, bolt-in custom tool boxes, luggage racks, fender extenders, air cleaners, winches, overdrives, limited slip differentials, steering stabilizers, free-wheeling front hubs, replacement tops, carpets, wide wheels, off-road tires, headers and manifolds, and lighting equipment for most popular 4WD cars including the Land Cruiser, Jeep Universal and Wagoneer, Bronco, Blazer and I-H Scout. Company also specializes in Chev V-8 conversion kits for the Toyota Land Cruiser, and carries dune buggy components and accessories. Catalog, $1.50.

Consumer Electronics
P.O. Box 43055
Cincinnati, Ohio 45243

The Model PYA Pyrometer, a battery-powered electronic instrument designed to measure tire temperatures from 60° to 300° F., is primarily used for tuning race car chassis. Price is $54.80. Free literature.

The Contemporary Historical Vehicle Association, Inc. (Special-Interest Cars)
71 Lucky Road
Severn, Maryland 21144

The CHVA covers all cars made during the period 1928-48, which they have termed "Action-era vehicles." Also included are a few later custom or limited-production vehicles like the 1949 Cadillac series 75 limousine. Most of these cars fit the special-interest category.

The principal Club publication is *Action Era Vehicle,* a bi-monthly magazine with information on proper restoration and automotive history.

The CHVA has ten regional affiliates plus a number of members in foreign countries. There are about four national meets each year, plus regional get-togethers. Membership is for a family and applications should be directed to CHVA, Inc., 120 Marydel Road, Linthicum, Maryland 21090. Yearly dues: $6.00 U.S.; $6.50 foreign.

Conti Enterprise Corporation
163-15 46th Avenue
Flushing, New York 11358

Distributors of ANSA free-flow exhaust systems and BWA Sportstar alloy wheels. ANSA exhausts are made for most Ferraris and Alfa Romeos, BMW 1600/2002 and Bavaria, Datsun 240Z, sports model Fiats and the Fiat 128 sedan, Ford Capri, Lamborghini, Maserati, MGB, Jaguar XKE, Opel, Porsche, Volvo and Saab 99. Tailpipes only are made for the Datsun 510, and for Toyota Corolla/Corona/Celica. Prices range from as little as $59.00 for an MGB system up to $345.00 for some of the more elaborate Ferrari models. BWA wheels are made for Alfas, BMWs, Datsuns, Vegas, Fiats, Lotus Europas, Mercedes, Opel GTs, Porsche, British Fords and Toyota. Company also distributes Mark Ten CD ignition systems. Free literature.

Continental
1727 Wilshire Boulevard
Santa Monica, California 90403

Foreign car goodies, rally equipment and other accessories for the enthusiast. Continental's padded seat cover individually fitted to the seats of many foreign cars costs $24.95 a seat and offers good lateral support. Complete competition seats are $49.95 or $64.95 for the high back model. Car covers are available in two fabrics for most foreign and domestic cars. A Porsche or VW "bra" is $34.50. Continental carries Heuer timing equipment, Stevens rally equipment, a complete line of AMCO accessories, Poli Italian air horns, Stewart Warner instruments, Koni shock absorbers and Chilton and Clymer manuals. Free catalog.

Continental Services
Box 355
Blue Bell, Pennsylvania 19422

New and rebuilt parts for 1940-48 Continentals and 1936-48 Lincoln Zephyrs. Miscellaneous repro parts include fender skirt rubber, fender welting, cowl vent and trunk gaskets, various rubber pads, LC gravel shields for $18.50 a pair, medallion hubcaps at five for $20.00, stainless steel nuts, bolts and washers for exterior engine parts and accessories (1936-48) at $65.00 for 1940-42 LC and Custom and $35.00 for all others, stainless steel fender kit with all nuts and fasteners at $25.00. Also most mechanical parts, wiring harnesses, sparkplug cable sets, batteries and cables. Literature available includes Ford Service Bulletins 1936-40 for $8.00; 1946 Ford, Lincoln, Mercury repair manuals for $5.00; 1936-48 Lincoln chassis parts catalog at $10.00. Free price list.

Conversion and Tuning Centre Ltd.
45a Tulse Hill
London S.W. 2
England

Performance induction systems, carb kits, cylinder heads, and cams for popular British and continental cars. Cars covered include Minis, Hillmans, Sunbeams, BMW 1600/2002s, British Fords, B.M.C. Cars, MGs, smaller Triumphs, Vauxhalls, Volvos, Opels, Lotuses, Peugeots, Saabs, Simcas, Renaults, Toyotas and Datsuns. Some components available for other cars such as Alfa 1750 and smaller Alfas, Alvis, Aston, Bond, Citroen, DAF, Daimler, Jensen, Humber, Jaguar, Lancia, Marcos, Mercedes, Morgan, NSU, and Rover. Catalog, 25p (about $.58).

Corbeau Equipe Limited
Duke Terrace
Silverhill
St. Leonards on Sea
Sussex
England

Corbeau racing and rally seats have been ranked with Recaro and Scheel seats by some buyers. Some models are available through U.S. accessory suppliers, but the full line of seats and universal sub-frame assemblies, as well as special sub-frames for particular makes, are available only from the horse's mouth. Prices range from $32.90 to $78.00 a seat. Sub-frames, front bars and runners are extra. Free literature.

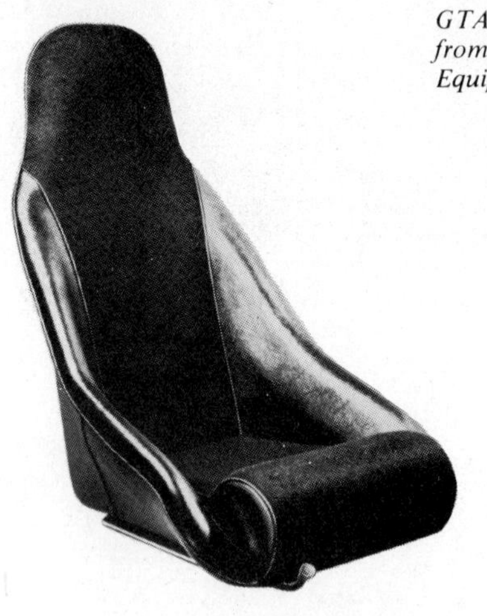

GTA "HB" seat from Corbeau Equipe Limited

Corvair Society of America (Corvair)
c/o Mr. William Garren
Treasurer
209 Lyndhurst Drive
Piqua, Ohio 45356

CORSA members receive a monthly newsletter, *CORSA Communiques,* a glossy quarterly magazine, *CORSA Quarterly,* and a membership roster. Other club publications include a *Corvair Specialists Guide,* listing garages around the country with Corvair expertise, and a *Corvair Reference Guide* which lists virtually every Corvair article, story and road test ever published. CORSA also has available decals, jacket patches, car badges and just about everything but dartboards with a Ralph Nader bullseye. The club is open to all those with an interest in Corvairs, including Lakewoods, Greenbriers and 95 Trucks. There are about 20 local chapters across the country. Yearly dues: $8.00; $2.00 for foreign postage; $1.00 for additional family membership.

Costruzioni Meccaniche Rho
20145 Milano
Via Canova 25
Italy

Manufacturers of the famed Borrani wire wheels, along with alloy and steel wheels for most European cars. Company publishes a catalog in four languages and is equipped to deal with overseas customers. Free catalog.

Grady Cox
Box 151
Avery, Texas 75554

Sells 1929-30 Chevrolet parts. Will supply information concerning parts available and technical information on Chevrolets of these years to all those sending a stamped, self-addressed envelope.

Warren Cox
P.O. Box 5383H
Long Beach, California 90805

Makes covers for classic, antique, and modern cars. Has more than 1,300 patterns on record. Fabrics are green drill, tan flannel, blue flannel, and waterproof tan coated on one side with Dupont Hypalon. A duffle type stowage bag made out of green drill material is available for each car cover. Prices range from $20.00 to $60.00. Free literature and material samples.

C-P Auto Products
3869 Medford Avenue
Los Angeles, California 90063

Cosmetic and small mechanical accessories for American makes and VWs. Cast aluminum valve covers, chrome wing nuts, chrome wire looms, oil-breather caps, valve cover breathers, air cleaners to fit most cars in low and high profile models, velocity stacks, chrome lug nuts and wheel locks, lift kits, rear shock extensions, lowering block kits, competition shock extensions, coil spring boosters, disc brake spacers to allow fitting custom wheels on disc-braked cars, carb adapters, wheel adapters, splash guards, distributor advance curve kits, carb bushing kits, fuel pump block off plates, carb stud kits, carb base gaskets, fuel fittings and clamps, air cleaner chrome wing nuts, mag wheel washers, aluminum spring lifters, rubber spring lifters, steering wheel pullers, hi-performance chrome valve stems and valve stem covers, NASCAR type hood pin kits, hood pin accessories, anti-theft door lock pulls, wood dash knobs and brake grips, tigerwood key fobs, hood locks, Chev spin-on oil filter adapters, chrome gas lines for Holley carbs, chrome fuel blocks, leather steering wheel gloves, baby moon hubs, license plate frames, chrome-plated easy-on fasteners, gaskets for exhaust and intake manifolds, valve cover gaskets, rear end gaskets, carb gaskets, header collector gaskets, stick-on wheel weights for mag wheels, carb air cleaner adapters, tire and wheel covers, and stainless steel pedal pads.
For VW: chromed air cleaners, valve covers, oil breather caps, oil filter adapters, timing discs, headers and exhaust extensions, nerf bars, quick shift kits, flop stops for anti-flip control, scoops, wheel adapters, lug nuts and wheel locks, door handles, wood door pulls, dash knobs, dash panels, brake sets and custom shifters. Catalog, $2.00.

Craig Corporation
921 West Artesia Boulevard
Compton, California 90220

Craig stereo components and sound system accessories include quad 8-track players, floor-mount auto-reverse stereo cassette/FM units, and floor or under-dash 8-track players with or without receivers. Craig also offers speaker kits for dash, doors, or rear deck. Free literature.

Powerplay floor-mount, autoreverse, Dolby System stereo cassette player with pre-set FM stereo from Craig Corporation

Crane Cams, Inc.
100 N.W. Ninth Terrace
Box 160-17
Hallandale, Florida 33009

Crane Cams are available in many profiles for practically any engine you can think of. Company will also regrind cams to order. If you want more pep in your OSCA, Bond Minicar, Crosley, Wolseley, Sprint Car, or your old family porthole Buick, Crane can provide a new or reground camshaft. Accessories available include aluminum rocker arms, valves, valve springs, pushrods, spring retainers, timing gears, degree wheels, and suchlike items. Catalog, $1.00.

Crank'En Hope Publications
450 Maple Avenue
Blairsville, Pennsylvania 15717

Reprints and distributes auto literature and shop manuals. Covers both vintage American and some foreign autos: 1938 Buick shop manual, $8.95; service manuals for 1934 Chev at $7.95; Model T Ford, $6.00; 1946-48 Lincoln Continental, $6.00; Mercedes to 1970, $7.95; Packard, 1935-39; MG T-series, $9.95. Maserati owner's manual, all models through 1960, $4.00. *Old Car Value Guide,* $5.00. *Glass Fiber Auto Body Construction Simplified,* $4.00. *Old Tire and Rim Handbook: 1915-27,* $4.00. 1912 Stanley Steamer Catalog, $2.00. Free catalog.

Crankhandle Club
(Vintage and Veteran Cars)
c/o M.J. Lewis
P.O. Box 1237
Cape Town
South Africa

Along with holding rallies and tours, the Club publishes a monthly newsletter, *The Cranker's Times* and offers spare parts and library privileges to members. Yearly dues for overseas members: $12.00.

The Crank Shop
121 West Hazel Street
P.O. Box 4096
Inglewood, California 90309

High rev and stroker crankshafts; up-graded replacement rods in steel, aluminum, and chrome moly; rod bolts and nuts; forged racing pistons; and machine shop services. A complete Pinto stroker kit and components is $644.23 with domed pistons, and $625.92 with flat-top pistons. The standard 1600 cc Datsun stroker kit is $666.72. Chrysler Hemi chrome moly rods are $634.90. Ford Boss 302 cranks with forged steel cores go for $210.00. Some machine shop prices are: aluminum welding at $15.00 an hour, complete V-8 assembly for $49.50, hot tanking at $7.20, align bore big blocks at $42.00, valve job $25.00, surface heads $22.50. Free information. Price quotes and technical information will be given over the phone.

Forged steel "Maxi-Rev" crankshaft from The Crank Shop

Crestline Publishing
Box 48
Glen Ellyn, Illinois 60137

Publishes histories of American cars—Ford, Buick, Chevrolet, Lincoln, Mercury, etc. Free literature.

Crime Detection Systems, Inc.
P.O. Box 790
Pearland, Texas 77581

Watchguard burglar and fire alarm system uses solid state components and works from 12-volt battery. Catalog of professional burglar and fire alarm equipment and accessories for car and home is $.50.

Michael G. Crosher
30 The Foxholes
Green Hill
Kidderminster
Worcestershire
DY10 2QR
England

Mr. Crosher is a Morgan Three-Wheeler specialist and can supply the following parts: brand new chassis, muffler and exhaust system components, gear and handbrake levers, brake and clutch pedals, rear lights, gas tanks, hose clip and rubber hose sets, front suspension parts, brake cables, lowering blocks for Twins, seat cushions and backs, tonneau covers, convertible tops, Hooley steering dampers, steering wheels, and quite a few other items. Many parts are individually crafted by hand. Mr. Crosher will also do complete restoration on all Morgans, including upholstery work, machine shop services, exhaust system fabrication, radiator rebuilds, welding of all metals, heat treatment, engine-turning of alloy dashboards, rebuilding Amal carbs, and general fabrication work. Free list of spares and services.

Crower Cams
3333 Main Street
Chula Vista, California 92011

High performance camshafts for most American engines and VWs. Cams come in both hydraulic and solid lifter models. Optional equipment includes heat-treated splitlock keepers, steel and Teflon valve stem seals, offset cam keys, advance and retard bushings, rocker stud pinning kits, adjustable and non-adjustable pushrods, rocker pivot balls, rocker lock nuts, aluminum roller rocker arms, ultra-lock grade-8 cam bolts, and hydraulic and mechanical lifters. Also makes fuel injection systems for small and large block Chevrolet engines, the 426 Hemi engine, and a blower injector on special order for supercharged engines. In addition, Crower markets clutches, heavy duty engine stands and racing accessories. Write for availability of catalog.

Curry-Fort Enterprises, Inc.
15424 Cabrito Road
Unit No. 7
Van Nuys, California 91406

Manufactures the Charger Mark I single-seater chassis for off-road racing. The basic frame is built from 1½″ O.D. mild steel tubing with M.I.G. welding used throughout. All hardware is aircraft or grade 8, and there is a 3-hoop roll cage structure. Also included are aluminum skid plates under seat, transmission and engine. Price is $595.00 assembled. Free literature.

Custom Speed Enterprises
21330 Gratiot
East Detroit, Michigan 48021

Among the racing accessories and miscellaneous goodies handled are fiberglass flex fans, cool cans, velocity stacks, plastic see-through valve covers for Chev V-8s, copper and asbestos head gaskets, valve cover and induction system gaskets, small racing hardware, high capacity oil pans, universal carb adapters, Holley carb modification parts, baby moon hub caps, pendulum pedal and slave cylinder kits, Moon hydraulic throttles, custom steering wheels, quartz driving lights, Stewart-Warner gauges, Sun gauges, Mallory ignition systems, Vertex magnetos, Thrush mufflers, Hilborn fuel injection systems, JR headers, Holley carbs, Offy and Edelbrock manifolds, Jabsco water pumps, Hooker and Vipar headers, traction bars, Gabriel and Delco shocks, VW intake manifolds and fiberglass body parts, Cragar and Ansen wheels, Mickey Thompson tires, Mr. Gasket and Hurst shifters, TRW pistons and rings, Jahns pistons, Grant piston rings, Velvetouch brake linings, Rocket racing wheels, performance valve train parts, B&M modified transmission components, MAS and CAE chassis components, Hays clutches, Zoom and Schiefer ring and pinion gear sets, Airheart disc brakes, Schiefer clutches and flywheels, Nomex clothing, competition seat belts, drag racing chutes, Lakewood traction bars and bellhousing safety blankets, Hedman headers, custom fiberglass scoops, and bucket seats. Also carries Corvette and Stingray fender flares; fiberglass body parts for 1955-57 Chev, 1948-53 Anglia and 1937-42 Willys; 'glass Vega and Pinto custom kits; and kits to transform the VW Beetle into a mini Rolls-Royce. Offers complete machine shop services including blueprinting, valve and head work, and engine balancing. Catalog, $1.00.

Cutlas Gear
& Manufacturing Co.
706 West 6th
Vinton, Iowa 52349

Manual and automatic free-wheeling hubs for 4WD vehicles. Free literature.

Nick Daidone
19 Wellington Court
Brooklyn, New York 11230

Original Borgward parts. Some hard-to-find items are door locks ($10.00 a pair), shift lever bushings ($1.00 each), oil filler caps ($2.00), front end parts, miscellaneous gaskets and seals, brake parts, etc. Send a stamped, self-addressed envelope with query.

Daimler and Lanchester
Owners Club
(Daimler and Lanchester
and B.S.A.)
c/o H.D. Saunders
Eastgate House
26 Top Street
Appleby Magna
Burton-on-Trent
Staffordshire England

Publishes a monthly magazine, *The Driving Member,* and a membership list. Holds monthly meetings and some rallies. Daimler SP-250 cars have their own section within the Club. Copies of technical literature are available on request. Yearly dues: U.S. $12.50.

Daimler Club
(Daimler)
c/o Clare K. Fulton
112 Hampshire Hill Road
Upper Saddle River
New Jersey 07458

Recently established Club devoted to information exchange, owners' directory and technical advice. Mr. Fulton is primarily interested in the Daimler SP-250, but also has information of interest to owners of other models. No dues at present. Send a stamped, self-addressed envelope with queries.

Dansk Jowett Klub
(Jowett)
c/o Niels Jonassen
Teglvaerksparken 12
3050 Humblebaek Denmark

Yes, there is a Jowett club in Denmark, although the current membership stands at only five. The Club's aims are "mutual aid in restoring and running Jowett cars and efforts to make the marque better known and thus find prospective owners of forlorn Jowetts." There is no membership fee.

Alan Darr
124 East Canyon View Drive
Longview, Washington 98632

Buys, sells and trades NOS Ford parts 1909-56. No catalog, send a stamped, self-addressed envelope.

The Darrow Co.
Fox Run Lane South
Newton, Connecticut 06470

Parts for steam cars. Currently available are pancakes, coil stacks and complete monotube steam boilers. Other products such as throttles and steam engines of the uniflow type, are either currently available or planned for the near future. Send a stamped, self-addressed envelope with query.

Datsun Competition Department
137 East Alondra Boulevard
Gardena, California 90247

Datsun has the right idea. Their catalog of optional parts reads like the menu in Alice's Restaurant.

For the 510 sedan and wagon, plus the popular Mini-pickup, you can get engine components from mild to wild to all-out Trans-Am racer. A good way to start might be with the SSS cylinder head ($105.00), streetable cam ($55.00), intake manifold (the SSS version is $24.00), twin SU carbs ($130.00) and the SSS distributor ($22.35). Better yet, get the whole SSS kit for $375.00 or the SSS slalom kit for $479.00.

Trans-Am types can build up their engines from a fully counter-weighted 6-bolt crankshaft ($131.89), an aluminum-finned baffled 6-quart oil pan ($125.00), a racing oil pump ($19.41), and a dual Solex carb kit ($247.15). Special pistons, valve-train components, bearings and other engine components are naturally available.

For the 510 sedans there is a 5-speed transmission, various gear ratios, and a limited-slip rear end with your choices of rear axle ratios. Limited slip differentials for the wagon and pickup are also available.

Datsun 510 owners also have a choice between a racing suspension kit, which will lower the car 2½", or a rally and off-road kit which increases ground clearance by 1½". Add competition disc brake pads (front) and shoes (rear), maybe an oil cooler, an electric fuel pump, and a 23-gallon gas tank, and you can decide whether to enter the Press-On Regardless Rally this year or just frighten all the Alfas and Porsches in the neighborhood.

Datsun 240Z owners are treated almost as well by the factory. For more beef under the hood there is a triple Solex carb kit ($475.00), a rally and slalom cam ($111.00) and a complete performance exhaust system ($180.00). A racing suspension kit goes for $552.10, while a rear spoiler is $60.00. Plexiglass headlight covers (not street legal) are $52.74 apiece. Then there's the 5-speed box with ultra-close ratios ($375.00) and a limited slip with various rear-axle ratios.

For the 240Z there are also competition brake pads (front) and shoes (rear), 5½" steel wheels, an oil cooler kit and an electric fuel pump.

Many parts are also available for the 1600 and 2000 sports cars (now out of production), the RL411 and other Datsuns. All parts can be ordered through your local Datsun dealer who should have the competition parts catalog on hand. And if he can't supply the goodies you need, Pete Brock at Interpart surely can. But that's another story.

Catalog free.

Datsun Owners Club of Southern California (Datsun)
363 Woodland Avenue
Brea, California 92621

Publishes monthly newsletter, *Datsun Owners News,* and has regular meetings and competition events. Is compiling a list of parts and accessories currently available for Datsuns. Yearly dues: $15.75; initiation fee $3.00; associate membership for spouses $7.75; national associate members (members outside the Southern California area) $4.00 with $2.00 initiation fee.

Lowell E. Davina
701 Deborah Drive
Roswell, New Mexico 88201

Mr. Davina, the owner of a Kurtis-Kraft auto built shortly after World War II in the U.S., was kind enough to give some information on the marque. There were 34 Kurtis-Krafts built. They used a variety of American engines such as the Hudson Hornet 6, Chrysler V-8 and Flathead Ford. The body was hand built and instrumentation was by Stewart-Warner. Replacement suspension components are available from CAE Racing Equipment (see separate listing). Frank Kurtis, the famous Indy car builder, now resides at Route 1, Box 158, Parker, Arizona 85344. He would probably be willing to supply necessary technical or historical information to Kurtis-Kraft owners.

Dayton Wheel Products, Inc.
2326 East River Road
Dayton, Ohio 45439

New Dayton wire wheels, in radial or crosslace patterns, are \$105.00 each in chrome, \$90.00 painted. Adapters are \$24.00 each and knock-off caps \$16.00. Complete 5-wheel sets (includes chrome wire wheels, adapters, knock-offs and hammer) are \$685.00. Painted 5-wheel sets are \$610.00. Standard sizes are 13″ x 5½″, 14″ x 6″, 14″ x 7″, 15″ x 6″, 15″ x 7″ and 15″x8″. Reversed rims, special offsets and special lacing patterns are \$15.00 extra for each wheel. Other services include Dunlop wire wheel rebuilding, Borrani wheel restoration (\$100.00, includes rechromed hubs, polished rims and new chrome spokes), and antique wheel rebuilding. Quotes for complete restoration are given only upon inspection of wheels. Prices are approximately \$100.00 in paint and \$350.00 in chrome, depending upon wheel condition. Free information and price list.

D.B. and Panhard Registry (Deutsch Bonnet, Panhard, Dyna-Panhard)
392 Franklin Street-B
Buffalo, New York 14202

Described as a "mutual-aid association of owners and fans of Panhard powered cars," the Registry primarily acts as a clearing house maintaining a list of cars and a library of information. There is also a newsletter which carries technical tips and information on parts sources. Membership is by voluntary contribution.

DC Ignition
4566 Spring Road
Cleveland, Ohio 44131

A division of Mr. Gasket Company, DC Ignition produces dual point high performance distributors for domestic vehicles and the VW. Other items in stock include high output coils, distributor components, degree rings, timing tapes, advance limiter kits, Delco and Mopar advance curve kits, Chevrolet distributor gears, spark plug terminals and boots, ignition wiring kits, numbered markers for ignition wires, and timing lights. Free catalog.

Deano Dyno-Soars, Inc.
1322 East Borchard Avenue
Santa Ana, California 92705

Performance parts for VW and other mini-cars. DDS makes big-bore kits, chopped flywheels, stroker cranks, aluminum oil sumps, windage trays, competition oil breathers, high-capacity oil pumps, remote full-flow oil filter systems, performance cams and valve train gear, high-velocity induction systems, headers, and other VW speed parts. If you want a complete 115-230 h.p. VW engine to drop into your sand buggy or Super Vee, DDS will oblige for prices ranging from \$925.00 to \$2,250.00. Another alternative is to buy a DDS rotary supercharger which is available for \$498.00 (with complete installation) for the VW, Colt, Vega,

Datsun 510, 240 Z, Pinto, Toyota 1900, and Mazda rotary. Now if you really want something that will look wholly sanitary bombing down the main drag or parked at the nearest McDonalds, DDS offers the VW Trike—a three-wheeler kit with bolt-together frame and fiberglass Manta-Ray style body. The cost is $795.00, not including a VW or Porsche engine/transaxle, which you must supply yourself. Other products which DDS manufactures or distributes include one-piece VW nerf bars, Weber and Holley carbs, 240 Z rear aluminum sun screens, VW close ratio gear sets, Webster competition transmissions, speed shifters, alloy 13″ wheels, and multi-carb kits for small Japanese cars including the Mazda rotary. Among the shop services which can be performed by DDS technicians are glass bead cleaning, hot tanking, Super Vee engine building, complete blueprinting services, transmission conversions for street and strip, and dyno tuning. Catalog, $2.00.

D.E. Competition
6215 Lancester Avenue
Philadelphia
Pennsylvania 19151

Racing and rally accessories include Hooker headers, Heuer timers, Smiths instruments, Raybestos and Ferodo disc brake pads, Deves rings, VDO instruments, Addco sway bars, Castrol lubricants, early Sprite competition wheel bearings, competition rods and main bearings for popular foreign cars, hood straps, Mocal oil coolers, Autobook workshop manuals, VHT aerosol lubricants and chemicals, Lucas battery switches, stainless steel brakelines, anti-seize and Loctite compounds, Marchal lights and air horns, AMCO accessories, MoMo steering wheels, Bendix and Carter electric fuel pumps, Hurst VW shifters, fuel filters, Bell helmets, Nomex and Fypro racing wear, and aircraft quality hardware. Also in stock at the D.E. emporium are Sprite racing engine parts, Talbot mirrors, Webster 4- and 5-speed transmissions which adapt to the VW transaxle, Formula Ford moly ring sets, Weber jets and competition contact points for the F/F, and budget engine tools. Free catalog.

Deist Safety Equipment
911 South Victory Boulevard
Burbank, California 91502

Nomex driving suits, breather face masks, on-board fire extinguishing systems, drag racing chutes and accessories, scatter shields in many models, seat belts and harnesses, tow straps, Baja bucket seats, and even drag chutes for bicycles so that budding drag racers get early practice. Write for catalog.

Delahaye Club
(Delahaye)
c/o Jean-Pierre Bernard
Les Milans
La Celle
St. Cloud 78
France

Members meet once every two months in Paris. There are also tours in the spring and fall. There is a Club bulletin and information on spare parts sources is disseminated to members. It is not necessary to possess a Delahaye in order to join, since all admirers of the marque are invited. All literature is, of course, in French. No dues.

J.R. Del Collado
196 West 69th Street
New York, New York 10023

Extensive listing of automobiliana includes show programs, auto emblems, color slides, color and B & W postcards, car models, and advertisements. Also brochures on experimental and show cars, Land Speed Record cars, and defunct makes—both U.S. and foreign. Some original owner's manuals and other books. List: $.75.

Delco Radio Division
General Motors Corporation
700 East Firmin
Kokomo, Indiana 46901

Manufactures radios for GM cars and Chrysler Imperials as well as heaters, air conditioning and automatic temperature controls for GM cars, and International Harvester and Jeep trucks. Publishes radio service manual and parts lists which can be consulted at GM dealers.

Delfosse Performance Products
11760 Sorrento Valley Road
San Diego, California 92121

Known for its high-quality gas pressure shock absorbers, which are made to fit most cars, Bilstein also distributes a line of VW performance parts under the name of FEBI, and is, of course, Delfosse Performance Products when not being Bilstein of America. Some VW parts designed to tempt a Bug owner are forged stroker crankshafts, swivel-foot valve adjustment screws, light weight flywheels and camshafts with various durations. Catalog, $1.00.

Demco
67 Oak Ridge Street
Greenwich, Connecticut 06830

Engine lubrication systems and allied products. Makes oil pump extensions for small and big block Chev and small block Ford V-8; oil pump drive tool, to obtain oil pressure prior to starting a new motor, for all Chev and Chrysler V-8 engines; oil pump pick ups for small and big block Chevs; oil pan and lifter valley baffles for most Chev engines; high volume oil pumps and high performance pump drive shafts for most Chev V-8s; and deep oil pans for Chevs. Several oil system products are sold together as complete oil system package for small and big block Chevs. Also makes TDC indicators, rocker arm stud supports for small block Chevs and degree wheels. Catalog, $.50.

Dempsey Wilson Racing Cams
63070 Miraloma Avenue
Anaheim, California 92805

Camshafts and valve train components strictly for racing cars. Manufactures flat and roller cams, H.F.O. (hard face overlay) cams, and cam and valve train kits. Catalog, $1.00.

Denzel Register
(Denzel)
c/o Carl H. Gatske
310 San Vincente
Salinas, California 93901

Mr. Gatske used to put out a yearly newsletter concerning Denzels, but dropped it when requests for information tailed off. He has worked on the restoration of three Denzels and visited Peter Denzel in Vienna, Austria, in search of parts and information. No parts are available, although the basic running gear is VW. Anyone in quest of further information about Denzels would be well-advised to contact Mr. Gatske.

V.W. Derrington, Ltd.
159 London Road
Kingston-on-Thames
Surrey KT2 6NY
England

Speed equipment for popular British cars. Derrington has performance kits for Mini-Minors, Spridgets, Vauxhalls, Hillmans, Triumphs, Austin and Morris cars, Singers, Sunbeams, Jaguars, Lotuses, and Marcos vehicles. Among the items in stock are headers, Weber carbs, Roadmax alloy wheels, Peco exhaust systems, Barwell-Derrington light alloy cylinder heads for B.M.C. cars, anti-roll bars, traction bars, lowering blocks, Serck radiators for Hillmans and Minis, speed shifter kits, Salisbury limited slip units, Tecalemit fuel injection for Cortinas and Twin Cam Fords, high-capacity oil pumps, Ford crossflow manifolds, Brooklands-type racing screens, polished valve covers, Monza-style and trigger-locking filler caps, oil cooler kits, Laystall-Lucas high-performance heads for T-series MGs, and Tuftrided cranks for British cars. Company also carries speed equipment for the Fiat 128 and some Continental cars. Catalog, $2.00.

Desert Classics
P.O. Box 1058
Nogales, Arizona 85621

This unique company specializes in remanufacturing 1956 Lincoln Continental Mark IIs (technically "Lincoln" was not part of the Mark IIs official designation) to authentic original condition. The interior is redone using hides from the original supplier, mechanical components are all renewed or replaced and the car is painted in original colors. Remanufactured cars are sold for prices at about the $12-14,000.00 level. Restoration services and parts are also available to current Continental Mark II owners. Continentals can also be special-ordered to be remanufactured according to customer specifications. Addresses for Desert Classic agents are: P.O. Box 105, East Meadow, New York 11554; P.O. Box 1058, Noyabo, Arizona 85621; and P.O. Box 2267, Whitten, California 90610.

A Continental Mark II "remanufactured" by Desert Classics

Desert Dynamics
6230 Maywood Avenue
P.O. Box 630
Bell, California 90201

Accessories for Chevrolet off-road vehicles. Rear spare tire carrier is $39.95 or $42.95 in a version which also carries two G.I. cans. Blazer trailer hitch—the class II heavy-duty model—is $24.95. A hydraulic steering stabilizer for all G.M. 4WD vehicles is $19.95. Other items for the Blazer are spare tire covers, roll bars and roll cages, safety belts and shoulders harnesses, electric winches, tow hooks, locking front hubs, front grille guards, transfer case skid plates, metallic brake linings and front disc pads, heavy-duty springs, coils to fit over shocks, dual exhaust systems, headers, chrome sidepipes, replacement steering wheels, floor carpet sets, center consoles, heavy-duty clutches, Stewart-Warner instruments, and dual battery selector switches. Some special van items are 12" diameter portholes ($29.50), metal or translucent plastic roof vents, two-way vents which can be opened in either direction ($29.95), rear spare tire carriers, roll cage kits, custom interior upholstery kits, and sliding door extending links to allow doors to clear wide wheels and tires. Pickup truck items include roll bars, motorcycle carriers, tonneau covers and auxiliary fuel tanks. For the LUV mini-truck, items available are a dual port manifold, camper top, interior upholstery kit and carpet set, outside mirrors, motorcycle rack, chrome side pipes, headers, alloy wheels, and replacement steering wheel. Free catalog.

Desert Vehicles, Inc.
440 Front Street
El Cajon, California 92020

Makes "rough country" suspension kit for all Chevrolet 4WD vehicles. Kit includes height raising blocks, positive arch

6-leaf springs, U-bolts and nuts, and heavy duty shock absorbers. Comes with complete installation instructions. Kit price is $249.95. Free information.

De Soto Club of America, Inc.
(De Soto)
Box 4912
Columbus, Ohio 43202

Who would ever have thought that the mundane De Soto, with its styling that has always tended toward jukebox modern, would suddenly become one of the hottest special-interest cars of all?
The very active De Soto Club has bi-monthly meetings and publishes a fat monthly newsletter titled *De Soto Days.* Want advertisements in the newsletter are free to members, while anyone with De Soto parts for sale can advertise without charge. As a result, *De Soto Days* is chock full of parts sources. The Club also has technical advisers who can supply information on the maintenance or restoration of particular models. Yearly dues: $6.00.

Detroit Automotive Products
11445 Stephens Drive
Warren, Michigan 48090

Manufacturers of the well-known "Detroit Locker" positive traction differential for passenger cars and trucks. The Detroit Locker is a positive locking differential which operates without friction clutches. It comes in both standard and special silent types. Free literature.

The Detroit Locker, or 250S series NoSpin differential, from Detroit Automotive Products

Deutscher Automobil-Veteranen Club
(Vintage and Veteran Cars)
7 Stuttgart
Krapfstrasse 29
West Germany

Holds veteran car rallies twice a year and publishes the news bulletin *Club-Mitteilungen* quarterly. Yearly dues: $20.00.

Devon Vintage Car Club
(Pre-1953 Cars)
1, Yeo Cottage
Cornwood
Devon
England

Club holds one rally a month, and has two concours annually. The monthly magazine, *Magnetozine,* contains information on Club activities and parts advertisements. There is also a spares section and a Club library containing out-of-print motoring books. A running roster of members is kept. Yearly dues: $3.60.

Diels
1111 Pennypacker Lane
Bowie, Maryland 20715

Parts for 1956-57 Continental Mark II. All parts usually on hand or can locate them. No repairs or restoration. Send a stamped, self-addressed envelope with queries.

D.J. Sports Cars Ltd.
Swains Factory
Crane Mead
Ware
Hertfordshire
England

The *raison d'etre* at D.J. Sports Cars is supplying replacement body panels in steel or fiberglass for the majority of British cars. They also have panels for popular sports cars such as Austin-Healeys, MG-TFs and Lotus 7s. All panel-fitting and chassis repairs can be done on the premises. Whilst having your car rejuvenated or updated, you can also opt for flared wheel arches (fender-extenders to Americans), a custom paint job in Metalflake or another up-to-date finish, or even a Velvetex "hairy" flocking spray, and pick up some odd goodies such as hood toggles and Dzus fasteners. Free parts and price list.

D.M.I.
5631 La Jolla Boulevard
La Jolla, California 92037

Complete machine shop services for VW engines. Also has many VW parts and some performance parts available. A special product is a Baja tank for the VW Beetle which holds 11.72 gallons. Free literature including list of machine shop services and prices.

DMS
9 Carlton Parade
Orpinton
Kent
England

To assist overseas owners of British cars, DMS will act as a purchasing agent for spare parts and accessories, and ship them directly by air freight to any international airport. The service is available both to private car owners and to racing teams which must obtain spare parts in a hurry. Write for further information.

Dodge Division
Service Department
Chrysler Motors Corporation
P.O. Box 1259
Detroit, Michigan 48231

Service manuals.

A. L. Doering
Manufacturing Co.
1 Station Plaza
Bayside, New York 11361

Spark plugs for domestic and foreign cars in various heat ranges. Consult catalog at parts house.

Downton Engineering
Works Ltd.
Salisbury
Wiltshire
England

Modifies various models of the MG, Morris, Mini, and Mini-Cooper for high-performance use. Some products are also applicable to other B.M.C. cars. Has conversions for the Mini 1000, Mini-Cooper 998 and 1275, Austin-Morris 1100, B.M.C. 1300, Maxi 1750, Austin/Morris 1800 Mark I, MG C, Spridget, Austin/Morris/Wolsley 6, and Austin 3 litre. An all-out conversion on the Mini-Coooper "S" is about $750.00 installed. Conversion includes lightening flywheel assembly, re-building and modifying engine with many new parts, fitting a tachometer, installing Koni shocks in front and bump stops in the rear, adding a pair of SU HS4 carbs with an exchange inlet manifold and new exhaust system, and other parts and services. Although all conversions are available for export, they may no longer be legal in some states on newer models. However, it is always possible to have a Downton conversion fitted to a cherry older model Mini or MG. Company will also prepare racing cars and rebuild vintage cars. By making suitable arrangements, a Yank might purchase an old Riley or Aston in Britain and have it restored before importing it. Free price list and parts sheets.

Drake Printing Co. 1000 West Eight Mile Road Ferndale, Michigan 48220	Service manuals for Pontiac.
Draw-Tite P.O. Box 126 Belleville, Michigan 48111	Draw-Tite has Class I and Class II hitches for domestic cars, pickup and commercial vehicles, and popular foreign makes. Carries both standard and equalizing hitches, along with tow bars, sway controls, utility ball mounts and air springs. Trailer dollys are also available. Free literature.
DRE 8913 La Crosse Skokie, Illinois 60076	Complete parts and maintenance service for Formula Vees. Services include engine rebuilding, chassis set-up and alignment, tune-ups, machine work, welding and trackside parts services. Among parts available are Bosch centrifugal advance distributors ($24.95), Rupert restraint systems (Formula car seat belt package including belt, harness, and submarine strap lists for $37.50), four-into-one exhaust system kit for updating older Formula cars ($55.00), two piece nose section for Zink FV at $40.00 for nose and $35.00 for windscreen/cowl, grade-8 metric hardware, special VW tools, Bell helmets and accessories, Solex carb parts, and other mechanical items. Some prices for machine work are: blueprint crank, $80.00; engine balancing, $49.50; and line bore 40 h.p. case (mains and cam), $62.50. Free literature.
D. S. Motor Engineering Co. Unit 3 1-7, Corsica Street Holloway London N. 7 England	The brand of car of interest here is the 6-cylinder Austin-Healey of recent memory. The Company can supply exchange engines or short blocks, plus many engine accessories. In addition, they have extractor exhaust systems; inlet manifolds for three Weber 40 D.C.O.E. carbs; the carbs themselves; most brake, suspension and steering parts; a large stock of body parts in both metal and fiberglass; and competition items such as rally springs, Koni shocks, lightened flywheels, widened front and rear fenders, wide wheels, competition clutch assemblies, oil cooler kits and rally camshafts. Free literature.
Duke's Wheels 4615 Texas Street Riverside, California 92504	Specializes in steel wheels for off-road vehicles and campers. Carries sand tires and drag racing slicks. One-piece double safety beaded steel wheels are $15.50 for size 13″x5½″ to $21.50 for size 15″x10″. Price for wider wheels is $1.50 for each additional inch for wheels wider than 11″. Company will also expand any stock wheel. A set of steel wheels and Beckett PaddlaTrak sand tires is $255.00 in size 13″x15″. Other items in stock include fiberglass seats ($19.00), steering brakes ($44.00), tire sealer, and aluminum gas tanks holding 3-9 gallons ($44.50 for the larger size). Free price lists.
Tom Dunaway Box 1974 Anderson, South Carolina 29621	NOS and repro Packard parts. Repro items are mainly medallions, mascots, plates, emblems, hub caps, and side mount mirrors. NOS parts include head and manifold gaskets, lenses, lightbulbs, and heater switches. Mr. Dunaway's particular specialty is new parts for Trippe driving lights. He also can duplicate any medallion or small metal part and can reproduce glass or plastic items in

unbreakable plastic. Send a stamped, self-addressed envelope with inquiries.

Dune Buggy Supply Co.
No. 10, 10th Avenue North
Hopkins, Minnesota 55343

Has fiberglass dune buggy bodies in various configurations at prices from $295.00 to $475.00. The standard model has the same style as the original Meyers Manx II. Other products include buggy lights and bumpers, windshields and windwings, exhaust systems, skid plates, roll bars, tow bars, air cleaners, steering brakes, steering wheels, wide VW bolt pattern wheels, wheel adapters, Gates and Mickey Thompson tires, Hurst shifters, VW frames (1961-65 unshortened version is $110.00), racing and off-road frames, fiberglass and convertible tops, bucket seats, carpeting, transmission and steering heavy-duty kits, Crown products engine adapters for Corvair to VW conversions, Corvair headers, fiberglass VW hood for Corvair engine, VW Bus air scoops, Bosch and Mallory high performance ignition components, Transvair conversion kits to adapt Corvair engine to VW, Baja Bug kits, fiberglass VW fenders to cover ultrawide tires, and Stewart-Warner instruments. Free information.

Dunlap Instrument Corporation
2254 Kingsway Drive
Cape Girardeau,
Missouri 63701

Those who are planning a race, gymkhana, or other competitive event, will be interested in Dunlap's catalog for race organizers. Items available include marker pylons, red fluorescent polyethlene plastic tube markers, Day-Glo orange tube markers, flag stanchion posts, marker and barrier tape, roller white line markers, headset and handset telephone systems (custom designed systems available), walkie-talkies, stopwatches, officials' vests, flags and flag sets, rally checkpoint signs, bull horns, portable PA systems, car numbers, sport seats, registration banners, timing banners, multi-sequence timing boards, digital electronic master clocks, score pads, and first-aid kits. Precision timers available include the Elekron "Sprint" Mark I timer, with one photo cell input, the Elekron Mark 80 timer with two photo cell inputs, the Veukron display timer and the Auto Score semi-automatic scoring unit to enable registering of lap times and laps of individual competitors. Free literature.

Durant-Star Owners' Club (Durant and Star)
c/o Gary Kaufman
3106 Plymouth Rock Road
Norristown
Pennsylvania 19403

Publishes an annual roster and eight newsletters a year. Aids members in locating spare parts and provides technical information. Along with the Durant and Star, the Club also covers vehicles sold under the names of Frontenac (Canadian Durant), and Rugby (export Star). Yearly dues: $8.00.

Dutton Sports Ltd.
Newcroft
Tangmere
Sussex
England

Dutton's 'B' Type car, based on Triumph Spitfire components, has been developed over the past two years and is now being exported to the U.S. and other parts of the British Empire. The basic kit consists of a fiberglass and aluminum body assembled to a multi-tubular space frame chassis. An extension gear lever, laminated windscreen, and rear lights are part of the kit price. Prospective owners must supply the factory with certain exchange parts such as a propshaft, steering column, and gear lever assembly. Suitable engines include

Ford V-6, MGB, British Ford 4-cylinder, BMC, Triumph and Alfa Romeo powerplants. There is also a racing version of the 'B' Type specially designed for club events such as the British Formula 1200. The newest Dutton vehicle, a 2-seater sportscar called the Malaga, is sold only as a completed vehicle utilizing either the 3-litre Ford V-6 engine or a 1600 cc Ford engine. Price for the 3-litre version is approximately $4,000.00 Free literature.

The "B Plus" from Dutton Sports Ltd.

Dynamite Sound
12248 Ventura Boulevard
North Hollywood, California 91604

Car radios, tape players, quadraphonic sound, and a variety of allied accessories can be found in the Dynamite catalog. Brand names include Panasonic, Lear Jet, Sanyo and A.F.S. Kar Kriket speakers. An 8-track stereo player is available for $50.00, while an AM-FM plus 8-track unit lists for $130.00. An AM-FM stereo cassette player with built-in record microphone is $225.00, while a quadraphonic AM-FM 8-track unit retails for $250.00. The most expensive speakers, the Kar Kriket 5″ variety, are $34.95 a pair, while others are as little as $7.95 the set. Accessories include a variety of power converters, stereo headphone jacks ($5.00), electric and manual antennas (the electric variety, in two models plus a custom one for 1968-73 VWs, is $24.00), mounting kits and brackets, a burglar alarm just for electronic accessories ($5.00), and a noise suppression kit for $1.90. There are also tape maintenance kits and cartridge or cassette carrying cases available. Free literature.

Dynaplastics
P.O. Box 3711
South El Monte
California 91733

Fiberglass hard tops for Triumph, TR 4, TR 4A, TR 250 and TR 6, Datsun Roadsters, Fiat 850 and 124 Roadsters, and Spitfires. Tops come in various styles including quarter window, porthole and landau arm versions. Prices are in the $200.00-plus range. Free literature.

Eaton Corporation
Special Products Division
P.O. Box 11085
Palo Alto, California 94306

Replacement bearings for most American cars. Consult catalog at wholesale and parts house.

Eaz-Lift
P.O. Box 489B
Sun Valley, California 91352

Draw bars and complete equalizing hitches with sway control. Eaz-Lift hitches are made for most severe-use towing applications. Accessories include a plastic ball cover in various sizes, trailer fishing pole holder, chrome trailer sleeve cap, and pull-down camper or trailer steps. Free literature.

Eckler's Corvette World
P.O. Box 5637
Titusville, Florida 32780

Cosmetic accessories and fiberglass body panels for Corvettes. A complete custom lift-up front end for 1968-72 models is $610.00. Fiberglass parts to replace the flip up head lamp assembly in 1963-67 Corvettes with an in-grille assembly are $48.00. A rear window kit for 1968-72 coupes, with GT roof panel, tinted rear window, window wells, flared wheel wells, Trans-Am style rear spoiler and rolled lower panel, is $470.00. A rear window louver kit for 1968-72 models is

Front spoiler from Eckler's Corvette World

$155.00. Also available are fiberglass bucket seats, many varieties of hood scoops, flared wheel wells for cars from 1953 to the present, trailer hitches, luggage racks, spoilers, Hooker headers and side pipes, and numerous other replacement panels and custom panels for all Corvettes. Catalog, $1.00; add $.50 for first class postage.

Eddy's Parts and Service
1200 South 7th
Centerville, Iowa 52544

Complete machine shop services with an accent on rebabbitting of Model A and old flathead V-8 engines. The company is also a T.R.W. parts jobber and carries NOS engine and suspension parts for some cars of the 1920s-1940s. In addition, radiator repair and automotive glass replacement are handled. Send a stamped, self-addressed envelope with queries.

Edelbrock
411 Coral Circle
El Segundo, California 90245

Edelbrock is an intake manifold specialist who sells manifolds for domestic cars, racing cars, and minicars. Street manifolds include Tarantula, Torker, single-quad high-rise, and minicar models. Competition manifolds are Edelbrock's tunnel-ram and cross-ram models plus the Hemi "Rat Roaster," and "Six-Pack" manifolds for Mopar engines. Also in stock are RV manifolds, linkage kits and fuel block kits for Holley carbs, polished aluminum valve covers, carb adapters, pressure fittings, and neoprene hose line. Catalog, $1.00.

EELCO Manufacturing
P.O. Box 4095
Inglewood, California 90309

Performance and dress-up accessories for American cars and VWs. EELCO has chrome air cleaners; die cast aluminum valve covers; chrome oil breather caps; Chev oil filter conversion kits; grade-8 hardware; universal carb adapters; gaskets of all types; Holley carb modification parts; dual-quad carb linkage kits; chrome, neoprene and vinyl gas line kits; "T" fuel block fittings; cool cans; aluminum fuel tanks; ignition wiring and terminals; crankshaft pulley timing tapes; distributor advance curve kits for GM and Mopar; Chev vacuum advance eliminator kits; Delco distributor advance limit kits; aluminum wheel adapters; disc brake spacers; Baby Moon hub caps; chrome wheel dust caps and rear axle covers; mag lug nuts and locking nuts; coil springs and raiser blocks; coil spring lifts and shock absorber extension kits; traction bars; hood and deck latches and accessories; shift lever T handles; anti-theft door lock knobs; and leather steering wheel covers. VW items include oil pressure gauge installation kits, stainless steel wire dividers, finned valve covers, ignition wire sets, Holley carb adapters, wheel adapters, walnut dash knobs, dune buggy cable ends, quick steering kits, and hood scoops. EELCO also offers a variety of safety belts and shoulder harnesses. Catalog, $1.00.

EFPE Company
30451 Little Mack Avenue
Roseville, Michigan 48066

Cibie quartz-iodine lights and related accessories including switches, relays, brackets, and wire. Free literature.

Cibie Super Oscar driving light from EFPE Company

Egge Machine Co.
136 East Alondra
Gardena, California 90247

Mechanical parts for many antique, classic and special-interest cars. If you need a distributor rotor for a 1926 Moon, or a timing chain for a Locomobile, or pistons for a 1926 Kissel Kar, you'll find the part you need in the Egge catalog. Their coverage is truly comprehensive—far too extensive to list in detail. Catalog, $1.00.

EIS Automotive Corporation
Middletown, Connecticut 06457

Drum and disc brake parts for domestic cars and trucks. Comprehensive listing includes older makes, such as Studebaker, and limited-production models like the Checker. Consult catalog at wholesale parts house.

El Cajon Machine & Wheel
10347 Prospect Avenue
Santee, California 92071

Spoke and "California Center" wheels for cars and vans. "JS" Series painted wheels, in sizes from 13″x7″ to 16″x20″ range in price from $32.50 to $63.00 apiece. ECM also makes aluminum gas tanks, dune buggy frames designed for VW or Corvair power and ramp-type trailers. Free literature.

Malcolm C. Elder
1 Grange Park
Steeple Aston
Oxfordshire
England

Mr. Elder specializes in selling vintage and thoroughbred British cars. He is accustomed to dealing with overseas customers, and can either respond to specific requests or send a list of his current stock. Does not deal in spare parts by mail. Write for further information.

Electrodyne, Inc.
P.O. Box 358
2316 Jeff Davis Highway
Alexandria, Virginia 22313

Specializing in Porsche and VW accessories, plus goodies for some other foreign makes. Electrodyne makes spoilers for the Porsche 914, Volvo P1800, Triumphs, Toyotas, Opels, Mazdas, Fiats, Datsuns, the Capri, and the small BMW. They also have spoilers for the Pinto and Vega, and for Ford and Chevy pickups. Porsche 911/912 owners can purchase a spoiler/bumper for $98.00 which replaces the entire front bumper assembly. There are also 911/912/914 wide fender flares ($190.00), 911/912 flared rear bumpers ($135.00), and a rear air scoop and rear license panel ($24.95 and $29.95 respectively) for the 911/912. Electrodyne also carries coco floor mats, AMCO Porsche accessories, 914 center seats, tartan seat covers for many foreign cars, BWA alloy wheels, 911/914 front stabilizers and 911 rear stabilizer bars, Porsche and Datsun 240Z bug shields, 356/911/914 cadmium plated tow bars ($69.95), trailer hitches, Deist safety harnesses, Michelin tires, Aeroquip brake lines, Mohn ski and bicycle racks, Scheel racing and rally seats, anti-sway bars for many foreign cars, Racemark steering wheels, Nomex clothing, Marchal & Hella lights, foglight flashers for the Porsche 914, VDO instruments, Semperit tires, Koni shocks, ANSA and Bursch free flow exhaust systems, Thunderbird (brand) extractor exhausts for all VWs and Porsches, Solex and Zenith carbs, Conelec electronic fuel pumps, Mahle pistons, Deves rings, Filtron filers, many replacement Bosch parts for Porsche and VW, Boge shocks and steering dampers, Stabilus hood and trunk gas springs for the 911/912, and numerous VW and Porsche specialty tools, replacement parts and performance parts. The new S.E.S. fuel injection system is now in stock. Catalog, $1.00.

Elegant Motors, Inc.
P.O. Box 20166
Indianapolis, Indiana 46220

Remember when you were a kid and dreamed of owning a boat-tailed, supercharged 856 Auburn Speedster, the classic playboy car of another era? Now you can make your boyhood dreams come true. Elegant Motors makes a fiberglass replica of the 856 Auburn which has the authentic look and the finest modern engineering. Under the 'glass you can have either Ford parts with a Cleveland engine, auto trans, and complete equipment down to a golf bag door, or Corvette parts with i.r.s. and all sorts of desirable equipment. The Ford version goes for a cool $15,500.00, while the Corvette-based car ups the price to $19,000.00. Then there are options. Air-conditioning, a supercharger, wire wheels, wide whitewalls, a "swirl-polished stainless dash facia," fitted matching luggage, a tonneau cover and so on. Auburn Speedsters always were honestly blatant cars and the Elegant Motors' version is no exception. For those with more talent than money, the fiberglass components are offered separately for $3,995.00 plus $100.00 for crating. The Elegant Motors showroom is at 829 Broad Ripple Avenue in Indianapolis, and you can stay at their suite while making up your mind about whether to get the genuine leather upholstery or settle for Naugahyde, and questions of that nature. Free literature.

Eliminator Tire & Rubber Co.
79 Enfield Street
Thompsonville
Connecticut 06082

Makers of wide 'glass tires for performance cars, and economy nylon tires. Free literature.

Elin Racing Apparel
501 Main Street
Rochester, Indiana 46975

T-shirts, jackets, and one-piece uniforms, custom printed or embroidered with team or company names. Screen printing in block or script letters is $2.00 a garment for the first 12 garments and $1.50 for each thereafter. Permabond block style letters are $.13 a letter with a minimum of $1.56. Thread embroidery in 2″ block or script letters is $.35 per letter for front letters, and $.15 for each back letter. Embroidered emblems are available from stock for most popular cars and in a variety of racer's emblems. Custom emblems and designs, along with specially designed apparel, will be quoted on request. Free literature.

Jumpsuit from Elin Racing Apparel

Elite Enterprises, Inc.
210 East Third Street
Cokato, Minnesota 55321

Makes Laser 917 fiberglass kit car for VW or Karmann Ghia chassis (no shortening necessary) and VW, Porsche 4-cylinder or Corvair engines. Standard kit is priced at $1,295.00 and includes reinforced gullwing doors, door handles, brake lights, front turn signals and parking lights, racing stripes, Plexiglass side windows, safety front and rear windshields, tail lights, LeMans type seats (not upholstered) and assembly manual. The deluxe kit version, at $1,895.00, includes NASA scoops, engine enclosure, gas tank and sending unit, headlight covers, heater and defroster ducts, racing mirrors, ram air ducting, bronze tinted side windows, and front and rear bumpers. The 917 super sports car kit includes all the features of the deluxe kit plus headlights, dash instruments, sliding rear window, upholstery kit with carpeting and headliner, VW wiring harness, mag type wheels with 60-series tires, and grill and nose insets opened and ducted for additional stability. Free information.

Mike Elling
SDC, 3603 Williamsburg Drive
Huntsville, Alabama 35810

Studebaker and Packard parts. Specialty is repair and reconditioning of radios, clocks, and instrumentation. Also has some shop manuals and Studebaker-Packard postcards. Send a stamped, self-addressed envelope for list of literature or answer to query.

Elmer's Auto Parts
Webster, New York 14580

Antique auto parts and antique cars for sale, restored and unrestored. Send a stamped, self-addressed envelope with queries.

EMPI
P.O. Box 1120
Riverside, California 92502
4030 Boston Post Road
Bronx, New York 10475

In 1956, EMPI started the whole VW/off-road accessories business and they are still just about the biggest in the field. The company sells complete kits to modify VW Beetles. The Baja 500 kit including mag wheels and dress-up components is $186.50. The Baja 1000 kit with cosmetic accessories and handling components sells for $427.50. Another version of the Beetle is embodied in the GTV series of kits which also consists of appearance and handling aids. Engine equipment available includes big bore kits for VW and Porsche 911; roller crankshafts; racing cams; modified piston rings; ZF limited slip differentials ($289); close-ratio gears; solid motor and transaxle mounts; high-lift rocker arm kits; performance valve train components; polished valve covers; ram induction kits; Zenith, Solex and Weber carbs; Bosch centrifugal advance distributors; heavy-duty oil pumps; dry element air filters; finned oil sumps; windage trays; fuel line kits; competition clutches; chopped and balanced flywheels; power pulleys; engine trim sets; carb overhaul kits for Zenith and Solex carbs; ignition wire kits; headers; megaphone exhaust pipes; alloy wheels in three styles; chrome lug bolts and wheel locks; wheel spacers; racing tire valve stems; front anti-sway bars; rear camber compensators for swing axle and i.r.s. Beetles; gas pressure shocks; complete dash instrument kits with a tach, oil pressure gauge, oil temperature gauge, ammeter and brake warning light mounted in walnut grained metal dash panel to fit 1973 and earlier Bugs ($118.95); individual instruments and dash panel replacements; vinyl or hardwood dash trim; wooden dash knobs; fresh air vents; pedal covers; coco floor mats; shift consoles; speed shifters; custom steering wheels and wheel covers; bumper guards; many small cosmetic accessories; and technical manuals. Catalog, $1.00. Engine parts catalog, $.50.

Enderle Fuel Injection
1282 Los Angeles Street
Glendale, California 91204

Fuel car blower injectors are available in magnesium or aluminum, with or without stainless lines. Magnesium model with stainless lines is $270.00. Mag gas injection unit is $235.00. Also available is upright gas or fuel injector unit. Port injection kit, to tune each cylinder on fuel, is $94.00 or $140.00 with stainless steel lines. Complete selection of nozzles and jets available. Also fuel pumps ($86.00-$96.00) pump overdrives ($70.00) with extra gear ratios available, high speed reliefs ($20.00 complete with jet holder), pump drives, drive components, fuel shutoffs and fuel filters. Injectors are available for 283-327 Chev, 396-427 Chev, 260-289 Ford, 426 Chrysler Hemi, 331-392 Chrysler, 290-390 American Motors, and Volkswagen. Other products include timing covers, fiberglass hood scoops in gloss black to fit Enderle and Hilborn injector units ($20.00), scoop and airhorn covers, barrel valves, hydrometers for checking the percentage of nitro you run, density gauges, distribution blocks and idle valves, a nozzle drill kit, complete flow bench, and various injector parts and fittings. Free literature.

Engle Racing Cams
1621 12th Street
Santa Monica, California 90404

Camshafts and valve train gear for American V-8 engines plus Vega, Pinto, Honda 600, Toyota 1600, Datsun 1600 and 2000, Datsun 240Z, and other foreign cars on request. Free information.

Envair
2205 Oakton Street
Evanston, Illinois 60202

Natural fiber custom car mats for every U.S. and foreign auto. Colors are natural plus a variety of reds, greens, and blues. Price for complete set is $21.95, or $14.95 for front only. Free literature.

Erskine Register
(Erskine)
441 East St. Clair Street
Almont, Michigan 48003

This is a registry of Erskine owners and their vehicles. A roster is mailed approximately annually. Can also aid Erskine owners in parts location. Membership: free to Erskine owners. Send a stamped, self-addressed envelope with queries.

Sig Erson Racing Cams
20925 Brant Avenue
Long Beach, California 90810

Street and competition camshafts for domestic 6s and 8s along with VW, Porsche, Austin-Healey, Anglia, Renault, Hillman, Sunbeam, Triumph, MGA & B, Spridget and Fiat. Also offers racing cam accessories such as Donovan cam gear drives, Chev hardened steel crankshaft sprockets, offset keys, Melling oil pumps, Cloyes timing chain sets, VW high-ratio rocker arms, performance valvetrain gear, distributor modification parts, carbide valve seat and spring seat cutters, degree wheels and valve gappers. Sig Erson distributor modification parts, carbide valve seat and spring Otto Parts (see separate listing). Catalog, $1.00.

ESB Brands, Inc.
P.O. Box 6949
Cleveland, Ohio 44101

Makers of Willard and ESB Brand batteries. Company publishes an informative brochure on battery construction and servicing, as well as wall charts on the same topics. Free literature.

Esslinger Hydraulics
712 Montecito Drive
San Gabriel, California 91776

Makers of "Buggy Reins," a hydraulic steering brake for use on dune buggies or other VW-powered off-road vehicles. The device consists of two floor levers which operate the left and right rear brakes respectively. They provide quick steering control, even on sand or gravel where front wheels may not respond to the steering wheel. The device can also be used to circumvent the differential by locking up a spinning wheel and causing power to be transmitted to the other wheel. Buggy reins come with either angled or upright handles and they do not interfere with normal braking control. The price is $47.00. Free literature.

E-T Industries
1000 Hill Road
Benicia Industrial Park
Benicia, California 94510

Mag style wheels in diameters from 13″ to 16″ and widths from 3.75″ to 13″. Also has chrome reverse and slotted wheels, wheel adapters, disc brake spacers, regular and locking wheel lug nuts, front end lift kits for many domestic cars, coil spring lift kits, shock absorber extension kits, shackle kits, chrome valve stems, tire marking kits, lug wrenches, and splash guards. Free literature.

Euram Imports
P.O. Box 2
Berkeley, California 94701

Imports Cromodora cast magnesium wheels, such as those which are original equipment on Ferrari GT cars. Models to fit many Italian cars plus Toyota, Datsun, VW, BMW,

British Ford, Mercedes, Opel, Porsche, Renault, and Mazda. Prices run from about $55.00 up. Also stocks Cromodora sports rear view mirrors in chrome or enamel colors. Free literature.

European Foreign Auto Wrecking
1700 Newton Avenue
San Diego, California 92113

Operates three salvage yards specializing in foreign cars. Along with the yard listed at the left, manages VW Auto Wrecking at 2863 Commercial Street in San Diego and Fords & Foreign Auto Wreckers at 2335 Newton Avenue. Will ship parts. Send a stamped, self-addressed envelope with queries.

Evans Auto Service
45 Prospect Street
Essex Junction, Vermont 05452

Repairs and rebuilds capillary-tube-type, dash-mounted temperature gauges. These include the King-Seeley or glass-tube type, as used by Auburn, Cord, Lincoln, Nash, Ford, etc., and the Bourdon-tube type as used by Duesenberg, Packard, Cadillac, Rolls, etc. Costs vary considerably, but basic repair charges start at $16.00. Send a stamped, self-addressed envelope with queries.

Excalibur Owners Club (Excalibur)
1864 West Washington Boulevard
Los Angeles, California 90007

The most potent item brewed in Milwaukee, of course, is Brooks Stevens' famed line of Excaliburs—sort of latter-day Mercedes SSKs with all the amenities and Corvette engines. And now Excalibur owners have united into a small but active organization whose activities include meetings with informal concours competition, and a quarterly newsletter, *Excalibur Driver.* No current information on dues, but those interested may write to Peter and Ruth Lambert at the address given to the left.

The Excalibur SS Series II Roadster

Exzostec, Inc.
P.O. Box 937
Paramount, California 90723

Mufflers and exhaust systems for U.S. and foreign cars. Stocks headers for Datsun, Pinto, Toyota, Vega, Porsche, VW, and dune buggies. Also lists exhaust system accessories and small hardware. Manufactures both Exzostec and Hornet exhaust system components. Free information. Consult catalog at wholesalers.

Paul Ezra
R.R. 2
Winamac, Indiana 46996

Repro parts for Model A and Model T. Stainless steel instrument panels, $35.00; chromed bumpers, $53.00 each; cowl lights complete with arms, $75.00 a pair. Zinc running board mouldings, $8.00 a set; Model A pickup bed flooring, $24.95 a kit. Send a stamped, self-addressed envelope for list of parts available and prices.

F & C Classic Auto Parts
4 Wayne Drive
Poughkeepsie, New York 12601

Hard parts for 1955-57 T-birds and Continental Mark IIs. The F & C catalog, for the 1956-57 Continental Mark II only, includes everything from a transmission front band anchor pin ($.50) to a short block assembly for $580.00. The $3.00 price of the Mark II Parts Catalog can be deducted from a first order of $15.00 or more. Write for availability of 1955-57 Thunderbird parts.

F & W Rallye Engineering
5N775 Campton Ridge
St. Charles, Illinois 60174

The specialty of the house is improved lighting systems and headlamp conversions. Along with being a distributor for Marchal lights and electrical accessories, F & W sells Penetrator headlamp conversion units with supplementary driving and fog lights available. Although these lights are not the quartz halogen type, the claimed candlepower is much higher than conventional lights and surpasses some quartz halogen models. Conversion headlights for quad-lamp cars are $18.95 for a low-beam pair and $16.95 for a set of high-beam lamps. A complete set of four sells for $33.95. Free information.

Falke Corporation
24 Frederick Street
Waldwick, New Jersey 07463

VW and dune buggy performance equipment and accessories. Engine goodies include big bore kits, stroker cranks, oil sumps and windage trays, high-capacity oil pumps, competition and street full-flow filter kits, cams, chrome moly push rods, high-lift rocker arms, intake and exhaust valves and valve train components, power pulleys, single and dual point centrifugal advance distributors, air cleaners, intake manifolds, and headers. Carbs available include Zenith, Weber and Holley. Also has racing clutches, gear sets, solid transmission mounts, speed shifters and nerf bars. Interior accessories available are walnut and foam steering wheels, steering wheel covers, Add-A-Dash kits for sedans and transporters, cocoa floor mats, seat covers, consoles for Bugs and VW type III, door sill and pillar guards, and custom window cranks. Carries a complete line of VDO and Racimex gauges and sending units. Front and rear flared fenders, recessed front hoods, rear deck lids with scoops, chromed tail lights, and striping kits are among the cosmetic items sold. Suspension equipment runs from heavy-duty sway bars and camber compensators, to Wito adjustable shocks, and is finished off with wheel adapters and mag wheels. Falke Corporation will build competition engines and short blocks in stage I, II and III versions. Parts and price list, $.50.

Fast Company
7A Dodge Street
Beverly, Massachusetts 01915

Formula car and sports racing car sales and preparation. Sells Royale cars and has parts available. Is dealer for Lexan face shields. Also has full line of performance street equipment for subcompact cars. Write for availability of catalog.

Federal Bearings Co.
Fairview Avenue
Poughkeepsie, New York 12602

Ball bearings in metric and SAE sizes for most applications. Free catalog to wholesalers.

Federal Mogul Corporation
North Western Highway & Lasher
Southfield, Michigan 48076

Along with supplying engine bearings for most cars, and modified bearings for competition American engines, Federal Mogul has an extensive catalog of replacement engine, drivetrain and chassis components for most popular postwar foreign cars. Although the catalog is available to wholesalers only, it lists many items not easily obtainable from other

Engine parts from Federal-Mogul

sources, and foreign car owners will want to gain an idea of its content at a local parts house.

Federation International Voitures Anciennes (Vintage Cars)
c/o A.J.B. Baily
82, High Street
Ware
Hertfordshire
England

FIVA is a federation of the principal car clubs in most European countries and some other areas of the world. A general assembly of member clubs is held once a year. Those interested in current information or addresses covering any FIVA member can get current literature from the Federation. So far as I know, there are no North American car clubs affiliated with FIVA, but there are FIVA members in Mexico, Brazil, Australia, South Africa and many other places. Free information.

Ferrari Owners Club (Ferrari)
3460 Wilshire Boulevard
Los Angeles, California 90010

Publishes monthly newsletter entitled *Ferrari,* which includes articles on racing and Ferrari history plus want advertisements. Also has twice a year illustrated membership roster. Has monthly meetings plus other events. Yearly dues: $20.00; initiation fee $10.00. Associate membership, at same price, offered to those who do not own Ferraris.

Ferrari Owners' Club (Ferrari)
c/o Sir Anthony Stamer, Bt.
Cedar Court
9 The Fair Mile
Henley-on-Thames
Oxfordshire RG9 2JT
England

Closely affiliated with the British Bugatti Owners' Club, this organization sponsors a special handicap class for Ferraris at each of the five annual Prescott Hillclimb meetings. There are also two sprint meetings a year at Goodwood Circuit in Sussex, and several touring and social events. Publications are *Ferrari* magazine and a Club newsletter—both quarterly. Technical advice and spare parts location round out the Club's services. Yearly dues: $12.50 single; $16.50 joint husband/wife membership. Life membership, $250.00.

Fiat Register (Pre-1940 Fiat)
c/o Capt. G. Liston Young
Dickinson & Morris, Ltd.
Melton Mowbray
Leichestershire
England

Schedules monthly meetings during the summer plus a dinner in February, and publishes an illustrated bulletin quarterly. Other services are technical advice, handbooks, and spare parts procurement. Yearly dues: $3.00.

Fiat Roosevelt Motors
532 Sylvan Avenue
Englewood Cliffs
New Jersey 07632

Fiat distributor. Service manuals.

Fantastic in Plastic. The dream car is a perennial at auto shows, usually appearing spotlit on a turntable and draped with scantily clad femininity. A few dream cars were landmarks in design; others are revered for their contribution to the American style known as High Camp. With the advent of high-impact plastics, the fashioning of dream cars was facilitated. If you can't tell the sheep from the goats, don't worry about it—GM, Chrysler, and Ford have the same problem.

1. 1933 Pierce Silver Arrow. Undoubtedly one of the most influential dream cars, the Pierce Silver Arrow was a last gasp effort with body by Studebaker. It owes a debt to some earlier German designs inspired by aerodynamic experimentation, but the exceptional execution sets it apart.

2. 1938 GM "Y-Job". Designed by the late Harley Earl, the "Y-Job" introduced disappearing headlights and an automatic cover for the convertible top-well. The bull nose became popular among customizers of the fifties.

3. 1950 GM Le Sabre. This one, also designed by Harley Earl, was probably the most popular of all dream cars. It inspired numerous home-built imitations and ushered in the era of bullet bumpers and extravagant tail fins.

1.
2.
3.

4. 1950 GM XP-300. Though cleaner than the Le Sabre, the XP-300 was still conceived in the Wurlitzer school of design, though it had some interesting mechanical innovations. There was an adjustable steering wheel and a supplementary carb for alcohol.

5. 1955 Corvette Nomad. The production Chevrolet Nomad station wagon is now a valuable collector's car and was a notably clean design. The Corvette Nomad, a more advanced design on the Corvette chassis, still looks desirable today.

6. 1956 Chevrolet Impala Dream Car. The compound-curved windshield and stratojet molding treatment were features on this GM effort which influenced later designs for intermediate cars.

7.

8.

9.

7. 1954 GM Firebird I. The Firebird I was the first gas turbine passenger car to be built. It was styled to resemble the Douglas Skyray, an Air Force jet fighter.

8. 1956 Firebird II. Firebird II with the same jet plane theme as I, but with seating for four. It was supposedly designed for the highway of the future on which radar-controlled steering would be possible.

9. GM Firebird III. The latest Firebird features a single-stick control system and an auxiliary piston engine in the nose to power all accessories.

10. 1973 Chevrolet XP 898. One of the better-conceived recent dream cars, the XP 898 has a fiberglass foam sandwich body and chassis and is powered by a Vega engine with an experimental cross-flow cylinder head.

11. Chevrolet Astro I. The low-slung Astro I has seats which rise as a canopy lifts, ending the need for curb-scraping doors. It is also very convenient for passing trucks underneath.

12. GM Runabout. This urban runabout and shopping car offers a hint on General Motor's recent thinking.

10.

11.

12.

118

Fiberfab
41060 High Street
Fremont, California 94538

This well-established maker of fiberglass kit cars has six basic models. The Avenger GT-12, a low-slung coupe, is designed for VW components although a Corvair engine can be fitted. The basic body kit is $995.00, with the cost of a preassembled body, all ready to drop on your bombed-out Bug, set at $2,695.00. There are numerous accessories to provide such amenities as upholstery, instruments, lighting, defrosters and windshield wipers.

The Jamaican is a body for British sports cars such as Triumphs, Austin-Healeys and the MGA. The parts to adapt this body to the VW chassis are also available. The Jamaican V-8, a body/chassis kit with differential, uses mainly Corvair and Chevrolet components which must be supplied by the builder.

The Valkyrie, the top-of-the-line model, is also for Corvair components plus a Chevrolet V-8 engine, and can utilize as much as 350 h.p. in its rear-mounted engine. A body/chassis kit with adaptors is $1,895.00 and there are many accessories available.

The Vagabond and Clodhopper are dune buggy shells, available for $545.00 and $345.00 respectively.

The Liberty SLR is a genuine replicar, as they say, combining the classic looks of a prewar British racing car (it has a more than passing resemblance to the MG K-3 Magnette) with a Ford V-8 engine and a front end from a Dodge pickup truck. The myriad accessories include everything from a badge bar for $10.00 to five wire wheels which are the genuine article at $595.00.

Other fiberglass parts include replacement front end panels for older Corvettes and E-Jags, VW fenders, custom front ends for Corvettes and Mustangs, front and rear sections for two-seat T-Birds, and a variety of other replacement body panels for various models of the Corvette. There are also custom bucket seats with upholstered covers in four models.

Making a kit car is not everyone's cup of tea. Even on preassembled models the builder usually must supply the engine and transmission, radiator, steering, rear end and front axles, fuel tank, wheels and tires, and many other items which are taken for granted on factory jobbers. However, for those with the inclination to poke around junkyards and the skill to get all the components together and functioning right, a kit car can be a real bargain and a fascinating pastime besides.

The Liberty SLR fiberglass body from Fiberfab

Those seriously considering a Fiberfab model can purchase the instructions in advance to determine whether they are up to the job. It might also be a good idea to check with the local motor vehicle bureau and determine how much of a hassle it will be to register a homebuilt car. Catalog $2.00.

Fiber Jet Co.
510 Tahoe Avenue
Roseville, California 95678

Specializing in dune buggy and VW accessories. Offers eight different basic buggy bodies including the Cobra, Enos 500, the Rough Terrain, Satan's Super "T", Beachcomber, Mountaineer, Sandhopper, and Toni II. Prices for the basic bodies in solid colors are from $139.00 to $320.00. Mylar Flake bodies about $45.00 extra. Also has 'glass tops, running boards, and consoles. Other products include Baja Bug kits, bucket seats, VW exhaust and induction manifolds, buggy tow bars and skid plates, shift kits, nerf bar bumpers, belly pan reinforcing kits, performance cams and valvetrain gear, and big bore kits. In addition, has mini camper and full-size pickup shells and compact two-wheel utility trailers which can be towed by VW-sized cars. Free literature.

David A. Ficken
Box 11
Babylon, New York 11702

Mr. Ficken, who publishes *Car Tips* magazine and the *Hershey* [Pennsylvania] *Directory of Vendors,* also buys and sells antique automobile literature. Send a stamped, self-addressed envelope with query.

Filter Dynamics International, Inc.
18451 Euclid Avenue
Cleveland, Ohio 44112

Manufacturers of Lee filters and a large number of accessory parts through various divisions. Lee products include Cyclone headers, Eelco accessories, EMPI VW components, ET Mags, and mufflers under the brand names of Goldin Goose, Tiger, Scat Cat and Lee. Free information.

Filter Products Division North American Rockwell Corporation
25000 Miles Road
Cleveland, Ohio 44128

Makes dry type and oil bath air filters for many applications. Some types of filters are suitable for use on off-road vehicles. Write for futher information.

Filtron Products Co.
7835 Burnet Avenue
Van Nuys, California 91405

Filtron polyurethane filters, treated with a special wetting agent, are known for their superior performance in off-road and other severe use situations. Filters are available for foreign and American cars as well as recreational vehicles and motorcycles. Filtron models can be used as replacements for dry element or oil bath air filters, and can be adapted to many custom applications. Prices range from approximately $6.25 for a Filtron "sock" to fit 2″ diameter neck carburetors to $29.95 for a 14″ diameter low profile filter with a spun aluminum housing. Free literature.

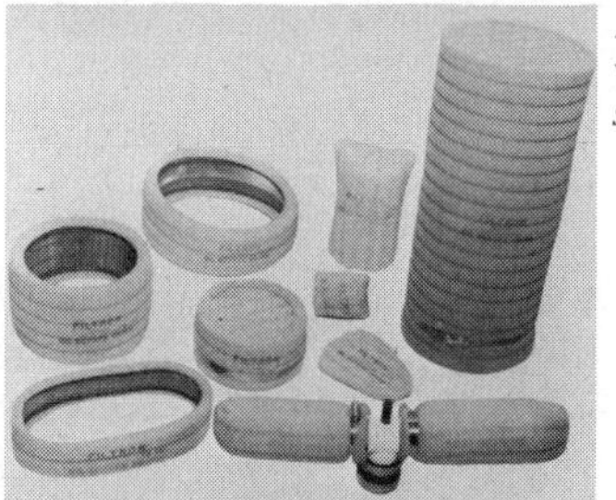

Filtron filters in various shapes and sizes

Flame-Out, Inc. 2670 East Walnut Pasadena, California 91107	Makes on-board fire extinguishing systems for race cars. Complete 5-pound system costs $200.00. Ten pound system retails for $276.00. Exchange refills are $55.00 for the 5-pound system and $85.00 for the 10-pound system. Free literature.
The Flathead Shop P.O. Box 770 Goleta, California 93017	Information service. For a fee ($2.00 an answer) will provide comprehensive information on 1932-53 Fords. Includes data on parts numbers, year-to-year changes, parts location, maintenance tips, accessories, etc.
Fleet Supply Company 2896 Central Avenue Detroit, Michigan 48209	Complete restoration services for all antique and classic cars. Company maintains a parts department, paint room, body shop, and machine shop. Prior work has been on Rolls-Royces, Duesenbergs, Packards, Model Ts and As, and many other cars. Send queries for further information.
Flex-A-Lite Corporation 5915 Lake Grove Avenue Tacoma, Washington 98499	The Flex-A-Lite fan, available for passenger cars, mini-cars, and most RVs, comes in both steel and aluminum versions and provides increased cooling with more fan blades and elimination of a fan clutch. Free literature.
Floyd Clymer Publications 222 North Virgil Avenue Los Angeles, California 90004.	Service manuals for U.S. and imported cars. Books on auto history. Free literature.
Ford Motor Co., Ford Europe **Ford Division** Dearborn, Michigan 48121	Handles British and German Ford distribution in the U.S.
Ford Parts Obsolete 1320 West Willow Long Beach, California 90810	Offering a complete line of parts and accessories for Ts, As and early Ford V-8s, the company can supply many rebuilt parts on an exchange basis. Some typical prices are: U-joint for 1909-27 ($15.95 new), axle housing, right or left ($7.50 used), complete engine and transmission gasket set for 1909-27 ($9.50), front hub for 1909-27 wooden wheel ($6.50), crankcase for 1912-24 and 1925-27 ($10.00 used), and transmission bands, both detachable and non-detachable models ($2.75). Machine shop services available for Ts include repouring and reaming mains and rods, plus a crank grind for $75.00; crank grind alone, $11.50; and reboring all 4 cylinders for $14.00. Model A fanciers can pick up a front axle dropped 2½″ ($23.95 exchange); steering wheels which duplicate original 1928-31 models ($25.50 to $32.95, depending upon model); a repro light switch and horn rod assembly ($13.95), new front and rear cross members ($19.95 and $24.50 respectively), and a muffler and exhaust pipe assembly in the original tapered design ($9.50). Many more mechanical parts and extensive machine shop service work available for As. Among other items offered are Walker street rod radiators, 1928-48 cooling system parts, radiator grilles and ornaments for all early Fords, 1928-48 fuel system components including rebuilt Tillotson, Zenith, AutoLite, Stromberg, Chandler Grove, and G/H Series carburetors and parts; rebuilt generators and starters; starter and ignition switches; wiring assemblies for lighting systems;

rebuilt distributors and distributor parts; headlamps and parts; tail lights; 1928-32 repro instrument panels; extensive wiring kits; fender brackets; running boards and molding; speedometers; windshield wiper components; rearview mirrors; shocks; and bumpers. Fiberglass components to duplicate 1928-41 and some later body parts, are covered in a comprehensive catalog listing. Many small trim items and upholstery fabrics are also offered. In addition, there is a large stock of 1955-57 Thunderbird parts on hand, however these are not catalogued. Catalog, $1.00.

The Ford Parts Specialists
98-11 211 Street
Queens Village, New York 11429

Hard parts for Model T, Model A, 1932-48 Ford and Mercury flatheads, Ford trucks, and 1956-59 Thunderbird. For Model T some listings are: exhaust manifold ($21.50), steering wheel with polished spider ($28.95), gull wing radiator cap ($8.65), model NH carb ($21.50), starter switch ($11.50), 1917-23 hood ($54.75), and aluminum script running board step plates ($12.95 a pair). For the Model A most wooden parts are available along with body sheet metal, fiberglass body components, seat springs, windshield frames, floor mats, running boards, and most mechanical components. There is a complete line-up of radiator grilles for Ford and Merc V-8s, mechanical parts for 1932-47 ½ to 1½ ton trucks, components for 1948-60 Ford trucks, "classic" T-Bird mechanical and body components, and Ford literature. Catalog, $1.00.

Ford Service Publications
P.O. Box 7750
Detroit, Michigan 48207

Service manuals for all Ford products.

Fort "T" Register (Ford)
c/o C.T.W. Pearce
16, Townsend Drive
St. Albans
Hertfordshire
England

Holds three competitive events each summer and publishes a bi-monthly magazine *T-Topics*. Yearly dues: full members, $4.20; associate members, $2.40.

Foreign Sale
6722 Expressway
Jacksonville, Florida 32211

Bi-monthly magazine in newspaper format devoted to advertisements for sports cars and other foreign vehicles, plus parts. Yearly subscription: $5.00 third class, $12.00 first class and $16.00 air mail.

Foresight Ventures, Inc.
841 31st Street
Oakland, California 94608

Sells alloy wheels in sizes 13″x5½″ through 15″x8½″, chromed steel wheels for cars and trucks, and oil cooler kits for engines, transmissions, and power steering units. Free literature.

Prowler XL alloy wheel from Foresight Ventures, Inc.

Forgedtrue Corporation
1480 Adelia Avenue South
El Monte, California 91733

Pistons, rings, and connecting rods for most domestic engines, plus pistons for more popular foreign engines. Free information.

Formula Tires
P.O. Box 9682
Minneapolis, Minnesota 55440

Makers of Desert Dog tires for street and off-road use. Street tires are as wide as 60 series. Free literature.

Formula Desert Dog tires

Formula Vee Association
c/o Mrs. J. Bannochie
Volkswagen House
Brighton Road
Purley
Surrey CR2 2UQ
England

Affiliated with the U.K. VW importer, this association administers Formula Vee and Super Vee races. Members, who are primarily drivers, receive regular newsletters advising them of race results and other matters of interest. Social activities are held throughout the year. The association has kindly provided the following list of British and Continental Formula Vee and Super Vee constructors: Crossle (Crossle Car Co., Ltd., Rory's Wood, Knocknagoney, Holywood, Co. Down, Northern Ireland), Lola (Lola Cars Ltd., Glebe Road, St. Peter's Hill, Huntington 7DS PE18, England), Royale (Race Preparations Ltd., Royale Works, Glebe Road, Huntingdon Trading Estate, Huntingdonshire, England); Supernova (Fallend Ltd., Fallend Works, Daux Road, Billinghurst, Sussex, England), Titan (Titan Cars Ltd., The Harley Works, Paxton Hill, St. Neots, Huntingdonshire, England), Elden (Design Formula, Wrotham Ltd, Tower Garage, Wrotham Hill, Wrotham, Kent, England), Veemax (Veemax Cars, 01730 Vantaa 2, Finland), Kaimann (Kurt Bergmann, Esslinger Hauptstrasse 13, 1220 Wien, Austria), Horag (Horag-Hotz Racing, 5400 Baden, Switzerland), Celi (Aldo Celi, Avenue Georges Henri 405, 1150 Brussels, Belgium), Motul (Motul-Tuning, 5060 Bensberg, Wipperfuertherstrasse 43, West Germany). Annual subscription for drivers is $8.40; associate members pay $2.40.

Forties Limited
16752 Huggins Avenue
Yorba Linda
California 92686

Devoted to the preservation and maintenance of 1940 Fords, deluxe 1939 models, and 1941 commercial models. Holds camp-outs, swap meets, round-ups and other traditional California activities. There are chapters in the San Fernando Valley, Orange County and San Diego. The club newsletter, *Forties Script* is published monthly. Along with advertisements for Ford V-8 goodies, a recent issue contained notice of a member wanting to sell a 1960 Mitsubishi dump truck, three 1952 Jowett Jupiters, a 1958 Goliath bus, a 1960 Hansa panel truck, an American Bantam body, a three-wheel Lambretta scooter, a home-built tractor with a Model T rear end, a BMW front end and frame, and other diverse and miscellaneous parts. You know there's still gold in those California hills. Yearly dues: $7.50; newsletter subscription, $5.00.

Warren Foster
504 Whipple Road
Tewksbury, Massachusetts 01876

Model A mechanical parts. Complete used engines; Sparton horn, $55.00; 21″ tire with tube and rim, $20.00; complete set of headlights with script lens, $30.00; short blocks, $60.00; bumper braces, $10.00 each. Also distributors, radiators and shells, rear ends, fenders, carburetors, transmissions, generators, starters, oil pumps, manifolds, and much else. Write to be placed on mailing list. Send style and model of car.

G. W. Foxcraft Products Corporation
P.O. Box 128
Huntington Valley
Pennsylvania 19006

Cartop carriers in various styles, deck lid carriers, ski and surfboard carriers, clamshell carriers, foreign car basket carriers, floor shift conversion units for domestic cars, jack safety stands, utility drain pans, rear coil spring lifter kits, front coil spring boosters, traction bars, fender skirt locks, universal rocker panel moldings, fender skirts to fit most cars, VW wheel adapters and replacement rear fenders, shock stud extenders, rear spring clamp kits, bicycle carriers, and portable steel ramps. Free literature.

Fram Corporation
Automotive Division
Providence, Rhode Island 02916

Fram makes oil, air, and fuel filters for domestics and imports. Also has a complete line of PCV valves. Filters and valves are available for the following imported makes: A.C. Cobra, Alfa, Amphicar, Audi, Aston, Austin, Austin-Healey, BMW, Borgward, Daimler, Datsun, Elva, Ferrari, Fiat, British and German Ford, Hillman, Humber, Innocenti, Iso, Jaguar, Lancia, Lotus, Mazda, Mercedes, Metropolitan, MG, Moretti, Morgan, Morris, NSU, Opel, Dyna-Panhard, Peugeot, Porsche, Renault, Riley, Rover, Saab, Simca, Singer, Standard, Subaru, Sunbeam, Toyota, Triumph, Turner, T.V.R., Vauxhall, VW, Volvo, and Wolseley. Consult application list at parts house.

Frankland Racing Equipment
P.O. Box 278-7th Avenue
& Highway 41
Ruskin, Florida 33570

Drivetrain components and braking systems for race cars. Frankland makes quick-change center sections, No-Spin differentials, True Track locking rear ends, hub assemblies, sway bar kits, Grand National rear ends and front assemblies for 1964-72 Chevelle, Chev spindles and steering arms, Chevelle upper and lower A frames, disc brake assemblies, and custom-fabricated chassis and drivetrain parts. Also sells Gabriel racing shocks and makes a wheel load ratio checker to determine the load at each wheel. Catalog, $1.00.

The H. H. Franklin Club (Franklin)
P.O. Box 66
Syracuse, New York 13215

The Franklin Club, with almost a thousand members, has an annual meeting at Syracuse in the middle of August. The Club magazine *Air Cooled News* is published three times yearly and contains a classified section and technical department. Franklin catalogs and technical manuals are available in photo-copy form through the Club. Also available are a Club roster, and bronze car emblems and jewelry. Yearly dues: $8.00.

Franklin Service Co.
1405 East Kleindale Road
Tucson, Arizona 85719

Complete car restorations, specializing in late model Franklins. While the mailing address is as listed, the shop is located at 1330 East Roger Road in Tucson. A limited number of spare parts are at hand. Send a stamped, self-addressed envelope with queries.

Frazer Nash Section of the V.S.C.C. (Chain-driven Frazer Nash and G.N. Cars)
65 Coventry Street
Kidderminster
England

Regular club activities include one weekend event in the United Kingdom every year and a touring event in Europe every other year. *The Chain Gang Gazette* is published three times a year. The club is also responsible for the manufacture of a wide range of new spare parts, and has original drawings of most components at hand. Although full members must own a chain-driven Frazer Nash or G.N. associate members are also accepted. Yearly dues: $3.60.

James Fred
Route 1
Cutler, Indiana 46920

Buys, sells and repairs pre-1950 automobile radios. Has tubes and vibrators available. Also publishes a newsletter entitled *Antique Radio Topics* ten times a year and an antique radio collectors directory. Send a stamped, self-addressed envelope with query.

Fred Opert Racing
17 Industrial Road
Upper Saddle River
New Jersey 07458

For those interested in sports car racing, a competition driving school is a good place to start. The Fred Opert school is based at Pocono Raceway and consists of three days of racing instruction, culminating in the student showing his stuff with a Formula Ford, for $500.00. Students who perform satisfactorily will receive an IMSA license. For an SCCA license, students who complete this course will be eligible after one weekend of SCCA instruction rather than the normal two. Fred Opert will also rent single seater cars to school graduates or holders of a National license who have had some single seater experience. The Opert cars you can rent and try harder with are a new Mk. 6B or Mk. 6C Titan Formula Ford ($800.00 per event), a Tui AM29 or BH3 Super Vee ($1,600.00), or a Brabham BT38/Hart Fuel Injection or March 722/Hart Carburetor Formula B ($1,600.00 per event). Prices are reduced for a contract covering four or more events. Prices include the supply of spares and tires, full transportation costs for the car to and from the circuit, the attendance of an experienced mechanic and the mechanic's room and board, the supply of a tow vehicle and trailer, and any labor required to prepare or repair the car—regardless of the cause of damage. Parts required to repair the car will be supplied unless damage was caused by a crash or by the driver exceeding a specified r.p.m. limit. Fred Opert Racing is also a distributor for Brabham, Titan, Tui, Brian Hart, Don Parker and Varley. Free literature.

Frigiquip Corporation
3805 NW 36th
Oklahoma City,Okla.73112

Aftermarket air conditioning systems for most cars. Includes custom through-dash systems for most vans and pickups, Courier, Datsun, Jeep, I.H., and LUV. Also rooftop air conditioners for trucks and motorhomes, rooftop condenser system for tough van and pickup cooling problems. Free literature.

Fritz Specialties
Route 4
DeSoto, Missouri 63020

New Model A items. Specialties are 1928-29 Ford lower landau bracket for sports coupe, Model A tire tools and jack handles and special ignition jumper. Also extra heavy, extra wide 19″ to 21″ rim strips for drop center wheels. Send a stamped, self-addressed envelope with queries.

Frontenac Club (Frontenac)
45 Greenwood Street
Tamagua, Pennsylvania 18252

Frontenac Speed Equipment was designed and built by the brothers Chevrolet—Louis, Arthur and Gaston. Nevertheless, the most famous cars were the "Fronty-Fords" of racing renown. In addition to Fronty equipment, Club members are those who fancy other sorts of vintage speed equipment including Rajo, Laurel, Roof, Cragar, Riley, Miller, and Duesenberg. Old race car drivers (meaning those who used to drive race cars and are now getting on in years), owners and builders are welcomed. The Club newsletter is *Castor Oil Fumes*. In addition, some Fronty parts are available through the Club. Technical advice and library services are additional features. Yearly dues: $6.00.

Fuel Injection Engineering Co.
25891 Crown Valley Parkway
South Laguna, California 92677

Fuel injection systems for most popular American engines and VWs. Chev small block fuel injection unit is $375.00. Set of 8 ram tube/air horn combos for unit at $32.00. Fuel pump drives can be Gilmer Belt, distributor or cam cover drive. Models for Chev, Chrysler 318 and 340, Chrysler Hemi, Valiant 6, and other popular cars. Turbocharged Chrysler fuel injector is $895.00 for early Hemi, $925.00 for later model. Turbocharger kit for all models, including two turbochargers, controller, wastegate and connecting ducts to inlet manifolds, is $1,495.00. Also Hilborn fuel injection units for various GMC blowers, F85 Olds aluminum V-8, Offenhauser, Offenhauser Midget, Offenhauser turbocharged, VW with dual port head, snowmobiles. Gilmer Belt Drive ($75.00), Cam drive ($62.50), distributor drive ($75.00), V-belt drive ($62.50) and Ford idler sprocket drive ($80.00) can be had with various engines. Also fuel pumps ($90.00-$165.00) and nozzles, plus complete fuel system hardware. Free information.

Hilborn fuel injector for Buick engines from Fuel Injection Engineering Co.

W. L. Fuller Inc. 1165 Warwick Avenue Warwick, Rhode Island 02888	Drills, countersinks, counterbores, plug cutters and taps. Free literature.
Fullerton Tire and Supply Co. 500 North Harbor Boulevard Fullerton, California 92632	Off-road and RV wheels and tires. Carries Jackman, A/P and U.S. Mag wheels; and Armstrong, Gates, Firestone, Goodyear, Thompson, Pos-A-Traction and Sand Tires Unlimited tires. Has many flotation, off-road racing and paddle tires in stock. Also distributes dune buggy frames and trailers made by Dirt Cars, Inc., as well as Gabriel shocks, wheel adapters, fiberglass fender flares for 4WD vehicles, Tri Phase air cleaners, and tire chains. Catalog, $1.00.
The Fulton Co. 1912 South 82nd Milwaukee, Wisconsin 53219	Makers of sunvisors in various shapes and materials. Free literature.
Bob Futterman Box 476 Riverhead, New York 11901	Specializes in upholstery and hard-to-find automotive fabrics. Has some old stock mohairs and bodycloths. Also has a few miscellaneous parts and manuals, but is not now emphasizing this aspect of his business. Will custom-make seat covers to order. Send a stamped, self-addressed envelope with queries.
Raymond Ganser Provost Alberta Canada	Special interest parts and literature. Parts for Chandler, Essex, Whippet, Chrysler, Pontiac, and many others. Shop and owners' manuals for Ford vehicles, including Canadian Monarch and Meteor. Also manuals for many British cars. Send a stamped, self-addressed envelope for lists.
Garton's Auto Parts 5th and Vine Streets Millville, New Jersey 08332	NOS parts for 1928-70 Fords, Mercury, Lincoln, Edsel. Also many Chevrolet parts, including mech. and chassis. Some parts for Pontiac, Buick, Olds, Cadillac, LaSalle, Graham-Paige and Hupp. Body parts and trim for 1932-54 Ford, plus most chassis parts. Mint original sales literature for Model A and Studebaker-Packard-Avanti. Stude shop manuals and parts books. Send a stamped, self-addressed envelope with query; free price list.
Gasket Material/Supplies **Carl Flinchpaugh** P.O. Box 2034 Whittier, California 90610	Gaskets for some pre-1948 automobiles and raw materials for making almost any type of gasket for all cars. Materials include various kinds of asbestos, cork, treated paper, Neoprene, Buna M and natural rubber. Also water pump packing, fuel pump diaphragm material, brass shim stock and punches. Has cork compound strips for headlamp lens seal on many classic and antique vehicles. Also available are fuel pump diaphragms for virtually all 1929-48 American cars. Free literature.
Gaslight Auto Parts P.O. Box 291 Urbana, Ohio 43078	A full line of parts for Model T, Model A, and early Ford V-8. Model A speed parts available include Rutherford valve covers ($19.95); front and rear tube shock mount kits ($18.75 each less shocks); Hartford type friction shocks ($31.50 a pair); Cyclone high speed cylinder head ($79.95 each); Dayton knock-off wheel hubs—either the two or three

ear variety—($16.95 each); 3¼″ drop front axle ($24.95); and other speed parts, such as cross and side drives, rocker arm covers and Ambler heads, which can be made up on a custom basis. Other Model A parts include 1928-29 front cushion springs ($31.60), 1928-31 oak pickup bed boards ($34.95), 1928-31 Coupe and Tudor vacuum wiper motor ($11.95), rebuilt starter motor ($39.95 exchange), and tire mount accessory mirror with chain and spring for attachment ($12.50). For Model T: aluminum high-speed flat head, finned for extra cooling ($79.95), Rajo polished aluminum valve cover ($24.95), Fronty polished valve cover ($25.95), polished aluminum exhaust and intake port cover for OHV motors ($8.95), finned and polished oil sump ($34.95), and front axle lowering brackets ($39.95 a pair). Free information. Those who are interested in original and repro speed parts for early Fords may write and ask to have their names put on the Old Speed List.

Gates Rubber Co.
999 South Broadway
Denver, Colorado 80217

Gates tires include 78-series radials, 60- and 70-series polyester belted tires, light truck and camper special nylon tires, and XT Commando and Sand Commando off-road tires. Free literature.

Gator-Bug
2823 190th Street
Redondo Beach,
California 90278

Makes chassis and frames for VW and Corvair mechanical components. Also fiberglass buggy bodies and VW parts. The Gator-Bug Sand Skate chassis is $350.00 for the 91″ wheel base and $385.00 for the 101″ version. The off-road racing chassis is $580.00; the Ascot Racer with short wheelbase is also $580.00. Other versions of the chassis and frame—all heliarc welded and with VW rear suspension, range in price from $425.00 to $550.00. Some chassis can be adapted for the Corvair engine and transaxle unit. Options include bumpers, steering components, shocks, flooring, fuel tanks, upholstered fiberglass seats, fiberglass Fire Fly antennas, steering wheels, sand tires, and many mechanical components. Company also makes custom buggies for Baja racers and the like. They can be built to take such engines as the Mazda Wankel and Honda. Also carries VW performance parts: big bore cylinder and piston sets; Zenith, Weber, and Solex carbs; intake manifolds; windage trays; Glyco bearings; and other mechanical parts. Free literature.

The Sport Buggy frame for VW or Corvair power from Gator-Bug

Gaylord Products, Inc.
1918 Prairie Avenue
Chicago, Illinois 60616

American distributors for the Panther West Winds Jaguar SS-100 repro car (see separate listing). Gaylord Products has recently set up a new distribution company: Panther (USA) Ltd. Free information.

Gebler Headers
6717 Ammendale Road
Beltsville, Maryland 20705

Makes custom headers for any application, including racing and show cars. Headers are priced at approximately $200.00 and up. Custom headers can be ordered through many local speed shops. Free information.

General Motors Restorers Club
P. O. Box 143
Highland Station
Springfield, Massachusetts 01109

This Club is no longer active. However, parts for older General Motors cars, which were formerly provided through the Club, can now be obtained from N.B. Pease and Company, 43 Foundry Street, Palmer, Mass. 01069. Free parts availability check list.

General Nucleonics/Tyco
2811 Metropolitan Place
Pomona, California 91767

Makes Speedatron CD ignition system for 12-volt negative ground automobiles. Basic unit costs $124.95. With Rev-Limiter the price is $139.95. The Speedatron Magnetic Pulse CD system for breakerless distributors is $159.95, or $174.95 with Rev-Limiter. Free literature.

General Technology of Arizona
455 West 1st Street
P.O. Box 1134
Scottsdale, Arizona 85252

Makes Swing-to tire carrier for rear of most 4WD vehicles, pickups or vans. Carrier swings away to allow rear door opening and is priced at $79.95, or $129.95 in chrome.
Other products are tailgate tents for Bronco, Blazer, Scout and Commando for $67.50; console front seat, for most 4WD cars and others with bucket seats and a column shift, which has a toolbox under the seat ($59.95-$64.95); fender cut-outs for the Bronco, allowing use of wide wheels; and extra front shock mounts for the Bronco at $21.95.
Fiberglass storage trunks, cleverly fitting around the wheelwells of Broncos, Blazers and Scout IIs, as well as pickup trucks, are $49.95 for Broncos and $69.95 for other vehicles. These trunks are lockable and they come with a 6 or 11 gallon water tank insert for another $25.00.

Blazer swing-to tire carrier by General Technology of America

Fuel tanks for the Blazer, GMC Jimmy and Scout II are made of 16-gauge steel with a treated and lined interior. They hold 37-40 gallons and cost $99.50 for the Blazer/Jimmy model and $107.50 for '73 Blazers and the Scout II. An 11-gauge skid plate for the tanks is a $29.75 option. Free literature.

E. W. George
2608 Gamma Circle N.W.
Huntsville, Alabama 35810

Antique, classic and special-interest auto appraisal service. Mr. George makes his evaluations after a comprehensive form on the car's condition is completed. The charge is $7.50 for each evaluation or $12.50 for two. Free information.

Germaine & Associates Fiberglass
235 North 16th Street
Sacramento, California 95814

Repro and custom fiberglass parts, bucket seats and dune buggy equipment. Hood scoops are available in just about any conceivable shape and size. They include Ramcharger, Tunnel Ram, Sox-type and Stingray scoops. Also VW bus standard and Big Boy style scoops. Among the bucket seat styles available are circle racing seats, Baja buckets, narrow dragster special seats, and double bucket seats. Stock and custom Model T body parts include poop decks, grille shells, pick-up bed tonneaus, fenders, dashboards, doors, and complete body buckets. Repro parts also available for early and late Chev, Corvette and Stingray, Ford Model A and V-8, Anglia, 1948 Fiat, Austin Bantam Roadster, 1933-42 Willys, and VW. Tilt or lift-off front ends available for Anglia, Prefect, postwar Chev, Corvette, Falcon and Mustang, Barracuda, 1933-42 Willys, Austin-Healey and Spridget, Opel Kadett and Jag XKE. A five piece Super Modified body is $195.00. Other products include Sprint Car tail and nose sections, Midget tail and nose section plus hood and cowl, complete Astra GT bodies, dune buggies in many styles, dune buggy hardtops, buggy roll bars and skid plates, and mechanical parts for buggies. Among the steel parts and accessories offered are chassis and frame components for 1923-27 Model Ts, and axles for Ford, Chev and Econoline. Free price lists. Write for availability of catalog.

German Auto Parts
P.O. Box 768
Idyllwild, California 92349

Hard parts for the VW and Porsche. Some VW parts on hand are: 40 hp cylinders and pistons ($48.00 for set of four); 1500/1600 cranks ($54.95); 40 hp cylinder heads ($37); Beetle and Fastback carb repair kits ($2.75 for 40 hp engine, $4.50 for others); Sedan and Bus oil coolers ($16.50); Front and rear shock absorbers ($6.95 a pair); and spark plugs ($.80). For Porsche: 1600N cylinder and piston sets ($140.00 for set of four); 356A/B main bearing sets ($16.95); 911 oil filters ($4.00); 911 air filters ($6.80); 356A/B master cylinders ($14.25); 912 regulators ($16.50); and 911/912 wiper blades ($3.50). Catalog, $.50.

Gidon Industries, Inc.
45 City View Drive
Rexdale
Ontario
Canada

Makers of Thrush high-performance mufflers, and Hush Thrush, quieter high-performance mufflers. The mufflers are designed for universal application and come with mounting hardware and instructions. Free information.

The Hush Thrush muffler from Gidon Industries, Inc.

Al Gigstead 1807 North Superior Appleton, Wisconsin 54911	Deals in antique auto literature, specializing in magazine advertisements. Also has some general items, mostly post World War II. Stock of more than 8,000 individual advertisements covers the years 1900-60. Send a stamped self-addressed envelope with queries.
Gilbert Metal Products 10816 St. Louis Drive El Monte, California 91731	Repro metal parts for Model Ts. Items available include 1909 Roadster and Touring front and rear fenders, 1909 running board aprons, 1910-11 Torpedo Roadster front and rear fenders and running board aprons, 1912-15 fenders and aprons, 1915 hoods, Edmund Jones headlights, and brass tail and side lights. Free literature.
Gil Manufacturing Inc. 4931 Santa Anita Avenue Temple City, California 91780	Makes auxiliary gas tanks for Datsun pickup and station wagon ($79.50), Blazer, Suburban, domestic vans, Toyota pickup and station wagon, Toyota Land Cruiser, all current pickup trucks (bed and saddle tanks), and many motor homes. Also has filler necks, compression fittings, hose, fuel line, tank selector valves, hose clamps, and gas tank caps. Free literature.
The 'Glas Works P.O. Box 3555 Inglewood, California 90304	Fiberglass repro parts for Model Ts, As and Ford V-8s. 1917-25 running boards are $20.00 each; 1923-25 turtle deck assembly for $75.00; 1930-31 front fenders, $40.00; 1930-31 rear fenders, $32.00; 1932 deck lid assembly (three or five window coupe, roadster), $50.00; 1932 roadster dash, filled and flat, $20.00; 1933-34 trans cover, $15.00; and radiator apron assembly, $12.00; universal hot-rod fenders, $30.00 a pair. Free parts and price listing.
Glen-Ray Radiators 2105 6th Street Wausau, Wisconsin 54401	Specializes in restoring radiators on vintage or classic cars. Send a stamped, self-addressed envelope with query.
Golden Lions **(Chrysler Corporation Cars)** 909 Edgewood Terrace Wilmington, Delaware 19809	The Golden Lions are interested in all cars built by Chrysler Corporation and its predecessor companies. They publish a bi-monthly newsletter with free want advertisements, and can serve as a source of parts, services, literature, insurance, and technical and historical information. Yearly dues: $6.00.
Golden Restoration, Inc. 410 Orchard Street Golden, Colorado 80401	Complete restoration services on all cars. Shop has wood, metal, painting and upholstery departments. Can restore cars from ground up. Also parts available for 1931 and older cars. Parts are not normally sold by mail; visitors are asked to search for the parts they require. Also operate antique car museum. Free information on restoration services.
Go-Power Systems 1890 Embarcadero Road Palo Alto, California 94303	If you happen to be in the market for an engine dynamometer (priced at $3,800.00 and up) Go-Power has models to fit every need. Free literature.
Gordon Spice **(International Spares)** **Limited** 12 B Central Trading Estate Staines	Specializing in competition parts for Formula cars, Ford, BLMC, Lotus, Ferrari, Porsche, Jaguar, Triumph, Datsun, Chevron, BRM, McLaren, etc. Offers an express parts service to ship competition parts or hard parts for British cars by air to the U.S. Shipments to customer's nearest

Middlesex England	airport can usually be expected within 48 hours. Will also make special parts or supply modified parts for any BLMC race engine or car. Carries large variety of accessories from such suppliers as Britax, Willans, Serck, Kangol, Leston, Speedwell, Oscot, I.A.P., Brown & Geeson, Hopkirk, Alexander, Mota Lita, Smiths, Fiamm, and other British and continental suppliers. Has comprehensive catalog of accessories available. Company will also act as wholesale distributors for competition or standard parts to U.S. retailers. Free literature.
Gordon's Restoring Service 504 Main Street Old Saybrook Connecticut 06475	Restorations of wood and cloth headliner on closed cars. No work done on convertibles. The entire job takes approximately two weeks. Mahogany is used to replace wood parts, while the customer generally provides his own material for headliner. Write for further information.
Gowen Auto Parts Box 729 Coffeyville, Kansas 67337	Has very large stock of parts for Antique and Classic cars from 1910-present. No catalog as yet. Send a stamped, self-addressed envelope with queries.
GP Speed Shop Ltd. Syon Hill Garage Great West Road Isleworth Middlesex England	Yes, there is a source for dune buggies in Great Britain. The GP basic kit consists of fiberglass body, hood, dashboard, some accessories and step-by-step instructions. Kit price is $336.00. Optional extras include a rollover bar, headers, wide wheels, leather-covered steering wheel, Marchal lighting equipment, racing bucket seats with runners and sub-frames, a wiring harness, folding soft top and side screens, fiberglass hardtop, front and rear bumpers, and mud flaps. The GP Beach Buggy version fits a shortened VW chassis (chassis-shortening is a service GP can provide), while the Super Buggy, at a slightly higher price, fits the full-length chassis. There is also an LDV model with a small pickup box at the rear. The Company also stocks 'glass, front and rear hoods and other traditional VW goodies. Free literature.
Graham Factory Service Auburn, Indiana 46706	Mostly NOS parts for Graham and Graham-Paige 1928-40. Also blueprints for most Graham parts. Some engine parts for Star and Durant available. Send a stamped, self-addressed envelope with query. Write for availability of catalog.
Grand/Safgard Automotive Products 5310 West 66th Street Chicago, Illinois 60638	Specializing in mufflers and muffler hardware. Products include high-performance "Goldin Goose" mufflers, O.E.M. Lee mufflers, glasspack Tiger and Quiet Tone mufflers, and Car Care factory replacement mufflers. Consult catalogs at wholesale parts house.
Greenland Company P.O. Box 332 Verdugo City, California 91046	Hood ornaments, Motometers, emblems, body plates and other accessories for Model Ts and As and other early cars. These are all repro items. The famous flying quail Model A hood ornament, with locking cap, is $19.95 or $24.95 with thermometer. A wreath-style Motometer with locking cap is $22.95, while a Jr. Meter without cap is $12.95. There are also plain rim Motometers and a version with 8″ wings.

Other "A" accessories include shell emblems, hub caps (heavy-gauge brass, chrome-plated, at $12.75 for a set of five), aluminum door sill plates, outside mirrors, floor mats and rumble seat mats, patent plates, and body plates.

For 1908-12 Fords and other cars, Greenland offers a solid brass generator for acetylene headlights. Price is $79.95 for regular or side mount.

Model T parts include windshield brackets, fender brackets, side lamp brackets and cowl light brackets. Also an overhaul gasket set ($9.95), crank handles, brass gas cap, crank clips, brass hood handles, a deluxe mahogany coil box with brackets for dash mounting, hub caps, hand-turned spark and gas knobs, exhaust manifolds, a wood steering wheel rim with brass spider, windshield support rods and hinges, plus many other items.

Greenland also has at hand front and rear bumper guards for 1933-34 Fords, emblem fobs for most popular antiques, 1928 Pierce-Arrow hood ornaments, a nifty selection of brass bell horns, Motometer dials for all cars, many repro body and chassis plates, a large line of miniature emblems, scripts and jewelry, Lincoln hub and trunk medallions, Cord taillight emblems, and much else. Free catalog.

Lyman E. Greenlee
P.O. Box 1036
Anderson, Indiana 46015

One of America's foremost Bugatti specialists has a very few parts plus copied manuals for sale. Also has much other literature on foreign and classic cars. Cotal Gearbox Manual (Xerox), $5.00; Talbot-Lago Manual including Wilson Preselector Gearbox information (Xerox plus English translation), $20.00; 1953 Kaiser Darrin folder, $5.00; English leather key cases with gold leaf embossed "Bugatti" or "Packard", $3.50. Send a stamped, self-addressed envelope for lists.

R. J. Grimes Ltd.
Hadleigh Garage
Marlpit Lane
Coulsdon
Surrey
England

Chrysler (Rootes Group) spare parts for all vehicles 1932 to the present. No catalogue, send international reply coupon with queries

Grimm Performance Products
1880 Whittier, Unit "E"
Costa Mesa, California 92627

Primary product is improved street cams for Datsun OHC engines. Will also custom grind cams for all import cars. Repairs and services most imports and can obtain many hard-to-find parts for older models. Will also do SCCA and professional rally car preparation as well as prototype engineering and fabrication. Free literature, Send a stamped, self-addressed envelope with queries.

Datsun 240Z spoilers from Grimm Performance Products

Grossman Motor Car Corporation 366 Route 59 West Nyack, New York 10994	Maserati distributor.
Jim and Hazel Grubbs' Village 5 & 10 2645 Marconi Avenue Sacramento, California 95821	Basically a clothing store with just the right duds to go with your Maxwell or 1913 Henderson motorcycle. Also antique Ford posters ($3.00), cast-iron model cars and coaches, antique and classic car puzzles, vintage car plaques, serving trays and coasters. Catalog, $1.00.
Guaranteed Parts Co., Inc. Seneca Falls, New York 13148	Ignition system components for domestic cars and trucks along with many foreign makes including A.C., Alfa, Aston, BMW, Borgward, Citroen, D.A.F., Daimler, Jaguar, Lancia, Lotus, Mercedes, MG, Morgan, Panhard, Porsche, Renault, Riley, Rover, Saab, Singer, Standard, Sunbeam, Triumph, Vanden Plas (Austin limousine), Vauxhall, VW, Volvo, and Wolseley. Also has carb overhaul kits for many U.S. and foreign makes, ignition and battery cable sets, insulated wire and terminal connectors, PCV valves, and replacement components for Chrysler electronic ignition systems. The Guaranteed line of "Grand Prix" high performance ignition parts are available for many domestic 6- and 8-cylinder engines including Corvair and Jeep V-6. Consult catalogs at parts house.
John R. Guerin 221 Herbert Avenue Fanwood, New Jersey 07023	Restoration of dashboards and other interior trim. Mr. Guerin is a woodgraining specialist and will send information sheet upon request. Send a stamped, self-addressed envelope with queries.
Dick Guldstrand Enterprises 11924 West Jefferson Boulevard Culver City, California 90230	Chassis components and racing accessories for Corvettes. An anti-roll bar is $32.00. Adjustable ball joints for 1963-72 models are $22.00 for the lower set and $20.00 for upper self-adjusting joints. Special rate springs available for big block and small block slalom and road-racing cars are $40.00 a pair. Among other suspension goodies available are heavy-duty steering rods, competition relay rods, control arm bushings, heavy-duty idler arms, modified trailing arms with steel ball joints, camber control arms, and a rear camber control bracket. Brake system components available are racing brake pads ($60.00 for four), Factory L-88 calipers, modified calipers to accept racing pads, Aeroquip steel brake lines, and metallic brake shoes for drum brake Corvettes. More items for the racer are 427 aluminum heads and modified oil pans, 350 heads, Carter electric fuel pumps, Hayden oil coolers, Traco remote oil filters, ignition wire sets, Traco small block heads and valve-train components, competition seat belts, racing mirrors, fiberglass bucket seats, plexiglass windscreens, SCCA legal front spoilers and roll bars, roll cage kits, Donn Allen safety fuel cells, small and big block headers, Jones tachometers, and magnesium and steel wheels. Catalog, $1.00.

Gull Wing Group, Inc.
(Mercedes-Benz 300-SL)
P.O. Box 2093
Sunnyvale, California 94087

The never-to-be-forgotten Mercedes 300-SL, both gullwing and roadster models, is kept a shining reality by the 500-plus members of the Group. Affiliates include six regional chapters, with more anticipated in the future.

Principal publication is the *300 Star Letter,* a substantial mimeographed monthly with chapter reports, technical tips, and advertisements for parts available and desired.

The club publishes a 275-plus page Tech-Tips Manual and has available Owner's Manuals, Factory Workshop Manuals and a Parts Catalog.

Another service is SPAS, a Scarce Parts Acquisition Service assisted by Mercedes-Benz of North America, Inc. Also members from time to time arrange for a limited number of accessories to be specially made up. Yearly membership: $15.00; outside U.S., $18.00

Vilém B. Haan, Inc.
10305-07 Santa
Monica Boulevard
West Los Angeles
California 90025

Sports and foreign car accessories in the Haan round-up include Maserati air horns; Nomex suits; driving gloves; Renauld sunglasses; Heuer timers; extractor headers for sports cars and small sedans; Autopower street and racing roll bars; Bell helmets; face shields; shoulder harnesses; custom car covers; replacment convertible tops for popular foreign cars; emblems and badges; Nardi steering wheels; Cibie, Hella, Raydyot, Lucas, and Marchal lights; rocker switches and switch panels; Lucas and Raydyot fender mirrors; international driving plates; Koni shocks; tire pressure gauges; Wanner grease guns; Monza quick-filler gas caps; Stelling & Hellings chrome air cleaners; alloy wheels; Porsche "bras"; sidewinder decals with car names in large letters; competition hood pin kits; custom hardtops for Datsun, Fiat, MG, Spridget, and Triumph; hardtop hoists; AMCO accessories; Krooklok steering wheel locks; sportscar jewelry; badges and badge bars; headlamp and driving lamp stoneguards; hood straps; fire extinguishers; custom dashboards and window winders; burglar alarms; splash guards; front spoilers; Brooklands racing screens; interior rally lights; Raydyot spotlights; custom bumper guards; gearshift boots; underhood spark plug holders; knock-off wheel hammers; Porsche and VW alloy ram pipes; Stahlwille metric tools; Curta calculators; Halda rally timers; Abarth mufflers; and Chilton and Clymer shop manuals. Free catalog.

H & E Enterprises
1118 North Thayer
Rhinelander, Wisconsin 54501

Screen process printing of T-shirts, sweatshirts and jackets. Made to order from logo or design. Wholesale and retail. Write for further information.

Hadley Chassis Engineering
1778 Monrovia
Costa Mesa, California 92627

Conversion kits for adapting the Corvair engine to the VW Beetle and Bus. Kit can also be used with dune buggies utilizing the VW chassis. Price for adapter kit for 1968-71 Bus is $119.50. Kit can be used with any Corvair engine and transaxle. Accessories are dual silencers ($44.50), remote oil filter kit ($14.95), oil cooler ($24.95), stainless steel throttle control assembly ($19.95) and Delco air shocks ($39.95). Hadley also has Transvair conversion kits to adapt the entire Corvair drivetrain to 1967 and earlier VW sedan and buggy chassis. Free information.

Halibrand Engineering
1506 West 228th Street
Torrance, California 90501

Famous for quick-change rear ends designed for championship, sprint cars and modifieds. Also front and rear hub assemblies, quick-change center sections, front and rear disc brake assemblies, torsion bar kits, in and out gearboxes, drive lines, cast aluminum race car grilles, and many components for Midget cars. Halibrand is also a prominent maker of magnesium wheels for racing. Most assemblies are sold by the individual component. Complete rear end assembly for Championship cars, with 3″ splined tubular axle and double unit spot brakes is $1,350.00. In and out gearboxes sell for $187.50. Magnesium racing wheels in sizes 4½″x15″ to 14″x16″ are priced from $71.50 to $134.00 each. Free literature.

Hallcraft's
244 Millar Avenue
El Cajon, California 92020

Wire wheels for dragsters and roadsters. Sizes are 16″, 17″, and 18″ in chromed steel or alloy. Heavy-duty 18″ alloy rims for early Ford spindles are $189.00 a pair. Free literature.

Hall Raceproducts, Inc.
9434 114th N.E.
Kirkland, Washington 98033

Fypro and Nomex flame resistant racing clothing and Phoenix on-board fire extinguishing systems. Complete model "3-2" 4-layer suit in red, white, blue or black, trimmed in contrasting color, with gauntlet gloves, boots, and respirator hood, will provide complete protection for the off-road driver. Price is $260.00. Phoenix systems are

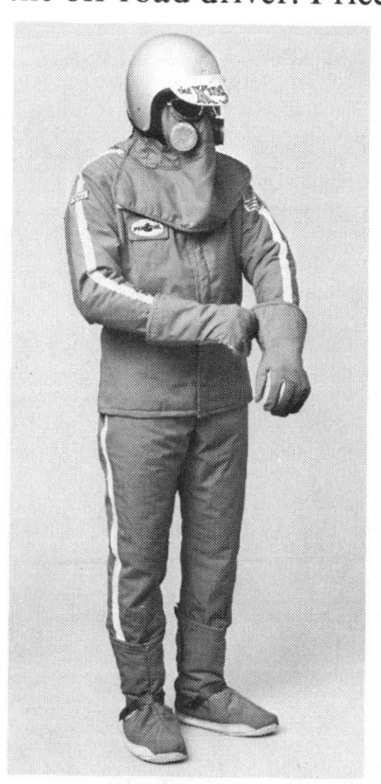

The "3-2" racing suit from Hall Race Products

available in an 11 pound model (total system weight 17 pounds), at $215.00; 5 pound systems, ($130.00), and 2½ pound systems, $95.00. Another product is a quality tire gauge in 0-15 PSI and 0-60 PSI models for $19.00. Free literature.

Hank's Vintage Ford Parts
14th & Elm Streets
Quincy, Illinois 62301

Ford Model A and T parts, books and accessories. Catalog, $.25.

The Masterpieces from Molsheim. According to rumor, Ettore Bugatti wanted to be a sculptor. And every component of every car produced at his almost feudal factory at Molsheim, France, looked as if it had been lovingly sculpted from steel. Today, the famous horseshoe-shaped radiator is a symbol for no-compromise construction of a type which the world is never likely to see again. Every Bugatti has a history and a pedigree, and every Bugatti owner has a priceless masterpiece.

1. 1926 Bugatti Type 35 Grand Prix. In the days when a sports car was a Grand Prix car with cycle fenders, the Bugatti Type 35, with men like Tazio Nuvolari and Achille Varzi at the wheel, was the racing car par excellence.

2. 1936 Bugatti Type 57 "Atlantique" Electron Coupe. The Type 57 is known as the finest Bugatti road car, and the Atlantique, with its rococo French coachwork, bulging with voluptuous curves, is a standout at any concours.

Hank the Crank, Inc.
7253 Lankershim Boulevard
North Hollywood
California 91605

Hank specializes in regular and stroker crankshafts for most domestic engines. Four basic models are the Street-Plus crank, offering a magnafluxed precision crankshaft at a relatively low price; the Stock-R-Plus model for Stock and Super Stock racing; the Rev-Now crank which offers ultimate performance in a non-counterweighted crank; and the Super-Rev all-out crank with counterweights. Also available are Forgedtrue pistons, chrome moly rods, chrome or moly rings and special rod bearings. Free information.

Harbor Industries
13025 Halldale Avenue
Gardena, California 90249

Specializes in engine hardware. Listings include adjustable valve cover wing nuts and hex valve cover nuts; valve cover breathers; VW air cleaners; replacement paper and foam air filter elements; adjustable gas regulators; lift top wire looms; wire dividers; Chev carburetor grommet kits; automatic choke block-off caps for Holley, AFB and Rochester carbs; universal carb adapters; carb heat insulators; shock extensions; up and down coil spring locks which can be used to raise or lower coil springs up to 3″; splash guards; valve cover gaskets for popular domestic engines; carb base and header collector gaskets; chrome gas line kits; finned valve cover breathers; chromed fuel blocks; bullet housings for dash instruments; chromed shift handles; hood pin and hood lock kits; distributor advance curve kits; chromed dash panels and switch panels. Free literature.

Hardins Speed Service Co.
3649 Illinois Street
Hobart, Indiana 46342

Manufactures Drag-Lite trailers for racing cars. Made of 2″x4″ box tubing, with steel ramps, 4-ply tires, 2-wheel brakes, lights, enclosed fenders, front wheel stop, ramp and ramp hangers, the price is $720.00. Options are 4-wheel brakes ($30.00), hydraulic brakes ($75.00), front jack ($11.00), spare tire and wheel ($30.00), and a boat-type winch ($25.00). Free literature.

Hardway Engineering Works
P.O. Box 4234
Tulsa, Oklahoma 74104

High performance street engines. Also manufactures Gladhander automatic brake bleed screws. Write for further information.

Don Hardy Race Cars & Equipment
9534 Forest View
Dallas, Texas 75238

Complete Super Twister V-8 Vega kit with headers, frame adapters, motor mounts, trans crossmember and mount, fuel-line changeover kit, heavy-duty front springs, upper and lower radiator hose, heater conversion kit, heavy-duty fan assembly, bolt package, decals and instructions; sells for $295.00. A V-8 Vega clutch linkage kit is $28.88; super heavy-duty radiator goes for $134.50; auto trans cooler for $19.88; 5-lug front hubs carry an exchange price of $35.00; while a complete 12-bolt Positraction assembly is $550.00. Ladder-type traction bars are $125.00 a pair and wheelie bars $79.95 a pair. Coil-over shocks with springs are $210.00 a pair. Among the smaller parts and fasteners useful to racers are aircraft quality U-joints ($7.50), tubing end adapters, clevis pins, rods ends, push-pull pins for quick disconnect, chassis brackets and Dzus fasteners. Also narrowed 12-bolt Chev axle assemblies, Adel clamps, front and rear disc brake assemblies, Vega pro stock spindles, Airheart single master cylinders and Don Hardy/Strange dual cylinders, buckets seats, Cragar wheels, 9″ Ford and 9¾″ Dana spools, aluminum water pumps for small-block Chev, Anglia spindles, M & H front drag tires, Pinto rack and pinion mounts, steering box assemblies, aluminum bellcranks, torsion bars for Funny Cars or street Roadsters, shoulder harnesses, and Don Hardy rear axles. Free catalog.

Harkin Machine Shop
115 1st Avenue N.W.
Watertown, South Dakota 57201

Complete bearing service including rebabbitting and boring of babbitted rods, heavy and precision insert bearings, cast and line bore cast-in-block main bearings and recasting early GM white metal main bearings. Write for estimate.

Harmon Electronics, Inc.
Grain Valley, Missouri 64029

Makers of "Tach II," a digital, direct reading tachometer for 4-, 6-, and 8-cylinder engines. Free literature.

Harmon's digital Tach II

Harnesses Unlimited
Box 140
Plymouth Meeting
Pennsylvania 19462

Stock harnesses for certain models of Packard and Lincoln. Custom harnesses for any car made from sample or pattern with all terminals identified as to function. All wiring harness components available. Send a stamped, self-addressed envelope with query

Hayden Trans-Cooler, Inc.
1531 Pomona Road
Corona, California 91720

Transmission and engine oil coolers include standard Swirl-Cool trans coolers, space saver coolers, Duo-Cool combination trans and engine coolers, high-performance coolers and VW models. Also has conversion kits to transform trans coolers to engine coolers, power steering coolers, and electric oil temperature gauges. Hayden's Duo-Cooler kit lists for $143.00. Free literature.

Hays Clutches & Flywheels
4566 Spring Road
Cleveland, Ohio 44130

Street and competition clutch components are the specialty of the house. Items in stock include aluminum and steel fly wheels, pressure plates, clutch discs, and throwout bearings for most American cars. Clutch/flywheel sets are also available for "Clutch Flite" and "Turbo Clutch" conversions. Hays, which is a division of Mr. Gasket Company, produces headers for many domestic vehicles including the Vega and Pinto. Free catalog.

Hays Ignition Systems, Inc.
17905 Sky Park Boulevard
P.O. Box CN
Irvine, California 92664

Manufacturers of magnetic impulse ignition systems to fit many late-model cars. Free literature.

Heald, Inc.
P.O. Box 1148
Benton Harbor
Michigan 49022

Sells kits for construction of 3-wheel ATV cars. Models include the Super Bronc ($279.95), Super Tryke ($369.95), and Super Bronc VT-812, with 12″ front tire, for $299.95. Free information.

The Super Tryke SST off-road three-wheeler by Heald, Inc.

Heath Co.
Benton Harbor
Michigan 49022

Electronic tune-up equipment and mobile shortwave radios in kit form. Free literature.

HECO
Dyersburg, Tennessee 38024

HECO's line of hydraulic steering stabilizers includes models for a number of domestic cars; 4WD vehicles such as the Land Rover, Datsun Patrol, and domestic 4WD pickups; VW and American vans. Company also makes pickup camper stabilizers, which fit between camper and truck body, to eliminate excessive roll and pitch. Most models of the HECO stabilizer sell for $23.95 or $27.95. Free literature.

Hedman Hedders
4630 Leahy Street
Culver City, California 90230

Headers for street or strip. Various models for motor homes, vans, dune buggies, pickups, and competition cars. Also for most U.S. cars. Price for basic model is $135.00. Husler model is $160.00. Super Huslers are $180.00 and Pro Huslers, $205.00. The Vega-Pinto-Capri mini-Husler is $70.00. Beetle and Dune Buggy Bugghedder is $58.00. Free literature.

Helm, Inc.
2550 East Grand Boulevard
Detroit, Michigan 48211

Chevrolet and Fisher Body service manuals.

Hemmings Motor News
Box 380
Bennington, Vermont 05201

The Bible for vintage and classic advertisers. Contains much for the contemporary and foreign car enthusiast also. Subscription rate: $3.50 a year for third class, $12.00 first class. Monthly.

Henry's Engineering Company
P.O. Box 2550
Landover Hills
Maryland 20784

Specializing in race car hardware. Company offers Aeroquip hose and fittings, race car rod ends, Stewart-Warner instruments, Teflon brake lines for all cars ($24.95 a set), hydraulic quick disconnects, external power plugs, aluminum fuel tanks, Adel clamps, surplus oil coolers (many sizes, $25.00), Dzus fasteners, aluminum ball valves and check valves, stainless steel safety wire, ATL fuel cells, tire pyrometers, Dri-Slide penetrating lubricant, and pressure fittings. Also stocks Hooker headers, Offy manifolds, and a complete line of S-K Tools. Catalog, $.50.

Herbert and Meek Automotive
11121 Magnolia Avenue
North Hollywood
California 91603

Kits for engine swapping. Makes kits to install standard engines such as Ford, Chev, and Buick V-8 of various sizes in classic T-Birds, Chev and Ford pickups of the 1950s, '55-'57 Chev, '62-'66 Chevy II, prewar Chev, Datsun pickup, Firebird, Mustang, Cutlass, GTO, Vega and Pinto. Should have, or will have shortly, kits for LUV, Courier, 240 Z, XKE and Toyota pickup. Accessories available to go along with engine conversions include high-capacity radiators for Vega and Pinto, special headers, remote oil filter systems, and a universal rear mount for transmission swaps. Also has disc brake conversion kits for 1940-64 Chev and 1964-65 Econoline. Free literature.

Heuer Timer Corporation
960 Springfield Avenue
Springfield, New Jersey 07081

Heuer stopwatches come in many varieties, including those in wristwatch form. Models are available to time 1/100,000th of an hour, to keep a continuous elapsed time record, or simply to serve as very accurate timepieces. Some Heuer timers are designed for dashboard mounting in rally cars. For those whose requirements are even more rigorous, Heuer has electronic quartz stopwatches with a digital readout. In addition, they have electronic pit timers which register and print out data on five cars per keyboard, electric eyes for automatic triggering, and a full line of system components. Free literature.

Hewlett Towing Service
81 Prince Avenue
Freeport, New York 11520

Local and long distance towing of antique and classic automobiles on the East Coast and in the Midwest. Write for further information.

Hickey Enterprises, Inc.
1645 Callens Road
Ventura, California 93003

A paradise for Blazer and Chevy pickup owners, the company is run by Vic Hickey of off-road racing and Baja Boot fame.

Here's how to outfit your half-ton or Blazer in full Hickey regalia. To make the underpinnings Sherman-tank-like, select dual shocks at each rear and front wheel ($160.00 for both mount kits plus four coil-over shocks), finned rear differential cover ($24.95), heavy-duty front cover ($19.50), front-axle truss assembly ($39.95), and skid plates for the transfer case ($19.95) and gas tank ($31.95).

Next you'll want high-grade safety wired cap screws for the steering box and transfer case ($4.95 apiece), a sturdy front end guard ($79.90 with push bar plates), a shimmy dampener kit ($12.50) and hydraulic steering stabilizer ($25.95), and rear anti-sway bars ($49.95).

Naturally you'll get a roll bar ($59.95 for Blazers) or roll cage ($159.95), or on the pickups you can get a roll bar with built-in motorcycle rack ($79.95 for the short bed model and $20.00 more for the long one.)

A virtual necessity is a winch. Hickey offers a fine electric winch at $469.50 complete, or the unique Sidewinder compact winch at $449.50. A small but serviceable electric winch which is easily detachable and comes with 35′ of cable

sells for $149.95. (The brand name is "Superwinch" and it fits practically any utility vehicle.)
Further down on the shopping list we come to auxiliary fuel tanks. A 38-gallon replacement tank for Blazers sells for $124.50. For 1973 Blazers there is a 43-gallon model which will cost an extra tenner. Or you could select a pair of wheel well tanks holding 13 gallons apiece and selling for $79.50 each. The 1973 models cost $10.00 more and they each hold an extra 2 gallons.
For a little more go in the engine compartment you would choose Hickey's powerhouse headers which range in price from $129.50 to $159.95, depending on the V-8 engine fitted. Hook these up to the Hickey dual exhaust system ($69.95, or $79.95 for the 454 cu. in. engine) which mounts up high for maximum ground clearance.
Cool the engine with an oil cooler ($99.50) and keep the transmission from overheating with another cooler ($59.95). Optimize the brakes with a disc-brake conversion kit for earlier Blazers (1969-70), which sells for $229.00 plus a core charge of $25.00 on the two hubs, and put Velvetouch brake linings on in the rear ($29.95).
In the interior you can add a jazzy AM/FM stereo with a tape deck for $159.95, and get a deluxe CB 23-channel receiver for $169.95.
There are quite a few more items the Hickey genie conjures up. Most of them fit the Blazer and half-ton pickup (along with their nearly-identical GMC counterparts), but there are a few for the LUV pickup and Chevy vans. Tonneau covers for the LUV are $59.00, and complete interior upholstery kits, which are made in various shades of Naugahyde and just slip into place, sell for $248.00. There are also trailer hitches for the Vega, El Camino and Van, and attractive aluminum or mag wheels in truck or car sizes.
The only trouble with the Hickey genie is that it requires money to work. So long as you have it, the genie will fulfill your every dream and then some. Whatever you don't see in the catalog, Hickey is ready, willing and able to make. Catalog $1.00.

Hides, Inc.
P.O. Box 30
Hackettstown
New Jersey 07840

For classic cars and other autos originally upholstered in leather, real hide is necessary to achieve that gennie look. A copious selection of genuine hides in Tuscan (smooth) or Milano (grained) finish can be had in nearly 60 colors from Hides, Inc.
The size of hides varies from 40 to 50 square feet and an upholsterer can easily determine how many square feet are necessary.
Those who want to know more can send for the fine sample book put out by Hides, Inc. or contact the company's vice president, T.P. Pooley, who is an antique car enthusiast himself and will be sure to come up with just the thing from his stock of imported and domestic hides. Sample book free.

Highland Enterprises
3164 Whitehall
Dallas, Texas 75229

Automotive books available include histories of Lincoln, Buick, Packard, and Studebaker, as well as collections of early auto advertisements. Free literature.

Phil Hill
266 Twentieth Street
Santa Monica
California 90402

Perhaps the most distinguished parts source in this book is the former world champion racing driver who has long been known as a Packard and Pierce-Arrow enthusiast. Among the repro items offered are Packard water jacket plates (for Standard 8, Super 8 and Packard 12 at prices from $61.25 to $65.00 a pair), hub caps, and running board covers ($200.00 a pair for various models). For Pierce-Arrows, an initial run of water jacket plates for 8-cylinder 1929-38 models is available at $79.00. Send a stamped, self-addressed envelope with query.

Hillman Register
(Hillman)
c/o D. S. Johnson
14, Queensway
Bletchley
Buckinghamshire
England

Although not a full-fledged club, the Hillman Register does list some social meetings and publishes a mimeographed newsletter, *The Hillman.* Technical advice, parts location, the manufacture of repro parts, and some library services are available. As a good source of spares for older Hillmans, Mr. Johnson recommends Grimes-Hadleigh Garages, Ltd., Marlpit Lane, Coulsdon, Surrey CR3 2YE, England. Yearly dues: $2.40; slated to be increased in the coming year.

Hillthorne Engineering Co.
Unit 2
Trumpers Way Trading Estate
Hanwell
London W. 7
England

A full-service machine shop equipped to work on vintage and racing car engines. Free literature.

The Hilmer Co.
Box 3537
Boulder, Colorado 80303

Makes portable manual winches for cars and light trucks. The smaller model, with a 5,000 pound capacity and a 70′ long cable, lists for $85.00. An 8,000 pound capacity winch with 135′ cable is $138.50. Accessories include a snatch block, ball and hitch clamp for mounting the winch to a bumper, and ball and bracket for square bumper mounting. For the larger model there is an automatic safety brake handle selling for $35.00. Free literature.

Historic Commercial Vehicle
Association of Australia
(Vintage and Veteran Cars)
c/o Mr. G. Travers
2319 Wylde Street
Potts Point 2011
New South Wales
Australia

American enthusiasts with an interest in older commercial vehicles may want to join this "down under" Association which covers such familiar makes as Reo, Mack, White, Studebaker and International, as well as British and continental trucks. Along with monthly meetings and bus tours, there is a monthly newsletter available on separate subscription. In addition, members have published some books on the history of commercial vehicles in Australia. Yearly dues: $10.50; newsletter subscription only, $6.00.

Historische Automobiel
Vereniging Nederland
(Vintage and Veteran Cars)
c/o P.A. van Eybergen
Baron Schimmelpenninck
van des Oyelaan
Voorschoten
Holland

Remember the Kleinschnittger? How about the Rovin, or the Brustch, or the Spatz? All of these interesting mini cars were the subject of a recent article in *Hav-Varia,* published 10 times a year by this club. The club has 5 regional sections, each of which organizes a series of events such as rallies, picnics and tours. The historic motor vehicles of interest to club members are divided into pre- and post-1940 categories. Spare parts location and library services are offered to members. Mr. Paul A. van Eybergen, Club

Secretary, who supplied the above information, is willing to answer questions on spare parts sources in Holland. Yearly dues: $12.00; entrance fee, $6.00.

Hobrecht Enterprises
8510 San Fernando Road
Sun Valley, California 91352

Street and competition roll bars for domestic performance cars, popular sports and foreign models, and 4WD vehicles. Company also makes single seat or dual seat frames for racing buggies. Free literature.

Hoe Sportcar
446 Newtown Turnpike
Weston, Connecticut 06880

When Duesenberg enthusiasts get together, as many did for a special event in 1973, the handiwork of Jim Hoe is sure to be on display. Mr. Hoe has been specializing in Duesenberg work since 1945 and is well-known in the field. At present, Hoe has worked his magic on most of the Duesenbergs around and now must turn to "lesser" cars. He is now doing a lot of Rolls and Bentley work, but can handle cars of all ages and makes. Does everything from minor repairs to full chassis restorations. Some body work is done on the premises, but not painting. Further information on request.

Hoffman Motors Corporation
375 Park Avenue
New York, New York 10022

U.S. distributors for BMW.

Holley Carburetor Division of Colt Industries
P.O. Box 749
11955 East Nine Mile Road
Warren, Michigan 48090

Under Holley and Mickey Thompson brand names sells performance carburetors for most American cars and VWs, electric fuel pumps, mechanical fuel pumps, ignition parts, spark plugs, speed shifters, headers, chromed wheels, wide tires, valve covers, and aluminum rods. Parts catalog, $1.00.

Holman & Moody, Inc.
P.O. Box 27065
Municipal Airport Station
Charlotte, North Carolina 28203

If you have been winning NASCAR-type races lately, there is no need to tell you who Holman Moody is. Their catalog pages, chockfull of those essential engine and chassis components for race cars, are required reading for every aspiring competitor. They can blueprint your engine ($1,200.00 for standard V-8s), Magnaflux your cranks and rods, Zyglo your pistons, check the wall thickness of your block with a Gamma sound gauge, make your block and head all sanitary with a sonic cleaning process, supply you with a complete roll cage, sell you a whole new dash with quick connect Camloc fasteners and Stewart-Warner instruments, install an on-board fire extinguishing system, sell you one of those nice Detroit Locker differentials, blueprint your differential, fit you out with a Nascar required nylon window screen, and put together a 429 Hemi engine ready to drop in right before the race begins. The Holman & Moody catalog is not available to just anyone, but if you're a racer or a retailer of racing parts, they'll send it.

Hone Manufacturing Co.
11748 East Washington Boulevard
Santa Fe Springs
California 90670

Hone overdrive models include Ford differential mount units, Universal Model 300 for most cars, and the Model 400 for Toyota Land Cruisers. Prices range from approximately $325.00 to $385.00. Reconditioned units, when available, are $275.00. New balanced driveshafts, necessary with some installations, are $100.00. Customer driveshafts can be balanced and shortened for $50.00. Other products include heavy-duty U-joint kits, a rear axle torque bar and a cooling system. Average installation charges for the overdrive unit are $100.00. Free literature.

Honest Charley, Inc.
P.O. Box M8535
Chattanooga
Tennessee 37411

Old Honest Charley hisself has been doing business down in Chattanooga for quite a few years now and built up a warehouse or two full of speed parts. It's hard to know where to begin with the Honest catalog, which is printed in the same small type and myriad little boxes used by J. C. Whitney. O.K., here goes. Holley carbs and fuel system accessories; Edelbrock induction systems; Hedman and Hooker headers; Hurst shifters; Hurst mounts for engine swapping; Offy manifolds; Superior custom steering wheels; Weiand manifolds; Zoom clutch parts; Mallory electrics; Ansen motor mounts; Grant custom steering wheels; Isky cams; Crane cams; Mickey Thompson headers; B&M auto transmission components; Cal Custom dress-up accessories; Mr. Gasket performance parts; Zoom rear axle gears; Trans-Dapt remote oil filter systems and engine-to-transmission adapter plates; all types of carb-to-manifold adapters; TRW pistons, rings and valves; Eelco fuel system components; Lakewood traction bars and safety accessories; Gabriel, Mr. Gasket, and Delco shocks; Accel ignition systems and alternators; Genuine Suspension traction bars; Tulsa oil and transmission coolers; E-T and Superior wheels; Compu-Dwell timing/dwell meters; Gibbs-Bowman tape players and speakers; A&A Fiberglass hood scoops; Cyclone header mufflers; Stewart-Warner instruments; Power Brute timing sets; Flex-A-Lite fans; stainless steel side rails for pick-up trucks; Clifford Research headers and manifolds for 6-cylinder engines; Auto Meter tachometers; Thrush mufflers; Recoton stereo headphones; American Racing Equipment wheels; replacement gears for cars with Muncie and Warner 4-speed transmissions; Fairbanks manual control Turbo-Hydro valve bodies; Radatron dash instruments; Quik Change oil drain kits; Grant piston rings; Jahns pistons; Hays clutches and flywheels; ScatCat and Tiger mufflers; Douglass header pipes and flanges; Marshs racing tires; Carter AFB carbs; Halibrand rear end units; Pos-A-Traction tires; metallic brake linings; Air Force surplus seat belts; fiberglass bucket seats; custom made leatherette seat covers; Delco Packard ignition wires and hardware; racing stripes; burglar alarm systems; Dixco tachs and tune-up equipment; VHT aerosol products; Fram filters; American Racing Equipment street spoilers; EMPI, Scat and Pacer VW speed equipment; Air Lifts; Thrush side pipes; Sun tachometers; Schiefer drivetrain components; crash helmets; Raybestos disc brake pads; Weber clutches and flywheels; freewheeling tow hubs; nylon racing jackets; and auto emblems. There are Honest Charley stores all over the South and Midwest, for those who prefer over-the-counter service. Catalog, $1.00.

Robert Hooks
2030 Sand Road
Vernon, Texas 76384

Mr. Hooks, who has 12 Rovers himself, sells used Rover Model 2000 parts. Send a stamped, self-addressed envelope with query.

Hoosier Machine Products
314-N S.E. 6th Street
Pendleton, Oregon 97801

Makes conversion kits for adapting popular 6-cylinder and V-8 engines to Jeeps, Scouts, and Kaisers. Prices are $93.00 to $142.25 for Scout conversions, and vary for Jeeps depending upon the model and engine installed. Also make conversion kit to adapt heavy duty, all-synchro Ford 3-speed or 4-speed transmission to Jeep or Scout transfer case. Cost of kit is $149.50, not counting the cost of the transmission. Free literature.

Charles H. Hornburg Jr., Inc.
9176 West Sunset
Los Angeles, California 90069

Western Jaguar distributor.

Horseless Carriage Club of America (Antique & Classic Cars)
9031 East Florence Avenue
Downey, California 90249

Sponsors several tours annually in different parts of the country—one especially for 1- and 2-cylinder cars. Holds annual convention during January in Los Angeles County. Has 80-plus regional groups with regular activities throughout the year. Club's bi-monthly magazine is *Horseless Carriage Gazette* with stories on auto history, Club activity, and members' advertisements. There are regular technical features and members' questions are answered. There are no requirements for membership in the national Club though full participation is limited to those owning pre-1916 autos. Yearly dues: $10.00 for whole family.

Horseless Carriage Enterprises
Box 321
Waupaca, Wisconsin 54981

Original sales and technical literature for 1895-1960 automobiles. Also sales catalogs, owners manuals and shop manuals. Free search service. Send a stamped, self-addressed envelope with query.

Horseless Carriage Shop
1881 Main Street
P.O. Box 170
Dunedin, Florida 33528

Complete restoration facilities including wood, upholstery, machine shop services, and painting. Has antique cars for sale on consignment. Is distributor for Universal, Dunlop, and Denman tires. Sells sealant products to form rubber bladder inside rusting gas tanks. Send a stamped, self-addressed envelope for color brochure and list of cars for sale.

Horstman Manufacturing Co., Inc.
730 East Huntington Drive
Monrovia, California 91016

Engine accessories for drag racing and other performance requirements. Products include small diameter crankshaft pulleys, chiller cool cans to cool gas for drag cars, alternator pulleys, water pump studs, chrome-moly head bolt washers, fuel system "Y" blocks, hardened rocker arm shafts for the 273, 318, and 340 Chrysler, forged steel rockers for 340 Chrysler engines, grade-5 header and intake manifold bolts, high performance water pumps for small block and big block Chev, and steel motor mounts for Chevs. Free information.

Horst Manufacturing, Inc.
RD No 2
Warren-Ravenna Road
Newton Falls, Ohio 44444

The last time you were broken down by the side of the road and someone yelled "Get a horse," that wasn't what he was really saying. He was really telling you to get a Horst with a Buick engine, transmission and drive train for reliability and easy maintenance. The unique Horstmobile is not a replica of anything. Instead, it is a hand-built, all steel car which is styled to resemble a classic era auto. The custom Horstmobile chassis has independent front suspension and leaf springs at the rear. Standard features are chrome wire wheels, a genuine walnut or maple dashboard with complete instruments including a compass and altimeter, power steering and brakes, and two sets of musical horns designed to play the songs of your choice. Paint and interior are specially selected to customer specifications. The price is a cool $21,500.00, so maybe the song you select on your musical horns ought to be a rousing Salvation Army tune. Free information.

H.P. Books
P.O. Box 50640
Tucson, Arizona 85703

Publishers of how-to books on hotrodding VWs, Corvairs, small and big block Chevys, and Datsuns. Also books on Holley and Rochester carbs, turbochargers, and Baja-prepping VW sedans and dune buggies. All books are $5.00. Free literature.

H.R.G. Association (H.R.G.)
c/o Ian Dussek
Hustyn
Packhorse Road
Bessels Green
Sevenoaks
Kent
England

Members of the H.R.G. Association, who are limited to current owners plus a few honorary guests, receive the *H.R.G. Association Gazette* once every two months and can participate in various social and competitive events. The association has purchased the old H.R.G. Works Parts stores. It also manufactures and encourages the manufacture of some new parts, produces updated technical models, and has at hand engineering drawings for many models. In addition, there is close contact with one of the original body-builders of H.R.G. cars so that most aspects of restoration can be handled through the Association. Of the more than 150 H.R.G.s that have been traced from the original production of about 280, almost all are owned by Association members throughout the world. Yearly dues: $5.00. An initial payment of another $5.00 is necessary for membership in the spares registry.

Hudson-Essex-Terraplane Club (Hudson-Essex-Terraplane)
23104 Dolorosa
Woodland Hills
California 91364

Club activities include an annual meeting and regional events sponsored by affiliates. Principle publication is the monthly magazine *White Triangle News* which contains notices of Club activities, historical information, and classified advertisements for parts. Technical advice and a parts locator service are other Club features. Yearly dues: $6.00. Foreign dues are $3.00, $6.00, or $9.00 depending upon whether the Club publication is sent by airmail or not, and also upon whether the treasurer is feeling charitable.

Carl Huether
54 Hobbs Road
Pelham, New Hampshire 03076

Sells and repairs radios for 1930-57 autos. Can do anything from minor repair to complete overhaul. Has stock of more than 150 radios on hand. Also deals in Chevrolet literature 1912-61 and has some general car magazines and manuals on hand. Send a stamped, self-addressed envelope with query.

Huffaker Engineering
22 Mark Drive
San Rafael, California 94903

Competition parts for MGB, Austin Healey 3000, Spridget, British Ford, and Formula Cars. MG items include pistons and rings, street and full race cams, valvetrain gear, lightened flywheels, modified carbs, special heads, front and rear anti-roll bars, headers, heavy-duty front and rear springs, and a Panhard rod kit. For the Austin-Healey there are similar engine goodies plus the Detroit Locker rear end. Also in stock are Spridget fender flares ($80.00 a set of 4, SCCA legal), competition components for the 948 cc, 1,100

Fender flares for popular sports cars from Huffaker Engineering

cc and 1,275 cc engines, complete race-ready Super Vee engines ($3,340.00), and Super Vee engine components. Huffaker also offers dyno tuning and engine machine work on Ford, MG, Healey and VW engines. Free literature.

Humber Register (Pre-1930 Humber)
c/o Michael L. Hall
Wards
108, Barnett Wood Lane
Ashtead
Surrey
England

Features a bi-monthly magazine with classified advertisements, a spares register, a technical library, and at least one rally a year. Yearly dues: $6.00.

Hunckler Products, Inc.
Roanoke, Indiana 46783

Automotive hardware in SAE and metric sizes. Has grade-5 cap screws, coarse and fine thread nuts and bolts, grease fittings, lock washers, wheel hub bolts, saddle-type clamps, expansion plugs, drain plugs, and solderless terminals. Assortments are available at many parts dealers under the name "Pik-A-Nut Paks." Free catalog to jobbers.

Hupmobile Club
Box AA
Rosemead, California 91770

Publishes *Hupp Herald* quarterly. Has parts coordinator who sends out lists of parts wanted and for sale. Members receive Club roster and technical advice. Yearly dues: $5.00.

Hupp Factory Service Department
Auburn, Indiana 46706

Mostly NOS parts for Hupmobiles 1918-40. Also blueprints for every part manufactured by Hupmobile. A few items for Star and Durant, mainly engine parts, are available. Send a stamped, self-addressed envelope with query. Write for availability of catalog.

Hurley Fiberglass Co.
P.O. Box 718
Newport, Arkansas 72112

Manufactures fiberglass pickup bed cover for all regular straight-sided pickups plus 1968 and later Ranchero and El Camino. Also has fiberglass fish transport tanks to fit pickup beds. Free literature.

Hurst/Airheart Products, Inc.
20235 Bahama Street
Chatsworth, California 91311

Disc brake assemblies and replacement parts for most cars. Also kits for dragsters, pro-stockers, midgets, super modified and sprint cars—even for go-carts and minibikes. Also master cylinders, special caliper tools, other brake system hardware. Free information. Order through retailers.

Husky Products Co.
P.O. Box 824
Longmont, Colorado 80501

Free-wheeling hubs, overdrive units, and other accessories for off-road vehicles. Products include spindle nut wrenches for most 4WD vehicles; front tire carriers for pickups; underslung rear tire carriers for pickups; rear mount carriers for vans and most jeep-type vehicles; overdrive units for pickups, Jeeps and Scouts; convertible tops for Blazer, Bronco, Scout, Jimmy, Commando, Jeep, and Land Cruiser; tonneau covers for pickup trucks, mini-pickups, El Camino, and Ranchero; and seats, seat cushions, carpeting bench pads and convertible top boots for 4WD vehicles. Free literature.

Hutton Motor Engineering
P.O. Box 351
Clarksville, Tennessee 37040

Parts and service for Lotus cars and Coventry-Climax racing engines. Inquire about availability of catalog.

Hydra-Motive Transmission Specialties, Inc.
3853 North Southport Avenue
Chicago, Illinois 60613

Racing transmissions and related components. The well-known Clutch-Flite and Clutch-Turbo transmissions, with a conventional dry clutch replacing the torque converter, are available for GM, Mopar and Ford bellhousings at exchange prices from $510.00 to $535.00. Stock auto transmissions available in rebuilt models for most cars. Modified transmissions include street and competition versions of the Torque-Flite, Turbo 400, Ford C-4 and C-6. Modified torque converters available for the same transmissions plus Powerglide. Catalog, $.50.

Hydra Products Co.
1320 West Santa Ana Street
Anaheim, California 92802

Makes auxiliary gas tanks with approximate 20-gallon capacity for mini trucks including the LUV, Courier, Mazda, Datsun and Toyota. Tanks come with mounting accessories and installation instructions. Free literature.

Ideal Manufacturing Co.
1107 South Seventh Street
Oskaloosa, Iowa 52577

Trailer hitches and towing equipment. "Kum-Along" tow bars are available for various models of the VW as well as Vega, Gremlin, and Pinto. Cycle carriers include both trailers and bumper add-ons. Other products consist of one- or two-wheel utility trailers, trailer chassis in many sizes and capacities, and accessories such as wheel chocks, utility tie-downs, trailer spare wheel and tire carriers, wiring and light sets, trailer jacks, hitches, couplers and balls, hand winches, tire pumps, safety skids, transmission oil coolers, and safety chains. Company also manufactures professional tools such as transmission jacks and engine hoists. Free literature.

IECO
2314-A Pico Boulevard
Santa Monica, California 90405

Engine equipment and accessories for VW and Corvair. Along with items such as intake manifolds, headers, electrical system parts, oil cooler kits, in-line gas filters, lightweight flywheels, shocks, sway bars, mag wheels, wood-rim steering wheels, nerf bars, driving lights, and tune-up instruments, IECO has some other parts of special interest. There are fiberglass scoops for sides and rear of Beetles, front and rear fiberglass fenders and lids, powdered metal brake linings, Judson superchargers, and off-road air filters for the VW. A complete "Dyno-Pak" tuning kit incorporating plugs, plug wires, gaskets, an in-line fuel filter, air filter and carb gasket kit costs only $24.95. Blueprinted twin port heads are $350.00 a pair. Delco airlift shocks go for $48.95 a pair, and SPG roller bearing cranks run from $199.95 to $329.95 depending upon the stroke. VW or Corvair catalog, $1.00.

VW Dyno-Pak by IECO

IMCADO Manufacturing Co.
P.O. Box 452
Dover, Delaware 19901

Leather products and some British car parts. Will make genuine cowhide hood straps for any car. Has straps in stock for Mini-Minor, Porsche, Spridget, MG, Jaguar, Ferrari, Stanley Steamer, pre-1928 Chev, Morgan, pre-1940 Bentley, Bugatti, Isotta-Fraschini, Stutz, Mercer, Model A, and other cars. Also has leather key fobs which may be fitted with customer-supplied crests. Non-leather products include racing windscreens in rounded or squared off styles, SU plenum chambers (cold air boxes), aluminum SU Filtrettes with fine mesh screens which fit between ram pipe and air-box installations, wheel spacers to fit Spridgets and Minis, and Spridget rear oil sump seals. Has many leather items for bicyclists also. Free information.

IMI Inc.
8363 Sunset Boulevard
Los Angeles, California 90069

Maserati western distributor.

Impacto Corporation
Box 415
Bernardsville
New Jersey 07924

Makes Plategard, plastic license plate protectors made of high impact ABS-type plastic. Price is $3.95, or $6.95 for two. Free literature.

The Imperial Barn Ltd.
125 Woodside Avenue
Briarcliff Manor, New York 10510

Parts for vintage, classic, and special-interest cars. Specialty is Franklin. Also generally have about 20 complete vehicles on hand. Parts are NOS and used. Send a stamped, self-addressed envelope with query.

Imported Car & Parts Trader
P.O. Box 749
Willoughby, Ohio 44094

Published 18 times a year in newspaper format. Extensive listings of foreign and sports cars for sale including many exotics. Sample copy sent free. Yearly subscription: $7.00 by first class mail and $3.00 by third class mail.

Import Parts Distribution Co.
Shox Northwest
2762 N.E. Broadway
Portland, Oregon 97232

Accessories for Volvo and VW. Volvo parts include front sway bar for P1800 ($33.95), competition front coil springs ($50.00 a pair), Bilstein and Spax shock absorbers, lightweight flywheels, mag wheels, overdrive units ($375.00), Deves rings, Mahle pistons, Vandervell bearings, front and rear crank seals, modified cylinder heads, SU carb and manifold sets, Filtron filters, electric fuel pumps, street and racing oil cooler kits, Ferodo brake pads, fiberglass body panels for 122S models, custom steering wheels, locking gas caps, interior floor mats, driving lights, Corbeau racing seats ($85.00 each), and VDO dash instruments. Also offers modified computer box, for fuel injection Volvos, with a manually controlled richness/lean adjustment. The cost is $75.00, on an exchange basis, with a core charge of $100.00. Carries all VDO instruments for VW. Free price list.

Increased cornering ability with chassis components from Import Parts Distributing

International Edsel Club
Box 304
Bellevue, Ohio 44811

Along with an annual convention, the enthusiastic State chapters of the Edsel Club hold their own monthly meetings. Club publication is *The Edseletter* published monthly. Parts location and technical advice are among the services offered to members. Active members must own an Edsel. Others can be associate members. Yearly dues: $5.00 for active members and $2.00 for associate members.

International Manufacturing
165 Industrial Park
Benicia, California 94510

Specializing in mag wheels in various types and sizes. Dial-fit system allows single wheel to fit many cars. A 13″ dial-fit mag can fit Pinto, Vega, Datsun, Toyota, Opel, Capri, Colt,

Cricket, Cortina, Falcon, Lotus, MG, BMW, Sunbeam and Sprite. Dial-fit models are also available for domestic cars and for special applications in sizes from 13″x5½″ to 15″x10″. Free literature.

International Racing Designs
19140 San Jose 'C'
Department D-11
Industry, California 91744

Specializes in design and construction of automobile transporters. The Penny Pincher model to transport dune buggies, sports cars and Formula cars has a base price of $154.70 in the economy kit and is $269.90 in the more complete kit. Weight capacity is 2,000 pounds. Optional equipment includes steel wheels ($19.00 a pair); 3,500 pound capacity coupler recommended for hauling cars over 1,200 pounds ($2.90); motorcycle rack; tire tie-downs; caster wheel and trailer jack; and wheel chocks. The Hefty Hauler kit, with 4,000 pound capacity, has a base price of $374.40 and offers the option of an electric brake package at $129.90. There are many frame and suspension accessories available for both trailers, including capacity upgrade kits, trailer widening packages, fenders, ramps, leaf springs, surge brakes, hydraulically-actuated disc brakes, trailer hand dollies, safety chain kits, motorcycle racks, tie-downs, lighting kits and wiring kits. Free information.

Race car transporter from International Racing Designs

International Rotary Engine Club (Wankel Engine Cars)
Box 2393
North Hollywood, California 91602

Organization devoted to collecting and disseminating information on rotary engines. Publishes monthly newsletter. Newsletter has technical articles and news about rotary engine development. Mr. Frank Gwodz, president of the Club, states that Mazda rotary engine accessories can be obtained through C.A.R.S., 11654 Sheldon, Sun Valley, California 91352, with discounts being offered to I.R.E.C. members. A catalog is available for $1.00. Yearly dues: $20.00 U.S., $22.00 foreign for charter membership; $12.00 U.S. and $14.00 foreign for associate membership. Associate members will also receive the newsletter.

International Truck Restorers
2026 Bayer
Fort Wayne, Indiana 46805

NOS parts and information on older International Harvester trucks. Send a stamped, self-addressed envelope with queries.

Interpart
100 Oregon Street
El Segundo, California 90245

Parts and accessories for the Datsun, Toyota, Vega, Pinto and Mazda. Under the leadership of Pete Brock, of racing Datsun fame, Interpart offers many performance components for all Datsuns, along with some items for other mini-cars. The famous Mulholland suspension kits are available for the Datsun 510, 240Z and pickup. The price of Mulholland springs is slightly over $90.00, and Mulholland stabilizer bars range in price from about $48.00 to $75.00. Other Datsun goodies are Spook spoilers for all Datsuns including the 1600 and 2000 roadster; Dellorto carbs; intake manifolds; Mikuni-Solex carbs and parts; Koni shocks; Hitachi-S.U. carbs; competition cranks and cylinder headers; oil coolers; high compression pistons; single point distributors; aluminum flywheels; racing clutch components; five speed transmissions; close-ratio gear sets; limited slip differentials; Detroit Locker differentials; stainless steel brake line kits; alloy wheels; custom steering wheels; Stewart-Warner instruments; Factory electric tachs; racing seats; lightweight fiberglass body panels for Datsun 510; roll cage kits; Mulholland brake components; headers; trailer hitches; consoles; hood and deck pins; clear plastic headlight covers for 240Z ($67.95); custom carpeting kits; and tape stripes. For the Toyota Corolla, Carina, Celica, and Corona, Interpart has spoilers, Mulholland suspension kits, intake manifolds, Dellorto carbs, headers, and trailer hitches. Similar items are available for rotary engine Mazdas, and the Vega and Pinto. Pinto, Vega, Datsun, Toyota, and Mazda catalogs, $1.00 each.

Intersil, Inc.
2000 Martin Avenue
Santa Clara, California 95050

Intersil's Cronus I stopwatch has a quartz crystal movement and digital readout. It measures 1/100th second increments up to 24 hours. It has four distinct functions: standard start/stop, Taylor/sequential, split, and event/time out. When not being used as a hand-held timer, it can be mounted on its base and used as an executive desk clock. The Cronus I runs on rechargeable nickel cad batteries and sells for $195.00. Free literature.

Jud Irish
30 Old Mill Road
Chappagua, New York 10514

Sells Ditzler paint for an authentic finish on many classic and special-interest cars from Auburn to Whippet. A chip of any formula paint is $2.00. Spraymaker tool with its own compressed gas power supply is only $2.50. One power unit sprays up to a pint. Power units cost $1.50 each and extra spray containers are two for $1.25. Other products include striping tape for $2.75 per 15-yard roll, antique Ford and Ditzler repaint manuals, engine enamel, and refurbishing manuals for 1937-48 Fords. Basic prices for lacquer or enamel are $4.50 a pint and $22 a gallon. Slight extra charge for maroon color. Send a stamped, self-addressed envelope for literature.

Irish Veteran & Vintage Car Club (Vintage and Veteran Cars)
10 Parkmore Drive
Terenure
Dublin 6
Ireland

Principal activities of the Club consist of two-day rallies in May and September along with a rally for veteran cars only in July. Sometimes a concours is held in conjunction with one of the rallies. There is a quarterly Club newsletter. Yearly dues: $3.50 single, $4.80 husband/wife. Club is an affiliate of the Federation International Des Voitures Anciennes.

Isis Imports Ltd.
469 Eddy Street
San Francisco, California 94109

Complete service for Morgans including sales, repair, and parts. Has many mechanical and body parts. Complete roadster ash body frames, $400.00; strengthened frame front cross axle assembly, $145.00; Monroe front shocks for

Morgan, $14.00 a pair; "Morgan" radiator badge, $8.50; script rear panel, $5.50, sliding sidescreens, $77.50; factory air cleaner, $50.00; hood strap in black cowhide with blue felt backing, $18.95; Moto-lita wood rim steering wheel, $47.95. Also service manuals, Morgan insignia jewelry, and complete cars in stock including Morgan 3-wheelers. Free parts list.

Ed Iskenderian Cams
16020 South Broadway
Gardena, California 90248

"Isky" is the grand old man of the engine performance equipment business. Along with modified cams for just about any modern car, he offers a complete line of valve train components plus blower drives and installation tools. Reading the Isky catalog and literature put out by the company is like taking a graduate course in engine modification. Catalog, $1.00.

Isotta Fraschini Owner's Association (Isotta Fraschini)
Midwest: 9704 Illinois Street
Hebron, Illinois 60034
East: Old York Road
New Hope, Pennsylvania 18938

A small but devoted group. Requirements for membership are owning an Isotta and a willingness to aid other owners. There are no regular meetings, no dues, and only an occasional newsletter. However the club has been in existence for more than twenty years with the simple objective of helping owners restore and maintain their cars. Services include a library of technical information and manuals available to members, and a supply of vital spare parts kept in stock. Parts not in stock are located, whenever possible. Yearly dues: none.

Jackman Steel Products
8527 Ablett Road
Santee, California 92071

On and off-road custom wheels in many sizes. A VW spindle mount wheel, in size 15″x3″, intended for applications where no front brakes are used, is $40.00. Five-bolt VW wheels are available in sizes from 13″x5½″ to 16″x20″. The standard bolt pattern, in five or eight spoke design, is available in the same sizes at prices ranging from $32.40 to $63.00. A duplex eight spoke wheel for size 16.5″ tires is $47.80 (16.5″x8.25″) or $50.20 (16.5″x9.75″). All wheels are available in three colors: Summit Grey, Inca Silver and Fleet White. Other products include JSP suspension units, which consist of an adjustable Gabriel shock absorber within a cast aluminum spring housing; heavy duty rack and pinion steering units, and complete mid-engine off-road vehicles, such as the recent JSP Special with a Mazda rotary engine and five-speed transaxle for off-road racing. Free literature.

Jack's Specialty Speed
2322 N.E. Davis
Portland, Oregon 97232

Largest single source of Ford V-8/60 engine parts. Parts are both new and used, and include used speed equipment and some V-8/60 transmission gears. New 1937-39 cylinder blocks are $65.00. New 1937-40 Magnafluxed connecting rods are $3.50 each. Reground 1937-40 crankshafts are $25.00 exchange. Martus water pumps sell for $32.50; Wico magneto caps are $5.25; rebuilt 1942-48 distributors to fit 1937-40 V-8/60 engines are $7.00 on an exchange basis. Another product line comprises Offy engine parts and chassis and body parts for Midget cars. A Kurtis Midget frame with spring front and cross bar rear is $450.00; Kurtis fiberglass radiator shell and hood go for $30.00

apiece; a Kurtis fiberglass tail is $60.00; and aluminum side panels, semi-finished, are $18.00 a pair. Among other items for Midgets are Halibrand wheels and spot brake components, roll cage kits, numerous suspension parts, Edmonds body parts, and a Cornis in-and-out box for $95.00. Racing accessories, such as clothing and helmets, and performance parts for Falcon and Chev 4-cylinder engines, complete the line. Free literature.

Jaguar Club of Southern New England, Inc. (Jaguar)
c/o Alan M. Levine
1897 Chapel Street
New Haven, Connecticut 06515

Club activities feature monthly meetings plus various competitive events, a Jaguar weekend at Waterville, New Hampshire, technical assistance and workshop sessions, parts-location and a member's discount on parts, plus a monthly publication, *The Spotted Cat*. Yearly dues:$10.00 single, $14.00 family.

Jaguar Drivers' Club (Jaguar)
c/o Mrs. Molly Wheeler
Norfolk Hotel
Harrington Road
London, S.W.7
England

The Jaguar Drivers' Club is officially recognized by the parent company and headed by the fabled Sir William Lyons. The Club publication, *Jaguar Driver* is sent to members monthly. Along with the parent Club, there is an SS Register section open to any person owning an SS or early Jaguar up to and including the Mark V. The SS Register puts out a bi-monthly bulletin and has a spare parts service which includes a number of repro parts. An annual rally and concours is held. Yearly dues: approx. $9.00; entry fee, $4.00.

Jahns Pistons
2662 Lacy Street
Los Angeles, California 90031

Jahns makes forged and cast aluminum alloy pistons for every application. Pistons are available for stock and racing engines, most imported cars, and a wide variety of antique and classic cars ranging from the American Underslung to the Waltham Orient. Pistons for experimental engines can be custom made. Free information.

James Auto Specialties
Box 151
Pasadena, California 91506

The James' stock of foreign car accessories and racing components includes Maserati air horns, siren burglar alarms, MG Mitten car covers, Italian racing goggles, Nomex apparel, leather driving gloves, Bell helmets, Talbot and Lucas

Hardtop hoist from James Auto Specialties

mirrors, Hella and Carello quartz lights, badges and badge bars, seat belts and competition shoulder harnesses, Stewart-Warner instruments, AutoPower roll bars for popular foreign cars, EMPI VW camber compensators, Koni shocks, Abarth exhaust systems, Bursch and Cannon foreign and compact car headers, Ansen wheels, Haan steering wheels, Monza quick-fill gas caps, Heuer timers, Curta calculators, VW and Bus air scoops, Blaupunkt radios, Becker radios, Semperit radial tires, and Stevens rally equipment. Engine-turned threshold plates for T-series MGs are $7.00 a pair. Engine-turned rear panels with license plate holders for 900-series Porsches and the Jaguar XKE are $25.90. Bursch headers for Porsche 356 cost $49.00 for the street model and $59.00 for competition. The Becker Europa AM/FM stereo radio is $218.00, while the least expensive AM- only Blaupunkt model is $49.00. James also carries many workshop manuals and a complete line of AMCO accessories. In a separate catalog Mr. James (his actual name is Richard James Carpenter) lists those 1955-57 Thunderbird accessories, which gave him a start in business. In 1955 he invented a small rope hoist to enable non-muscular types to lift off their removable hardtops. In an improved model, with nylon rope, the hoist is still available and lists for $10.95. Other items for classic T-Birds are traction bars, Marchal headlamp conversions, hardtop locks ($9.95 each), automatic transmission locks ($9.95), wide whitewall tires by Lester, English leather steering wheel gloves, carpets, trunk mats, tonneau covers, burglar alarms, cockpit covers, license plate frames, chromed engine goodies, and many original body parts supplied by Ford. General catalog, $1.00; Thunderbird catalog, $.50.

Janasz Corporation
236 California Street
El Segundo, California 90245

Distributors of the Swedish Deves piston rings to fit American and European cars. Deves rings are available for all standard makes and for exotic cars like the Goliath, Moskvich, Borgward and Wolseley. Free information.

Jardine
7565 Acacia Street
Garden Grove
California 92641

Truck and recreational vehicle headers. All models are priced at $125.00. Smog fittings for Chevy and GMC vehicles are available at $15.00 extra. Free literature.

Jensen Owners Club (Jensen)
c/o L. C. Jackson
40 Station Road
St. Margarets
Hertfordshire
England

Club activities comprise area meetings plus annual Open Days. The Club's first national rally was held at Beaulieu in June 1973. There is also a regular newsletter and an informal program to aid members in parts location. Membership is open only to Jensen owners. Yearly dues: $7.20 in Great Britain, $9.60 overseas.

Jerrari Equipment, Inc.
P.O. Box 283
1415½ Aviation Boulevard
Redondo Beach
California 90277

Performance accessories and goodies for foreign and sports cars. Specialty is Fiats. Has fiberglass spoilers for many foreign cars including Datsun, most Fiats, Honda 600,

Mazda, Opel, Porsche, Toyota, Triumph and Mini pickups plus Vega, Pinto and Capri. Catalog, $1.00.

Spoilers available from Jerrari Equipment, Inc. include models for the Fiat 124 Coupe (top) and Capri

Jersey Old Motor Club (Vintage and Veteran Cars)
c/o J. W. Sweeny
5 Boulevard Avenue
Millbrook
Jersey
Channel Islands
England

Unless you happen to be visiting Jersey in the Channel Islands, you won't be much interested in Club activities (although they include treasure hunts and untimed cavalcades), however there is a quarterly Club publication, *Jersey Old Motor Club Gazette* and the dues are a bargain. Yearly dues: approximately $2.50.

Jim's Antique Ford Ranch
Route 1, Box 13
Corner Z & N Highways
Wentzville, Missouri 63385

New parts and accessories for Model A. Leatherette spare tire cover with script emblem is $10.95 in white, tan or black. Stone guards for radiator are $69.95 standard or $79.95 de luxe. Rumble step plates $2.75. Motometer locking cap with wreath rim and flying quail cap in either standard or thermo variety are both available. Wind wing brackets are $14.50 for closed cars, $15.50 for open cars. Trunk racks with oakwood strips are $65.00; with chrome steel bars, $50.00. Other products include spare tire guard ($23.50); explosion whistle ($14.95); Aermore exhaust horn with cutout ($29.95); Ahoooga horns (6-volt, $11.95, 12-volt, $12.95); chrome Schrader valve caps ($.75 for a set of five); spare tire locks in black or chrome; motometer wings in polished aluminum, brass, or chrome plate; accessory shift knobs in onyx or walnut with script; full line of accessory mirrors; suction cup ash tray; and rumble seat grab bars. Various tools available include crank lug wrench ($4.95), screwdriver as original ($1.95), script tube repair kit ($1.75), script tool bag ($2.95), spoke wheel brush ($1.00), script oil can as original ($3.95), wheel puller ($.80) and Williams water pump wrench ($3.00). Along with a very complete assortment of mechanical parts, offers many sheet metal body parts, rumble seat items, instrument panel replacements, special bolt kits, oil-filled shocks, floor mats, and rubber items. Catalog, $.25.

Fred L. Johnston
Valley View Park, Lot 36
Tuckerton Road
Reading, Pennsylvania 19605

Mr. Johnston's avocation is the sub-mini car. His specialty is the BMW 300-600-700 and he also has new and used parts for Fiat 500-600, NSU, Crosley, Austin/Bantam, and even the infamous Subaru 360. Send a stamped, self-addressed envelope with query.

Jowett Car Club
(Jowett)
c/o A. N. Wright, Secretary
Ambleside
Clun Road
Craven Arms
Shropshire
England

Javelin and Jupiter fans will be glad to know that standards are still being kept up in England. Members receive a list of spare-parts suppliers (in England) and can call on the services of the Club's technical information officer, spares officer, and librarian. Club magazine *The Jowetteer* is mailed regularly and includes technical information and classified advertisements. Jowett owners' handbooks and maintenance manuals are available through the Club, and, for the super-enthusiastic, there is even a Club tie. Yearly dues: $4.80, husband/wife joint membership $6.00; there is also a nominal initiation fee.

Jowett Car Club
(Jowett)
c/o Malcolm S. Bergin
P.O. Box 39058
Auckland
New Zealand

Jowetteers seem to be particularly active worldwide. The New Zealand Club has three regions which hold a variety of events, and there is a national rally each year. The Club magazine, *Flat-Four* is published quarterly. Technical information sheets and a membership and car register are also issued. The Club has its own library and can supply advice on parts location in New Zealand. Mr. Bergin himself has Jupiter parts on hand, while Mr. Stephen Wickens of 13b Lambley Road, Titahi Bay, is a specialist in prewar Jowett parts. Yearly dues: not specified.

Jowett Jupiter Club
(Jowett Jupiter)
c/o Bryce D. Eicholz
3106 Eastern Avenue
Sacramento, California 95821

Mr. Eicholz, a Jowett enthusiast and member of marque clubs around the world, has recently started a U.S. Jupiter register. If sufficient response is forthcoming, he will begin a semi-annual or quarterly newsletter. Write to him for technical advice or further details.

JR Products Corporation
3220 Kurtz Street
San Diego, California 92110

Racing chassis components, headers, roll bars, and engine stands. Has many traction bars for Super Stock, Pro Stock, and Modified cars. Also shock adapters; Mopar pinion snubbers; tube axles for Ford, Chev, Econoline and Anglia spindles, with drops from zero to 6″; dual spring kits; transverse front spring kits; Anglia spindles; Vega and Pinto front and rear sway bars; 1955-57 Chev crossmember assemblies; Camaro/Chev II (1968-71) and Firebird subframes; 1962-65 Chev II subframes; and '23 T Chassis constructed from 2″x3″ .120 wall square box tubing. Chassis components in stock include radius rod/axle plates; radius rod brackets; spherical rod ends; front and rear radius rods; spring mounts; rear spring clamps; adjustable front and rear snubbers to replace those on JR traction bars; U-bolts; tapered self-aligning rod ends for 1928-48 Fords, 1960-63 Econolines and 1949-54 Chevs; radius rod ends; driveshaft retaining loops; and spring perches. Roll bars are available for most American cars, the Blazer, Bronco and VW. Also VW competition roll cages and bumper/skid plates. Other products are universal tow bars; engine stands; engine hoists; headers for U.S. and foreign cars as well as street roadsters; and Vega and Pinto exhaust systems. Also offers machine shop work plus the design and construction of complete race cars. Free catalog.

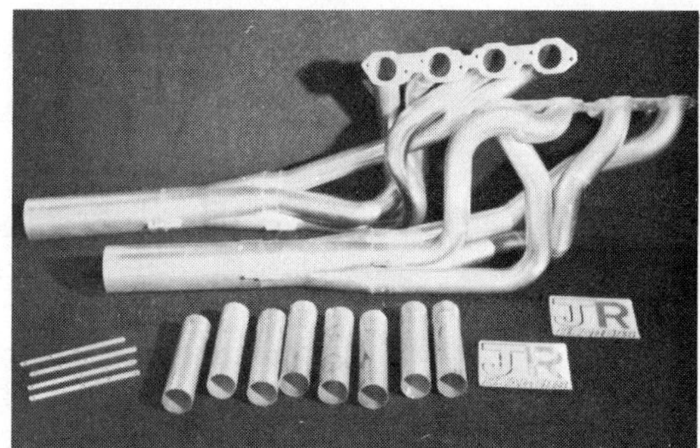

Headers for the 427 cu. in. Chev Camaro (for Super Stock and Pro Stock use only) from JR Products Corporation

J.R.R. Co.
P.O. Box 2220
Alderwood Manor
Washington 98036

Antique and classic car carburetor repair for autos from 1902-52. The company performs its services for restoration shops across the country as well as for individuals. Among the more esoteric makes of carburetors they work on are Secor Higgins, Senrab, Old Nick, Floatless, Palubla Syphon, Van Briggle and Shakespear. About 300 of the more common carbs are kept on hand for exchange purposes. Send a stamped, self-addressed envelope with query.

Judson Research and Manufacturing Co.
Conshohocken, Pennsylvania 19428

Judson's electronic magneto is the largest selling such device on the aftermarket. The price is $59.95. Free literature.

Kaiser-Frazer Owners Club (Kaiser & Frazer)
4015 South Forest
Independence, Missouri 64052

Club holds an annual national convention each summer and there are many regional meets and gatherings. Publications are *The K-F News Bulletin* monthly with classified advertisements free to members, *The Kaiser-Frazer Quarterly* with many technical articles, and a membership roster. A parts warehouse is maintained by the Club and contains many NOS items acquired when the Kaiser-Willys factory went out of business. Also aluminum car plaques and T-shirts available with Club emblem. Yearly dues: $10.00, associate memberships for other members of family are $5.00 each.

Fred and Dan Kanter
P.O. Box 33G
Morris Plaines
New Jersey 07950

A prime source of parts for all model Packards, 1930-56, and for the Facel-Vega, 1954-65. The more than 100,000 Packard parts in stock include bumpers, brake parts, clutches, electrical and engine components, fuel system items, exhausts, instruments, springs, steering and suspension parts, transmissions, rear axle components, wheels, hubcaps, trim and emblems, and body parts. Manifold gaskets for the 1932-39 V-12 go for $18 and head gaskets are $14. Shock absorbers for the 1937 Super-8 sell for $35 apiece. Front and rear axles for the 1930-32 Super-8 and Twin Six are $100 each complete with brakes. Seat cushions and jump seats to fit the 1931 model 845, 7-passenger sedan are $100. For those who own later model Packards, a Delco distributor for the 1965 V-8 is $45; a torsion level delay switch sells for $25; fuel pump kits are $7.50; and a complete rebuild kit for 1950-56 Ultramatic transmissions sells for $75 with $10 core deposit. It is claimed that new and used parts in stock for the Facel-Vega comprise the largest store in the U.S., and complete cars are also for sale. Other items available from Fred and Dan Kanter include Packard literature of all types and wide white wall tires of polyester tubeless construction in 14″ and15″ sizes. Free parts and price list.

Kar Manufacturing Co.
49 Main Street
Monson, Massachusetts 01057

Along with a variety of dune buggies, this company makes fiberglass "Funny Cars" for street use. The Mini-Camaro, designed to fit a shortened VW chassis, is $525.00 for the basic body available in a choice of 36 Metalflake colors. Options include a windshield kit, snap-on convertible top, interior side panels and carpet kit, and bucket seats. A fiberglass Z-28 Camaro replica body, at $595.00 a copy, has options which include flip-up doors, seats and carpets, windshield kit, and headlights. The Z-28-style body is designed to fit an uncut VW chassis. Another version of the Z-28 is a true street Funny Car with a flip-up body in the customary style. It is designed to fit a special chassis available in kit form at $1,095.00. The total kit including body, chassis, seats, dash, and interior liner is $1,690.00. Dune buggy bodies available are the Shorty 70, on a VW chassis chopped 24″, the "T" Tub on a stock VW chassis, the aerodynamic Wildcat, on an 80″ wheel base, and the Kar-T, also on an 80″ wheel base and resembling a cross between the Model T and the Lotus 7. Many accessories are available for each dune buggy type. A number of other buggy body styles, formerly manufactured by Poty Enterprises under the Sand Rover name, have now been taken over by this company. Other products in the Sand Rover line include fiberglass VW parts and a one-wheel utility trailer. Catalog, $1.00.

Kaslaw Enterprises
P.O. Box 3571
Wilmington
North Carolina 28401

Accessories for American and imported cars with the exception of Volkswagen. (Company operates VW Enthusiast Association for Volkswagen owners.) Dealers for many major brands of aftermarket accessories. Prices are claimed to be below retail. Queries on product availability and prices are given 24-hour service. Write for "open quotation" form.

KC HiLites
Box 243
Saugus, California 91350

Driving lamps, fog lamps, flood lamps, lamp brackets and shields, and interior lights. The KC Daylighter, a 230,000 beam candlepower driving light, is shock mounted for off-road use. Price is $24.95. The Mini Fog light, which comes with brackets and vinyl protective cover, is $8.95. Brackets for adapting KC lights to 1965-73 Ford are $2.95 each; those for the 1967-72 Chevrolet are $3.25 and a model for the 1973 Blazer and Jimmy is $1.95. Brackets for adapting lights to most pushbars and front end guards are $3.25 each. Foam-padded vinyl lamp covers in yellow, red, green, blue and white are $1.95. Free literature.

K-D Manufacturing Co.
Lancaster, Pennsylvania 17604

Makes a full line of specialty tools for many U.S. and foreign cars. Catalog can be consulted at most wholesale parts houses.

Keller's Auto Ranch
R.D. No. 1
Ronks, Pennsylvania 17572

New and used parts for antique cars. Specialty is wiring harnesses. Makes some custom harnesses. Wiring specialties are both wholesale and retail. Send a stamped, self-addressed envelope with query. Dealer sheets available.

Kelmark Engineering
5130 North Okemos Road
East Lansing, Michigan 48823

Makers of the Laser 917 kit car using an uncut VW chassis and a mid-engine Chev V-8 or GMC V-6. Will also sell transverse mid-engine Chev V-8 transaxles and frames for kit cars at $1,775 per unit. A kit to put all 1965 and later GM V-8s and V-6s in stock bodied VWs, or any other body designed to bolt to a VW floor pan, is $695.00. A shifter kit designed to be used with the Hurst 4-speed is $99.95. In-line mid-engine adapter kits are available for Chev V-8 to Corvair transaxle, Chev 4-cylinder to Corvair, Buick aluminum 215 V-8 to Corvair, Buick 198 and 225 V-6 to Corvair, Corvair to VW, and V-6 or V-8 to VW. Parts to modify the Corvair engine to take six carburetors are another product offered. In addition, the company sells complete transverse transaxles for Chev V-8, Chev-4 and Buick V-6. Kelmark distributes the Ja-Mar hydraulic steering brake ($49.95). Free information. A booklet on the Laser 917 bodies is $2.00.

Bob Kennedy
8609 Oceanview
Whittier, California 90605

Mr. Kennedy specializes in woodgraining and states that he is able to duplicate any original grain pattern on an early car. All finishes are done in lacquer with designs being hand worked. Pieces are supplied buffed and waxed, ready for reassembly. His specialty is early Ford V-8s. Send a stamped, self-addressed envelope with queries.

Kennedy Engineered Products
10202 Glenoaks Boulevard
Pacoima, California 91331

This company can supply adapters to install a wide variety of engines in the VW Bug, Karmann Ghia or VW Bus. Adapter kits available for V-6 Buick/Jeep, V-8 aluminum B-O-P, Chev 4 and small block V-8, and German Ford V-4 engines. Kits will also bolt to Porsche transaxles. Newly-available kits for Pinto, Saab V-4 and Datsun 1600 engine in VW, and for aluminum V-8 in Corvair. Accessories include fiberglass engine cover for back of VW Bus, replacement 6-volt ring gear for flywheel rebuilds, 12-volt tachometer, radiator filler neck and cap, beefed-up differential spider gears, transaxle side plates, transaxle cast magnesium ribs to be welded on Bug or Bus transmissions to strengthen weak points, heavy-duty VW clutches and complete Saab V-4 or Ford V-6 industrial engines. Also has adapters for mid-engine installations. Catalog, $1.00.

1963 aluminum Olds V-8 in VW-based sand buggy

Ken Tool Manufacturing Co.
768 East North Street
Akron, Ohio 44305

Professional tools available include bead breakers and expanders, tire irons, lug wrenches, impact wrenches, front suspension hand tools, power tire changers, mechanics' creepers, jacks and jack safety stands, wheel valve stem tools, tire gauges, wheel balancers, tubeless tire vulcanizers, pullers, drain plug tools, grease and lubrication tools, battery service tools, tune-up equipment, engine valve and piston tools, brake system service equipment, tap and die sets, parts cleaning tanks, and torque wrenches. Free information to wholesalers.

Keystone A&A Industries
728 River Road
Richmond, British Columbia
Canada

Alloy wheels, roof racks and RV accessories. Keystone has a wide variety of aluminum, steel and all-magnesium wheels for mini cars, imports, domestic vehicles, racers and small trucks. Also carries chrome wheel hub covers, mud flaps, splash guards, wheel-cleaning compound, regular and locking lugnuts, valve stems and stem covers, wheel adapters, spacers, adhesive wheel weights, bicycle bumper carriers, utility roof racks, ski racks, roof racks with boat roller attachments, fiberglass pickup bed tops and steel step bumpers for mini-trucks, interior carpets and bed tonneau covers for Japanese trucks, and portable generators. Free literature.

Kimble Engineering Ltd.
8 Painswick Road
Hall Green
Birmingham 28 OHH
England

Mostly MG T-Series hard parts and cosmetic items. A few parts for earlier MGs and other British cars. Carries S.U. carb kits and rebuilt fuel pumps. Parts and price list available with prices in U.S. dollars.

King Motoring Specialties
6704 North Crescent Boulevard
Pennsauken, New Jersey 08110

Goodies for the sports and foreign car enthusiast. Desmo "boomerang" mirrors, Astrali steering wheels, Scientific and Chilton repair guides, Nomex and Fypro racing clothes, shoulder harnesses, signal boards for racing pits, Bell helmets, Semperit tires, Koni shocks, Heuer timers, Stelling & Hellings air filters, Porsche and VW "bras", Smiths instruments, Stebro and Abarth free-flow exhaust systems. Cooper free-flow exhausts for British sports cars range in price from $19.95 (Sprite/Midget) to $33.95 (Triumph Spitfire Mk III and GT-6). King's own headers for popular foreign cars start at $49.95 for VW models and range up to $125.00 on some Triumphs.

Along with Cibie, Carello and Lucas quartz halogen lights, King carries the British Miller line at moderate prices. A variety of lamp covers and stoneguards are also available.

For those who have it and want to begin flaunting it, King offers tape stripes, in black or white, which incorporate the name of the car in big, bold letters. The price is $12.95 a pair. Other dress-up items include fancy door handles, walnut dash panels, plaques and badges, and the Amco line of bumper overriders, luggage racks, insignia floor mats, tonneau covers, consoles, ski carriers and leather or walnut shift knobs.

For those who don't have it and are looking for something to flaunt, Astrali aluminum wheels at $49.95 a copy are good-looking status raisers. They are available in size

13″x5½″ for many foreign cars. Wheels size 5″x10″ to fit Minis and Hondas are $42.95. In larger and wider sizes, American Racing Equipment mags are offered.

A suitable *pièce de résistance* would be Italian Svezia air horns with five chrome trumpets playing "Colonel Bogey," "La Cucaracha," "Never on Sunday," etc. A set of horns (12-volt only) in the tune of your choice is $54.95. For the diffident there are dual plastic horns (6- or 12-volt) at $19.95.

A fairly extensive line of anti-sway bars, SCCA-approved roll bars for sports cars and small sedans, and finned valve covers for British sports cars and VWs, are other items offered under the King brand name.

Sunday mechanics and proto-racers will appreciate King's Mini Jack, a one-ton capacity hydraulic floor model which would be a handy item at track or shop. There are also jack safety stands at $6.95 each and heavy-duty scissors-type jacks at $9.95. Catalog, $1.00.

Capri with Astrali aluminum wheels from King Motoring Specialties

---

Kingsbury Tire
3340 East Anaheim Street
Long Beach, California 90804

Sells Armstrong off-road tires and Jackman and Dan Gurney Eagle Wheels. Also has wide steel wheels at moderate prices. Free catalog.

Dick Kingston Restorations
134 East Avenue H-6
Lancaster, California 93534

Complete auto restorations, wire wheel service, custom spoke work, and chrome plating. Also builds complete bodies including woodwork and metal shaping. Stocks large supply of 1916, 1919 and 1922 4-cylinder Stutz parts. Write for further information.

Kissel Kar Klub
(Kissel)
c/o E. E. Husting
Frost Pond Road
Locust Valley, New York 11560

Mr. Husting kindly writes to inform us that club members get together informally, although there have been two organized meetings in recent years. The members, who must either be Kissel owners or have been associated with the Kissel Motor Car Company, receive help in locating spare parts and keeping their cars up to snuff. There is also a club publication, *The Kissel Kar* published "approximately annually." Mr. Husting states that some Kissel 8-cylinder engine parts were similar to those used in Lycoming 8-cylinder engines, and parts are available through the Auburn-Cord-Duesenberg Company. Otherwise the only parts generally available are gears, gaskets, and tires. Yearly dues: none.

Chris Koch
6 East Cherry Street
Wenonah, New Jersey 08090

NOS Ford parts 1932-59. Also original Ford literature. Send a stamped, self-addressed envelope with query.

Koehler's Model "A" Shoppe
Route 256
Churchton, Maryland 20733

Complete line of antique Ford parts plus Ford hi-performance items such as cams, counterbalanced cranks, ignition systems, intake and exhaust systems, race car bodies, Miller grille shells and chassis. Also complete restoration services for any car. Specialty is restoration of race cars. Parts fabrication on special order. Queries with a stamped, self-addressed envelope.

Koenig Iron Works
Box 7726
Houston, Texas 77007

Manufactures service bodies and tool boxes for pickup trucks, and power winches. Service bodies of galvanized steel come in various models with compartments utilizing the spaces around and over the rear wheel arches of pickup trucks for storage space. Regular and heavy-duty models include panel door locks and have optional equipment such as overhead ladder racks, telescopic top with tailgate enclosure, and rear bumper with step plate and optional recess for trailer hitch. Models are available to fit the new compact trucks such as Chevy LUV and Ford Courier. Tool boxes are available to fit in bed of pickup truck or above sides. For larger trucks there is an under-body tool box. Winches are available in both electric and power take-off models. They are individually engineered for specific 2WD and 4WD vehicles. Free literature.

Kool-Fuel
Racing Products, Inc.
215 S.E. Second Street
Oklahoma City, Oklahoma 73125

Traction bars and fuel coolers. Fuel coolers, for pro-stock racers, come in single and dual coil models for $42.60 and $69.40 respectively. Weld-on chassis aids are ladder bars ($101.60) and wheelie bars with 36″-44″ arm length ($136.00) which both fit all cars. A universal adjustable shock relocator is $14.70. Other products include a pre-load adjuster kit ($16.00), spring clamp kit for leaf springs ($14.70), adjustable driveshaft loop ($18.66), traction bars for most Chevs, Chrysler and American Motors cars with leaf springs ($48.00), traction bars for most Fords with leaf springs exc. Pinto ($48.00), adjustable traction bars for Chev-Chrysler-American Motors or Ford ($74.50), coil spring traction bars for most mid-range GM cars ($48.00), Vega coil spring traction bars ($42.80), van traction bars ($67.00), various coil spring bars for full-size GM and Ford cars, an economy clamp-on traction bar for leaf springs ($24.70), super U-bolt kit to go with traction bars ($20.00), universal degree wheel ($9.30). Free information.

Kugel Komponents
8056 Westman
Whittier, California 90606

Chassis components for street rods. Parts available for Deuce roadsters and early Ford V-8s include front end kits ($75.00), reversed rack and pinion steering ($50.00 exchange), Jag rear end kits ($140.00), lower control rod bracket kits, torsion bar hangers, Jag brake pedal assemblies with master cylinders, tube front end kits, trans coolers, split wishbone kits, and universal ignition wiring kits. Also has alternator supports for small block Chev V-8, shocks to go with Jag front end, Jag front and rear hubs, and combination engine stands and hoists. Offers complete chassis fabrication service for labor price of $8.00 an hour. Free literature.

Kustom Headers
P.O. Box 328, 1331 W. Cedar
Standish, Michigan 48658

Headers, sidemounts and exhaust accessories for American cars and VWs. American car headers come in two series. The All-Star Line models are $115.00 and the competition headers are priced from $150.00 to $300.00. Header mufflers are $15.95. Flat black headers and side pipes, available for various Chevrolets and Corvettes, are priced from $275.00 to $300.00. These headers are also available with chrome side pipes or fully chromed. Sidemount header mufflers are $25.00 apiece. Exhaust accessories include straight tubing, collector extensions, formed collectors, flange plates, and temperature resistant paint. Free literature.

Kwik-Way
902 17th Street N.E.
Cedar Rapids, Iowa 52402

Power equipment for wheel balancing, exhaust gas analysis, rod reconditioning, brake system service, head work, glass bead cleaning, parts cleaning, refacing valves, boring VW engines, cylinder boring, block reconditioning, magnetic particle inspection, crankshaft grinding, wet surface grinding, and power hoisting. Free literature available to professionals.

L & S Bearing Co.
6 South Pennsylvania Avenue,
Oklahoma City
Oklahoma 73101

Wow have they got bearings! Bearings for cars, trucks, farm tractors, boat trailers, snowmobiles, and maybe even little red wagons. For both American and foreign cars, just about every bearing ever needed is listed in the comprehensive catalog put out by this company. Consult catalog at wholesale parts house.

Ron Ladley
1117 Sydney Street
Philadelphia,
Pennsylvania 19150

Mr. Ladley, who is a founder of the Willys Club of America, sells Willys cars and parts, 1937-42. Also Willys trucks and literature. Send a stamped, self-addressed envelope with query.

Lagana
RFD 1
Canterbury,
Connecticut 06331

Model A parts exclusively. Rebuilt engines, generators, starters, carburetors, distributors and tons of other parts. Complete line of Ditzler lacquer for custom mixing any original Ford color. Mr. Lagana formerly operated the Automotive Obsolete Company in Flushing, New York. Send a stamped, self-addressed envelope with query.

Lagonda Club
(Lagonda)
c/o Mrs. Valerie May
68 Savill Road
Lindfield
Haywards Heath
Sussex
England

This is the parent club of the American Lagonda Organization. There are numerous social and competitive events, a monthly newsletter, a quarterly glossy magazine called *The Lagonda,* technical advice, spare parts location and the manufacture of new parts, and library services. Those seeking parts sources are advised to write to Capt. Ivan Forshaw, The Pines, 415 Ringwood Road, Parkstone, Dorset, England. Yearly dues: $10.00; entry fee $2.40.

The Lagonda Club
(Lagonda)
c/o R. T. Crane
10 Crestwood Trail
Lake Mohawk
Sparta, New Jersey 07871

This is the American branch of the English club which is located at 35 Cobold Avenue, Eastbourne, Sussex, England. The Club publishes a quarterly magazine and monthly bulletins in between. In addition they have a technical and spare parts advisor and have now embarked on a program of manufacturing needed parts that are not now available. Yearly dues: $10.00; initiation/registration fee $2.50.

Lakewood Industries
4800 Briar Road
Cleveland, Ohio 44135

Makers of safety bellhousings, bellhousing blankets, roll bars, seat belts, traction bars, portable engine stands, metallic brake linings, and brake rebuild kits. Traction bars are available in street or competition models for many domestic cars. Write to company for the name of your nearest distributor. Literature available through distributors.

Street/strip roll bar from Lakewood Industries

Lancia Motor Club (Lancia)
c/o Mrs. Betty M. Rees
New Grass
Down Ampney
Circencester
Gloucestershire, GLY 5 QW
England

Driving tests, concours, film shows, and occasional rallies and races comprise the principal activities of the Lancia Motor Club. Publications include a monthly news sheet, a journal issued three to four times a year, and an annual membership register. The Club maintains a comprehensive technical library and has initiated the manufacture of parts for some models as the demand arises. Technical advice and parts location are other services available. Yearly dues: $7.20; Entrance Fee, $2.40.

John Lane
6321 Crossview Road
Seven Hills, Ohio 44131

Specializes in sale of water pumps for cars from the teens to about 1950. All pumps are rebuilt and can be sold in job lots or individually. Among cars for which pumps are available are Essex, Durant, Oakland, Graham Hollywood, and Cord. Also a limited number of early car radios and heaters, and a very comprehensive inventory of all types of Victor and Fitzgerald gaskets for early cars. Send a stamped, self-addressed envelope for lists.

Lang Automotive Engineering
20 Jackson Avenue
Vancouver 4
British Columbia, Canada

Calling all Beetles. VW power pulleys or stock diameter replacement pulleys are to be had for $18.00 at Lang. A sand seal pulley kit ($28.95) and drag racer's degree wheel ($13.95) are other products offered.

For real high winders a crankcase and rocker cover breather kit ($25.20) would be a good choice. There are also finned rocker arm covers, a belt and pulley guard, and a fuel pump block-off plate for those installing the electric variety.

Changing clutches? Lang makes a clutch alignment pilot tool ($3.60) which will be a big help.

The Lang Super Sump ($29.95) increases oil capacity 40

percent, while a spin-on filter bracket ($9.54) will keep things sanitary. For those going to a custom system on all VW and Porsche 4-cylinder engines, there is an oil cooler block-off, with O-ring sealing, for $9.72. Also a special oil by-pass check relief valve and spring, increasing oil pressure to 60 pounds, for $5.10.
A mini sump to fill all VW engines except the 411 extends the pickup 1½″ and may be tapped for a remote pickup system. Lang's mimeographed catalog tells all. Catalog, $1.00.

Larry's Thunderbird Parts
48 Monument Plaza
Pleasant Hill
California 94523

Parts for classic T-Birds, 1955-57. New and used parts. Repro seat covers, door panels, kick panels, carpets, drop curtains, arm rest covers, headliner ($21.95), vinyl floor covers (behind seat) $6.00, dash covers, garnish rail sets, windlace sets, quarter side cardboards, backrest cardboards, and soft tops ($65.00). Also, 1955 and 1956, rubber trunk mat ($39.95), trunk side cardboards, center trunk hardboard, firewall cover ($19.95), firewall grommet set ($3.95), firewall cover fasteners ($2.95 a set), inside mirror, hood pad ($4.95), license frame sets ($4.95), hard and soft top weatherstrip sets. Most mechanical parts shown in exploded view in catalog, and there is a detailed price list. Catalog, $1.00.

Lea Francis Owners Club
(Lea Francis)
c/o D. Purdy
54 Gresham Way
Shefford
Bedfordshire
England

Admirers of the marque will be glad to know that the Lea Francis Club numbers 190 members, and holds concours events and driving tests, as well as social meetings each year. There is an L.F.O.C. newsletter plus a magazine called *The Leaflet* published twice a year. The Club holds spares for some pre-1935 cars, and has a register of spare parts available. Yearly dues: $5.00.

Leather Stuff
P.O. Box 18
Provo, Utah 84601

Along with watchbands, belts, pocketbooks and sundry items of that nature, makes hand-tooled leather keyfobs with car emblems (Ford, Chevrolet, Hudson, Land Rover and many others), Chevrolet insignia or Ford Script rings (brass $6.00, silver $12.00), Ford or Chev brass belt buckles ($6.00), and belts with Ford or Chev emblems branded in ($12.00 with buckle). Also some items with VW emblem. Free information.

Le Baron Bonney Co.
14 Washington Street
Amesbury,
Massachusetts 01913

Supplies upholstery, sidewall, headliner, carpeting, trim, fasteners, welting, windlace, and other materials for interior restoration of Fords (Model A and early V-8) plus most other cars. Also has available complete interior kits, top kits, sidecurtains, top boots, tire covers, and upholstery installation services for Model A and early V-8 Fords. A complete selection of upholstery, side wall, panel, and headlining fabrics is $1.00. A selection of carpeting, bindings, and carpet fasteners is also sent for $1.00. A third selection at the same price is leathers and vinyls, topping and trim. Prices and material samples on Ford items sent upon request. It is necessary to state specific model and year of Ford. Add $.25 for first class mail.

The Soft Machines. Ever since Marinetti and the Futurists, the dynamism and functional mechanics of the automobile have inspired art which is both witty and penetrating. Here are some recent examples.

1. "One Way" by Red Grooms, 1964. (Courtesy John Bernard Myers Gallery; collection of Mr. & Mrs. Walter Nathan.) Oil on canvas. This is an urban scene both familiar and prosaic. A snapshot of the eternal traffic jam.

2.

2. *"Untitled" by Don Eddy, 1971.* (Courtesy Sidney Janis Gallery; photo by O.E. Nelson.) Acrylic on canvas. The hard-focus reality of shiny metal surfaces and assembly-line production. The automobile as "hollow, rolling, sculpture."

3. *"Red Volkswagen" by Sig Rennels, 1971.* (Courtesy O.K. Harris; photo by Eric Pollitzer.) Latex and acrylic. In contrast to the hardware of machine-rolled steel, there is the soft machine which exists as a pleasure object alone, useless and unashamed.

4. "Radiator, Hard Model" by Claes Oldenburg, 1965. (Courtesy Sidney Janis Gallery; collection Mrs. Ethel Krauschaur; photo by Geoffrey Clements. Corrugated paper and enamel. Another whimsy of a distinguished modern artist.

5. "Soft Engine Parts No. 2, Air Flow Model No. 6 (Filter and Horns)" by Claes Oldenburg, 1965. (Courtesy Sidney Janis Gallery; photo by Geoffrey Clements.) Stenciled canvas, wood, and kapok. The underpinnings of the soft machine. The final cadaverous dissection of a cancerous organism.

6. "Soft Engine, Air Flow Model No. 6" by Claes Oldenburg, 1966. (Courtesy Sidney Janis Gallery; photo by Geoffrey Clements.) Stenciled canvas, wood, and kapok. And here is the soft engine, impotent, magnified, and somehow ridiculous. A technological dinosaur in decay.

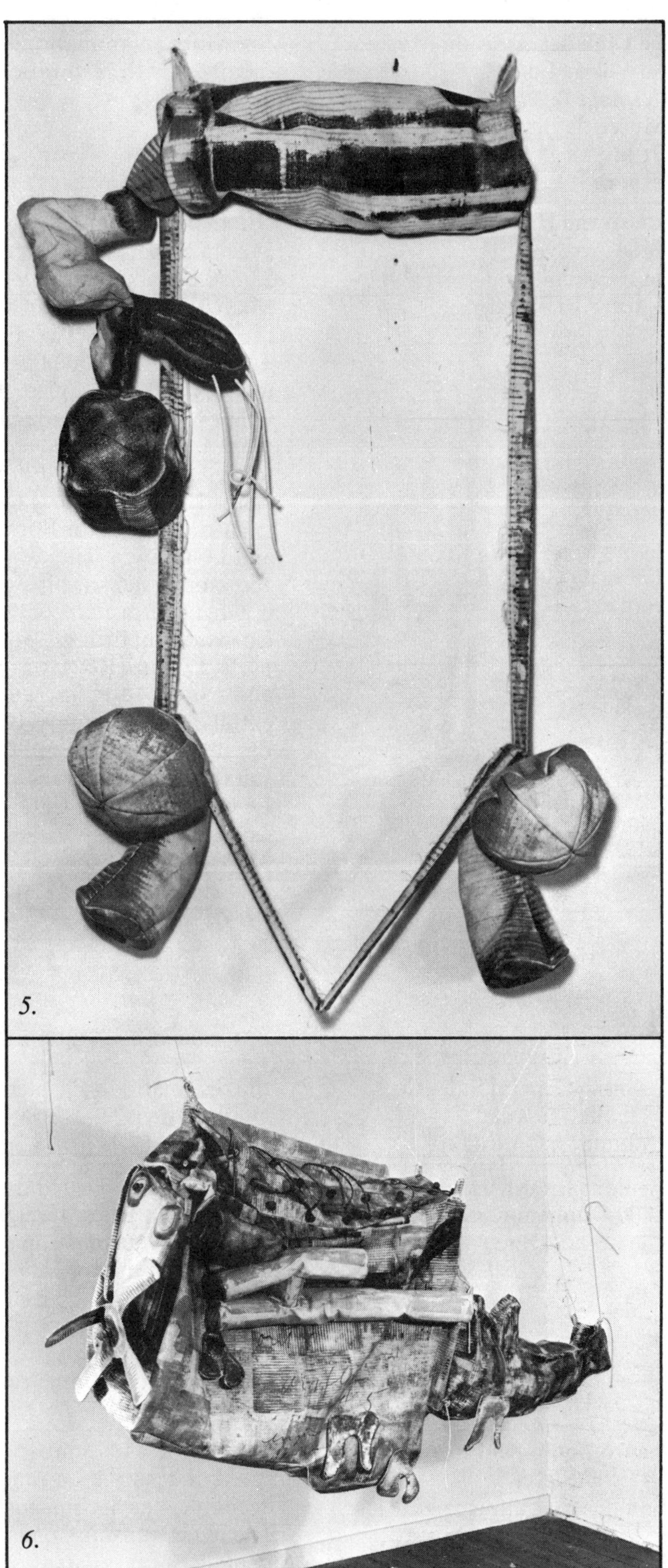
5.

6.

Le Club des Amis du Musee du Val de Loire (Vintage & Veterans Cars)
Musee de Briare-45
Briare
France

Sponsors an annual rally for veteran cars and assists members with restoration of their vehicles. Yearly dues: $4.00

Le Grand Race Cars
1104 Arroyo
San Fernando
California 91340

Offers three complete Formula cars ready to go racing. The Mk. 15 Super Vee is $6,950.00 in race-ready form or $3,850.00 in kit form *sans* engine, gearbox and tires. The Mk. 13F is $5,489.00 in race-ready form or $3,195.00 for the kit. The Formula B car fitted with customer furnished Ford T/C engine is $8,500.00, while the disassembled kit retails for $6,400.00. Complete plans are also available for each car. Other products include racing bucket seats, Formula Ford parts and accessories, engine-to-gearbox adapters for Alfa to Hewland, English Ford to Hewland, Brabham (short), Lotus 23 (long), Chevy to LG600 and FT200 to 1600 Ford; exhaust systems for Formula cars, Formula Ford wheels and Le Grand racing wheels, race car trailers and racing accessories such as pit signal boards and lap charts. Company is a distributor for Koni racing shocks, Hayden oil coolers, Cosworth oil fittings, Conelec fuel pumps, Girling spare parts, Loctite, Revgard rpm limiter, Hewland gearboxes and parts, Moon instruments, Flame-Out on-board fire extinguishing systems, Hurst/Airheart disc brakes, and Lazenby dry sump pumps. Many other mechanical parts suitable for racing cars, and small fittings, are listed in the Le Grand catalog. Catalog, $2.00.

New sports racing model for big league competition from Le Grand Race Cars.

Lehman General Sales Co.
1835 Stelzer Road
Columbus, Ohio 43219

Makes small sandblasters, handy for home use. Operating air pressure is 50 to 200 pounds. Model C blaster is $44.50 and model D-90 is $58.50. Free literature.

Lempco Industries Inc.
5490 Dunham Road
Cleveland, Ohio 44137

Makers of standard and automatic transmission replacement parts, foreign car (VW, Opel and Toyoglide) automatic transmission components, air conditioner service parts, water pumps for Chrysler 6-cylinder cars, air conditioner charge kits, timing gears and chains, U-joints, motor and transmission mounts, power steering parts and tools, universal transmission and clutch spring tools, and special air conditioner service tools. Catalogs available to jobbers only.

Lenco Equipment Co., Inc.
1425 'E' Street
San Diego, California 92101

Racing transmissions and associated parts. The Lenco two speed underdrive transmission, with clutch reverser available, has become justly famous in drag racing circles. The basic transmission is $810.00 in aluminum and $875.00 in magnesium. Also offers 3- and 4-speed racing

	transmissions suitable for dragsters, Funny Cars and Pro Stock cars. Quick-change rear end units, available for all Ford, Chev, Mopar, Dana, Pontiac and Olds rear ends, are $250.00. Other parts available include clutch throwout bearings and collars; aluminum late-style Ford center sections; Ford pinion supports; rings and pinions; axles; driveshafts; complete drivelines; clutch stands; fuel pump overdrives; cylinder sleeves for Ford, Chrysler, and Chev engines; and spools to lock up Ford and Chrysler rear ends and eliminate a conventional differential. Catalog, $1.00.
Les Amis de Delage (Delage) Chateau des Ducs de Bretagne 44-Nantes France	Although American friends of the Delage cannot take advantage of on-the-spot activities, they may receive periodic bulletins and obtain help in locating spare parts. The bulletins, of course, are in French, although the secretary-general of the Club, Jean Lorfray, will answer questions in English. Yearly dues: $11.00.
Leslie Enterprises P.O. Box 772 Atwater, California 95301	Foreign car and dune buggy accessories. Upholstered bucket seats run from the "Total Comfort" at $37.95 to the "Total Roundtrack" at $89.95. For VWs and Buses there are Baja kits, scoops and fender flares. A kit to convert the VW Beetle to a mini-Ford 1937 look is $200, a Datsun spoiler goes for $25, and a Pinto spoiler is $32. Headers are available for VW, Porsche, dune buggy, Pinto and Vega. There are also VW intake manifolds; dune buggy windshields; custom shifters; oil coolers; steering wheels; VW valve covers; VW vinyl wood-grained dashboards; and a very full line of buggy accessories including roll bars, skid plates, steering brakes, bumpers, windwings, wire looms, shortened clutch cables, and headlights. Other items include tow bars, wheels and wheel adapters, VW motor mounts, Pinto scoops to replace the rear window at $60.00, and similar scoops for the Vega. Catalog free.
Les Leston Products 315 Finchley Road London NW3 6EH England	Outfitters for the gentleman racer. Along with driving suits and various brands of helmets, Leston sells a magnetic pit signaling kit, stop watches, racing and rally numbers, the Robotimer multi-sequence timing board, a handy little PVC-covered clipboard with pen and pencil holders and space for a stopwatch, along with sports clothing for the race goer and his bird. Free catalog.
Gerald J. Lettieri 132 Old Main Street Rocky Hill, Connecticut 06067	Gaskets for American cars 1914-60. Gaskets are NOS, head gaskets, pan, manifold, etc. Also some auto literature and miscellaneous mechanical parts. Send a stamped, self-addressed envelope with query.
Leverage Tools, Inc. P.O. Box 68 Glenvil, Nebraska 68941	Manufactures vise-type locking pliers in many models including C-clamps, sheet metal holders, welding clamp pliers, long-nosed locking pliers, and battery service pliers. Also makes bracket to convert any Lever Wrench to a portable vise. Free literature.
Arnold Levin 2835 West North Shore Avenue Chicago, Illinois 60645	Early brass lamps, horns, carbide generator tanks, carburetors, wooden coil boxes and other miscellaneous parts for antiques and classics. Also complete antique and classic autos for sale. Send a stamped, self-addressed envelope with query.

W. Kenneth Lewis 4915 Baymeadows Road No. 8-D Jacksonville, Florida 32217	Classic and foreign auto literature. Some workshop manuals, much automobiliana. If you are looking for an Amphicar owner's manual or a fact sheet on the Mohs Ostentatienne Opera sedan, Mr. Lewis may be the man to supply it. Free listing.
Lexol Corporation West Caldwell New Jersey 07006	Makes leather preservative for classic and antique cars. Price $1.75 a pint and goes up to $6.00 for gallon can. Free literature.
Lightspeed Panels The Station Leaholm Whitby Yorkshire England	One of the most interesting of British kit cars is the new Magenta made by Lightspeed Panels. The car is based on British Leyland 1100 and 1300 running gear and uses an MG 1100 radiator grille. The roadster body has an early MG look from the front, and resembles the smaller Morgan from the rear. The basic kit consists of a main body section, combined bulkhead and dash, front panel which holds the number plate and hood catch, hinged hood which incorporates the MG grille, battery tray molded in position, an anodized aluminum windshield frame and brackets fitted with laminated glass, roadster top and side screens, roll bar, spare wheel mounting bracket, and other miscellaneous parts. Seats are an optional extra. The body can be supplied in seven different colors. Cost of the basic kit is approximately $850.00 Free literature.
Lincoln Continental Owners Club (Lincoln Continental Continental Mk. II) P.O. Box 549 Nogales, Arizona 85621	Includes both pre and postwar Contis plus the Continental Mk. II and special-interest Lincolns and Continentals of the 1949-67 period. National meets, regionals, rallies and swap meets are some of the activities enjoyed by the Club's (approximately 2,000) members. Publications include *Continental Commments,* a quarterly containing technical comments, pictures and data, and *Continental Bulletin,* a bimonthly newsletter with information on Club activities and classified advertisements. Members also receive a computerized Club roster listing fellow members and their cars. Yearly dues: $10.00.
Lincolns Corvettes, Inc. 12220 Aurora Avenue North Seattle, Washington 98133	Mr. Lincoln's auto salvage yard has an extensive section devoted exclusively to Corvettes. Along with listing complete cars for sale in damaged condition, the Lincoln catalog includes body parts for all Corvettes from 1953 to the present. There are also Corvette radios, steering wheels, instrument clusters, hub caps, bucket seats, soft tops, complete engines and transmissions, rear axle assemblies, front and rear suspension components, and brake parts. Among the brand new items in stock are Goodyear and Firestone street and race tires, racing fuel cells, hood scoops, fiberglass body components including custom fender flares, and roll bars. Prices of many used component are based upon condition. Also in stock are components for Porsches, Jaguars, Mercedes, Alfas, MGs, BMWs, and other foreign vehicles. Shipping rates are quoted in the catalog. Company will do race car preparation, roll bar installation, and general Corvette repair work. Catalog, $2.95.

Lincoln Village
2862 Westwood Lane, No. 5
Carmichael
California 95608

Specializes in 1951-53 Lincoln Continental convertibles and sedans. Can supply many parts, as well as complete cars unrestored and restored. Reprinted 1951 shop manuals are $8.50. Send a stamped, self-addressed envelope with queries.

Lincoln Zephyr Owners Club (Lincoln Zephyr, 1941 and 1942; Lincoln Custom, 1940-48 and 1956-57; Continental Mark II; 1946-48 Lincoln)
6628 Verna Street
Library, Pennsylvania 15129

One of the most active special-interest car clubs in existence, the LZOC holds many regional meetings and publishes a bi-monthly magazine, *The Way of the Zephyr* which contains historical articles and technical tips along with many parts advertisements. The Club also publishes an annual roster and has reprinted Lincoln service bulletins avaiiable. Club members can also order license plate frames, badges, decals, and jacket patches. Technical advice and parts location are services available to members. Yearly dues: $8.00 U.S., $10.00 overseas.

Littelfuse, Inc.
800 East Northwest Highway
Des Plaines, Illinois 60016

Stocks all types of fuses, fuse holders, circuit breakers, emergency fuse kits, fuse pullers, and in-line fuse holders. The company's *Comprehensive Automotive Fuse Guide* can be consulted at most parts houses.

Little Dearborn Parts
2015 Washington Avenue North
Minneapolis, Minnesota 55411

Parts for Model T, Model A, Ford V-8, Lincoln and 1955-57 Thunderbird. Most items listed are mechanical parts and trim accessories. Model T cylinder heads are $28.95 used. Valves are $2.25 each. An intake manifold of the early aluminum dogleg type is $9.95. An outside oil line accessory kit lists at $6.95. Model A crankshaft pulley is $4.95. Radiators go for $57.50 on an exchange basis. A rebuilt starter is $18.50 exchange with a core charge of $5.00. 1930-31 chromed cowl lights list at $23.95 a pair. Chrome plated replacement grilles for 1934-35 Ford V-8 are $39.95. A 1932-36 Greyhound hood ornament is $24.95. Lincoln parts available, mainly for 1936-48, include a V-12 major engine overhaul gasket set at $19.95, and rebuilt V-12 1936-48 distributors at $18.50 exchange. Also has radiator grille and bumper parts for 1949-51 Ford. Catalog, $1.00.

Logghe Stamping Co.
16711 13 Mile Road
Fraser, Michigan 48026

Funny Car and Dragster chassis and body components. LSC offers three versions of a Funny Car chassis, with the all-out version which includes independent front suspension going for $2,950.00. Funny Car accessories include Airheart disc brake systems, battery boxes, remote battery plug-ins, Dana or Spicer heavy-duty rear axle assemblies, aluminum fuel tanks, shortened driveshafts, Ford ring and pinion assemblies incorporating a Detroit Locker unit, Girling master cylinders, Funny Car chrome packages, and front wheels with Pirelli tires. There are also magnesium bulkheads and nose supports, aluminum interior panels, and fiberglass bodies with integral front and rear spoilers available in most current Chrysler, Ford and Chev body designs. In the Super Pro dragster line, LSC offers a chrome moly chassis, front axle and torsion bar assembly, shortened rear axle housing assembly, disc brake systems, aluminum handcrafted bodies and nose pieces, Donovan billet couplers and axles, P&S steering boxes and billet Anglia spindles, Lakewood bellhousings, 17″ dragster spoke wheels, and Crowerglide and Hayes combination direct drive units. Company also offers an NHRA gasser chassis to accommodate any Willys or Anglia style body, a Super Pro Altered chassis which is adaptable to 1923 T roadster or similar bodies, street rod chassis, Solar bucket seats, street roadster motor mounts, custom aluminum fuel tanks, front axle assemblies, brake and spindle kits, shortened driveshafts, coil-over shocks, rear traction bars, Chev steering arm kits, Ross steering boxes, steel windshield frames, and 1923 T bucket fiberglass bodies with pickup beds. Hardware in stock includes Heim joints, 4130 chrome-moly tubing, grade-8 cap screws, and Aeroquip hoses and fittings. In the racing accessory line, LSC has American Racing Equipment mag wheels, competition harnesses, fire-resistant race hoods with respirators, drag chutes, fire suits, trans shields, and M&H drag racing tires. Free information.

Lotus West Car Club, Inc. (Lotus)
P.O. Box 75972
Los Angeles, California 90005

Among the benefits of club membership are a technical data system in which technical articles are sent free to members as they appear, and previously-published articles may be ordered individually or as a complete set for $5.00. Lotus West's monthly newsletter is called *Stress Cracks.* There are also Club meetings, participation in competition, and tune-up and maintenance clinics. The Club maintains a list of parts sources and places which offer a discount to members. Yearly dues: $10.00, or $15.00 a couple.

LPS Research Laboratories, Inc.
2050 Cotner Avenue
Los Angeles, California 90025

Aerosol spray chemicals including lubricants, ignition drying sprays, cleaners and instant cold galvanizers. Free literature.

Lucas Engineering
Box 174
Culver City
California 90230

Antique car tires plus some Ford repro accessories. Tires come in sizes such as 350/400x19″, 550x19″, 500x20″, 450x21″, 30x3½″, 440x23″ and 500x24″. Wide whitewalls are available. Also fire engine tires. Other products include complete Model T steering wheels with brass or chrome center spiders, $29.75; Model T exhaust cut-outs, $7.95; Model A manifold clamps, $2.35; explosion exhaust whistles (guaranteed loudest ever) for $11.75; adapters for Model T and A, 4-cylinder Chevrolet and most pre-1920 Buicks, $2.00. Aermore exhaust horn with solid brass tubes is $18.75. Whistle control valves are $8.75 for Model T and $11.75 for Model A. A locking kick pedal costs $2.75 with a cable kit going for another $.45. Have fun! Free literature.

Joseph Lucas North America, Inc.
30 Van Nostrand Avenue
Englewood, New Jersey 07631

Distributor for Girling brakes, Lucas quartz halogen lights, India electric horns, Lucas Pacemaker batteries, the Lucas 12-volt sports coil, Girling motorcycle shocks, Girling strut-repair inserts to replace McPherson type struts on various models of BMW, Peugeot, Porsche, Fiat, Triumph, VW, Plymouth Cricket and English and German Fords, and the Lucas Flexilight, an interior gooseneck lamp which is a favorite of rally drivers and campers. Free literature.

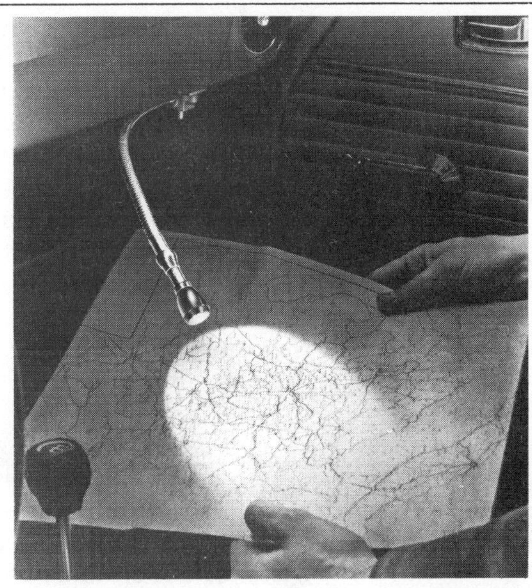
The flexilight by Joseph Lucas of North America, Inc.

M&H Tire Co.
309 Main Street
Watertown, Massachusetts 02172

Tires for drag racing, dirt track competition, Midget cars, Trans-Am cars and asphalt oval racing. Free literature.

McCreary Tire & Rubber Co.
Box 749
Indiana, Pennsylvania 15701

Racing and road tires. Sells 60-series and 70-series belted polyester street tires, drag slicks, dirt/asphalt mini-stock tires, and treaded tires for oval stockers. Free literature.

McGard, Inc.
852 Kensington Avenue
Buffalo, New York 14215

Makes wheel locks to fit many types of mag and steel wheels, including VW. Available in metric thread sizes. Also cadmium plated transmission bolts for U.S. and some popular imported cars. Free literature.

McGurk Engineering
16020 South Broadway
Gardena, California 90249

Camshafts and valve train gear for Chev 4, 6, and V-8 engines, Chrysler V-8s, Ford V-8s and Pontiac V-8s. Dual, triple and 5-carb manifolds for Chev and GMC 6-cylinder engines. Chev V-8 6-carb manifolds. Pistons for 1937-62 Chev 6-cylinder engines, and small and large block Chev V-8. Also oversize valves and complete stroker assemblies for GM engines; lightweight flywheels and clutch parts; roller rocker arms for small and large block Chev V-8; matched timing gear sets for 4- and 6- cylinder Chev; Ford V-8 timing sprockets; Mallory ignition equipment; Ford and Chrysler adjustable rocker arms; professional engine tools such as cam timing kits and cc-ing kits; high volume oil pumps; silicone chrome valve springs; and small engine hardware. Makes dry sump oil pumps for VW, and complete competition front drive units—consisting of front timing cover, dual oil pump, direct drive water pump, and set-up to drive Hilborn fuel injection—for Chev 4, 6, and 8-cylinder cars. Price is $450.00. Free information.

Mike McKennett
1250 NW Bella Vista Avenue
Gresham, Oregon 97030

Fiberglass repro parts for prewar Ford cars and trucks. Exact fiberglass repro of cardboard dash insulators for all 1932-48 Fords is $35.00 (specify model and year). Precut insulation material to fit behind fiberglass cover, $15.00.

Right-hand kickpanel with formed pocket for an authentic glove-box radio installation on 1933-34 Fords, $35.00. Flat kickpanels (left or right) for all cars 1928-48, in brown or black, $10.00 per side. Soon available will be headliners for pickups. Free information.

Dick McKnight
P.O. Box 375
Tully, New York 13159

Specializes in antique, classic and other early auto and truck literature. Send a stamped, self-addressed envelope with query.

Mack's Auto Sales
2290 East Avenue
Akron, Ohio 44314

New and used parts for Studebaker, Packard and Avanti. Send a stamped, self-addressed envelope with queries.

McLeod Industries
11491 Dillow Street
Westminster, California 92683

Clutch pressure plates, discs and flywheels for most performance applications. Clutches fit popular American cars and include Borg & Beck, Diaphragm and Long types. Discs include sprung hub and solid hub varieties. Flywheels are steel or aluminum, and include a new adjustable-weight flywheel. Accessories available include throw-out bearings and pressure plate bolts. Free literature.

Mac Tools, Inc.
Washington Court House
Ohio 43160

Full line of tools for the amateur and professional mechanic. SAE and metric socket sets; special VW tools; hand tools for front end alignment; electric test equipment; wheel balance and alignment systems; tap and die sets; air conditioning service tools; pneumatic impact and grinding tools; torque wrenches; and precision measuring instruments. Free literature.

Magna-Com, Inc.
1350 East Wilshire Avenue
Santa Ana, California 92705

Sells the solid-state Auto-Volt unit to convert the output of any alternator to a 110 volt DC plug-in power source. The unit is manufactured by Pemm Power, Inc. in Fullerton, California, and Magna-Com is the distributor.
A 50 amp alternator with the Auto-Volt unit will supply as much power as a motor of about two horsepower, according to Magna-Com, and this is enough to run 15 to 20 100-watt light bulbs or power anything from a hot plate to a saber saw so long as it is the type that runs on DC. In order to supply this power, however, the engine must be kept running at a fixed rpm higher than idle. Thus an auxiliary throttle control at $2.95 is a wise investment. The Auto-Volt itself costs $19.95 and other accessories are battery charging cables for $8.95, a welding attachment claimed to weld up to ¼″ steel for $18.95, and a complete welding kit, with helmet and gloves, for $39.95. Free literature.

Maison de Vitesse
1060 East Main Street
El Cajon, California 92021

Porsche 911 and 914 aficiandos will enjoy perusing the stock at Maison de Vitesse. Items available include front and rear spoilers, fender flares, mag wheels, rear license panels, headlight covers, racing seatbelts and harnesses, and a 2.5 litre Big Bore kit for the 911. Price of the latter is $400.00. A 911RS Carrera rear spoiler is $185.00 and a front spoiler goes for $85.00. Cromodora 14″x6″ mag wheels for the 914 are $58.00 each. Free literature.

Malion Reinforced Plastics, Inc.
460 Conchester Highway
Twin Oaks, Pennsylvania 19014

Makers of custom fiberglass body components. Using carbon reinforced Carboncopy techniques, the company has done fiberglass repairs and modifications on everything from Indy cars to Pro-Stock Vegas. They will design and produce body parts for any racing car to order. Free information.

Mallory Electric Corporation
1801 Oregon Street
Carson City, Nevada 89701

Mallory ignition systems and components include high-performance coils, dual point distributors, "Rev-Pol" distributors and transformers, magnetos, CD ignition systems, ignition modification parts for 8-cylinder domestic cars and the VW, electric advance distributors, tune-up kits,

Tune-up kits for foreign cars available from Mallory Electric Corporation

switches, spark plug covers, wiring kits, tachometers, rev limiters, vibrating timers for distributors and magnetos, and cable terminals and dividers. Free literature.

Mal's 'A' Sales
4968 South Pacheco Boulevard
Martinez, California 94553

Hard parts, accessories, body parts, and tools for Model A, Model T and early Ford V-8. Cast aluminum bumper clamps are $9.50 a set of four for 1930-31 models. Hand windshield wiper assembly is $5.95. Air Maze filter (copy of original for early Zenith carbs) is $9.95. "Float-A-Motor" set to replace original rear motor mounts and eliminate excessive vibration is $19.50. For those seeking a sportier Model A, a skull gear shift knob ($3.95) and wolf whistle that connects to the exhaust system ($4.95) are offered. A natural wood luggage rack with chrome frame goes for $65.00. Among the tools offered are a rear wheel drum knockoff ($.95), brake rivet set tool ($3.90), square hole drain plug wrench ($2.75), grease gun ($6.95), distributor cam wrench ($.80), and valve guide knockout tool ($2.75). Body parts for As include a rumble seat step ($2.75), rechromed instrument panel ($6.00 exchange price), and a pickup runningboard set for $49.95. A rebuilt engine with a 90-day guarantee carries an exchange price of $289.50. There is also an extensive listing of fabrics and welting, along with many rubber parts. For the Ford V-8, hood nose ornaments are $8.95, 1932-35 chrome hubcaps with V-8 emblem are $5.95 and 1935-36 floor mats are $24.50. Other floor mats are available at prices from $14.75 to $24.95. Model T parts include brake rod anti-rattle sets ($5.95), Ruckstell patent plate ($1.90), brass bulb horn ($12.75), and black tire cover with white script ($9.50). There are also many Ford books in stock. Catalog, $.25.

Mamba Developments Ltd.
Washer Lane Works
Kings Cross
Halifax HX2 7DX
England

Mamba aluminum alloy wheels come in 10″ sizes to fit Minis, and in the popular 5½x13″ size. They can be finished in natural aluminum or with the hub and spokes painted matte black, Bugatti blue, canary yellow, or Ferrari red. The wheel center cap carries the Mamba Snake

Trademark, and all wheels are sealed for use with tubeless tires. Free information.

Manchester Vintage Car Club (Vintage and Veteran Cars)
c/o Royston Dawber
The Spinney
1, Copperfield Road
Cheadle Hulme
Cheadle
Cheshire
England

Along with holding monthly meetings, a program of competitive events, and the annual Vista Road Rally, Club publishes a monthly newsletter and an annual roster. Yearly dues: $3.00; family membership, $.60.

Marauder GT
c/o Randy Berry
R.R. 1
Potomac, Illinois 61865

Makes Marauder GT fiberglass kit car. Also does fiberglass custom work, makes tube and monocque frames, and fabricates custom independent suspensions. Other services include painting, all types of welding including TIG, and construction of complete fiberglass and aluminum bodies. Sells speed equipment of all types and operates tune-up and engine building shop. Buys and sells all types of cars, with specialty being roadable racing cars. The Marauder GT kit car is a dune buggy-like body made to fit a shortened VW pan. Basic price is $398.00, with unusual option being gull-wing fiberglass top. The Marauder GT Mark II, which sells for $4,500.00 minus engine transmission and wheels, is basically a group 7 racing car for the street and can be fitted with Pinto, Wankel, or Porsche 914 engine. It is a mid-engine car with pop-up headlights. Available transmission is the Hewland 5-speed. The complete car, ready for the street, goes for $8,500.00. Free literature.

Maremont
168 North Michigan Avenue
Chicago, Illinois 60601

Makers of Gabriel shock absorbers to fit just about any car you can think of. Models include front and rear coil spring heavy duty shocks, adjustable racing or street shocks, and air shocks that compensate for heavy loads. Consult catalog at wholesalers.

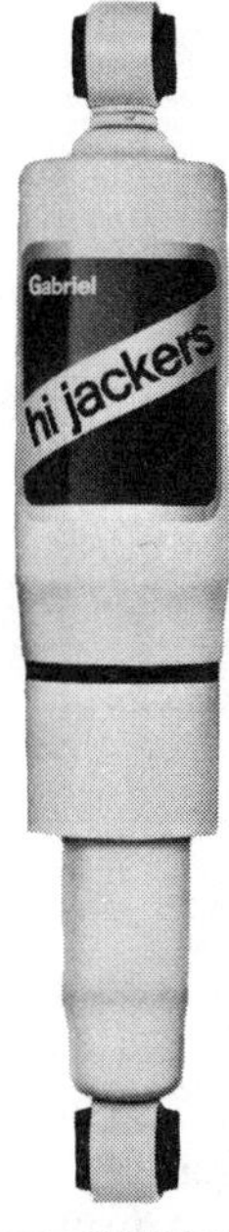

Gabriel "hi-jack-ers" air shocks from Maremont

Mark Auto Co., Inc.
Layton, New Jersey 07851

New parts for Model A and Model T. Many small mechanical parts and electrical items. Wiring harnesses, distributor parts, hood lacing sets, rubber gaskets, pedal shaft sets, and much else. Catalog, $1.00.

Marquette Manufacturing Co.
3800 North Dunlap Street
St. Paul, Minnesota 56112

Tire service equipment including power and manual tire changers, wheel balancers, tire lubricants, and hand tools. Free information to service garages.

Marson Corporation
130 Crescent Avenue
Chelsea, Massachusetts 02150

Paint guns, body filler, spray undercoat and fiberglass repair products. Also sells engine enamels, touch-up paints, polyethylene car covers, hand and hydraulic riveters, body repair tools, fiberglass curtains, car and wheel maskers, primer putty, muffler cement, engine block mender, aluminum and steel backup plates and allied items. Consult catalog at wholesalers.

Masonville Garage
Box 57
Masonville, Iowa 50654

Model A coupe bodies with fenders, running board aprons, running boards, radiator apron, and trim moldings are $1,295.00, while fiberglass roadster body kits sell for $1,145.00. Among the many other Model A parts and accessories available are front motor support kit ($1.95), connecting rods ($23.95 exchange), rebuilt transmissions ($99.95 exchange), radiators ($57.50), exhaust manifolds ($18.75), script ammeters ($1.30), point sets ($.75), tail light lenses ($.85), running board step plates ($11.50), chrome plated bumpers ($45.00 exchange), 1930-31 radiator stone guards ($64.75), rumble seats upholstered in black leatherette ($79.95), top kits ($15.00 for coupe and pickup, $22.50 for Tudor and Fordor), and rebuilt engines ($345.00 exchange). Some fiberglass parts for non-Ford cars include early Chev fenders and running boards, Chev and GMC

	pickup fenders, and fiberglass parts for International-Harvester, Willys, Corvette, and other cars. Masonville Garage sells plans for building a 1928-29 Model A "Huckster Wagon" body for $10.00. Catalog, $.35.
Maupin Auto Salvage, Inc. Box 463 Hutchinson, Kansas 67501	Has a 21-acre yard plus 50,000 square feet of warehouse space jammed with antique and special-interest car parts. About 715 parts cars are on the premises, and they range from a horse-drawn hearse right up to 1964 models. Although mail orders are accepted, most customers make a pilgrimage to Hutchinson and spend the day browsing around. Send a stamped, self-addressed envelope with query.
Max-Trac Tire Co. P.O. Box 227 Cuyahoga Falls, Ohio 44222	Distributor for Mickey Thompson sports and racing tires. Free literature.
Don R. May Enterprises 1927 North Hills Drive Raleigh, North Carolina 27609	Trackmaster car trailers. Among options for trailer are 12-volt winches and cables, tie down chains, front tool boxes, hand winches and cables, and electric brakes. Trailer has tandem axle assembly with 4,000 pound capacity. Surge brakes are fitted on one axle and the empty weight is 1,550 pounds. Free literature.
Mazda Motors of America, Inc. 3040 East Ana Street Compton, California 90221	U.S. distributor; service manuals.
Ray Melander 123 Westgate Road Des Plaines, Illinois 60016	Complete wiring for 1949-51 Willys Jeepsters. Main ignition harness for 4- or 6-cylinder is $45.00. Tail light and gas tank wiring with new loom sells for $18.75 in the 3-lead version. Also handles wiring for overdrive units. Wiring diagrams available for $1.50 each. Free parts and prices.
Mercedes-Benz Club, Ltd. (Mercedes-Benz) c/o G.A.F. Coward 153 Russell Road Birmingham B13 8RR England	Club activities include rallies, gymkhanas and social events. Primary publication is the bi-monthly *Mercedes-Benz Club Gazette.* Among the services offered to members are technical advice, spare parts location, a guide to manufacturers of non-available spare parts, and liaison with other M-B clubs throughout the world. Yearly dues: $8.00; initiation fee, $1.50.
Mercedes-Benz Club of America, Inc. (Mercedes-Benz) Box 4550, Dept. A Chicago, Illinois 60680	Three national events sponsored by the Club are the Tri-O-Rama, generally held at Pocono Raceway, the Midwestern Gemutlichkeit at Elkhart Lake, Wisconsin, and the Western Caravan held at various West Coast locations. Along with these get-togethers, the Club sponsors an annual pilgrimage to Stuttgart for four weeks. The nine Club regions and 30 sections hold many other events throughout the year. Principle Club publication is *The Mercedes-Benz Star,* a bi-monthly magazine. Spare parts purchases and swapping are handled through the *Trading Post* column in the magazine. Also available is a Mercedes *Vintage Car Register*

which costs $5.00. Yearly dues: $15.00; fiscal year begins October 1.

Mercedes-Benz of North America, Inc.
One Mercedes Drive
Montvale, New Jersey 07645

U.S. distributor; service manuals.

Mercer Associates (Mercer)
c/o Prof. Bill Cains
MGT Department Texas Tech
Lubbock, Texas 79406

An informal group of lucky Mercer owners. A newsletter is issued at regular intervals, and members exchange advice. No dues.

Mercury Tube Industries, Inc.
3015 Dolores Street
Los Angeles, California 90065

Sells side pipes (including a flame-painted model and others with stars and stripes, "Keep On Truckin" slogans and car company names), mufflers, dual exhaust systems, and exhaust system components. Free literature.

Merritt Products
800 West Eight Street
Azusa, California 91702

Makes fiberglass Baja bucket seats for sports and racing cars. Seats are cast of rugged polyethylene and have snap-on Naugahyde covers over a foam padding. The basic fiberglass shell is $43.50. Other models come with or without a high seat back and side arms. The top of the line Pro-Seat with

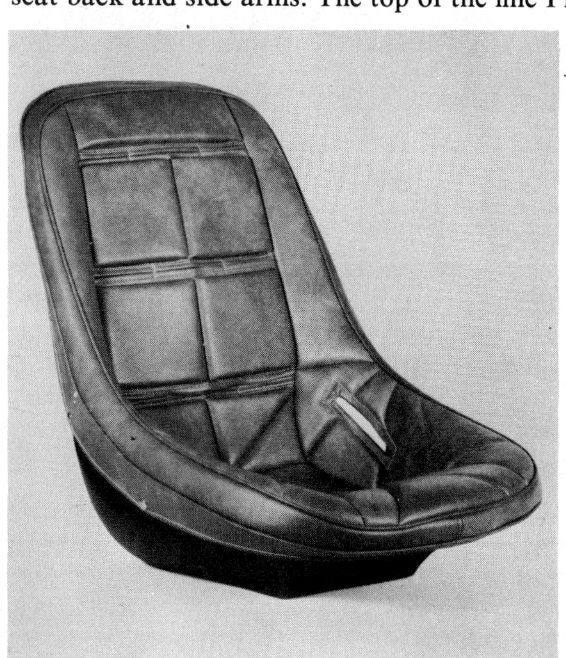

Baja Super Seat from Merritt Products

arms and high back is $279.50. Also make adjustable mounting platform, VW mounting plate, and competition seat belts. Free literature.

Messerschmitt Owners' Club (Messerschmitt)
c/o Les Klinge
39 Sylvan Way
West Caldwell, New Jersey 07006

Mr. Klinge, "King of the Schmitts," is the prime mover in this Anglo-American Club dedicated to the likeable little 3-wheeled bubblecars of years past. The Club newsletter, *Kabin News,* is a monthly and goes to about 70 members in the U.S. and more than twice that number in Britain.

Parts, service manuals and technical advice are offered to all Club members. Mr. Klinge notes that *all* parts are currently available—where original parts cannot be located, new ones are made up.
An informal annual meeting takes place in August at Mr. Klinge's house. Members also get together at the Hershey, Pennsylvania swap meet in October. Yearly dues: $6.00.

Metalflake, Inc.
P.O. Box 950
Haverhill, Massachusetts 01830

Makes the type of paint George Barris uses and Tom Wolfe wrote about in *The Kandy-Colored, Tangerine Flake, Streamlined Baby*. Product line includes metallic chips available in 36 colors, Glowble super-reflective flake, Mirra metallized polyester iridescent flake, acrylic based Candy Apple paints in 15 colors, silver and gold metallic ground coats for use with Candy Apple colors, Vreeble transparent acrylic crackle finish in 6 colors, and Flip Flop Pearls—paints that change colors when viewed from different angles. Free literature.

Metro Moulded Parts
2617 Washington Avenue North
Minneapolis, Minnesota 55411

Reproduction rubber parts for early American cars. Items in stock for Model T, early Chevrolet, American Bantam, Packard, Pierce-Arrow, Auburn, Cord, Graham, Willys, Chrysler, Lincoln, La Salle, and other makes. A few foreign car items in stock such as Mercedes pedal pads ($8.00), Riley pedal pads ($7.00), and Jaguar pedal pads ($7.00). Other parts in stock include step plate pads, tailight bases, booster brake diaphragms, hood corners, body bumpers, door bumpers, beaded mounting pads, bumper grommets, gravel shields, shift boots, and windshield bases. Sells rubber stripping, sheets, slabs, and vent window mouldings in bulk. Will make some parts to order. Catalog, $1.00.

Metz Owners Club
(Metz)
216 Central Avenue
West Caldwell
New Jersey 07006

At present, activities are limited to maintaining a roster of Metz owners. There is a technical library from which free information can be supplied to new Metz owners. The address above is that of *Antique Automobile,* whose classified advertisement manager, Mr. Franklin B. Tucker, is the Metz man.

MGA Twin Cam Registry
(MGA Twin Cam)
c/o James R. Treat
256 Galaxy Drive
Circle Pines, Minnesota 55014

Dedicated to preservation and restoration of T/Cs. Aside from a registry, the group also publishes a quarterly newsletter, *La Bete,* gives technical advice, helps locate parts, offers free newsletter advertisements to members, and sells T/C literature. Photocopied workshop manuals are $12.00, factory newsletters (48 pages) are $3.50 each, driver's handbook (64 pages) is $4.00. Also stocks BMC timing data for racing at $.50 a copy, summary factory newsletter on tuning for $.50, back-issues of club newsletter for $.50. Yearly dues: $5.00 for T/C owners, $10.00 for non-owners. One-time registration fee is $2.00.

MG Mitten
36 South Chester
Pasadena, California 91101

Foreign car and racing goodies. MG Mitten can supply custom made covers for any car in five different fabrics. In waterproof Golden Mink or Silver Mink prices range from about $34.95 to $59.50. At somewhat lower prices a water repellent Duricon fabric is offered. Among other products are convertible tops for most foreign cars, small car headers,

Car covers for foreign and domestic cars available from MG Mitten

Hobrecht SCCA approved roll bars, driving gloves, racing side stripes, hard top hoists, custom steering wheels, Imcado hood straps, competition bucket seats (GT8 seat with black leather-cloth and brushed nylon cord center plus provision for full racing safety harness is $89.00), VW cosmetic accessories and Koni shock absorbers. The company carries a number of accessories specifically for Mini-Minor including wheel spats ($16.95 a set of four), alloy wheels, Paddy Hopkirk engine valve cover buttons which allow removal of the valve cover without a wrench, fly-off hand brakes, mechanical door stays, wheel spacers, Add-A-Dash kits of wood grained vinyl, quick-removal grille buttons and workshop manuals. Other popular lines include Stelling & Hellings air filters for foreign cars; P/S mag wheels; Par-A-Bolic velocity stacks; front and rear anti-sway bars; Abarth exhausts; Cannon auto alarms; Hurst shifters for VW and Toyota; Judson ignition systems; Smith's instruments; AMCO accessories; Bell helmets; Nomex and Fypro clothing; Stevens rally calculators; competition shoulder harnesses and seatbelts; pit signal boards; Heuer timing equipment; dashboard timer mounts; interior lights for rally cars; Carello driving lamps; Talbot mirrors; Stebel air horns; alloy valve covers for Spridgets, Austin-Healeys, TR2 and 3, and MGA & B; universal wheel spacers; luggage racks and ski carriers for small sedans; gear shift boots; locking gas tank caps; and shop manuals from Chilton, Clymer, Intereurope, Elfrink, Autopress and KGM. Catalog, $1.00.

Midland-Ross Corporation
Power Controls Division
490 South Chestnut Street
Owosso, Michigan 48867

Power brake hard parts for domestic cars. Free information.

Midstates Jeepster Association
312 South Sterling Street
Streator, Illinois 61364

Club features two annual meets, one in Illinois and one elsewhere. Meets are open to all 1948-51 Jeepster owners, whether members of the club or not. There is a monthly newsletter through which a member can place free classified advertisements. Although most mechanical parts are still obtainable, Jeepster body parts have become scarce and the club has been instrumental in the remanufacture of some parts by jobbers. Yearly dues: $5.00—covers whole family.

Midwest Auto Specialties
5063 Turney Road
Cleveland, Ohio 44125

Specializing in engine and drivetrain performance components, company lists Edelbrock manifolds, Offy manifolds, Holley and Carter carbs and components, Mr. Gasket accessories, Mallory electrics, Vertex magnetos, Accel ignition components, tune-up equipment, Hurst shifters, B&M racing transmissions and components, Borg-Warner 4-speed transmissions, Schiefer rear end gears, Lakewood traction bars, Gabriel shocks, NMW bolt-on tow bars and freewheeling tow hubs, Lakewood safety bell-housings, Velvetouch brake linings, Ansen chassis components, Schiefer and Hays clutches, Frankland quick-change units and limited slip differentials, Airheart disc brake systems, Halibrand racing components, Ross steering units, fiberglass bucket seats, safety fuel cells, P.S.I. tubular front axles, CAE chassis components, drag racing tires, all-magnesium wheels, up to 19″ wide, General Kinetics and Crane camshafts, Moroso drive train components and deep sump oil pans, Cragar wheels, Stewart-Warner instruments, Grant helmets and piston rings, Jahns and TRW pistons, Crower roller cams, Cyclone and Hooker headers, Thrush mufflers, Mickey Thompson tires, Sun tachometers and Flex-A-Lite fans. Also in stock are fiberglass body panels for Chev, Ford, Corvette, Pontiac, Mustang, Anglia and Willys; burglar alarm systems; Grant steering wheels; HP books; and Nomex driving suits. Small hardware of all types is listed in comprehensive catalog. Catalog, $.50.

Mike the Pipe
128 Stanley Park Road
Wallington
Surrey
England

A large part of Mike Randall's business consists of contract work for the British Motor industry. Of more interest is the availability of custom exhaust systems for racing or other applications. There are some stock specialties though these frequently change. No catalog. If you are in the market for a one-off exhaust system let Mike the Pipe know what you have in mind.

Milanese FAP
Box 413R
Mount Arlington,
New Jersey 07856

Hard parts and accessories for Alfa Giulietta, 1750, 1900, 2000 and 2600. Parts include ball and roller bearings, transmission and driveshaft components, engine bearings, ATE and Girling brake and clutch kits, disc brake rotors, speedo and tach cables, chrome air cleaners, carb repair kits, coils, clutch release bearings, disc brake pad sets, Mahle and Borgo pistons, engine filters, generators, flywheel ring gears, valve adjusting pads, engine gaskets, tune-up parts, oil seals, voltage regulators, starter drives, radiator hoses and caps, thermostats, timing chains, valve train components, and windshield wiper blades. Company also handles AMCO accessories for Alfa, Marchal electrical products, Delta CD ignition systems, metric tools, BWA Sportstar alloy wheels (14″x6″, $55.00 a wheel), ANSA free flow exhaust systems, Milanese steering wheels in mahogany or Italian leather ($59.00), locking gas caps, and the Intereurope Alfa workshop manual. Catalog, $.50.

Milbar Corporation
530 Washington Street
Chagrin Falls, Ohio 44022

Specialty tools include snap ring pliers, safetytwist pliers which combine plier action with a twisting mechanism for safety wiring, diagonal cutting pliers, a close-clearance ratchet wrench and other items. Free information. Order through your retailer.

Milesmaster Inc. of America
Exeland, Wisconsin 54835

Sells a fuel pressure regulator and filter for universal application ($6.95), and a battery heater to aid starting on those cold mornings. Free literature.

Milestone Car Society
(Special Interest Cars 1945-64)
2422 Inglewood North
Minneapolis, Minnesota 55404

The Milestone Car Society is devoted to those post war vehicles which are considered to have future classic status. Cars such as the Mercedes 300-SL, Lincoln Continental Mark II, Kaiser Darrin and Packard Caribbean are what the Society is all about. Along with sponsoring various meets and social events, the Society has a quarterly glossy magazine *The Milestone Car,* and a monthly newsletter *The Mile Post.* In addition, a roster and data manual on outstanding postwar cars is published annually. At present, the Society is compiling a roster of the nation's wrecking yards where special-interest parts may be found. Yearly dues: $10.00. If you join between January 1 and May 30, dues are $5.00 for the rest of the year. For those who are not members of any car club which recognizes one or more milestone cars, there is a $2.50 initiation fee. Add $3.00 for overseas postage.

Mill Accessory Group
Two Counties Mill
Eaton Bray
Near Dunstable
Bedfordshire
England

Mill Accessory Group spells M-A-G, and that's the sort of wheels they sell. There are rally wheels and road wheels, aluminum wheels and SuperLite wheels, standard wheels and wire wheels. They fit continental and American cars, as well as most British models. To go along with their jazzy wheels, M.A.G. offers a complete line of Paddy Hopkirk accessories. There are fender extenders, wheel spacers, rally

G.T. wheels made by Mill Accessory Group are cooked in three-stage camel back oven for long-lasting finish

seats, custom steering wheels, suspension lowering kits and short front springs for English Fords, leather bonnet (that's hood to you, Yank) straps, Hopkirk racing helmets, radio aerials built into sun visors, or printed on a narrow strip of self-adhering clear vinyl, rally sump guards (crash pans), for a number of British cars, leather driving gloves, ignition water proofing kits for 4- and 6-cylinder cars, Betalight tritium gas-illuminated dashboard switches and keyhole surrounds, sportscar trunk racks, and anti-theft lug nuts working on a special master head/key principle. Many Paddy Hopkirk accessories are designed particularly for Minis. Another interesting device sold by M.A.G. Ltd., is the Sovy brake fluid indicator which uses a light on the dash to indicate when the master cylinder is low. It is available for 12-volt systems using single master cylinders only. Price is circa $5.00. Free literature.

Miller & Norburn, Inc.
Box 8811
Durham, North Carolina 27707

Performance components for recent BMWs. Items available for 1600-2002 models include street and racing cams, Venolia forged pistons, headers, Bilstein shocks, front and rear sway bars, ($24.95 and $23.95 respectively), heavy-duty springs ($89.50 for set of four), quick-ratio steering boxes ($110.00), limited slip differentials ($360.00), 4.11 and 3.90 ring and pinion sets ($125.00), negative camber plates, and Ferodo brake pads. Cams are available for both 4- and 6-cylinder cars on an exchange basis. Other items include Alpina cams, Weber carb conversion kits, Stebro exhaust systems, Racemark steering wheels for 4- and 6-cylinder BMWs, Scheel rally seats, Marchal driving lights, BWA Sportstar alloy wheels, Premier crash helmets, trailer hitches and car covers. Miller and Norburn has established prices for all machine shop and tuning services for BMWs. Free catalog.

Miller-Haven Enterprises
2944 Randolph Avenue
Costa Mesa, California 92626

Miller-Haven has in the past been well-known as a supplier of Baja Bug and Bus parts. In the future, they will no longer sell air scoops and other fiberglass items. Instead, they are concentrating on building off-road racing engines and transmissions, plus VW mechanical accessories. Items in stock include an aluminum skid plate for the Bug ($44.95), Armstrong tires and wide wheels, a ready-to-go dynotuned 1900cc Baja engine ($1,995.00), VW engine performance parts, Tri-Phase air cleaners, oil cooler kits, heavy-duty oil pumps, Cibie and Wipac lights, exchange stock transmissions ($125.00 with core charge of $50.00), heavy duty transmission parts, 4-speed and 5-speed Webster racing transmissions, and a number of off-road accessories such as tire bead breakers and spark plug air pumps. Their newest product is a bolt-in rollbar for VWs "The Thing," which sells for $50.00. Catalog, $.50.

Miller Racing Enterprises
133 Fairground Road
Xenia, Ohio 45385

Fiberglass body panels for British cars. Has parts for Austin-Healey, Spridget, Sunbeam Alpine and Tiger, Ford Anglia, Capri, Consul, Cortina, Sunbeam Imp, Hillman Husky, Hillman Minx, Jaguar XKE, Morris 1000, MG-A, B, and C, Mini-Minor, Mini Estate and Van, Porsche 356, older model

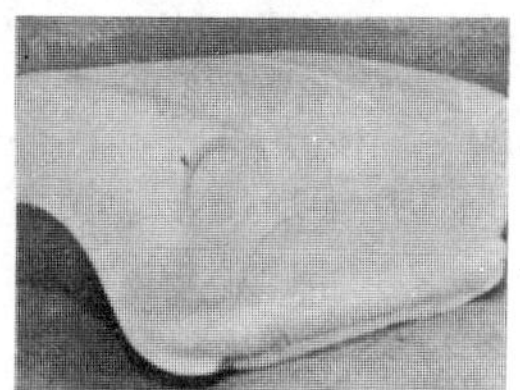
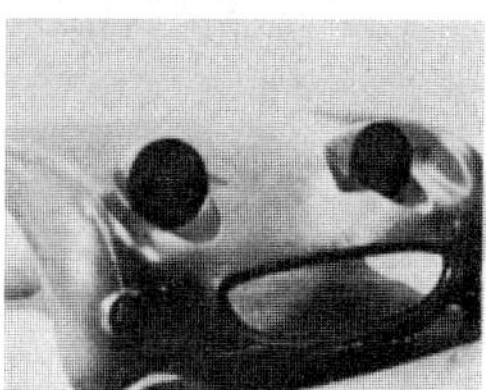
Fiberglass fronts for the Mini (left) and Mark I Sprite by Miller Racing Enterprises

Rovers and Rover 2000, Vauxhall Victor, MG/Austin 1100, Triumph Spitfire, GT 6, Herald, Vitesse and TR-series. Plans to shortly offer hardtops, windows and windshields for British sportscars and sedans. Free literature.

Miller Special Tools
Division of Utica Tool Co., Inc.
32615 Park Lane
Garden City, Michigan 48135

Special service tools for Chrysler Corporation cars including Cricket and Colt. Also carries hydraulic lifting equipment and safety stands. Free information.

Milne Bros.
1951 East Colorado
Pasadena, California 91107

Jeep parts and accessories include roll bars, tow bars, cage kits ($39.95), wide steel wheels, Armstrong and Gates tires, Whitco, Kayline, Warn, and Meyer accessories, service manuals, and rubber fender extension material for all Universal Jeep models at $1.50 a foot. Free price list.

Milodon Engineering Co.
7711 Ventura Canyon Avenue
Van Nuys, California 91402

Milodon's specialty is engine performance parts for drag cars. They offer a "VII Litre" aluminum engine block for the 426 Chrysler Hemi which is claimed to represent a savings of 130 pounds. For popular domestic engines there are 4-bolt main caps, precision gear drives, oil pump pickups, high

"VIII Litre" engine block from Milodon Engineering

volume oil pumps, cool cans, oil pump extensions, spark plug tube seals (for late Hemi heads), Hemi water fillers, fuel shut-off valves, high capacity oil pans, dry sump oil pans, windage trays, chrome rocker shafts, aluminum bronze valve guides, degree wheels and Ford C-6 transmission case supports. Catalog, $1.00.

Mini City
P.O. Box 1083
Rochester, New York 14603

Has complete line of high performance parts and cosmetic accessories for Minis. Fender flares are $34.00 a set of four; rubber hood clamps are $4.25 a pair; a locking gas cap is $4.50; a steel sump guard goes for $26.50, while headlamp stoneguards are $10.50 a pair. Spun aluminum blanks to replace headlights for competition are $2.95 each or $9.95 with chrome wire screen. Steel door stays to replace the retaining straps on both doors are $4.95 a pair, and a fly-off handbrake retails for $2.95. Other available accessories include bucket seats, complete dash panel replacement, full line of Smiths instruments, Smiths rear window defroster, carpeting, inside door handles, polished aluminum valve covers, velocity stacks, competition ignition equipment, an engine stabilizing kit, and Abarth or Stebro exhaust systems. There is a full line of British Leyland special tuning parts including fiberglass body parts, plexiglass windows, suspension and brake system parts, improved cooling, close-ratio gear sets, a limited slip differential, performance heads, cams, and clutches, and other mechanical goodies. To complete the line there is replacement Lucas electrical equipment; Lega, Speedwell, Cosmic and Minilite wheels; Goodyear, Semperit and Bridgestone tires; plus workshop manuals, parts lists and books on Mini modifications. Catalog, $1.00.

Mini Owners of America, Inc.
P.O. Box 2872-D
Pasadena, California 91105

Club is divided into seven sections as follows: Chicago area, 606 Herkimer Street, Joliet, Illinois 60435; Dayton, 2064 Norway Drive, Dayton, Ohio 45439; Los Angeles area, P.O. Box 2872-D, Pasadena, California 91105; New Jersey, c/o Lee Middleton, Whitenack Road, Far Hills, New Jersey 07931; San Francisco area, P.O. Box 2584, Menlo Park, California 94025; Seattle, SAMOA, 1610-40th, Seattle, Washington; Tucson, P.O. Box 4237, Tucson, Arizona 85717. Club activities include a monthly newsletter, *Mini News,* and events both social and technical in each area. There is a classified section for members, in the newsletter, and parts location plus technical advice available. Also jacket patches, decals, jewelry and badges. Yearly membership: $10.00; initial fee $5.00. For those outside a club area, yearly subscription is $3.00.

Mini Sport
7 Church Street
Padiham
Lancashire
England

Offers many versions of the Mini-Minor and Mini-Cooper engine as well as new gearboxes on an exchange basis or outright. Other products available are Tuftrided cranks, emergency fan belts, hood safety pins, rally and race car numbers, Salisbury limited-slip differentials, close-ratio gearboxes with either straight or helical gears, lightened flywheels, race and rally cams, heavy-duty oil pumps, competition clutches, final drive crown wheels and pinions, performance exhaust manifolds, sport cylinder heads, Weber carbs plus special inlet manifolds, air filters for Weber and SU carbs, Mini "Madadash" vinyl-finish dash kits, many suspension and brake components, rollbars made by John Aley to fit British road and competition cars, oil cooler kits, Mini sump guards, Mamba alloy road wheels, fender extenders for Minis and British Fords, Don Barrow illuminated map magnifiers, Cibie headlamps, Kangol crash helmets and harness safety belts, Rally seats, and a complete line of replacement fiberglass panels for Minis. Performance parts and fiberglass body parts are available for a number of other British cars including Fords, Spridgets, Austin/Morris 1100s and others. Mini Sport also offers many machine shop services including Tuftriding, shotpeening connecting rods, regrinding cranks, cylinder block reboring, flywheel lightening, engine balancing, etc. Catalog, $.75.

Mintun Fiberglass
1065 Memorex Drive
Santa Clara, California 95050

Under-dash consoles for VWs. Fiberglass consoles with space for gauges, radios, and switches, fit Bug, Super Beetle, Ghia and Variant. Color is black, tan, or white, and all models are priced at $22.95. Also handles other fiberglass parts for VW. Free literature.

Miracle Power Products Corporation
1101 Belt Line Street
Cleveland, Ohio 44109

Lubricants available include dry and wet graphite, moly gear lube, all weather grease, silicone spray, and similar products. Free literature.

Mitcham Motors
472 London Road
Mitcham
Surrey
England

Modified cylinder heads available on an exchange basis for popular British cars including B.L.M.C. "A" Series, Ford, Vauxhall, Triumph, and others. Nikki Twinchoke carbs with inlet manifold, air cleaner, and necessary linkages, available for B.L.M.C., Ford, Vauxhall Viva, Opel Kadett, VW and small Fiats. SU carb kits and modified cams are also in stock. Other items carried include leather-rimmed steering wheels, exhaust manifolds, and rally jackets. Machine shop services and the fitting of accessories are among the jobs done on the premises. Free information.

Mitchell
146 South Palm Avenue
Alhambra, California 91802

Makers of Caltone exhaust systems, headers, and mufflers. There are mufflers for popular foreign cars, VW and Porsche headers, Audi twin bullet mufflers, Blazer dual exhaust kits, Mini-pickup side pipes, and Pinto dual exhaust systems. Mitchell also has chrome tail pipes, Pinto and Vega headers, pipe components with precision bends, muffler blanks, and specialty hardware. Free information. Consult catalog at a local parts distributor or speed shop.

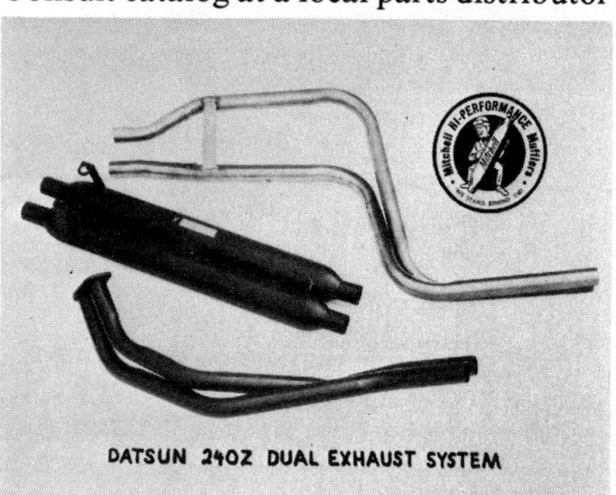

Datsun 240Z dual exhaust system by Mitchell

George M. Mitchell
Thrums-Cleish
Kincross
Scotland

Mr. Mitchell purchased the stock of the Jowett Company when they went out of business and can supply all Jowett Javelin and Jupiter spare parts. Also does Jowett restoration and rebuilding. Will ship parts anywhere in the world. Send international reply coupon with queries. Parts and price lists will be supplied.

The Shazam Cars. Remember Captain Marvel going down into an old abandoned subway station and saying "Shazam." That was the magic at the root of his super powers. The Shazam cars, produced in the immediate postwar era, had their own sort of magic that was every bit as mysterious. Straight-through pipes and lowering blocks, frenched headlights and a "necker's knob" on the steering wheel—those were the magic accessories that showed you were a contender in the midnight drag races down Main Street and a backseat Lothario to boot. And then Detroit got the message from overseas and began producing sports cars as well as the runty but stout-hearted Nash Metropolitan and the big, V-8-engined supercars that were to become so much a part of the American scene. Remember the D.A. haircut? Sneaking a smoke in the school parking lot? Getting instructions from some older kid on how to open a brassiere with one hand? Those were the years when cars became an intrinsic part of the American social scene and a driver's license was a ticket to nirvana.

1. *1947 Kaiser.* A serious contender in the early postwar era. Styling by the fabled "Dutch" Darrin.

2. *1949 Ford Sedan.* Mom and Dad bought one just as soon as they became available after the War. You put on straight-through pipes and tried downshifting to second gear at 60. It made so much noise that you hoped the guys would never discover that there was only a puny 6 under the hood.

3. *1953 Chevrolet Corvette.* Conceived as a GM dream car, the Corvette went into production and became the revered granddaddy of the big bad 'Vettes of today.

4. *1950 Oldsmobile 88.* This was the "racer's edge" way back when. With a "Rocket 88" engine and zoomy styling, an Olds 88 had class.

5. 1955 Chevrolet Bel Air. 1955 was a vintage year for Chevrolet. Cars of that year were completely restyled with an egg crate grille like a Ferrari and a V-8 engine with enough power to get up to 60 in 9 seconds flat. Just try it in your new Chevrolet and see how much progress we've made.

6. 1955 T-Bird. Maybe it wasn't a real sports car. But the two-seater T-Bird of 1955-57 was a true postwar classic and still is. What's the word—Thunderbird!

7. 1960 Nash Metropolitan. The Austin-engined Metro was one of the first American attempts to compete with "them funny little furrin' cars" for the economy sweepstakes. Sales were good and the indomitable Metro was very much a part of the American scene.

8. 1956 Chrysler 300B. The Chrysler 300s were the archetypical super cars of their era—clean and bold with more horsepower than the competition.

8.

Roger Mitchell
8361 Louise Drive
Denver, Colorado 80221

Chevrolet cars and parts. Specializes in 1955-57 hardtops and Nomads. Send a stamped, self-addressed envelope with query.

Model A Ford Club of America (Model A Ford)
Box 2564
Pomona, California 91766

The Club, which claims to be the largest car club in the world devoted to one make of automobile, has chapters all over the U.S. and in many foreign countries. Each chapter schedules its own activities, including tours, meets, and gymkhanas, while there is a national convention and car show in even-numbered years. The principal Club publication, *The Restorer* is published bi-monthly and includes a free classified advertisement service to members. Among the products sold by the Club are lapel pins, license plate frames, enamel badges, decals and patches. Yearly dues: $5.00 U.S., $6.00 overseas. Additional family memberships are $1.00.

Model A Restorer's Club (Model A Ford)
P.O. Box 1930 A
Dearborn, Michigan 48121

MARC is divided into local regions with each region having its own activities. There is a national membership meeting in March and a Trophy Meet in the summer. The bi-monthly Club magazine is *Model 'A' News* which carries news, technical information, and advertisements (free to members). Yearly dues: $6.50.

Model A's and Things
432 West Michigan Avenue
Port Washington
Wisconsin 53074

Most everything for Model As. Rebuilt Zenith carbs are $22.50 exchange. New Tillotsons are $16.75. Rebuilt starter drive, $4.25; rebuilt distributor, $14.95 exchange; intake manifold, $18.60; exhaust manifold, $19.25; ignition coil with bracket, $3.95; pair of cowl lights, complete, $25.95; replacement 6V Ahoogah horn, $12.95. Many small items

1931 Model A restored with parts from Model A's & Things

such as speedometer decal set, $.75; bumper clamp paint, $.85; door handle pad, $.30; grease fittings, $.18 to $.80; engine green spray paint, $1.30 and distributor cam wrench, $.80. Catalog, $.25. Send a stamped, self-addressed envelope for list of NOS parts available.

Model T Ford Club International (Model T Ford)
c/o The Allerton
711 North Michigan Avenue
Chicago, Illinois 60611

An annual tour, annual restoration contest, photo contest, and the annual banquet meeting held each January, are some Club features. Publication is the bi-monthly *Model T Times* magazine which carries technical and service data along with classified advertising and information on Club activities. There is a technical staff which will respond to specific queries. There are local chapters of the Model T

Ford Club around the country. Yearly dues: $8.00, $9.00 outside U.S. Associate membership for spouse is $2.50 a year.

The Model T Ford Club of America (Model T Ford)
P.O. Box 711
Oceanside, California 92054

Founded in 1955, the Club now has over 6,000 members and a chain of almost 50 chapters in most states. Each year an annual meeting is held in January at Los Angeles. There is also an annual tour (probably to Dearborn in 1974 and San Diego in 1975). The Club's bi-monthly magazine *The Vintage Ford,* is noted for its quality. Yearly dues: $9.50; $11.50 overseas.

Modena Sports Car Service Ltd.
770 11th Avenue
New York, New York 10019

Lamborghini distributor.

Modern Classic Motors
201 West 2nd Street
Reno, Nevada 89501

Ferrari distributors.

Moderntools Corporation
P.O. Box 407
Woodside, New York 11377

Precision tools such as dial calipers, vernier calipers, height gauges, and centering microscopes. Write for literature and price lists.

R. K. Mogey
76 King George Road
Warren, New Jersey 07060

Makes speedster type body, to fit Model T chassis, out of ¾″ waterproof, plastic-coated plywood. Framing is selected hardwood, steel reinforced. Dash is formica. Body complete in primer is $495.00, or $345.00 in kit form. Double bucket seats are $150.00 and come with trim installed but no upholstery. Set of four fenders in primer is $240.00. Classic speedster-style heavy gauge steel, 13-gallon gas tanks, are $145.00 with brackets. Also available is brass and aluminum stock. Write for further information.

Mohawk Rubber Co.
1235 Second Avenue
Akron, Ohio 44309

Makers of bias-ply and belted tires in many patterns. For performance use the Super Mag 60- and 70-series tires and the Ultissimo Costeel steel-belted 78-series tires will be of interest. Free literature.

Monroe Auto Equipment Co.
Monroe, Michigan 48161

Monroe makes O.E.M., heavy-duty, overload, air adjustable and RV shocks. Models available for most domestic and import cars, and for trucks and motor homes. Also makes 70/30, 90/10, 45/55, 75/25 high riser and 50/50 shocks for drag racing, oval track vehicles, and circuit racing. Catalog, $1.00.

Montgomery Ward
619 West Chicago Avenue
Chicago, Illinois 60607

Wards offers tools, tires, seat covers, batteries, tune-up equipment, radios, tape players, exhaust system components, headers, alloy wheels, shocks, and rebuilt parts for most American cars along with the VW. Rebuilt engines go for as little as $250.00 (1957-59 Mopar 6), while short block assemblies carry an exchange price of $175.00 and up. Wards also lists pistons and gaskets, remanufactured cranks, rebuilt carbs, electric fuel pumps, alternators, starter drive assemblies, voltage regulators, solenoids and switches, rebuilt generators and starters, water pumps, radiators, remanufactured auto transmissions and U-joints. There is a complete listing of replacement front end parts, wheel bearings, drum and disc brake components, and rod and main crankshaft bearings, along with some oil pumps, timing chain and sprocket kits, overload springs, air levelers, steering stabilizers, convertible tops, pickup truck bed covers, air filters, Fenton alloy wheels, Cyclone and ScatCat headers and header mufflers, and Hurst shifters. Wards Powr-Kraft hand tools are known for good value, and there are also specialty tools, hydraulic jacks, wheel balancers, and lubrication equipment. For RV enthusiasts Wards stocks bolt-on and equalizing hitches, utility trailers, car-top carriers, trailer jacks, jalousie windows for campers, transmission and engine oil coolers, auxiliary gas tanks for pickup trucks, trailer brake controllers, free-wheeling hubs, trailer johns and sinks, stoves and refrigerators, LP gas appliances, 12-volt lighting fixtures, RV air conditioners, van spare tire carriers, trailer safety skids, pickup truck camper stabilizers and tool boxes, bicycle and motorcycle carriers, and compasses. For the younger members of the family, of any age, there are crash helmets, mini bikes and trikes, go-karts and kart accessories. Wards least expensive helmet, meeting all current Z90 standards, is $12.99. If you wander off into another section of the 1,200 page Wards catalog, or for that matter in a different area at your nearest Wards store, you can find welding equipment, air compressors, power shop tools, and other things to dream about when your rich uncle dies. As you may know, the Wards catalog is theoretically available to all but actually rather hard to obtain. Unless you are a regular customer, your best strategy is to make a pest of yourself at the catalog counter of your local Wards store until the lady gives you one to get rid of you.

The Montreal Volvo Owners' Club (Volvo)
Box 38, Main P.O.
Montreal, Canada

Has monthly meetings and publishes a newsletter each month containing news, information, and technical tips. Can supply owner's manuals and back issues of the newsletter. Yearly dues: $6.00; entry fee, $2.00.

Moog Automotive, Inc.
P.O. Box 7224
St. Louis, Missouri 63177

Replacement chassis components, coil springs, shock absorbers, and power steering parts for current and older domestic cars, and some foreign models. Moog also has load-compensating coil springs for cars and trucks, single leaf helper springs, coil lifters, and special chassis tools. Consult catalog at parts house.

Ed Moran
3300 Netherland
Riverdale, New York 10463

Sells owners' manuals and sales catalogs for many foreign cars of fairly recent vintage and some earlier American makes. Also has issues of vintage car club publications. Large stamped, self-addressed envelope will bring list.

Mor-Drop Axles
600-29th Avenue
Oakland, California 94601

Dropped axles for Fords, Chevrolets and pickups. Fords are available from Ts and As to Twin I-beam on modern pickup. Chev and GMC pickup to 1957. "T" axle is $20.00

exchange price plus $30.00 core charge. 1942-48 Ford is $14.00 plus $15.00 core charge. Twin I-beam is $50.00 plus $50.00. Chev is $25.00 plus $30.00 core charge to 1954, $25.00 plus $50.00 core charge to 1957. Early Ford chromed axle is $55.00 extra. Chev, late Ford and GMC are $65.00 extra chromed. Many other axles carried in stock and prices quoted on request. Free price list.

More Opel
Box 15143C
Seattle, Washington 98115

The Compleat Opel for street or racing use. Speed accessories available for Manta, Ascona, Kadett and GT. Accessories include frame strengtheners, engine and fuel tank skid pans, plexiglass windows, fiberglass body parts, roll bars and roll cages, front and rear spoilers, heavy-duty motor and transmission mounts, sport and rally front and rear springs, Watts linkage for rear axle, racing lower control arms, front and rear sway bars, Koni shocks, quick steering kits, and complete suspension kits. Modified driveline components include clutches, flywheels, driveshafts, close- and wide-ratio 4- and 5-speed transmission kits, ring and pinion carriers, and limited slip differentials. For go-power, More Opel offers dynotune kits, and hop-up kits in mini, midi and maxi forms. Also has racing versions of 1,100 cc, 1,900 cc and 2,000 cc Opel engines. Other accessories consist of alloy wheels up to 8″ wide (Europa Racing Wheel available in any width and any offset), adjustable brake pressure regulators, competition brake equalizers, front and rear vented disc brake assemblies, sport or racing brake pads and linings, cams and valvetrain gear, Group-2 cylinder heads, dry sump lubrication systems, headers, Weber and Solex carbs with manifolds, Solex carb parts, air filters, oil cooler kits, custom steering wheels, airfoil windshield wipers, racing side mirrors, stripe kits, rally light bars, Cibie lights, Halda and Heuer timing equipment, competition seat belts, Recaro seats and Bell helmets. Dynotune kit for 1968-72 1,500 cc and 1,900 cc engines is $12.50. Superkit with dual Solex carbs, sport camshaft, heavy-duty valve springs, and headers—adding about 40 hp to stock Opel engine—costs $515.00. The sport suspension kit for Opel 1900, Manta and Ascona is $214.60, while the racing suspension kit is $333.35. Catalog, $1.00.

Charles Morford
1220 West 4th, Dept. A
Davenport, Iowa 52802

Doing business under the name "Reprints Unlimited," Mr. Morford offers photostatic copies of hard-to-find manuals, such as the 1916 Briscoe owners manual ($2.00), 1931 Rockne owners manual ($2.50), 1920 Case owners manual ($3.00), and 1916-28 Chev parts book ($3.00). He also has some bumper stickers of interest to old car fans, such as one reading, "Owned by a little old lady who beat hell out of it." Free information.

Morgan Car Club, Inc.
(Morgan)
8600 16th Street (B-2)
Silver Springs, Maryland 20910

The Club has an annual meet in the Pocono Mountains (Peter Morgan himself was there in 1972), and other social meetings. Along with publishing a monthly newsletter, *The Rough Rider,* the Club maintains a list of Morgan parts sources and a membership roster. Yearly dues: $10.00; family membership, $15.00.

Morgan Motor Company
Pickersleigh Road
Malvern Link
Worcestershire
England

Mr. D.D. Morrill of the Plus Four Club (see separate listing) writes to say that, although there are no authorized Morgan Parts Dealers in the U.S., the Morgan factory can still supply many necessary items. The Plus Four Club keeps some of the more popular parts in stock and can provide them to members at a slight discount.

Morgan Plus Four Club (Morgan)
c/o Lily Lavender,
Membership Chairman
447 Wren Drive
Los Angeles, California 90065

Devotees of the anachronistic and superb Morgan are an international group, though social activities and regularly scheduled competitive events are confined to California only. Other benefits of Club membership are a monthly newsletter, *The Format,* a spares registry "containing many strange and wonderful Morgan spares available to members only," technical advice through the technical chairman, and an annual roster. Available-to-members items include badges, pins, decals, a reference notebook containing past technical articles printed in the newsletter, and the *Morgan Manual.* One must be a registered owner of a Morgan to join, although associate membership is granted to some non-Morgan-owners by the Club board of directors. Yearly dues: California residents, $10.00 plus first-year initiation fee of $10.00. Non-Californians, $7.50.

Morgan Sports Car Club (Morgan)
c/o C.J. Smith
23 Seymour Avenue
Worcester
England

Close to the mecca at Malvern Link, this Club is headed by P.H.G. Morgan, Esq., himself. Trials, rallies, and hill climbs are on the list of competitive events, and members even have their own racing team. There is a monthly newsletter, and a very interesting bi-monthly magazine entitled *Miscellany.* A recent issue of the magazine carried a good number of articles on Morgans in competition and a story of a club member who traveled from Capetown to Rhodesia in a Mog pulling a fair-sized trailer. Not for the faint at heart or weak at stomach. Yearly dues: $5.00, due on April 1. After October 1 dues are $2.50 for the rest of the year.

Morgan Three-Wheeler Club (Morgan Three-Wheelers)
c/o Brian Clutterbuck
Elm Cottage
Clock Lane
Bickenhill
Warwickshire
England

Club activities include sprint meetings, sponsorship of some vintage racing events and hill climbs, and social meetings. Club publications are a monthly *Bulletin,* collection of *Bulletin* articles *(The Best of the Bulletin),* a catalog history of Morgan Trikes *(The Three-Wheeler),* and an annual membership roster. Services include a formal technical advice procedure, the provision of spare parts (many new and used parts are available directly through the Club), and a car register. Yearly dues: $6.00 for Morgan owners, about $4.80 for associate members who do not own Morgans. The Club has about 40 U.S. members at present.

Dewitt Morley
Box 1194
Rochester, New York 14603

Mr. Morley is a machinist who specializes in working on antique and special-interest cars. At present he is limiting his activities due to lack of shop space, but those in the Rochester area might want to consult him.

Moroso Performance Sales Inc.
737 Canal Street, Building 23
Stamford, Connecticut 06902

For Pro Stock or Modified racers, as well as for the stoplight Grand Prix boys, Moroso offers a complete line of racing products. Among the items listed are deep sump oil pans and oval track oil pans for many U.S. cars, high-output oil pumps for Chev engines, extended oil pick-ups, high voltage batteries of lightweight construction, lifter valley oil baffles, Muncie transmission gear sets, slick shifted sliders and hardened synchro hubs for Muncie and Borg-Warner 4-speeds, trick front springs, mechanical tachs,

Some products from Moroso Performance Sales Inc.

mechanical shut-offs (rev limiters) along with dual drive adapters, degreed harmonic balancers, lightweight water pumps, deep groove racing pulleys, cool cans, fuel block Y-kits, quick-change cam timers, lightweight fiberglass hoods and scoops, heat treated spider gears, heavy duty differentials—limited slip—for GM cars including Corvette, and the usual decals and T-shirts. Catalog, $1.00.

Morris Register
(Pre-1940 Morris)
28 Levita House
Chalton Street
London N.W.1
England

The many events run by this Register and its affiliates each year include informal social gatherings, known as "Noggins and Natters," plus two major gatherings and an annual run to Brighton. There is a monthly newsletter and quarterly journal, as well as a formal program to disseminate information on restorations and spare parts availability. Information manuals on early Morris 8s, 10s and Minors, plus a collection of road tests, are sold by the Register. Yearly dues: $6.00 for the first year, $4.80 thereafter. Associate members who do not own a prewar Morris vehicle must pay a further entry fee of $2.50. Family membership is an additional $2.40.

Moss Motors, Ltd.
P.O. Box MG
5775 Dawson Avenue
Goleta, California 93017

If you own a T-series MG or MG-A, this is where it's at. Moss carries an extensive line of MG hard parts and useful accessories. Major assemblies are depicted in their catalogs in disassembled form and each little part is numbered and priced, so that, for instance, if you are looking for a thingamajig in your TC's rear axle, you can match it up with the catalog piece and see that it is No. 265 170, a silentbloc bushing, and that the price for two is $3.25.

Moss carries not only an extensive line of engine, power-train and chassis parts, but also those miscellaneous body and interior items which are so difficult to find. There are wood parts, rubber parts, door parts, lock sets, interior piping, medallions, hub caps, and just about anything else required to restore an MG to pristine original condition. For those who prefer the pzazz to the pristine, there are fiberglass body panels, polished aluminum valve covers, engine-turned "facia" and other panels, Brooklands racing screens, antenna bumpers, windwings and luggage racks.

For ageing enthusiasts who no longer appreciate the wind-in-the-face and cold toes feeling, there are fiberglass hardtops and a Moss heater kit for $60.00.
Other items featured are replacement Tompkins steering kits for TCs ($32.50) and a complete selection of Whitworth wrenches and other MG-like tools. A tool kit with the essential spanners plus hammer, screwdriver and pliers goes for $13.65. A 25-piece tap and die set is $49.00 and tyre irons similar to the original are available at only $1.25 the pair. There are also some Austin-Healey parts. T-series catalog, $.50, MG-A catalog, $.50.

Motor
250 West 55th Street
New York, New York 10019

Annual books on domestic and foreign car, and truck repair. Free literature.

Motorola Automotive Products
9401 West Grand Avenue
Franklin Park, Illinois 60131

Tachometers, transistorized ignition systems, and alternators. Motorola also makes many small electronic components and brackets. Consult catalog at parts house.

Motor Racing Equipment, Inc.
1412 East Borchard Avenue
Santa Ana, California 92705

Among the racing and rally accessories offered are Bell helmets, Nomex and Fypro clothing, Moon air density gauges, Maserati air horns, Carello lights, Aeroquip hoses and fittings, Racemark bucket seats, oil coolers for British racing cars, Stewart-Warner and Smiths instruments, B&B racing clutches, Girling and Lockheed brake parts, Lucas fuel injection units, Weber carbs, Formula Car wings, Ampep rod end bearings, Moon durometers (rubber hardness testers), Varley aircraft-type batteries, Koni double adjustable shocks, Jones-Motorola and Smiths tachs, Dunlop "bump steer" gauges and tire pyrometers, Graviner on-board fire prevention systems, Ferodo brake pads, pit signal boards, VW shift levers and dash panel kits, VW Bus fiberglass deck lids with scoops, Porsche and VW aluminum oil sumps, VW Beetle front spoilers, foreign car headers, Datsun 240Z and Fiat 124 spoilers, Pinto fiberglass hoods with built-in scoops, and AMCO accessories. Also offers machine shop services, chassis alignment, Hewland gearbox overhaul, Lola chassis parts, and has in stock or can obtain parts for every current racing engine. Catalog, $1.50.

Motorsport East
P.O. Box 261
Owings Mills, Maryland 21117

Renault high performance equipment. For the R8/R10 there is a tubular combination intake and exhaust manifold with installation kit, designed to take a Weber carb, which sells for $73.88. The Weber 28/36 dual throat carb is $88.06. Modified distributors are $40.81. A 9:1 compression ratio ported and polished cylinder head, with special valves and heavy-duty valve springs is $111.68. High-performance camshafts are $73.88 for the type 688 engine and $79.46 for the type 810 engine. Many other R8/R10 performance components are available including piston-liner kits, Allard superchargers, headers, increased capacity oil pans, S.E.S. electronic carb kits ($117.35), Gordini quick-ratio steering boxes, Stiffer coil springs, competition oil coolers and pumps, heavy-duty engine and transaxle mount kits, Hermes

Aerofoil spoilers, front sway bars, Spax and Koni shocks, Gordini brake pads, roll bars, free-flow exhausts, 5-speed Gordini transaxles and Gordini clutch components, limited slip differentials ($358.00), and optional axle ratios. For the 4CV, Dauphine and Dauphine Gordini there are reground cams, increased displacement kits, free-flow Devil exhaust systems and carb conversion kits. For the R16TS, not originally sold in the U.S., there are a number of performance components listed. Hard parts and a complete line of hop-up items are also available for the R12, R15, R17 and Lotus Europa. Accessory items include Gotti mag wheels, Weber carbs, headers, and sway bars. Shop services include engine rebuilding for R12, R15 and Lotus Europa. Complete speed components available for the Hemi-807 Renault/Europa engine can raise horsepower to 175. As a service, the company maintains a register for Renault R8 Gordini vehicles. Parts and technical information for the R8 and R12 Gordini are available. Complete R12 Gordinis can be imported by the company, although they are only legal for off-highway use. Catalog, $.50.

Motor Wheel Corp.
1600 North Larch Street
Lansing, Michigan 48914

O.E.M. wheels for most American cars and light trucks of fairly recent vintage. Wheel and hub groups for mobile homes and travel trailers. High-flotation trailer wheels. Special mag-type wheels in 14″, and 15″ and 16.5″ sizes for most American cars. Styles are Spyder, Magnum 500, Rally, and Multi-Style 100 and 200 for light trucks. Also chrome wheel nuts. Full line of brake drums, hubs and disc rotors for American cars and light trucks. Principal parts catalog contains excellent section on proper mounting and demounting of mag-type wheel, also has template for determining 5-lug bolt circle size. Free literature.

Mr. Bug
P.O. Box 11728
Santa Ana
California 92711

National sales representative for J. Miller & Co., American Automotive Products, J C Enterprises, Hamman Tool Co., Stellings & Hellings, Sig Erson Racing Cams, L & J Fiberglass, RC Company, and Globe Automotive Products. Free literature on the products of each company.

MRE, Inc.
1412-R Borchard Avenue
Santa Ana, California 92705

Foreign car accessories plus servicing and parts for competition gearboxes and aerospace-type fittings. Custom wound coil springs are $75.00 a pair. A Moon air density gauge with box for gauge and spark plugs is $80.00. Small fittings in anodized aluminum alloy, steel, and stainless steel are available in many sizes. MRE is a distributor for Stewart-Warner and Smiths instruments, Bell helmets, Maserati air horns, Carrello lights, Aeroquip brake lines, English Automotive Products B&B racing clutches; Can-Am and Formula car wings, Weber carbs, Varley aircraft type batteries, Koni shocks, Ferodo brake pads, Heuer timers, Abarth exhausts, and AMCO accessories. Another aspect of this company's business is service and parts distribution for competition engines and gearboxes. They will rebuild Hewland and Weismann transmissions, including Magnafluxing, and offer parts and service for the following racing engines: Bartz, Bolthoff, BRM,

Cosworth, Falconer-Dunn, Foltz, Hart, Lotus, Lucas, Morand, MRE, Piper, Racing Services, Repco, Traco, Vegantune, and Webster. They also offer machine shop services; chassis alignment and bump steering, chassis and suspension parts for Lola Graviner on-board fire extinguishing systems; fiberglass spoilers for Datsun, Fiat, Mazda and other small cars; a fiberglass deck lid with scoops for the VW Bus ($59.95); Porsche and VW aluminum oil sumps; books about racing; and Ampep rod end bearings finish out the list. Catalog, $2.00. A Hewland gearbox workshop manual, $5.00.

Mr. Gasket
4566 Spring Road
Cleveland, Ohio 44131

Mr. Gasket's extensive line of performance and cosmetic components covers most American and many foreign vehicles. Items are also sold under the brand names of Hays, Andeck and DC Ignition (see separate listings). Mr. Gasket specialties include all gaskets, rocker arm gear, cams for domestic vehicles, valvetrain components, stock and modified synchro rings for T-10 Borg-Warner and Muncie 4-speed gear boxes, timing chain and sprocket sets, power pulleys, oil pans and windage trays, fuel line fittings, chrome moly clutch linkages for 1955-57 Chevs and 1967-72 Camaros, cool cans, carb adapter kits to adapt Holley and Carter AFB carbs to various manifolds, Holley and Rochester carb performance parts, velocity stacks and air cleaners, hood and deck locks, burglar alarms and anti-theft devices, wheel adapters, clear plastic valve covers and finned aluminum valve covers, mechanical fuel pumps, aluminum quick change rear covers for GM cars, race quality bolts and nuts, fiberglass and aluminum flex fans, chrome oil breathers, air filters and fuel line kits, an extensive line of aerosol sprays for lubrication and degreasing, touch-up paint, quick shifters for domestic 4-speed boxes plus VWs, air shocks and special shocks for drag racing, traction bars, pinion snubbers, front and rear lift kits, shock extension kits and electric tachometers. Catalog, $1.00.

Mr. Roadster
6918 Simpson Avenue
North Hollywood
California 91605

Street rod freaks will drool over Mr. Roadster's new 1923 T aluminum frames ($295.00), especially the version fitted out to mount a Jag rear end and coil shock springs ($325.00). Other figments of the street rodder's fancy are 1926-32 space frames, radius rods and dropped axles, axle plates, Jag suspension conversion kits (front and rear), disc brake plates to convert Jag rear ends to quick-change Airheart discs, roadster headers, wire wheels for Ford and Chev spindles, torsion bars, leaf springs, windshield kits, polished brass radiators ($275.00 with transmission cooler), brass steering wheels with wood rims, roadster headlights and light brackets, disc brake kits, blower drives, hydraulic gas linkages, and Weber carbs for street engines. For 1953-56 Ford pickup trucks, Mr. Roadster sells wide 'glass rear and front fenders ($70.00 a fender), fiberglass front splash pans, and aluminum or brass polished and finned rear end covers. Fiberglass hoods and tailgates should be ready as you read this. Other fiberglass bodies from the fertile Mr. Roadster molds are 1923 and 1927 T roadster, and 1932 Bantam roadster. Also the ubiquitous Deuce roadster bodies. Free information.

John Muir Publications
P.O. Box 613
Santa Fe, New Mexico 07501

VW service manual, *How to Keep Your Volkswagen Alive: A Manual of Step-by-Step Repair for the Compleat Idiot,* $5.50.

Murray Motor Co.
Box 546
Colby, Kansas 67701

Mr. Murray, a former De Soto/Plymouth dealer, has many NOS Chrysler parts dating back to 1934. His prices for parts are those last listed in the Chrysler parts price books. Send a stamped, self-addressed envelope with queries.

Myers Model A Shop
4808 North Seneca
Wichita, Kansas 67204

Duplicate wood parts for all models of the "A". Parts are made from oak. Parts sheets clearly show all assemblies in question. Send a stamped, self-addressed envelope for parts sheets.

Nance Speed Equipment
444 West 29th Street
Wichita, Kansas 67204

Sprint car, drag racing and performance street vehicle accessories. Complete fiberglass sprint car body, $225.00; '32 Ford coupe one-piece body, $115.00; '30 Model A Victoria fiberglass body, $115.00; aluminum wrap around bucket seat, $45.00 without upholstery; fiberglass bucket seat with upholstery, $58.50; 19″ wide race car radiator, price on request; dry sump oil tank for Sprint car, POR. Also has Clifford manifolds for 6-cylinder Ford and Chev; Holley carbs; Mallory distributors; Vertex magnetos; many popular high performance camshafts; wheel centers and blanks for do-it-yourself constructers; Chevy race car headers; many Sprint car components; steering wheels for Sprints and Midgets; steering units by Erlbacher, Schroeder and Ross; Lakewood bell housings; CAE in and out gearboxes; Airheart disc brake assemblies; heavy duty clutch and transmission parts; Halibrand rear ends; drop center or straight solid front axle assemblies; Sprint car, Super or Modified frame kits; and many other chassis components. Catalog, $1.00.

Narrangansett Restoration Co.
P.O. Box 36
Kingston, Rhode Island 02881

Parts for Lincoln Continental and Lincoln Zephyr, along with electrical system components for all early cars. New 1940-41 fuel pumps, $9.50; carb rebuilding kit, $6.00; 1940-41 repro air cleaners, $75.00; electric fuel pump kits, $45.00; 1941-48 spark plug wire kits, $17.50; kingpin sets, $13.00; engine gasket sets for Zephyr and Custom 1936-48, $20.00; and Continental and Zephyr colors—laquer or enamel—$22.50. Other parts include brake system components, ignition parts, rubber products, exhaust systems, cooling system components, hydraulic window and convertible top cylinders, trim pieces, service manuals and small body parts. Also has Continental and Zephyr interior rug kits. Electrical components for antique and classic cars include wiring diagrams for cars from the 1900's to 1960 ($1.00), automotive wire loom, neoprene tubing, Greenfield metal conduit, heat-shrink tubing, braid-covered and lacquered vacuum and air hoses, custom battery cables (will duplicate original patterns), solderless terminals, and electrical wiring in various colors and gauges. Complete custom wiring components for Continental, Zephyr and 1946-48 Lincoln. Harnesses available for such early cars as Auburn, L-29 Cord, Ford Model T and A, Lincoln K and KB and prewar Buick, Cadillac, DeSoto, Dodge, and Airflow. Also has harnesses for some early Pontiacs, Oldsmobiles, Studebakers, Mercurys, Pierce-Arrows, and many early Packards including 1940 Packard Darrin. Harnesses, lights, wiring and some switches for MG T-series, and Jaguar XK. Many types of upholstery material, leather, headliner and carpeting available by the yard. Will do complete restorations for a basic labor charge of $12.00 an hour. Specializes in custom upholstery and carpeting. Free information.

The Nash Car Club of America (Nash, Rambler, Jeffrey, Ajax, Lafayette, Nash-Healey, Metropolitan, Hudson, Jeffrey and Nash Trucks)
635 Lloyd Street
Hubbard, Ohio 44425

Sponsors annual national meet plus numerous regional meets and get-togethers. Publishes bi-monthly, *The Nash Times,* containing technical information, restoration tips, and a question and answer column. Maintains a library for members' use, has parts locator service, and has some projects for parts remanufacture. Yearly dues: $5.50 U.S., $6.50 foreign.

Doug Nash Racing
36360 Ecorse Road
Romulus, Michigan 48174

High performance transmissions and accessories. Carries parts for Muncie, Ford T&C, Mopar-New Process and Borg-Warner T-10 and Super T-10 transmissions. Has parts to modify transmissions for heavy duty or competition use. Pro/Shift Conversion Kits available for these 4-speed transmissions include hardened or "blueprinted" input shaft, second and third gears, sliding sleeves and solid hubs. Complete Pro/Shift competition transmission assemblies and new lightweight quick change transmissions also available. Free information.

National Abarth Register (Fiat-Abarth and Simca-Abarth)
c/o Peter C. Linsky
9910 S.W. North Dakota Street
Tigard, Oregon 97223

This recent group plans a yearly registry of Abarths on the North American continent. Listing of cars will be by type so that owners of similar vehicles can contact each other. Requirements for joining are current ownership of an Abarth, in any condition, and there will be free space for classified advertisements by owner-members in the Registry. Membership fees are not fixed as yet (they will probably be about $5.00), so those interested are asked to send a letter describing their cars to Mr. Linsky, and he promises to send details on the Registry, plus a questionnaire in return.

National Automotive Service
P.O. Box 10465
San Diego, California 92110

Annual on car repair. Free information.

Naylor Brothers
Airedale Garage
Hollins Hill
Esholt
Shipley
Yorkshire BD17 7QN
England

Specialists in restoration and component remanufacture for all T-series MGs. Complete wooden frames or any individual wood parts for all T-series. Also aluminum body parts, wire wheel hubs and brake drums, and some mechanical components. Price list free.

Don Neale
Box 67
Gabriels, New York 12939

Special-interest car parts for cars from the 1920s to the 1940s. Will also custom build exhaust systems for vintage cars. Offers complete car restorations and sells antique, classic, and special-interest cars. Send a stamped, self-addressed envelope with queries.

Neal Products
4960 Naples Place
San Diego, California 92110

Neal offers hydraulic clutch linkages for VW and Corvair ($49.95), hydraulic throttle controls ($59.95), hydraulically-actuated steering brakes ($69.50), polished aluminum gas tanks with capacities from 3½ to 9 gallons, solid motor mounts for VW, and brake and clutch pedal assemblies without master cylinders. Catalog, $1.00.

Nederlandsche V.W. Brillenvereniging (VW)
c/o W. J. Nieboer
Laan v.d.
Vrijheid 162
Groningen
Netherlands

This is a club devoted solely to pre-1953 (i.e. split-window) Beetles. The "brillen" in the club title means a pair of spectacles according to Mr. Paul Harris of the British Volkswagen Owner's Club. There was no time to contact Mr. Nieboer before publication of this book. However, serious split-window enthusiasts looking for parts or sympathy are advised to contact their Dutch brethren.

David Newell
1481 Hamrick Lane
Hayward, California 94544

Mr. Newell, who is president of the Corvair Society of America, has supplied some of the information about Corvairs in this book. He deals in Corvair parts and literature, as well as complete cars, and knows whereof he deals. Send a stamped, self-addressed envelope with query.

New Era Products
4480 Broadview Road
Cleveland, Ohio 44109

Burglar prevention systems and tune-up equipment. The Auto-Guard electronic protector works by isolating the ignition coil so that an engine cannot be started even if it is hot-wired. New Era tune-up items include a power timing light, engine analyzer, dwell/tach unit and 5-in-1 electronic tester. Free literature.

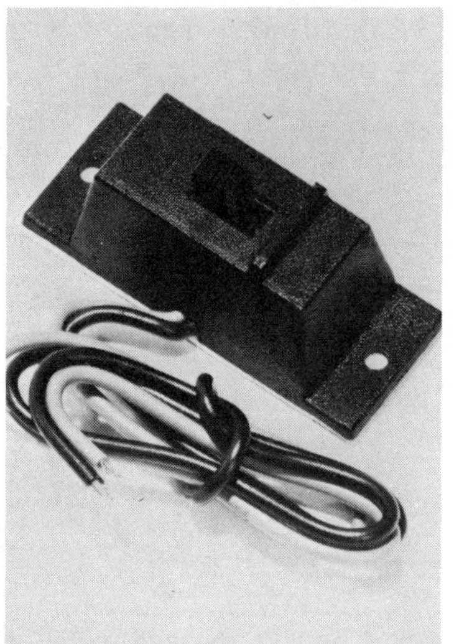

New Era Products Model AG-100 Auto Guard burglar prevention device

Newman & Altman, Inc., Standard Surplus Division
407 West Sample Street
South Bend, Indiana 46621

The Newman & Altman team of Avanti fame have also acquired some of the parts stock of Studebaker-Packard and offer components for cars 1946-66. Their catalog lists new short blocks, exhaust system parts, parts books, owners' manuals and front end suspension and steering parts. A replacement block assembly for the 232 V-8, fitted to 1951-54 Studebaker cars and 1954 Stude trucks, lists for $185.00. Other short block assemblies are priced at $225.00 to $445.00. Free information.

Newman & Altman's Avanti II

David Newman (Camshafts) & Co.
Farnborough Way
Farnborough
Kent
England

Performance cams and cylinder heads for British cars and VWs. Also has cams for Simca, Renault, Fiat, Volvo, Toyota, and Alfa. Most cams are available with various lifts and durations. Cams and cylinder heads are sold outright or on an exchange basis. Free catalog.

NHK Spring Co. Ltd.
1-3-6 Uchisaiwaicho
Chiyodaku
Tokyo
Japan

Coil and leaf springs, torsion bars and special springs for Japanese cars. The U.S. office for this Japanese concern is at Room no. 203-205, 23300 Greenfield Road, Oak Park, Michigan 48237. Free information to jobbers.

Nickey Chevrolet
4501 Irving Park Road
Chicago, Illinois 60641

Nickey is a Chevrolet dealer famous for selling high-performance and racing cars off the floor. Their version of a Camaro comes with either a 427 cu. in. 430 hp engine, or with a 454 cu. in. engine developing up to 450 hp. The car comes with a 4-speed Muncie transmission, power front disc brakes, heavy-duty radiator, Positraction, and special modified suspension. Similar performance versions of the

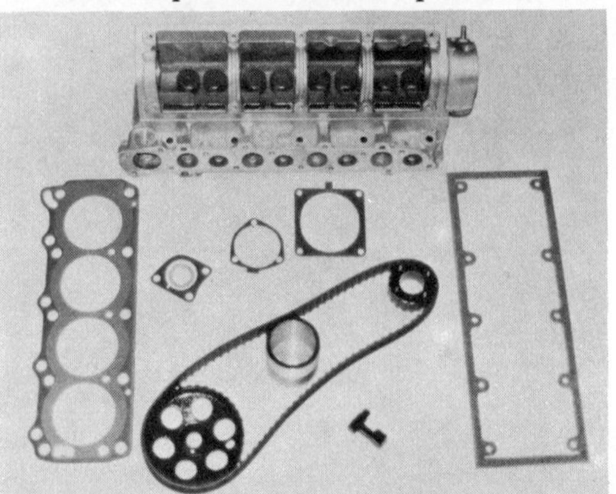

Nickey Chevrolet Vinegarroom Vega conversion kit includes cylinder head, water pump gear, and gaskets

Chevelle, Nova, and Corvette are offered. The company's Vinegarroon Vega kit, claiming a horsepower boost of over 40 percent, features a complete cylinder head with valves, cam, springs and lifters; special water pump hub; degreed cam gear, cam belt tensioning tool and all gaskets. The kit is advertised as being completely street legal and the exchange price is $149.95. Other offerings include a full line of Factory high-performance parts; TRW cams, pistons, and valve gear; Holley carb/manifold combos; Accel ignition kits; Air Lift springs; Arrow and Stewart-Warner instruments; Lakewood bell housings; American Racing Equipment wheels; adjustable spoilers; racing clutches; Offy and Edelbrock manifolds; Hooker, Appliance and Kustom headers; Zoom transmission gears; Hurst shifters; Nickey traction bars; and Cure Ride drag shocks. Catalog, $1.00.

N.M.W. Mfg., Inc.
355 East 54th Street
Elmwood Park, New Jersey 07407

Traction bars and towing systems. Bolt-on ladder bars for GM intermediates, $64.00. Weld-on ladder bars for most cars, $64.00. Weld-on Stingray traction bar, $46.87. Bolt-on tow bar for many U.S. cars and VW, $39.95. Bolt-on

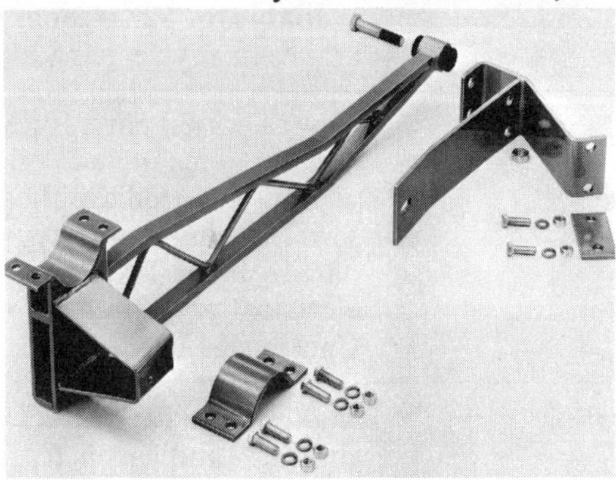

Bolt-on ladder traction bar from N.M.W. Mfg., Inc.

tow tabs to adapt bar to second car are $15.00, or $11.00 for universal model. Other products are free-wheeling tow hubs ($79.00) and universal driveshaft loop ($15.00). Catalog, $1.00.

Norris Cams
14762 Calvert Street
Van Nuys, California 91401

Performance camshafts and valvetrain components. Along with domestic models, Norris has cams for the following foreign cars: 1956-present Porsche (five models), Alfa, Austin-Healey, Spridget, BMW 4-cylinder, Datsun 4- and 6-cylinder, Fiat OHV and DOHC, British Ford, Capri, Lotus, Jaguar, MGA and B, Opel OHV and SOHC, Renault and Gordini, Triumph 4- and 6-cylinder, Toyota, VW, and 4-cylinder Volvo. For the VW, Norris stocks windage trays, degree wheels, power pulleys, high pressure oil pumps, oil coolers, and swivel foot valve adjusting screws. Catalog, $1.00.

The North-East Club for Pre-War Austins (Austins to 1939)
c/o T. Pelton
Fox and Hounds
Newfield
Bishop Auckland
Durham England

Along with specializing in vintage Austins, the Club is the principal organization in Northumberland for vintage car enthusiasts. Owners of all makes are invited to join. The Club publishes a monthly newsletter, an occasional magazine, and an annual calendar of events. In addition, members receive the quarterly magazine of the Austin 7 Clubs Association. Yearly dues: $2.40.

Northern Star Industries, Inc.
690 Muney Avenue
Lindenhurst, New York 11757

Almost any sort of wheel cover you can imagine is manufactured by Northern Star Industries. They can match the original covers on Buicks, Chevrolets, Dodges, Fords, Mustangs, Mavericks, Mercurys, Montego/Comets, Cougars, Oldsmobiles, Plymouths, Duster/Valiants, Pontiacs,

Jeeps, and other popular cars and trucks. There are also slotted VW wheel covers, covers for other foreign cars, and universal models in chrome and simulated chrome. Rubber sidewalls to mount under tire rims or under wheel covers are also available. Free information.

Novak Enterprises
Box 1324
Whittier, California 90609

Makes components to mount Chevrolet V-8, Chevy II 4-cylinder, Vega, Buick V-6, and Ford V-8 engines in various models of the ubiquitous Jeep, and adapt the engines to Jeep transmissions. Among other products are heavy-duty spring shackles, shackle bolts, extra length axle snubbers, and other heavy-duty components to go along with Jeep engine conversions. Has instruction articles on each conversion, and also on steering and brake installations, available for $2.00 each. An article on installing Mercury brakes in any Jeep is $1.00. Free catalog.

NTG Services
Dept. P.
Barking Tye
Ipswich IP6 8HU
England

New and used parts for MG T-series and YA/B models. Special items include oil filter conversion kits for MG TCs, walnut veneered dashboards, steel running boards for T-series, wiring looms, reprinted workshop manuals and parts lists for TA/B and TC. Has most available mechanical, electrical parts and rubber moldings for older MGs. Catalog, $1.00.

Nu-Metrics Corporation
P.O. Box 18072
Cleveland, Ohio 44118

Makes Digi-Tach direct reading digital tachometer. Also shift light indicators to go along with other tachometers. Options with Digi-Tach are a rev limiter, and an optic scan sensor which reads engine speed directly from a mark painted on the harmonic balancer or crank pulley. There is no possibility of ignition interference. Free literature.

Objects of Fiberglass
5612 East LaPalma Avenue
Anaheim, California 92806

Fiberglass body parts for Jeeps, Broncos, Couriers, and Ford vans. Fenders, hoods, floor boards, and firewalls available for CJ5 and CJ2A Jeeps. Also has Jeepster fender extenders at $27.95 a pair. A Bronco hood with scoop is $139.95. Ford van rear extenders go for $27.95. A new product is a Bronco fiberglass full top with no windows on the side. Free literature.

Obsolete Auto Parts
Route 1, Box 72
Decatur, Texas 76234

NOS parts for GM, Mopar, Ford, Studebaker, Packard, Kaiser-Frazer, and many other makes, including some obsolete ones. Mostly mechanical items but some sheetmetal. Send a stamped, self-addressed envelope for parts list.

Obsolete Chevrolet Parts Co.
506 West Marion Avenue
Nashville, Georgia 31639

Hard parts and accessories for 1918-59 Chevrolets. Offers many small mechanical parts, emblems, molded rubber items, repro fiberglass body parts, and Chevrolet literature. Speed and cosmetic accessories include Edelbrock manifolds, reworked small block oil pumps, polished aluminum differential covers, hood and deck pin sets, aluminum valve covers, Hooker headers, 1928 and later windshield frames, chrome radiator caps, aluminum step plates, and Hurst engine conversion motor mounts. Complete engine gasket sets with copper head gaskets for most early Chevs are

$12.00. 1931 repro rumble seat lid is $75.00, and early Chev front and rear fenders are $36.50 to $48.50 apiece. Many mechanical parts are also at hand for early pickups and 1953-55 Corvettes. In the literature library, reprinted tune-up data/wiring diagram sheets are $1.00 to $1.10 apiece. There are also owner's manuals, Fisher body manuals, parts lists, sales literature, service bulletin reprints, and workshop manuals. The very helpful catalogs which Jim Tygart publishes cover Chevrolets 1918-48 in one volume, and 1949-59 in another. Most parts are identified in detailed diagrams, and there are engine specifications and model identification data. Catalog, $1.00.

Obsolete Ford Parts
311 East Washington Avenue
Nashville, Georgia 31639

Parts for Ford, Lincoln and Mercury 1928-56. Has new or repro parts for Model A, Ford V-8, early Mercury, 1928-59 Ford trucks, T-Bird (1955-57) and post-war Lincoln. Also stocks many original 1928-69 Ford, Mercury, Lincoln, and Ford truck shop manuals. Great variety of both mechanical and body parts available. 1928-48 catalog, $.50; 1949-56 catalog, $.50; complete literature catalog, $.25.

Obsolete Parts Co.
Box 326
Gallup, New Mexico 87301

New parts for cars vintage 1925-50. Parts are for many American makes including Chrysler, GM, Ford, Oakland, Whippet, Star, K-F, Nash, Willys, Reo, Hupp, Studebaker, etc. Among items available for various makes and years are carb kits, $10.00; valve cover gaskets, $5.00; pan gaskets, $5.00; diff housing covers, $2.00; water outlet gaskets, $.50; timing chain and gear covers, $3.00; water pumps, $10.00, fuel pumps, $12.75; oil pumps, $14.00; valve springs, $.75; wrist pins, $1.25 each; piston rings, $12.75 a set; pistons, $4.00 each; starter switches, $3.00; horn relays, $3.00; generator cutouts, $5.00; starter brushes, $2.50 a set; generator brushes, $2.50 a set; distributor caps, $4.00; plug wire sets, $6.00; coils, $10.25; points, $2.50; rotors, $1.75; and many chassis, brake and exhaust system components. Free listing.

Pete O'Connor
290 South Elm Street
Windsor Locks
Connecticut 06096

NOS parts for many cars 1929-52. Mostly mechanical parts although a few body parts and accessories are in stock. Send a stamped, self-addressed envelope for list of parts. Specify make and year of car.

Octagon Car Club
(Pre-1956 MG)
c/o H. Crutchley
36 Queenville Avenue
Stafford
England

Holds competitive events—such as trials, gymkhanas and treasure hunts—throughout the year. Publishes a monthly bulletin, *Octagon,* and operates a spare parts service split into three categories: OHC cars, T-type cars, and sedans. The Club also maintains a spares stockpile and has a number of projects for the manufacture of new parts. There is a library service which makes available to members service manuals and spare parts lists for most models from the 18/80 on. Overseas membership in this Club is increasing and there are plans to hold some meetings abroad. Yearly dues: $4.20, family membership is $4.80.

Octagon Sports Car Ltd.
19-21 Grosvenor Park Road
London E. 17 England

Parts for T-series MGs. New and rebuilt parts available. Machined and polished aluminum rocker covers with flip-over oil filler caps, as originally fitted to early production

MG TCs, are $60.00. Reconditioned 19″ wire wheels, as originally fitted to TA, TB and TC MGs, are $42.00 apiece. Brooklands type windscreens are $14.00 each.

MG TC luggage rack from Octagon Sports Car Ltd.

Reconditioned XPAG engines are $360.00 for outright purchase and are also available on an exchange basis. Most mechanical parts and some fiberglass and metal body panels, plus interior trim, seats and carpets, are all available. Service manuals for TC, TD and TF are $5.50. Price list $1.00.

Off-Road Advertiser
P.O. Box 340
Lakewood, California 90714

Magazine covering 4WD, off-road VWs and pickup trucks. Strong West Coast orientation. Subscription rate: $3.00 for 1 year (12 issues).

Old Car Parts Co.
211 East Lake Street
Minneapolis, Minnesota 55408

Stocks auto body replacement panels for cars from 1949 to the present, and also the following parts for 1941 to the present cars: pistons, piston rings, gaskets, timing gears and chains, engine bearings, camshafts, oil pumps, hydraulic lifters, U-joints, exhaust system parts, remanufactured engines, and crankshafts. Send a stamped, self-addressed envelope with query.

Old Cars
Iola, Wisconsin 54945

Printed in newspaper format and published twice monthly, *Old Cars* amply fulfills its motto, "The Newspaper of the Hobby." In its pages you will find news of all the big meets and auctions plus feature articles of interest to enthusiasts. There are many car and parts advertisements in the "Motor Mart" section of the magazine. Yearly subscription: $4.00.

Oldsmobile Division
Service Department
General Motors Corporation
Lansing, Michigan 48921

Service manuals.

100+ International Accessories
Hainge Road
Tividale
Warley
Worcestershire
England

Manufactures a 3-point competition harness, a full line of accessory leather steering wheels and aluminum road wheels in most popular sizes. The 100+ alloy wheel application list shows wheels to fit most American and popular foreign cars, along with some off-beat makes such as the Bond, Clan Crusader, Ginetta, Mitsubishi Colt, Reliant GTE and Skoda. Free information.

On-Guard Corporation of America
350 Gotham Parkway
Carlstadt, New Jersey 07072

Manufactures sirens, burglar alarm systems, wheel locking lugs, stereo lock mounts, spotlights, battery terminals, electric hood locks, "shepherd's crook" pedal-to-steering wheel locks, electrical switch locks, and ignition components for popular domestic cars. Free catalog to jobbers.

Osterreichischer Motor-Veteranen Club (Vintage and Veteran Cars)
c/o Henry Goldhann
Neue Weltgasse 5, 1130
Vienna XIII
Austria

This is the main vintage car club in Austria. The Club sponsors two rallies a year and holds monthly meetings at the Hotel Eder in Vienna. Along with a monthly publication, *Austria Motor Journal,* Club members receive help in locating spare parts, library privileges, and technical advice. Yearly dues: 200 Austrian schillings (about $12.00) plus a one-time-only initiation fee of $6.00.

Otto Parts, Inc.
P.O. Box 3212
South El Monte
California 91733

Corvair speed equipment. Finned oil pan to fit all Corvairs is $40.00, or $42.50 with an additional oil temperature sending unit boss to monitor temperature at the pick-up point. Finned rocker arm covers in either 4- or 6-bolt pattern are $36.00. Owners of turbocharged Corvair Spyders are offered a ceramic-fiber insulation kit to wrap around the exhaust and gain horsepower. A high output oil pump is $25.00. Other products offered are Sig Erson cams, "O" ring seals for pushrod tubes and lower head stud seals, gasket sets, big bore head gaskets, a head nut kit, spark plug thread inserts, and a damped spring-loaded idler kit to maintain uniform fan belt tension. Catalog, $1.00.

Owatonna Tool Co.
Owatonna, Minnesota 55060

Makes specialty tools such as manual and hydraulic pullers, axle and suspension service tools, brake system tools, torque wrenches, chain wrenches, flare nut wrenches, clutch aligning tools, hydraulic presses, engine stands, and cranes. Free literature to jobbers.

Pacer Performance Products
5345 San Fernando Road
Los Angeles, California 90039

VW, dune buggy and import car accessories. Products include headers, ram induction manifolds, nerf bars, speed shifters, wheel adapters, valve covers, and many cosmetic accessories. Catalog, $1.00.

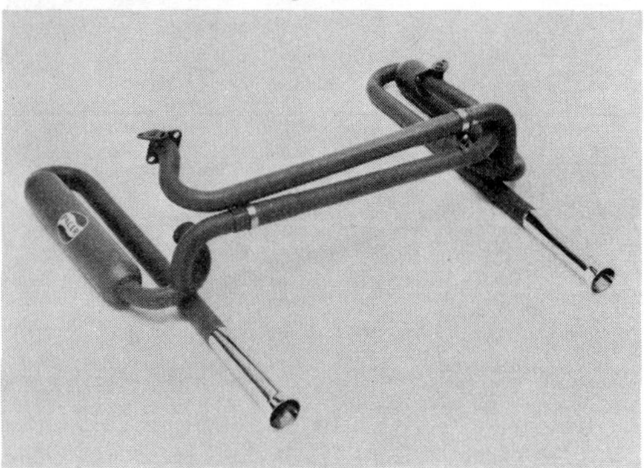

Pacer Performance Products' Green Hornet exhaust system

Pacific-Italia, Inc.
P.O. Box 315
Hillsboro, Oregon 97123

Alloy wheels for domestic cars and mini-cars. Also has VW headers, ski racks, VW "bras," and air scoops in stock. Free literature.

Packard Automobile Classics (Packard)
P.O. Box 2808
Oakland, California 94618

Holding its 20th anniversary this year, the club has regional affiliates throughout the country. Principal publication is a beautiful quarterly magazine, *The Cormorant,* which contains much material of technical and historical interest. In the months when the magazine is not printed, the club issues *The Cormorant News-Bulletin,* which includes free advertising for members as well as service tips and parts sources. A membership roster is published each summer. Tours, social activities, and competitions are held by various regions. The national club offers advice on restorations and allied matters through its technical committee. Yearly dues: $10.00, associate membership—for the wife or husband of a member—$2.50. Dues are pro-rated for those joining late in the year. Life membership, $200.00.

Packards International Motor Car Club (Packard)
P.O. Box 1347
Costa Mesa, California 92626

Local regions have their own activities, while national events are a membership meeting in January and an annual tour and trophy meet in the summer. Club publications are a quarterly magazine and a 'News Counselor' between issues. Members are given free advertising in each. Yearly dues: $10.00; sample magazine is $2.00 with money applicable to membership.

PAECO
213 South 21st Street
Birmingham, Alabama 35233

Comprehensive line of foreign car performance equipment includes engines in four stages of development for Alfa, Austin-Healey 6-cylinder, Spridget, Mini-Cooper, BMW 2000-series, Capri and Pinto 2-liter, Datsun 4- and 6-cylinder, Fiat 850 and 124, British Ford, Jaguar 6-cylinder, Lotus 1600 DOHC, MGA and B, Opel GT, Porsche 1600, Sunbeam Alpine, Spitfire, Triumph TR-series and GT-6, Volkswagen 1200 and 1600 cc and Volvo 1800. Engines are either sold outright or on an exchange basis. Typical prices (for Capri/ Pinto) are $680.00 (stage 1—160 hp), to $1,120.00 (stage 4—

Competition foreign car clutches from PAECO

220 hp), additional price for outright engine is $350.00. Company also sells Sun tachs, Purple K fire extinguishers, Jahns pistons, PAECO cams and valve gear, crankshaft installation kits, Uni-Syn carb synchronizers, Judson electronic magnetos, lightweight flywheels, Cosmic wheels, Abarth exhausts, Isky cams, front and rear sway bars for popular European sports cars and sedans, bearing kits, timing chains, ring gears, Nomex clothing, bucket seats, Bell helmets, shop manuals, street and competition roll bars, oil filters, oil coolers, headers, Stebro exhaust systems, scattershields, Weber carbs and manifolds, fuel pressure

regulators, Bosch ignition parts, racing plugs, racing brake pads and linings, spoilers, PAECO telescopic shocks, Armstrong lever shocks, shock fluid, Spridget axle shafts, and Triumph and Porsche big bore kits. Free catalog.

Page's Model A Garage
Main Street
Haverhill, New Hampshire 03765

Offers Model A and B bright parts—rechromed and reproduction—either outright or on an exchange basis. Brake lever, $10.50; front bumper, $59.50; gearshift lever, $9.50; headlamp body, $15.50; instrument panel, $12.50; radiator shell, $50. Also many rebuilt mechanical parts on exchange basis or outright, sheet metal parts and replacement wood items. Original Ditzler lacquers available at $5.50 a quart (add $1.00 for maroons and reds). Special parts list for 1930-31 Ford station wagon. Also many complete Model As in all body styles and other antique Ford cars and trucks for sale. Send a stamped, self-addressed envelope for lists. List 44A—Model A wood items; List 44B—Model A bright parts; List 44F—Ford books currently in print; List 44SW—wood and metal parts for 1930-31 Model A station wagon; List EEE—Non-Ford auto literature, $.16; List FFF—original Ford literature includes Edsel, Lincoln, T-bird, etc.; List MMM—6-page list of car magazines, tour guides, old maps, etc.

Palley's
2263 East Vernon Avenue
Los Angeles, California 90058

Palley's surplus military items include a wide variety of hardware, tools, electrical components, and what-is-it? gizmos. Small hardware assortments, such as aircraft bolts and gear mixes, come in gadgeteer-size packages. Available tools include precision calipers and micrometers (these are new, imported items) and aircraft wrenches, most of which may not be too practical for auto mechanics. They also carry new power drills, bench grinders, and other home shop tools. Real surplus items, for the hard core gadgeteer, include antennas, control boxes, miscellaneous switches, field telephone equipment, large generators, arc welders, electric motors, inverters, linear actuators, centrifugal and squirrel cage blowers, aircraft heaters, special-purpose gear boxes, air compressors, pressure tanks, accumulators, aircraft instruments, compasses, small aircraft fittings, hydraulic pumps, fuel pumps, hand pumps, pump and motor units, slave cylinders, hydraulic valves, check valves, relief valves, cryogenic valves, electronic test kits, portable power supplies, test stands, and even some medical equipment. If you can figure out what it is, you can probably find a use for it. And the price is right. Catalog, $1.00.

Palmar Products
22191 Old Santa Cruz
Highway
Los Gatos, California 95030

Manufactures running board moldings for classic cars. One model, for 1929-31 Franklins is $45.00. Another, duplicating an original used by more than 28 early car manufacturers, sells for $25.00. Free information.

Panoptic Corporation
1795 Massachusetts Avenue
Riverside, California 92507

Recreational vehicle accessories offered include temperature monitors (a 5-sensor temperature monitor lists at $54.95), water level monitors, battery condition monitors, monitoring consoles, and dual battery charging systems. Free literature.

Pantera
Lincoln-Mercury Division
P.O. Box 880
Detroit, Michigan 48231

Ford's most glamorous entry in the sports car sweepstakes can be seen at selected dealers. Those with no dealer nearby may want to send for an interesting brochure on the Pantera by Jan P. Norbye. Ford will also supply the address of the nearest dealer who carries the car. Free brochure.

Pantera International
(De Tomaso Pantera)
1774 South Alvira Street
Los Angeles, California 90035

Club sponsors rallies and tours, and holds regional events through chapters. Publishes *Pit News* (Pantera International Technical news), and the *P. I. Price List* with performance items and custom accessories available at a substantial discount to club members only. Technical questions are personally answered. Jacket team patch and a paperweight are sent to new members. Yearly dues: $15.00.

Panther West Winds
West Winds
Oatlands Chase
Weybridge
Surrey
England

What is it that looks like a Jaguar SS100 and is fitted with a new Jaguar 4.2 liter 6-cylinder engine or the redoubtable Jaguar V-12? The answer is that it's a new Panther J72—one of the finest replicars ever to come winding around the mountain bend. The chassis is a tubular one with beam axles located by a 5-link system and disc brakes all around. The gearbox is also a Jaguar unit, fitted with Laycock overdrive on top gear. The body is hand-beaten aluminum, and the dash is made from traditional burl walnut. Although the looks are appropriately vintage, the Panther, with its fat tires on 6″ rims, can really wing it in ways no SS100 ever could. The time from 0 to 60 is 6.4 seconds (according to an Autocar road test) and top speed is approximately 115 mph. Want one? Better be prepared to spend about $8,000 for the standard model and another grand or so for the V-12 Panther, which should be a fantastic performer. Free information to serious customers.

Parkdale Hi Performance Centre
Box 3421, Station "C"
Hamilton
Ontario
Canada

One of the largest speed shops in Canada, Parkdale carries headers by Hooker, Thrush, Mickey Thompson and Hays; Holley and Carter carbs; Edelbrock, Offy and Weiand manifolds; Accel and Mallory ignition systems; a complete line of Mr. Gasket accessories; Hurst shifters; Gabriel shocks; Spark-O-Matic shifters; Crane cams; TRW pistons and valve gear; B&M racing transmission components; Manley oil pumps and pistons; Hays and Schiefer clutch components; Moroso differentials, deep sump oil pumps and fiberglass hood scoops; Zoom and Schiefer drivetrain components; Lakewood bellhousings and traction bars, alloy wheels by American Racing Equipment, Cragar, Mickey Thompson and Appliance; M&H and Concorde racing tires; Cal Custom dress-up items; Genuine Suspension underpinnings; Grant steering wheels and helmets; Stewart-Warner, Sun and Smiths dash instruments; Sig Erson cams; A&A Fiberglass bucket seats, hood scoops and VW/Rolls Royce kits; sound systems by Automatic Radio and Tenna; Andeck exhaust systems; and many parts for VW and mini-cars. Also handles hard parts for domestic cars including remanufactured clutch assemblies, reconditioned radiators, and used engines and transmissions. Catalog, $1.00.

John Parker
828-E East Walnut
Fullerton, California 92631

Parts and engine rebuilding for Kaiser, Frazer, Henry J, Willys, and Kaiser Darrin. Send a stamped, self-addressed envelope with query.

Parrish Plastics
Department A
5309 Enterprise Boulevard
Bethel Park
Pennsylvania 15102

Fiberglass hard tops for most popular sports cars. Tops are available in primer, paint, or vinyl. Prices range from about $135.00 for the least expensive tops in primer to $195.00 for the most costly one in vinyl. Headliner is a heavy woolen material, rear windows are made of shatterproof plexiglass and fasteners are chrome plated turnbuckles. Free literature.

Pauter Machine Co.
367 Zenith Street
Chula Vista, California 92011

VW performance parts include stroker kits with modified Chev rods, counterweighted crankshafts, heavy-duty gland nuts, lightened flywheels, big bore kits, solid motor mounts and motor/transaxle hangers. Company also makes

Chevy rod stroker kit for VWs from Pauter Machine Co.

complete off-road buggy frames with full roll cage. Single-seater models are sold only in welded-up form. Price for two-seater Enduro II frame kit without suspension components is $129.95. Complete welded kit with suspension components is $365.00. A four-seater kit is available for $10.00 to $20.00 more. Additional hardware for the buggy builder includes steering shaft mounts, steering wheel and shifter brackets, and pedal brackets. There are also bucket seats, quick-steering plates, and transaxle supports listed in the Pauter catalog. Machine shop services, along with heliarc welding and mandrel tube bending, are offered. Catalog, $1.00.

PECO
Sandford Street
Birkenhead L41 1AZ
England

PECO free-flow exhaust systems are original equipment on Rolls-Royce and Jensen cars. Aftermarket systems for many sports and foreign cars are offered. PECO also makes custom steering wheels. Principal American outlet is SCU Industries, Inc. (see separate listing). Free literature.

Pendleton Tool
2209 Santa Fe Avenue
Los Angeles, California 90058

Makers of the Proto line of tools for professional mechanics. Complete line of metric and SAE wrenches, torque wrenches, pullers, body and fender tools, special purpose tools, precision measuring instruments, tool boxes, and engine diagnostic equipment. Free literature.

Fords in Your Past. Henry Ford was not the first auto manufacturer to conceive of mass production, and his cars were not always the lowest-priced ones on the market. But Ford found the formula for the universal car—the Tin Lizzie that was economical to buy and maintain, easy to drive, and seemed to keep on going forever.

1. Model T Ford. The Model T was Henry Ford's mainstay, and it established a record for longevity of production that is practically unrivaled. Only the Silver Ghost Rolls, the VW, and the Jeep can match the Model T's record.

2. *Ford's First Car.* In 1896, Henry Ford built his first car, constructed by hand in a one-room workshop. It has a 2-cylinder engine, tiller steering, and a top speed of about 10 miles per hour.

3. *Model A Ford.* Most people said that Henry Ford could never do it again. The Model T was out of production and Ford was reported to be having great difficulties with his new model. But the "A" was a winner from the day it appeared in Ford showrooms. Designed and developed by numerous Ford employees, it was ultimately the genius of Ford himself that was responsible for making all the right decisions.

Penny Wise Motoring
140 Abbey House
Victoria Street
London S.W.1
England

PWM magazine is the British equivalent of *Hemmings,* though still an infant in comparison to *Hemmings'* mighty size. Actually *PWM* is the journal of The Vintage Transport Enthusiasts' Club which runs rallies and the British equivalent of swap meets, but Yankees only get to subscribe to the magazine, and it goes to the U.S. via Air Mail. *PWM* is published fortnightly—which means every two weeks, Bud. Yearly subscription in U.S.: $19.95.

Roger Penske Performance
2110 33rd Street
S.W. Allentown
Pennsylvania 18103

Distributor for Fabroid race car bearings and rod ends and for Goodyear Blue Streak tires. Free literature.

Perfection American
Route 5, Dovesville Highway
Darlington
South Carolina 29532

Clutch assemblies for domestic and foreign cars, timing gears and chains, transmission gears, ring and pinion gears, flywheel gears, and auto transmission hard parts. Catalogs available to jobbers only. Company publishes *Ring and Pinion Gear Setter Manual* for $1.00.

Perfect Plastics Industries, Inc.
1304 Third Avenue
New Kensington
Pennsylvania 15068

For a complete and streetable dune buggy with classic Manx looks, the Boss Bug should more than fill the bill. The basic body is $399.95, while a kit with seats, headlights and most of the small stuff needed sells for $100.00 more. From that point you can scrounge around local wrecking yards or go first-class and make your selections from P.P.I.'s extensive menu of accessories.

Boss Bug from Perfect Plastic Industries, Inc.

Another kit car is the Tuff Tub, designed for the full-length VW chassis and looking somewhat like a Fad "T."

Perfect Plastic Industries' Tuff Tub

There are also 22 different fiberglass hood scoops designed for popular domestic cars. They either bolt on or bond in place (an installation kit is available) and come in a wide variety of styles from hi-risers to Grumpy Lumps.

Entire hoods with built-in scoops are available for Corvettes, Camaros, Mustangs and Novas, while strip racers—or those who get their kicks from driving Q-ships on the street—may opt for replacement front end shells. The front ends are available for 1955 Chevys (natch), 1971-73 Vegas, 1962-65 Chevy IIs, 1967-69 Camaros and 1970-73 Mavericks. Fenders, grill panels and bumpers are also available for these cars.

At the rear end you can select spoilers for various models of the Mustang, Camaro and Firebird. There are also universal spoilers and airfoils, and front and rear spoilers for the 240Z.

Rounding out the fiberglass line are fender flares for Corvettes, replacement panels for Triumph TRs and Austin-Healeys, VW fenders, hoods and scoops, and a trio of bucket seats including a circle track model which is really trick. Catalog $1.00.

Performance Associates
1512 Bexley Drive
Austintown, Ohio 44515

Distributors of Mobelec C-D ignition systems, coils and lights. The C-D system is available in Model E 20 for 4- and 6-cylinder cars, and 8-cylinder cars to 6000 rpm ($99.95 with coil); there is also an E 40 Model for 8-cylinder cars and 12-cylinder cars to 6500 rpm ($124.95 with coil). Optional extras for both models comprise a speed limiter ($39.00) and tach adapter for $12.00. A 6-volt non-breakerless system is available on special order. Fiberglass body parts are listed for the Austin-Healey (front shroud, $246.00; door sills, $20.00; boot lid, $85.00; other parts), MGA, MGB, TR-3 and TR-4. Full range of fiberglass fenders and hardtops available on special order. Another item carried is the Colortune 500 test plug for carb adjustment. Price is $14.95. Free literature.

Performance Associates Mobelec breakerless CD ignition system

---

Performance Marketing
1320 North Miller, Unit "H"
Anaheim, California 92806

Products for racers include Firestone racing tires, Borg & Beck clutch components, Hewland roll bars, seat belts, racing hardware of all types, Nomex and Fypro clothing, and Bell helmets. Among the services offered to the racer are sandblasting, Magnafluxing, Zygloing, glass beading, cadmium and nickel plating, custom shatterproof windshield fabrication, rollbar fabrication, welding, sheet metal work, fiberglass repair, bent tube and chassis repair, epoxy frame painting, chassis setting, custom oil pans, oil tank repair and fabrication, mag wheel repair, gearbox services, custom coil springs, tire mounting and balancing, rewiring and bolt upgrading, radiator repair and fabrication, on-board fire system installation, and the fabrication of special trailers. The company also sells face shields for Bell helmets manufactured from Lexan impact-resistant plastic. Clear shields are $7.95, and tinted versions are $8.95. Free literature.

Per-Lux, Inc.
804 East Edna Place
Covina, California 91723

Per-Lux Fogcutters and Model 200T all-weather lights use special louvers inside the lamp to aim their beams low on road. Free literature.

Per-Lux Fogcutter auxiliary lamp with louvers to direct light

John T. Peters
Wyndover Lane
Stamford, Connecticut 06902

New and used parts for Austin-Healey 100-4, 100-6 and 3000 series. Repro parts include louvered fiberglass bonnets and rubber moulding. Also hard to get parts imported from England. Send a stamped, self-addressed envelope with query.

Petersen Manufacturing Co. Inc.
Dewitt, Nebraska 68341

Makers of the well known Vise-Grip locking hand tools. Vise-Grip is a registered trademark of the company and I hereby apologize for using it freely, in the past, in lower case. Vise-Grip variants include locking chain pliers, "C" clamp pliers, welding and sheet metal pliers, and either straight or curved jaw locking pliers in 5″, 7″, and 10″ sizes. There are also Vise-Grip pinch-off pliers especially designed for refrigeration work but handy for the home mechanic. Free literature.

Peterson Publishing Co.
8490 Sunset Boulevard
Los Angeles, California 90069

Publishers of *Motor Trend* and *Hot Rod.* Publications on auto repair and modification. Free information.

Peugeot, Inc.
107-40 Queens Boulevard
Forest Hills, New York 11375

U.S. distributor; service manuals.

Peugeot Owners Club (Peugeot)
P.O. Box 7363
Columbus, Ohio 43209

The focus of Club efforts is a monthly publication, *The Lion of Belfort,* which serves as a forum for members to share technical problems and maintenance tips. The Club is considering initiation of a rebuilt parts exchange service for members. One club chapter in the Los Angeles area meets monthly for discussions and social events. The ownership of a Peugeot is not required for membership. Yearly dues: $5.00.

Phil's Auto Top
2204 Ashland Avenue
Evanston, Illinois 60202

Carries VW and dune buggy hard parts and performance accessories. Has convertible tops for most dune buggy bodies (prices are $134.95 and $144.95); top materials in flowered vinyl-coated nylon and "leopard skin"; buggy bucket seats; headers and intake manifolds; Thompson tires; Wito shocks; Sig Erson cams; Ja-Mar hydraulic brake system locks; Thermo-Chem coolers; Neal hydraulic linkages; Chenowth roll cage frame kits; Andeck headers; S.E.S. fuel injection units; and Transvair conversion kits. Is also distributor for Alondra, Bosch, Dee Engineering, International Coach Works, Tri-Mil Industries, T. Hoff Inc., Glyco, SPG, Segal, E.I.E. Inc., Venolia, Filtron, Neway, Scat, Thomas Automotive, Manley, C-P, Kolbenschmidt, and R.C. Fire Extinguishers. Carpets, tops, and upholstery can be made to order. Catalog, $1.00.

Pierce-Arrow Society, Inc.
(Pierce-Arrow)
c/o Bernard J. Weis
135 Edgerton Street
Rochester, New York 14607

Along with holding an annual meet around the first weekend in August, the Society has three regions—Delaware Valley, Lake Erie, and Northern California—which have their own activities. The Society's quarterly magazine, *The Arrow,* is supplemented by bi-monthly service bulletins and a newsletter with advertisements, *The Emporium,* sent with each mailing. Other publications are a cumulative index of technical information, a membership roster and car register, and a parts and service directory. The club maintains a technical committee to answer members' questions on restoration and maintenance. Yearly dues: $7.50.

Pierce Racing Parts
115 Lauderdale Street
Montgomery, Alabama 36111

Despite the name, Pierce makes add-on air-conditioning units for most Japanese cars (including Mazda and 240Z) plus the Capri. Prices range from $229.95 to about $250.00. Free literature.

Hank Pinckney
100 Prince Street
Fairfield, Connecticut 06430

NOS Oldsmobile parts, 1941-57. Send a stamped, self-addressed envelope with query.

Pioneer Distributing Co.
172 Tunnel Road
Marietta, Ohio 45750

Makes all sorts of fasteners used on antique and later cars, including the "common sense" types. Also has repro hood ornaments including Flying Lady, Cadillac style Flying Lady, Bucking Ram, Greyhound, and RA Stutz. Antique jewelry available with crests of Chrysler, Chevrolet, Essex, Plymouth, Pontiac, Ford Oval, Packard, Dodge, Buick, Studebaker, Cadillac, Kaiser Frazer, plus A.A.C.A. and M.A.R.C., includes keychains, lighters, and men's and women's jewelry. Free literature.

Pirelli Tire Corporation
60 East 42nd Street
New York, New York 10017

Manufactures tires to fit most American and foreign cars. Pirelli Cinturato tires are radial and come in a variety of high-speed configurations. Two excellent booklets put out by the company, *Pocket Guide for Imported Cars* and *Pocket Guide for American Cars* give the correct sizes to fit most cars, along with recommended inflation pressures. Free literature.

Pirrana Performance Products
P.O. Box 158
Port Credit
Mississauga
Ontario
Canada

Distributors of Mobelec CD ignition systems, Mobelec coils and fog lamps, and Lynx Ram-Flo fireproof and washable air filters. Also stocks exhaust manifolds. Free literature.

Washable air filters from Pirrana Performance Products

Plymouth 4- & 6-Cylinder Owners Club (Plymouth)
c/o R. E. Bender
Rd No. 1, Box 360
Jeannette, Pennsylvania 15644

Club holds at least three national meets each year. In spring, summer and fall. The summer meet is traditionally held at New Hope, Pennsylvania, and the fall meet at Hershey, Pennsylvania. Several chartered regional organizations across the country also hold meets. Club publication is the *Plymouth Bulletin* a bi-monthly which includes technical advice and an extensive classified section. Dues are assessed by calendar year. Those joining before October 1 are considered members only through December 31 of that year but receive available back issues of the Club publication. Ownership of a 1928-48 Plymouth is not a prerequisite for membership, but each applicant must be sponsored by one active member. Yearly dues: $8.00.

Pontiac Owners Club International (Pontiac and Oakland)
Box 612
Escondido, California 92025

Main goals of Club are technical information and parts exchange. Has annual national meet, and publishes quarterly magazine, *The Silver Streak News,* which carries technical and historical articles plus extensive Pontiac and Oakland parts advertisements. Advertisements are free to members. Another publication is an annual membership roster. Club also maintains a library for members' use. Yearly dues: $5.00. Associate membership for husband or wife, $2.00.

H. Porsche Accessories
348 Vermont
Los Angeles, California 90004

A nifty rear deck spoiler for the Porsche 911 is available for $64.85. The spoiler bolts on with hand tools in less than an hour. Free information.

Porsche Audi
600 Sylvan Avenue
Englewood Cliffs
New Jersey 07632

Service manuals.

Porsche Club, Great Britain (Porsche)
c/o T.A. Woods
Mill House
Cock Green
Felsted
Dunmow CM6 3NA England

The Club holds social events and pays the entry fees for British members participating in competition. *Porsche Post* is the Club's quarterly magazine. Services are technical advice and spare parts location. Yearly dues: $9.60.

Pos-A-Traction
622 North La Brea
Inglewood, California 90302

Pos-A-Traction makes the Torque-Master and Torque-Sixty belted polyester tires and Stagger Block nylon on/off-road tires. The Torque-Master is a 70-series tire while the Torque-Sixty is an ultrawide 60-series.
The company also distributes Bridgestone Racing Tires which are designed strictly for the track and come in dry, all-weather, and wet versions.
The aluminum wheels made by Pos-A-Traction are the Mag-Star (sizes 10″x5″ and 12″x5″); the Torque-Dish, for most foreign and domestic cars in sizes which range from 13″x5½″ to 15″x8½″; and the Truck-Dish, for 8-lug wheels, in sizes 6.75″x16.5″, 8.25″x16.5″ and 9.75″x16.5″. All provide room to clear disc brakes.
On orders of four tires or wheels, there are no freight charges. The manufacturer may also offer discounts to mail-order customers. Literature, $1.00.

Pre-Fifty Auto Parts
c/o Max C. Morton
339 Blue Creek Road
Jacksonville
North Carolina 28540

Model A parts and mechanical parts for many early standard American makes. Clutch plates, $6.00-$8.00; mufflers, $9.00; master cylinder kits, $2.00; U-joints, $4.50-$9.95; wheel cylinders, $3.95; wheel cylinder kits, $1.00; rings at $1.00 a cylinder; fuel pumps, $4.95; tie rod ends, $1.95; brake linings, $3.00 each; brake shoes, $5.00; water pumps; gaskets; distributor caps, $1.59; points, $.50; rotors, $.50; condensers, $.50; generators, $15.00; regulators, $5.00; generator cut-outs, $1.50; generator brushes, $.50 each; starters, $15.00; starter drive springs, $1.00; starter switches, $2.00; starter brushes at $.75 each; dimmer switches, $1.00. Many other small mechanical parts. Free price list.

The Pre-War Austin Seven Club (Austin Seven)
c/o N.H. Barr
7 Leopold Street
Derby DE1 2HE
England

There is an annual Club rally and a Club camping holiday, along with monthly meetings, social runs and occasional special events. Cars covered include the Austin Seven and Big Seven along with foreign equivalents. A periodic magazine called *The Austin Ear,* the quarterly Austin Seven Association Magazine, and a monthly newsletter are mailed to members. This Club can also give you the gen on where to get NOS and repro parts. Technical advice and library services are available. Yearly dues from $3.60.

Progressive Dynamics, Inc.
P.O. Box 168, Kalamazoo Street
Marshall, Michigan 49068

RV and off-road vehicle accessories. Items available are power converters and inverters, automatic dual battery isolation systems ($10.75), battery chargers, ground fault warning devices, automatic circuit breakers, electronic static filters, 12-volt incandescent and fluorescent lighting fixtures, assist grips, gauged air pressure pumps, water entrance pressure caps, flexible high pressure water hoses and fittings, L.P. gas pressure regulators and cylinder gauges, and water tank gauges. Free information.

Progressive 4x4 Truck Accessories
6605 Lash Lane
Los Angeles, California 90068

Mail-order-only accessories for 4WD vehicles and pickup trucks. No catalog available at time this was written. Send queries.

Protective Treatments, Inc.
420 Dellrose Avenue
Dayton, Ohio 45403

Products for automotive windshield installation and allied work include auto glass sealant tape, body and glass sealer, rubber joint sealer, caulk strips, glass cleaner, and primer. Also makes protective chrome and vinyl side moldings which can be cut to size. Free information.

Pulfer and Williams
5059 Washburn South
Minneapolis, Minnesota 55401

If you want to know which of six different radiator emblems was used on your particular 1911 Stoddard Dayton, Pulfer and Williams can tell you and supply any of the six. They will reproduce emblems or scripts for any car, and also radiator ornaments. Their files contain 50,000 references and they keep more than 500 different name plates in stock and ready to be sent out. Among stock items are many Bugatti brass plates and enamel radiator emblems; Cadillac/La Salle items; emblems and mascots for Cord, Lincoln, Packard, Stutz and Rolls-Royce; plus many insignia for modern cars. They also have such things as motometer name plates for cars like the Thomas Flyer, Dagmar, Metz 25, Nyberg and Ogren. Will also supply enamel miniatures to be made up into modern keyholders and watch fobs, full line of motometers, and car related jewelry. Some NOS or used emblems in stock. Catalog, $1.50.

Pull-A-Long/J-J-J, Inc.
10215 South Harlem
Oak Lawn, Illinois 60455

Trailers for dragsters, race cars, snowmobiles, cycles and utility use. Enclosed dragster trailer has overall length of 25′ 6″, includes 4-wheel electric brakes, ramp door, baggage door, motor door, front shelf, cable jack, safety chains and safety brake switch. Options include Mor-Ryde axles, floor tie-down mounts, chains and load binders, 30-gallon water tank, extra doors and lights, motor rack, brake control, wheel track, built-in cabinets and motor track and trolley. Additional height and length trailers available. Cycle trailers come in two and three rail models. Custom trailers available. Free literature.

Pure Air Products
P.O. Box 218
Basking Ridge
New Jersey 07920

Makers of the Sojo Ozo-Auto ozonizer to destroy odors within cars. Price of small unit is approximately $37.50. Free information.

Quality Products Co.
P.O. Box 2202
Castro Valley, California 94546

Radiators and radiator cores for Model T, Model A, 1901-05 Oldsmobile, and 1908-10 Buick. Radiators are made from heavy-gauge yellow brass. Radiator parts, including

Repro Model T 1911-12 radiator made by Quality Products Co.

brackets, braces, flanges, pipes, and walls, available for the the Model T. Complete radiator prices run from $260.00 up. Do-it-yourself radiator kits available for Model T only. Another interesting product in stock consists of plated replacement covers to fit most Prest-O-Lite acetylene tanks. Free literature.

Quick Cable Corporation
2501 Eaton Lane
Racine, Wisconsin 53404

Battery cables and ignition wires for most cars and trucks, American and foreign. Also sells insulated copper cable, terminal clamps and associated hardware, and kits for custom making battery terminals and spark plug cables. Consult catalog at wholesalers.

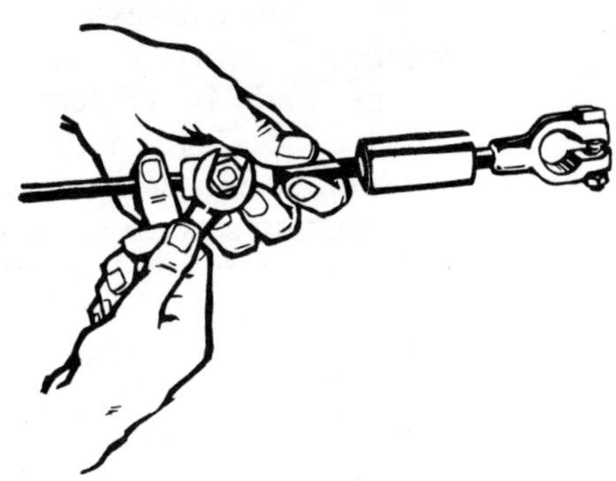

Battery cables of any length made quickly with kits from Quick Cable Corporation

Quicksilver Racengines
1101 Gude Drive
Rockville, Maryland 20850

Company has four divisions which offer a variety of parts and services. Quicksilver Racing Enterprises, Inc. imports parts for European and Japanese cars. Quicksilver Racing Engines, Inc. sells Formula Ford, Super Vee, Formula 5000 and Stock Car racing engines. Dyno facilities are available. Quicksilver Racing Mechanics School offers a five-day course covering both race car preparation and trackside servicing for $500.00. Quicksilver Racengines can handle a wide variety of machine shop services for competition and street engines. Free information from any company division.

Race America
P.O. Box 20373
Dallas, Texas 75220

Sells and can supply parts for Merlyn Formula Ford cars, models Mk-11, Mk-17, Mk-20, and Mk-24. The complete Mk-24 race-ready vehicle with Goodyear slicks is $5,895.00. Options are inboard rear brakes ($250.00), an on-board fire extinguisher system, and Aeroquip steel brake lines. Write for literature and price lists.

The Merlyn Mark 24 Formula Ford from Race America

Racemark
P.O. Box 178
Ballston Lake
New York 12019

Racing apparel and accessories. Nomex and Fypro clothing, on-board fire extinguishing systems, fiberglass bucket seats, and leather padded or wood custom steering wheels. Free literature.

Racer Brown
9270 Borden Avenue
Sun Valley, California 91352

Performance camshafts and valve train components. Cams are available in many grinds for most domestic cars and for popular foreign makes such as Alfa, Austin-Healey, Sprite, Datsun 4- and 6-cylinder, British Ford, Fiat, Jaguar, MG, Porsche, Renault, Rootes Group, Triumph, VW and Volvo 4- and 6-cylinder. Also available for most sub-compacts including Gremlin, Vega, Colt, Cricket, and Pinto. Some accessories listed are roller lifters for small block Chev; rocker arm adjusters; offset cam bushings for Chev and Mopar; screw-in rocker arm studs; super-duty valve locks; special distributor drive gears; lightweight fuel pump push rods for all Chev V-8s; roller timing sprocket and chain sets for small and big block Chev plus Mopar; degreed crankshaft dampers; small block Chev nose plugs; and camshaft gear drive assemblies for Chev and Mopar. Racer Brown sells specially-formulated engine break-in compounds, and is a distributor for Edelbrock, Forgedtrue Pistons, and Donovan Engineering. Machine shop services, such as cylinder head work, available. Catalog, $1.00.

Racer Walsh Co.
124 Orange Avenue
Suffern, New York 10901

The compleat Pinto performance store. Among the more mouth-watering goodies offered are an Offy 4-barrel manifold and Holley carb, Trans Am headers ($82.00), Isky cams, competition front disc brake pads ($23.00), front and rear sway bars ($39.95 each), street and racing roll bars, and various suspension bits for competition use. Other items offered for the Pinto are Weber dual side draft carbs,

Racer Walsh modified Pinto

Jahns pistons, stainless steel valves, oil cooler kits, Sun and Stewart Warner instrumentation, street or competition traction bars ($54.00 and $80.00 respectively), Koni shocks, ATL fuel cells, Ansen wheels, and Mallory distributors. The company also builds and sells complete Pinto race cars and Pinto engines for IMSA, SCCA, and Midget competition. Free catalog.

Race Shop
239 Greenwood Avenue
Midland Park
New Jersey 07432

In addition to being the North American importer for March racing cars, Race Shop also offers sales and service on all Formula 5000, Formula B & C, and F & F cars. Chassis and engine parts are kept in stock. Company builds Lotus

Twin Cam engines for Formula B and also specializes in servicing the BMW 2-liter racing engine. Free information.

Racetronics
770 Broadway
Raynham
Massachusetts, 02767

Specializes in VW-based race cars, offering complete engine and transaxle service which includes engine dynamometer services, air flow testing and chassis tuning. Also offers service for street VWs and other imports. Write for availability of special parts and service catalog.

Racing Exhaust Specialties
2710 16th Avenue South
Department D
Minneapolis
Minnesota 55407

Under brand name of "Headers by Ed" supplies equal length headers for Chev, Camaro, Chevy II, Chevelle, Dodge, Plymouth, Challenger, Barracuda, Duster, Demon, Swinger, Corvette, Stingray, GTO, Le Mans, 442, Cutlass, Mustang, Cougar, Fairlane, Meteor, Montego, and other domestic cars. Will also custom make headers to order. Another option is "experimental" collectors which can be supplied in various lengths and diameters so that the most efficient combination can be found. Also supplies header mufflers and hardware. Free literature.

Racing Head Service
4174 Elvis Presley Boulevard
Memphis, Tennessee 38116

Blueprinted engines for the stocker and super stocker. Modified short block assemblies run from $850.00 to $1,450.00 while heads go from $575.00 to $840.00. Porting and polishing and most machine shop services available. Also cams for most popular performance engines. Free literature.

Radatron Corporation
2424 Niagra Falls Boulevard
North Tonawanda
New York 14120

Dash instruments for the VW. Radatron's three-in-one oil-amp-cylinder head gauge (with four cylinder head senders and a four position switch) lists for $64.82. Free literature.

James Ragsdale
134 James Street
Morristown, New Jersey 07960

Mr. Ragsdale specializes in Studebaker parts, but also has on hand many other NOS parts for other special-interest cars and sells original automobile literature. No catalog, send a stamped, self-addressed envelope.

rah enterprises, inc.
P.O. Box 748
Windomere, Florida 32786

Getting tired of the new cars with their emission controls and seat belt interlocks? Try the PPV or People Powered Vehicle which will go as fast as you can pedal. The vehicle comes with a 3-speed transmission and side reflectors.

The PPV (People Powered Vehicle) by rah enterprises, inc.

Colors are green, blue, yellow and black, while the body top and seats are snow white. Although prices have not been firmly established as yet, it should cost in the $350.00 range. Free literature.

The Railton Owners Club (Railton)
c/o Barrie McKenzie
Fairmiles
Barnes Hall Road
Burncross
Sheffield S30 4RF
England

John R. Bond and other American enthusiasts for this marque are happy that brother enthusiasts across the sea have things well in hand. Monthly and national meetings are all in England, but there are 165 members throughout the world and they receive the Club bulletin each month. Also available to members is a register of the 200-plus cars in existence, a technical manual, a car badge and tie, and much help on restoration and the procurement of spares. The Club holds a stock of parts and has remanufactured unobtainable ones from time to time. The Spares Registrar, Mr. Richard Hirst, who has been kind enough to supply the information here, will help members locate a wanted part and will shortly be issuing a directory of all known current sources for spares. Along with Railtons, the closely allied Brough Superior cars and early Hudsons are covered in the Club's domain. Yearly dues: $6.00; plus about $1.00 initiation fee.

Rally International
370 East 134th Street
Bronx, New York 10454

A candy store for the feverish rallyist, where goodies abound. The Stevens and Halda lines of rally equipment are sold, along with Heuer timers, Curta calculators, quartz halogen lights from Marchal and Cibie, and the admirable Lucas-Butler Flexilight. But that's just the beginning.

The Compleat Rallyist will have a hard time choosing between the Autonav Rally Computer ($495.00 with a position display for $250.00 and a driver guide going for $90.00), the Zeron 330 computer ($415.00 with reversible odometer), the Zeron 440 unit ($550.00), the Heuer/Robo computer ($425.00 without accessories), and the Rallecomp computer ($439.50). The functions of each are explained in detail in Rally International's catalog.

As long as we're dreaming, why be chintzy? Let's throw in the Sheetz-Gull rally computer readout ($175.00), the Al-Fab Gemini trip counter with three registers ($120.00), and the Rallyphone transistorized intercom system (with noise cancelling microphone fitted to a user-supplied helmet) which goes for a mere $250.00 and has an on/off switch to shut out your wife on Sunday drives.

Zeron rally computer from Rally International

Dear Santa, please also bring an Alpina calculator (a mechanical unit working like the Curta and selling for $148.00), and a Grimes Navigation Light ($31.95) which is rheostat controlled, has a 360° tilting base, and will focus to spot or flood in either red or white or anywhere in between. (A red light is far less distracting to the driver at night.)

And don't forget the Lufft Auto Compass, a superior unit for $10.00, and an add/subtract differential pulse counter ($92.00).

There are other models of Grimes lights, selling for as little as $6.95, and a manual calculator called the Bohn Contex 10 which is almost as small and versatile as the newest electronic calculators and is made from rugged Swedish steel. It sells for $119.50.

To keep sophisticated timing equipment on time, Rally International offers the Tunaverter, a small receiver which attaches to any AM radio and converts it to receive WWV and CHU time signals in four different dial locations. The Tunaverter's price is $27.50.

Those who go rallying on a more modest scale will want to look at the Autopacer Speed System Mark 3 ($19.95), which consists of a set of speed, factor and finder cards in a quick-access box with color-coded tabs. Also the Taylor Rally Calculator ($7.95), a circular scale, and Rally International's handsome, PVC-covered, clipboard with plastic top sheet plus pen and pencil holders and space for a stopwatch to clip on ($4.95).

An essential item for both the rallyist deluxe and the seat-of-the-pants competitor is a dash-mounted plexiglass board which holds rally instructions or maps and has suction cups and hinges for mounting ($6.75).

For rallymasters and clubs there are scorecards, checkpoint signs (custom-built), rally forms, time slips and arrival and departure logs. There is also a checkpoint timing line, which works like a gas station signal bell, and comes with 300′ of wire. It operates on 12 volts, hooking to a car battery with alligator clips, and costs $30.00.

The catalog includes sage and humorous advice from Russ "Alligator" Brown, 1971 SCCA rally champ, which shows how the alligator got its name (apologies to Kipling). For those who want more, a fine selection of rally books is offered. Catalog $1.00.

Rally Rails
1700 S. Western Avenue
Gardena, California 90247

Rally Rails are aluminum bars which fit in pickup truck stake holes and go along the top of the bed sides. Along with their cosmetic appeal, the rails make convenient tie-down points, especially when used with the company's Easy Loader tie-down straps. Rally Rails are available in 8′ sizes for domestic pickups and 6′ versions for mini pickups. The latter require drilling for installation. Free literature.

Ram Automotive Co.
4525 Cleveland Avenue N.W.
Canton, Ohio 44709

Competition and street clutch components for domestic cars. Also has clutch cap screw sets and nylon release bearings. Free information to wholesalers.

Ramsey Corporation
P.O. Box 513
St. Louis, Missouri 63166

Piston rings for racing and high-performance engines. Free literature.

The New Wave. First there were the MG-TCs, underpowered and hard-riding on their spindly 19″ wire wheels. But they looked rakish and impudent, buzzing down the road like frightened bumblebees and always ready to take on the nearest porthole Buick. Then came Jags, Healeys, and the thundering American-engined Allards on the race courses. The Glen, Thompson, Sebring . . . if you couldn't afford to buy one of the new British sports cars, you could always buy a copy of *Road & Track* and dream a little. Those pioneering sports car enthusiasts passed each other with a friendly wave. There was an elaborate etiquette determining who waved first.

1. 1949 MG TC. They sold for about $2,000 new, and a good one will bring twice that today. The MG TC was an aesthetic pinnacle, MG lovers lamented when the more practical but stolid TD was introduced.

2. 1952 Allard J2X. With Ford, Chrysler, and Cadillac engines, Sidney Allard's hot rod burned up the race courses under the able guidance of A. Erwin Goldschmidt, Masten Gregory, Phil Walters, and other early stars. They reigned until the combined onslaught of the 4.1 Ferrari and XK-120C Jaguar finally signaled an end to the era of the big, cycle-fendered thunderers.

1.
2.
3.

3. 1954 H.R.G. Though not the fastest, most expensive, or handsomest of cars, the H.R.G. was the ultimate in *snobbisme.* H.R.G. owners were always entitled to wave last—perhaps in recognition of their fortitude in enduring the kidney-shaking suspension.

4. 1952 Jaguar XK-120 Convertible. Sir William Lyons always had a genius for offering fast, stylish cars at less than half the price the competition was asking. The early XK had its faults mechanically, but conceptually it was a masterpiece. The Jaguar XKs were the first postwar imports to offer real performance at an affordable price. They were a solid success.

5. 1958 Austin-Healey 100-6. A few years after the introduction of the XK Jaguar, the Austin-Healey came along with almost as much performance and a substantially lower price. Fitted out with 6-cylinder engines and modified styling, the "Big Healey" was an outstanding bargain that lasted until the dawn of emission controls.

6. 1957 Jaguar XK-SS. Based on the racing "D Jaguar," the limited production XK-SS was another milestone. It led directly to the "E Series" Jaguars of today.

4.

5

6.

Ramsey Winch
5531 Admiral Place
Tulsa, Oklahoma 74115

Makes both electric and PTO winches for 4WD vehicles and pickup trucks. Also has winch kits, which include heavy duty front bumpers, for Scout II and other 4WD off-road vehicles. Free literature.

Ramsey Winch makes the DC-200 Winch to fit popular 4WD cars

Rancho Jeep Supply
6309 Paramount Boulevard
Long Beach, California 90805

Hard parts and accessory components for all Jeep models. Rancho overdrive units, for most pickup trucks, Universal Jeeps, Broncos, and 1961-65 Scouts, are available either new or rebuilt, with prices ranging from $179.50 to $289.50. Self-adjusting 10″ brakes for Universal Jeeps are $99.95. Eleven inch brake kits for Jeepsters, Jeep station wagons and pickups, and CJ series Jeeps are $149.50. Along with many hard parts, Rancho carries engine and transmission adapter kits, Whitco carpets, Kayline tow bars and roll bars, sissy bars, jerry cans and can carriers, Offy four barrel kits for the Jeep V-6, Stewart-Warner gauges, free-wheeling hubs, Kayline seats and convertible canvas tops, Heco steering stabilizers, Meyers metal tops for CJ5 Jeeps ($399.05 for standard model, $437.37 for deluxe), and wide steel wheels. Also in stock are winches by Koenig, Ramsey and Warn. Free catalog.

Ranger Automotive Co., Ltd.
E.J.S. House
258 Leigh Road
Leigh-on-Sea
Essex
England

One of the more interesting kit cars utilizing the BLMC 1100/1300 base, is the Ranger 4-seater roadster. The kit includes a welded steel space-frame chassis plus floor pan. BLMC components needed are the engine, sub-frames, steering, dash, fuel tank, wheels, exhaust system, seats, windshield, and lights. The car can also be provided in a pickup version. Options include hard and soft tops plus a variety of speed equipment. A rollbar and tow bar can also be supplied. Cost of the kit is $588.00. Free literature.

Rankin Obsolete Parts
Box 341
Anderson, South Carolina 29621

NOS parts for GM, Ford and Chrysler cars 1928-70. Many small mechanical parts include brake kits, ignition items, fuel pumps, water pumps and kits, gaskets, tie rod ends, king bolt sets, lenses, gas and radiator caps, fan belts, spark plugs, clutch discs, suspension parts and many other items. Send query with a stamped, self-addressed envelope.

Rapid Cool
306 South Center Street
Santa Ana, California 92703

Makers of "Transaver" for cooling automatic transmissions on all cars, "Enginsaver" for engine cooling on most foreign and American cars with a model for the air-cooled

VW and Porsche, full-flow oil filter systems for VW and Porsche (4-cylinder only), and oil pressure booster kits to boost pressure on VW Beetle and Porsche 356 and 912 models to 50 psi. An interesting accessory is a filter support for spin-on cartridges to prevent the mount from cracking or vibrating loose under the stress of off-road travel. Free literature.

Ratner
R.D. 2, Box 572
Lakewood, New Jersey 08701

Parts for Willys Jeepsters. Also complete restored cars. Firewall board—waterproof black—$10.50; muffler, $9.75; oil gauges, fuel gauges, temperature gauges and ammeters, $3.75 to $4.50; repair kit for Carter YF carb, $6.00; overdrive parts; water pumps; oil pumps; body parts; convertible tops; chassis and steering components; all rubber parts; carpeting; and side curtains are some of the further items available. Send a stamped, self-addressed envelope for parts and price list.

Rat's Hole
P.O. Box 11-111-DT
St. Petersburg, Florida 33733

Your one stop shopping center for T-shirts reading "Dirty Old Men's Club" and heat transfer decals with slogans like "Rated X" and "Beep Beep Yuras." If you like this sort of thing, Rat's Hole surely has a sticker for you. Catalog, $.75.

Redi-Strip Co.
2528 Merced Avenue
South El Monte
California 91733

Billing itself as the "metal laundry," Redi-Strip will undertake rust removal from any size object made from any ferrous metal. According to the company, its alkaline electrolytic immersion process will not harm organic components, such as rubber and plastic, and will not cause hydrogen embrittlement. Complete paint stripping services are also offered. A typical de-rusting job would run under $200.00 for a prewar coupe body and $50.00-$70.00 for a small frame. Rust removal is also done on individual parts, and it is suggested that they be pooled for shipping. Free literature.

Red Triangle Auto Services, Ltd.
Common Lane
Trading Estate
Kenilworth
Warwickshire
England

When the late lamented Alvis Company merged with British Leyland, Red Triangle took over the entire stock of Alvis spare parts. They are now the official suppliers of parts and service for all Alvis Cars. Send a stamped, self-addressed envelope with queries.

Reese Products, Inc.
P.O. Box 940
Elkhart, Indiana 46514

Towing systems and accessories. Reese equalizing hitches with sway control are suitable for towing the largest trailers. Other products include stabilizers, plastic ball covers, hitch box covers, levels, Lectra Jacks, tire mount kits, hydraulic tongue jacks, coil overload springs, utility hitch bars, hitch pins, and the Hydra Jac leveling/stabilizing system for travel trailers. Free literature.

Renault Inc.
100 Sylvan Avenue
Englewood Cliffs
New Jersey 07632

Renault distributor; service manuals.

Renault West Service Center 702 West 190th Street Gardena, California 90247	Service manuals.
Reo Motors Register (Reo) c/o Peter A. Anderson The Bellbirds The Entrance Road Erina Heights, 2251 New South Wales Australia	Ransom E. Olds would be happy to know that his favorite car is still well-represented and treasured in faraway places. Mr. Anderson has a huge library on Reo vehicles, and also acquired a stock of NOS parts from the former Australian agents. Although not maintaining a formal club, he is willing to supply technical information and help locate Reo parts.
Repcoparts USA, Inc. 6281 Chalet Drive City of Commerce Los Angeles, California 90040	Hard parts for most imported cars. Repco makes pistons, valve gear, U-joints, clutch components, ring gears, ignition parts, filters, hydraulic brake assemblies, disc brake pads, oil seals, engine mounts, water pump repair kits, wiper blades, and many other parts. Also distributes Scientific workshop manuals, and manufactures automotive reconditioning equipment for professional mechanics. Catalog available to jobbers only.
Repro-Tiques Route 4, Box 130 Hot Springs, Arkansas, 71901	Custom-made gas tanks, generally constructed from galvanized metal. Price for tanks with lengths to 29¾″ and circumferences to 35¼″ is $45.00. Slight additional charges for extra length or extra circumference. Other options are tanks with concave ends (to 14″ diameter) for an additional $5.00, Ford script on tanks for $5.00, brass or aluminum castings at $5.00 and up. Prices include installation of factory or customer-furnished fittings. Also Ford Model T reproduction gas tanks, caps, mounting brackets and muffler shells. Prices for Model T gas tanks range from $45.00 to $60.00. Write for further information.
Republic Gear Co. 20200 East Nine Mile Road St. Clair Shores Michigan 48080	Republic makes transmission gears for domestic cars, starter drives and flywheel gears, solenoids, motor and transmission mounts, U-joints, oil pumps and pump repair kits, valve train gear, timing gears and chains, valve train components, power steering hose, and hard parts for most automatic transmissions. Catalogs available to jobbers only.
The Restoration Engine Shop R.D. 1, Box 228 Jamesburg, New Jersey 08831	Complete facilities for rebuilding antique and classic automobile engines. Can also handle entire restorations. Send a stamped, self-addressed envelope with queries.
Reynolds Head & Block Repair 2318 Charles Page Boulevard Tulsa, Oklahoma 74127	All classic and vintage castings restored. Will work on trucks, tractors, steam engines, pumps, compressors, and any other parts in cast iron, steel or aluminum. Free literature.
Rezzino's Box 1215 Scranton, Pennsylvania 18501	Large selection of antique, classic, and special-interest car parts for sale. A few particular specialties are Chrysler products parts, (primarily 1940 and up, but also some older), replacement rocker panels for cars of the late 1940s and after, and Kaiser-Frazer (along with some

Henry J) parts. Also carries reproduction watch fobs with straps. Send a stamped, self-addressed envelope with query.

Bob Rich
1024 West 15th
Wichita, Kansas 67203

Parts for Packards (mostly postwar) and miscellaneous parts for cars 1912-50. Timken roller bearings, pistons, piston pins, brass distributor gears, head gaskets and other mechanical parts. All parts NOS. Send a stamped, self-addressed envelope with query.

Chester Riggins
Box 68
Dunnville, Kentucky 42528

From his Dunnville Garage & Restaurant Mr. Riggins writes that he has been doing interior wood sets on Model As for nine years and that one of his 1931 Ford Deluxe roadsters has been first place and best of show down Kentucky way for the past two years. Interior wood for the 1928-29 roadster is $28.75. For the 1930-31 roadster and 1932 B roadster, interior wood goes for $29.75. A set of ten wooden body to frame blocks is $9.75.

Mr. Riggins has no catalog, but he does have Model A parts on hand and will do complete restorations, especially on Model A roadsters.

Riley Car Club
of New Zealand
(Riley)
P.O. Box 6624
Wellesley Street
Auckland
New Zealand

Holds an annual national rally plus regional events. The Club operates a spare parts service, and two members are currently compiling a parts-interchange catalog. There is a bi-monthly magazine, along with monthly newsletters published by regional affiliates. Yearly dues: $5.00, family membership, $6.00.

Riley Register
(Riley)
c/o A.P. Dunn
162, Leicester Road
Glenhills
Leicester
England

The Register sponsors an annual rally at Coventry and local meetings throughout Great Britain. Publications are a quarterly bulletin, a newsletter with an advertising supplement eight times a year, and a membership list. Membership is open to owners of Rileys built prior to September 1938; others may become associate members. The Register also maintains a library service, loans tools to members, and has some spare parts available. Yearly dues: $7.20.

Rite Autronics
3485 La Cienega Boulevard
Los Angeles
California 90016

Electric and mechanical dash instruments, panel housings, bullet housings, dash installation kits, switches and switch panels, electric tachs, auto coolant return systems, CD ignitions, electric troubleshooting equipment, remote starter switches, vacuum and fuel pump monitors, compression testers, timing lights, dwell/tach meters, battery cell testers, voltmeters, exhaust gas analyzers, ignition analyzers, and tune-up kits for the home mechanic. RAC's exhaust analyzer, priced at $131.60, would make a fine Christmas gift for ecology-conscious amateur mechanics. If that's more than you want to spend, RAC makes a budget tachometer which lists for $20.15. Free literature.

Road & Track
Box 2280
Newport Beach
California 92660

Famed auto magazine has catalog of accessories, mainly books, model cars and jewelry. Perhaps the ultimate kit car is a ⅛ scale model of a 1932 Rolls-Royce Phantom II with over 2,000 parts. In kit form it sells for $159.95 and is

28″ long when assembled. If you don't want to bother with the assembly, it can be supplied already completed, in a glass case, for $525.00. Other cars in the series are a 1931 Alfa-Romeo Grand Sport Spyder, 1931 Alfa 8C 2300 Monza Spyder and 1907 Fiat Racer.

Models in 1/43 scale come at the more down-to-earth price of $3.95. These are die cast metal, fully assembled. Also in 1/43 scale are a line of carefully-detailed classic car models at $7.25 per copy. Operating models of the futuristic Mercedes 111 and Porsche 917, in 1/16 scale and powered by flashlight batteries, are $15.95. A powered model of the Porsche 911 Targa in 1/19 scale is $9.95.

Kit fanciers will be taken with a line of plastic and metal cars and engines, in 1/16 scale, which contain 100 to 300 parts each. They range in price from a Mazda Wankel engine with 130 parts for $5.95, to a Bugatti Royale with detailed engine at $18.95.

The books available from R & T are copious and they range from practical repair manuals to elegant coffee-table books like Jesse Alexander's *At Speed* for $59.50. There are also racing posters at $2.00 each and classic car prints for $1.50. Jigsaw puzzles depicting classic cars or racing scenes are $3.00.

Sets of Road & Track road tests, reprinted from the original issues where they appeared, are available at prices from $3.00 (14 BMW tests) to $6.50 (32 Fiat tests).

Rally accessories, insignia jewelry and desk top items are also offered. Catalog $.50.

The Roadster Shop
16 Fieldhedge Drive
Sommerville, New Jersey 08876

Sells chrome and brass polish, made without corrosive chemicals or harmful abrasives, for $2.00 per 8 oz. bottle. Free information.

Brass and chrome polish from The Roadster Shop

Roaring 20 Autos, Inc.
R.D. 1, Box 178-G
Wall, New Jersey 07719

Operates car museum with about 100 cars on display. Entire inventory is priced for sale. Write for further information.

Rob de la Rive Box
Reben 22
5612 Villmergen AG
Switzerland

Mr. Box, who has been mentioned favorably in publications of the Ferrari Club of America, sells Ferraris, Maseratis, and Lamborghinis. He has a large stock of new and used parts for these cars and is also a prime source of parts for prewar Lancias and the 356 Porsche model. As a service, he is willing to reproduce Ferrari, Maserati, and Lamborghini owners' books for cost price. Send international reply coupon with queries.

The Roberk Co.
88 Long Hill Cross Road
Shelton, Connecticut 06484

Car antennas in power booster and unbreakable stainless steel models. Also slip-on universal antenna repair masts. Company also makes license plate frames, many types of exterior mirrors for cars and trucks, and windshield wiper blades. Free information.

John Roby
3703 Nassau Drive
San Diego, California 92115

Sells both out-of-print and in-print auto books, plus aerospace and nautical books. Catalog $.25.

Rocket
3501 Union Pacific Avenue
Los Angeles
California 90023

Accessories for popular domestic cars and the VW. Rocket offerings are: engine chain-downs, 12-volt utility lights, leather steering wheel covers, walnut dash trim for the VW and Pinto/Vega, custom door and window cranks, VW sport shifters, shifter knobs and pedal pads, cocoa floor mats, quartz driving lights, finned aluminum differential covers for GM cars, splash guards, VW nerf bars, chrome exhaust pipes, fiberglass hood scoops, front spoilers for small cars and vans, polished aluminum valve covers, valve cover breathers, chrome crankcase breather caps, hood pin kits, ignition wire dividers, low-restriction air cleaners, velocity stacks, fiberglass engine fans, stainless steel 6-blade fans, engine and transmission oil coolers, remote oil filter kits, mag wheel locks, tire pressure gauges, chrome wheel centers and dust covers, disc brake spacers, universal wheel adapters, burglar alarms, hood locks, and locking fuel line blocks. Disc and drum brake parts available include sintered iron brake linings, organic brake linings, self-adjuster conversion kits, and disc brake service hardware kits. Driveline components offered are nylon throw-out bearings, 4130 alloy clutch linkages, shifter repair kits, brass synchro rings, ring gear spacers, and driveshaft loops. Rocket electrical and ignition products consist of rpm controls, distributor curve springs, wiring kits, tune-up kits, distributor caps and rotors, performance coils, ignition system hardware, and remote starter controls. In the way of engine goodies there are timing gear and sprocket sets, hardened crankshaft keys, performance valvetrain components, high capacity oil pans, windage trays, heavy-duty oil pump springs, oil pressure regulator kits, and high-lift rockers. To complete the line-up Rocket has headers, VW intake manifolds, resonator mufflers for Japanese cars, header and standard mufflers, super duty hardware, electric fuel pumps, high-output mechanical pumps, fuel system fittings, carb adapters, automatic choke conversion kits, header choke stoves, carb linkage assemblies, chrome fuel line kits, carb jets,

	engine and exhaust system gaskets, aerosol paints and chemicals, shocks and shock extensions, up and down coil spring locks, traction bars, pinion snubbers, front and rear lift kits, spring spacers, spherical rod ends, and a complete line of steel and alloy wheels. Two catalogs, $4.00.
Rock-ett Products 2124 North Lee South El Monte California 91733	Rock-ett Products consist of roll bars, sand bars and cage kits for most 4WD vehicles including the Land Rover and Suzuki; custom roll bars for the VW Beetle and Datsun pickup; tow bars for popular 4WD vehicles; 11″ brake kits for Jeeps, Jeepsters and Wagoneers; full floating axles for Jeeps and Jeepsters; and Rancho overdrive units. Suzuki roll bars are $43.00 ($48.00 for heavy-duty version), and Jeep brake kits go for $149.50. Free literature.
Roddick Tool Co. 1023 North Pauline Street Anaheim, California 92801	Makes bolt extracters and internal pipe wrenches. Free literature.
Rolls-Royce & Bentley Owner-Drivers Club (Rolls-Royce and Bentley) c/o John Compton The Coach House Whistlers Wood The Ridge Woldingham Surrey England	The Club owns an impressive Inn in Surrey and is open to members from 9:00 A.M. to 11:00 P.M. daily, except Monday and Tuesday evenings. Although Club publications are only on an occasional basis, spare parts location, technical advice, and library privileges are available to members. Membership is open to anyone throughout the world who holds a genuine interest in Rolls and Bentley cars. For a nominal fee the Club will test and report on any car in which a member is interested—certainly a boon for Americans who are intending to import a Rolls or Bentley sight unseen. Yearly dues: approximately $15.00.
Rolls-Royce Club Midland (Rolls-Royce and Bentley) c/o Miss Susan Taylor 49, Wolverhampton Road South Birmingham, 32 England	This very active Club holds numerous events, publishes a monthly bulletin plus Rolls-Royce bibliographies, and offers technical advice to members. Associate membership, for Yanks, is about $3.60 a year with a small initiation fee.
Rolls-Royce Enthusiasts Club (Rolls-Royce and Bentley) c/o Lt. Col. E. B. Barrass Lincroft Montacute Road Tunbridge Wells Kent England	This very large Club sponsored more than 50 events last year, including the Great Alpine Commemorative Rally. Publications include *The Bulletin* bi-monthly and a membership list bi-annually. Open to owners of all Rolls-Royces plus Derby and Crewe Bentleys, the Club has a technical advice service, manufactures some repro parts, and will help members to locate all spare parts. Yearly dues: about $12.00.
Rolls-Royce Inc. P.O. Box 189 Paramus, New Jersey 07652	U.S. distributors for Rolls-Royce and Bentley.
Rolls-Royce Owners Club, Inc. (Rolls-Royce and Bentley)	The Club's activities center around the exchange of technical and historical information. A technical committee provides advice on restoration, and much information is

1822 North Second Street
Harrisburg
Pennsylvania 17102

contained in the bi-monthly magazine, *The Flying Lady*. There is an annual national meet plus regional meets held at various times of the year. Members receive a directory and register of members and cars, and can order many Rolls and Bentley technical manuals and replica catalogs through the Club. There is also a variety of jewelry and insignia clothing available. New prospective members must have a sponsor who has been a member of the RROC for at least two consecutive years. Yearly dues: $15.00.

Rolls-Royce Owners Club of Australia (Rolls-Royce)
c/o D. Watkins
28, Dendy Street
Brighton 3186
Victoria
Australia

The address at left is for the Victoria Branch of the Club which has a number of regions in the country. The Club publishes a quarterly magazine, while each branch has its own monthly newsletter. Each branch sponsors competitive and social events, while some maintain lending libraries, sell technical publications, and aid members with restorations. Yearly dues: $10.50.

Ronco Corporation
Blue Bell
Pennsylvania 19422

Vertex magnetos are known for their dependable operation and superior quality. Both street and competition models are available. Ready to install units are $179.50 for 4-cylinder cars to $224.50 for 8-cylinder versions. Options include mechanical tach drive, degree ring, starting relay, kill switch, key type switch, radio suppressed rotor and protective cover. Free literature.

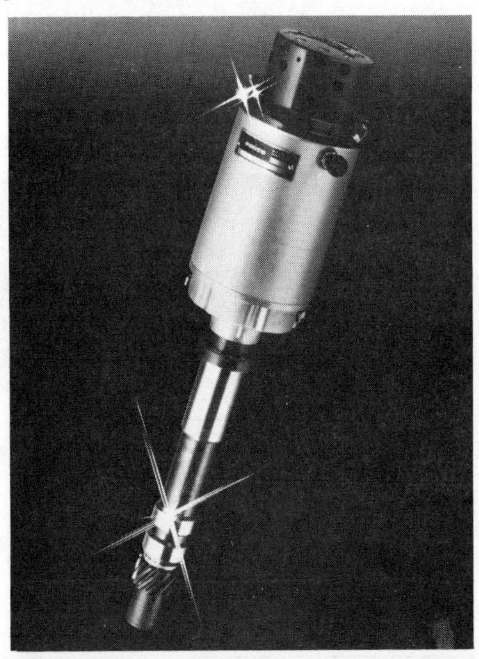

Vertex Magneto from Ronco Corporation

Ron's Bug House
1807 North "E" Street
San Bernadino
California 92405

Ron's line of VW accessories includes SPG, Okrasa and SCAT cranks; big bore kits; SCAT and EMPI cams and valvetrain gear; plenum and ram manifolds; Holley, Zenith and Weber carbs; velocity stacks; Bosch and Judson ignition equipment; oil coolers; heavy-duty oil pumps and windage trays; extractor exhaust systems; lightweight flywheels; competition clutches; off-road drivetrain accessories; most popular quick shifters; interior and exterior cosmetic items; fiberglass body parts and scoops for Type I, II, and III models; dune buggy exhausts; buggy bumpers and skid plates; Bilstein, Koni and Gabriel shocks; and buggy electrical and brake system accessories. Catalog, $1.00.

Ron's Parts
P.O. Box 1466
Lawrence
Massachusetts 01842

Packard and Oldsmobile parts. Packard stock includes mechanical parts from 1935-56 and body parts from 1945-56. Oldsmobile stock is mostly engine parts. Send a stamped, self-addressed envelope with query.

Rootlieb T Hood Works
545 South Center Street
Turlock, California 95380

Aluminum and steel Model T hoods which duplicate originals. Also fenders, aprons and engine pans for Ts. Fenders made for other cars by special order. Write for prices.

David Niles Rosen
364 Tompkins Street
Cortland, New York 13045

Primarily deals in parts for 1953-62 Corvettes. Also complete cars for sale. In addition, handles some Cadillac and other NOS parts. Send a stamped, self-addressed envelope with query. Write for availability of catalog.

Rossi Transmissions
2826A Metropolitan Place
Pomona, California 91767

Racing transmissions include versions of the Powerglide, Turbo-Hydro, Torqueflite and Ford C-4 and C-6. A street and strip version of the Turb-Hydro goes for an exchange price of $275.00. Competition and super-competition models are priced at $325.00 and $375.00 respectively. A Sportsman Turbo-Hydro, for RVs and tow cars is $425.50. Also sells high-stall-speed torque converters, trans coolers, aluminum transmission pans, and shift kits. Catalog, $1.00.

Modified power glide transmissions from Rossi Transmissions

Rotiform Corporation
2008 Cotner Avenue
Los Angeles
California 90025

Makes a digital direct-reading speedometer in models with or without speed warning lights. The "with" model sells for $94.95. Free literature.

Roto-Faze Ignitions & Equipment
1152 East 65th Street
Inglewood
California 90302

Roto-Faze ignition systems are available for most domestic cars and VWs. The Roto-Faze Magnum model distributor, at $133.00, is also available at a slightly higher price for special engines such as the Offy 168 cu. in. supercharged racing engine. Coils are $20.00 each. Other electric accessories include plug wire and terminals, and block converters for Mopar engines. A CD ignition system, for use on maximum performance engines, is also available.

	Some special fuel system accessories made by the company are Isoport blower manifolds, and Thinline fuel hydrometers. Free information.
Rover Owner's Association (Rover) c/o W.G. Duffield Meteor Works Solihull Warwickshire England	Coordinates activities of Rover clubs worldwide along with clubs devoted to the Land Rover. The American affiliate is the Rover Owner's Association of North America, 76 Washington Street, East Orange, New Jersey 07017. The Rover Owner's Association publishes a quarterly newsletter plus a monthly bulletin to clubs, both of which are circulated only to affiliate members.
Royal Industries **Brake Products Division** Stewarts Lane Danville, Kentucky 40433	Disc brake assemblies for foreign and domestic cars. Also makes brake shoes for riveted or bonded brakes. Consult catalog at wholesalers.
Royal Industries **Grant Division** 16960 Gale Avenue City of Industry California 91744	Manufacturer of Grant piston rings for all cars, including most every foreign make. Also makes standard line of safety helmets, replacement steering wheels, steering wheel adapters. Free literature. Order through your wholesaler.
Royann Enterprises Box 1209 Rapid City South Dakota 57701	Dealers in shop manuals, catalogs, and other automotive literature. Send a stamped, self-addressed envelope with query.
Jim Russell International Racing Driver's School P.O. Box 911 Rosemond, California 93560	Based at Willow Springs International Raceway, the School offers eight lessons for the budding racing driver. Lessons one through six cost $65.00 each and lessons seven and eight are $75.00 each. The full eight lessons are $500.00. Students drive Merlyn Formula Fords. Free literature.
Mason Rust Route 1, P.O. Box 471 Ashland, Virginia 23005	Parts for Mercedes-Benz 300-series. Send a stamped, self-addressed envelope with query
S & W Race Cars Walnut and Cedar Streets Spring City Pennsylvania 19475	Race car chassis construction and speed equipment. A complete funny car chassis is priced at $5,579.50 to $5,779.50. A fiberglass body with front and rear windows goes for $1,200.00. A complete front engine dragster chassis is $3,545.00, while a complete rear engine chassis sells at $3,712.50. All parts are available individually. Free price lists.
Saab Motors Inc. 100 Waterfront Street New Haven, Connecticut 06506	U.S. distributor; service manuals.
Saab Owners Club (Saab) c/o J. Holdham Fosterbrook High Street Westerham Kent, England	There are three annual Club meetings where concours competitions and driving tests are held. One meeting is at Beaulieu, one at Woburn and the third held at various locations in the Midlands each year. *Saab Driver,* an informative magazine with advertisements, is issued

monthly. The Club offers technical advice, some spare parts, rally information, and the loan of service manuals. Yearly dues: $4.80; $7.20 for husband/wife membership.

Safety Racing Equipment Inc.
P.O. Box 72
Eau Claire, Michigan 49111

Drivetrain components, mag wheels, disc brakes, and fuel cells for racing cars. Products include hubs and hub components, quick-change axle assemblies, axle shafts, component parts for the Halibrand Championship rear end, racing seats in aluminum or fiberglass, safety belts and seat harnesses, couplings for closed drivelines, 15″ and 16″ all-magnesium wheels, Hurst/Airheart disc brake assemblies, EDCO universal magnesium calipers and vented discs, and ATL safety fuel cells. Free information.

The Salmson Register
(French Salmson)
Ard-na-Greina
Morley Lane
Haslemere
Surrey
England

Holds two or three informal meetings yearly, generally in conjunction with a sister club, the Amilcar Register. A major rally is held each September. The *Salmson Register Bulletin* is published quarterly. Other services are the location and remanufacture of spare parts, and technical advice on request. Yearly dues: £1 in Britain, $3.60 overseas.

Lin Sample
102 Garfield Street, No. 5
Ashland, Oregon 97520

Literature on antique and classic cars. Most items pertain to electrical and mechanical service. Send a stamped, self-addressed envelope with query.

Sanderson Headers
1379 North Carolan
Burlingame, California 94010

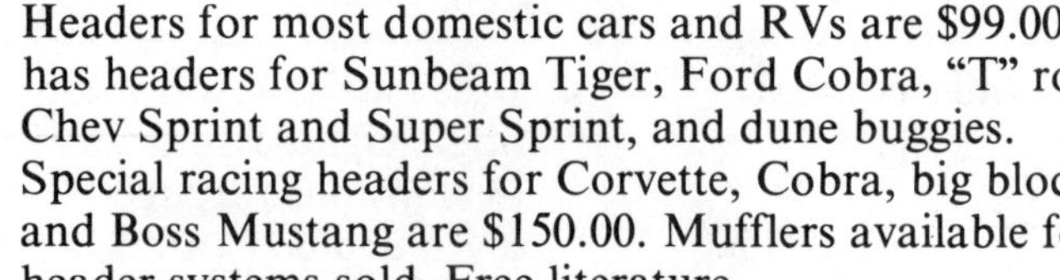

Headers for most domestic cars and RVs are $99.00. Also has headers for Sunbeam Tiger, Ford Cobra, "T" roadster, Chev Sprint and Super Sprint, and dune buggies. Special racing headers for Corvette, Cobra, big block Ford and Boss Mustang are $150.00. Mufflers available for all header systems sold. Free literature.

San Fernando Buggy Center
1533 Truman Street
San Fernando, California 91340

Dune buggy frames, chassis components, and accessories. The Hi Jumper Ascot buggy frame ($160.00 in kit form, or $360.00 welded) is designed for oval track racing; the Duster is designed for off-road racing; and the Rustler ($579.00 with accessories) is the basic chassis used by the famed Fritz Kroyer for desert racing. Accessories available include bucket seats, a fiberglass hood and side panels, foam steering wheel, rear motor cage, steel wheels and mud or sand tires, a competition shoulder harness, and the Neal cutting brake. The company carries Per-Lux, Cibie, and K-C HiLites lighting equipment; Bilstein shocks; Crown drivetrain components; close-ratio VW gears; skid plates; steel motor mounts; auxiliary rear shock mounts; heavy-duty torsion bars; aircraft universal joints; front I-beam mounting kits, Filtron air cleaners; Tri-Mil headers; and Buggy Whip fiberglass flag poles. To haul your sand machine out to the dunes, the Buggy Center offers a lightweight 2-wheel trailer ($135.00), or a heavier ramp trailer ($150.00 in kit form, $325.00 welded). Free literature.

Sand Toys Co.
1731 West Lincoln
Anaheim, California 92801

For those who would like to try some off-road racing in the popular 1200 cc class, Sand Toys offers a welded frame for $245.00, 36 hp engine set up for dirt at $150.00, and a crash box transmission for $55.00. Other parts a buggy-builder might need include a front axle ($60.00), seats ($36.00), an aluminum 5½-gallon gas tank ($40.00), lights ($16.00), tires and wheels ($165.00), and other accessories. A complete ready-to-go rail is $999.00. Other offerings for VWs and buggies include Filtron and Tri Phase air filters, fiberglass Baja Bug kits (from $74.95), Baja bumpers, chrome tubular bumpers, Neal pedal assemblies and cutting brakes, Big Bore kits, Weber and Holley carbs, oil coolers, extractor exhausts, full-cage roll bars, skid plates, Sedan and Bus air scoops, plenum intake manifolds, off-road tires, VW seat covers, and many fiberglass Beetle parts. Free literature.

Sandwinder Company
2746 Main Street
Riverside, California 92502

Got a yen for some off-road racing? Sandwinder offers the chassis and much more besides.

The basic Challenger chassis in single or dual-seat version is designed for a rear-mounted engine and constructed of mild steel tubing, suitably triangulated. The price is $495.00. Another hundred bucks gets you the mid-engined Midi chassis (also available in a dual-seat version at $649.00) with brackets for a Porsche 911 steering box and VW master cylinder and pedal cluster assemblies.

You can buy a reconditioned Porsche steering box for $99.95, spring plates ($39.95 or $64.95 for the mid-engine variety), torsion bars for the rear-engined chassis ($79.95), a "midi" shift-linkage kit ($69.95), aluminum or fiberglass dash panels ($16.95), front skid plate ($19.95), rear skid plate ($29.95), fiberglass hood and side panels ($179.95), and other racing essentials.

Also available are heavy-duty axle tubes for pre-1968 transaxles (Type I and Type III), reinforced side-plates for swing axle and IRS VWs, and fiberglass seven-piece Baja Bug kits of appealing design. The kits cost $195.00, with an accessory installation kit going for another $49.95. It consists of Dietz 820 headlight assemblies, hood tie-down straps and hooks, chromed rear deck-lid hood pin assemblies, and fender welting.

Now here's an unusual item for drag-racers, funny car fans, and Q-ship lovers. A complete flip-up VW front, fenders and all, handcrafted of 'glass and weighing only 22 pounds. The gun-lay-up version goes for $149.95 and the hand-lay-up model is available for 20 bucks more. It fits standard Beetles only and pre-1967 headlight assemblies are required. Literature, $1.00.

Satra Motors Ltd.
Canada Road
Oyster Lane
Byfleet
Surrey
England

If you happen to own a Moskvich and need spare parts, or if you'd like to import one (paying due attention to emission control and safety regulations, of course), Satra Motors is your nearest source. Free literature.

Scales Air Compressor Corporation
88 Windsor Avenue
Mineola, New York 11501
185 Woodward Avenue
Ridgewood, New York 11237

Through its rebabbitting service division, Scales will pour and machine babbitt bearings to any specification within one day after receipt of connecting rods. Rods should be shipped by United Parcel or parcel post.

Scales also distributes most major brands of air compressors and accessories, including after-coolers, dryers, filters, regulators, silencers and safety devices. Complete service is available on all brands handled. Free literature.

Scarborough Faire
Box 112
Rehoboth
Massachusetts 02769

Specializing in hard parts for the MGA. Most parts available, including replacement body panels, new tops, and upholstery. Also has chrome trim items such as the trunk lid Octagon ($2.50), and vent grille 'MGA' ($5.95). Rebuilt 1500 and 1600 engines with new oversized pistons are available. The Mk. II cylinder head is $100.00. A rebuilt clutch pressure plate is $19.35 on an exchange basis, with a $3.00 core charge. Catalog, $.50.

Scat Enterprises
P.O. Box 4096
Inglewood, California 90309

Performance parts for VW, Porsche, Corvair and Japanese cars. Dual port competition heads for all VW engines, except type IV, are $236.80 a pair. Dual port heads for use with most competition or street manifolds with slight port enlargement are $524.42 a set. Twin 40 mm Weber carb racing kit for VW is $341.06. Plenum ram induction manifold for single port heads is $33.22. Zenith 32NDIX carb rebuild kit is $12.35. Other products include spun-aluminum velocity stacks for VW and Porsche 4-cylinder, street and competition full-flow oil cooler kits, windage

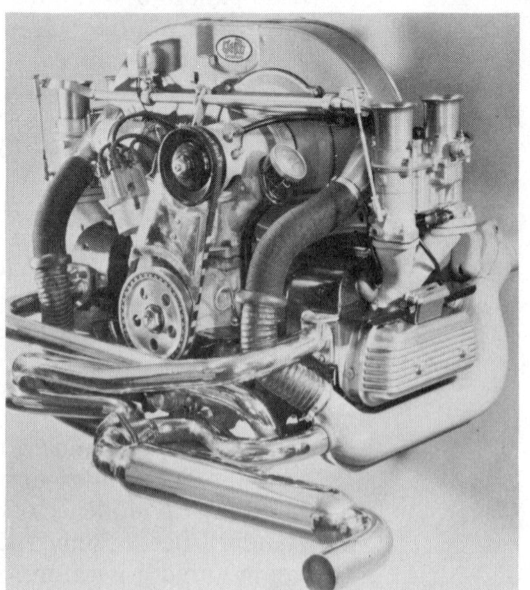

VW stroker engines from Scat Enterprises

trays for VW and dune buggy, lightweight flywheels, transaxle supports and straps, heavy-duty spider gear kits for swing-axle VWs and Porsches as well as newer VWs with IRS, drag lockers for VW and Porsche transaxles, close-ratio competition gears for VW boxes, VW and Porsche nerf bars, fiberglass Baja Bug kits, side scoops and fender flares for VW bugs, VW Bus fiberglass deck lids with built-in scoops, and Beetle front spoilers. VW Type IV/Porsche 914 items include 76 mm welded stroker crankshaft ($177.86 with $75.00 core charge), lightweight aluminum pushrods, performance cams and valve train components, Weber and Solex carb kits, oil cooler kits and headers. For the 4-cylinder Porsche available items include SPG roller bearing cranks, 1700 cc piston and cylinder kits, aluminum oil sumps and adapters to convert Porsche manifolds to accept 48IDA Weber carbs. For the Capri/Pinto there are stroker and carb kits, headers, and fiberglass hoods with built-in scoops. Carb kits and headers are also available for the Toyota Corolla and Opel. Company also carries Crown Corvair-to-VW conversion kits and heavy-duty Corvair items. Corvair hop-up accessories include ram induction manifolds to adapt Holley or Carter AFB 4-barrel carb to Corvair 140 hp engines, headers, valve components, and an optimum advance distributor kit. Catalog, $2.00.

Schaeffer & Long, Inc.
210 Davis Road
Magnolia, New Jersey 08049

Complete restoration services for any auto. Mechanical work, fabrication of parts, painting, wood work and upholstery are all handled. No parts are sold separately. Write for further information.

J. Schneider
19 South Union Street
Bayshore, New York 11706

Has *all* parts for Cadillacs 1938-48. Send a stamped, self-addressed envelope with queries.

Schott Metal Products Co.
2225 Lee Road
Akron, Ohio 44306

Replacement body parts for American cars and pickup trucks plus a few imports such as VW and VW Bus, Anglia, Metropolitan, and Vauxhall. Some metal panels are available for older domestic makes such as Willys, Hudson, Nash, and Studebaker. Catalog, $1.00.

Schrillo Company
16750 Schoenborn Street
Sepulveda, California 91343

Power steering units for 4WD and competition cars. A Ford unit for the Bronco and pickup trucks is $298.50. Power steering units also available for Midgets, Sprints, Modifieds and Championship cars. The Schrillo power units are adapted to Schroeder steering. A new division of the Company offers products for the Toyota Land Cruiser, including roll bars, dual front shock mounts, and Cibie lights. Free literature.

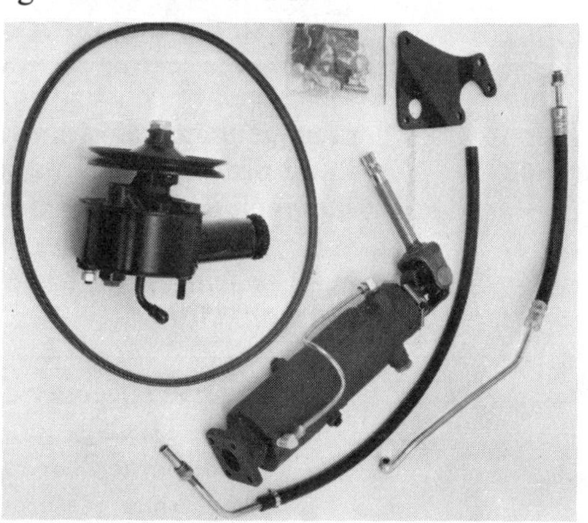

Schrillo's Bronco power steering kit

Conrad E. Schwager
4503 North Knoxville Avenue
Peoria, Illinois 61614

Used auto parts for American makes 1928-58. Parts for Buick, Cadillac, Ford and others. Also specializes in trading interesting cars. Limited partial restorations. Send a stamped, self-addressed envelope with query.

Scientific Motors Ltd.
c/o Howard Nudelman
President
12119 Edgecliff Place
Los Altos Hills
California 94022

U.S. distributors for the M.R.E. Formula Ford originating in England. The car can be converted to Formula Three specifications. Scientific Motors carries an extensive parts inventory and will also do chassis tuning and machine shop fabrication for any Formula Car. Free information.

David Scott-Moncrieff and Son Ltd.
2 Macclesfield Road
Leek
Staffordshire ST13 8LA
England

Specialists in Rolls-Royce and Bentley. Classic and modern Rolls and Bentleys shipped to overseas clients. Company makes all shipping arrangements and price is approximately $550.00 to ship and insure. All cars are right hand drive, and the majority of coachbuilt bodies are aluminum. Free stock list.

SCU Accessories
35093 Schoolercraft Road
Livonia, Michigan 48150

Foreign car goodies and performance parts. Has Cosmic wheels, Peco free-flow exhaust systems, Spax shock absorbers, adjustable outside mirrors in racing styles, Peco wood and leather rim steering wheels, Stadium fog and driving lights, Intereurope workshop manuals, Bort front and rear spoilers for Vega and Pinto, and the Wood Jeffreys electric fan kit for all cars and light trucks. The electric fan is claimed to improve performance and economy and reduce engine wear. Catalog, $1.00.

Scuncio Chevrolet
446 Putnam Pike, Route 44
Greenville, Rhode Island 02828

This Chevrolet dealer has gone the factory one better and sells Vegas complete with 350 cu. in. V-8 engines. The basic model is a Hatchback or Notchback with a 370 hp LT-1 Chev V-8 with solid lifters, 11:1 compression, aluminum high-rise manifold, dual feed Holley, tubular headers, electric fuel pump and chrome air cleaner. A Don Hardy installation kit is used, with heavy duty front springs, flex-fan, HD radiator and Saginaw 4-speed gearbox. Many options are available. Another V-8 Vega model, available both on coupes and wagons, features the same basic equipment plus a narrowed Chev 12-bolt rear end with heavy duty brakes, Positraction, 14″x6″ mag wheels with E70x14 belted tires, dual exhaust system, Hurst shifter and other equipment. Free literature.

Sealed Power Corporation
2001 Sanford Street
Muskegon, Michigan 49443

Makers of Speed-Pro engine parts for performance and racing engines. Best known product is the patented Head Land piston ring. Other items available for most domestic cars include forged pistons, cams, tappets, rocker arms, and valve train gear. Also has engine bearings including main bearings, con rod bearings, and camshaft bearings. Catalog, $1.00.

Sears, Roebuck & Co.
303 East Ohio Street
Chicago, Illinois 60611

Sears has five specialty catalogs of interest to auto enthusiasts. Their general car catalog is titled *Parts for Automobiles and Trucks* and lists a great many hard parts along with tools and accessories.

For most post-1962 American cars, Sears has air filters, oil filters, PCV valves, gas-line filters, spark plugs, plug wire sets, ignition parts, coils, exhaust system parts and fiberglass-packed mufflers, rebuilt engines or short blocks, fuel pumps, carb rebuild kits, clutch parts, rebuilt transmissions, crankshaft repair kits, rocker arm assemblies, main and conrod bearings, U-joints, pistons and ring sets, valves, cams, timing chains, gasket kits, alternators, rebuilt generators and starters, solenoids, radiators, radiator and heater hoses, water pumps, fan belts, front-end parts and steering stabilizers. Also regular, heavy-duty, overload and air shocks; coil and leaf springs plus helper springs; master cylinders; wheel cylinders and other brake parts; wheel bearings; oil seals; floor mats; seat covers; batteries; replacement heaters and aftermarket air-conditioners; trailer hitches; tow bars; outside mirrors; convertible tops; car covers; and burglar alarms. Prices are favorable.

Sears' general auto catalog also lists a large variety of Craftsman tools, repair manuals, engine test equipment, lube supplies, Edelbrock manifolds, Holley carbs, Penske and Hurst shifters, Cragar and Penske wheels, quartz halogen lights, instruments, seat belts and harnesses, dune buggy accessories, floor jacks, hydraulic presses, and tire-changing equipment.

Hard parts for foreign cars are listed in Sears' *Imported Car Replacement Parts and Supplies* catalog. Cars covered include all VWs, Alfa, Audi, Austin, Austin-Healey, BMW, Citroen DS, Datsun, Fiat, British Ford, Hillman, Jaguar, MG, Mercedes, Morris, Opel, Peugeot, Renault, Rover, Saab, Simca, Triumph, Vauxhall, Volvo, and some others. Parts available include filters, ignition kits, brake and clutch parts, shocks, exhaust systems, gaskets, carb rebuilt kits, some front end and power-train parts, taillight assemblies, and electrical system components. There are also trailer hitches, car covers, replacement convertible tops, AMCO luggage racks and seat belts.

For VWs the import car catalog lists rebuilt engines, EMPI accessories, Holley carbs, a Schiefer clutch/flywheel set and seat covers. Craftsman metric tools are also listed in this catalog.

For Jeep owners, Sears puts out a *Parts for Jeep, Utility Vehicles and Jeepsters* catalog which is quite comprehensive. It lists hard parts for all Jeep Universals, both military and civilian, locking differentials, a Jeep roll bar, pintle hooks, manual winches, a military-type gas can carrier for $6.19, front free-wheeling hubs for $39.99, King-Seeley and Stewart-Warner dash instruments, steel or aluminum tops and half-tops, Jeep seat covers and floor mats, chromed steel wheels up to 8″ wide, and rear-mounted spare tire brackets.

Sears *Power and Hand Tool* catalog lists the whole Craftsman line and contains home mechanic essentials like bench grinders, drill presses, arc and oxy-acetylene welding outfits (the cheapest gas outfit is $97.50), power hacksaws, metal-turning lathes, air compressors, impact wrenches, and tool boxes in all sizes.

Sears *1973 Catalog of Accessories for Mobile Homes, Recreational Vehicles and Camping* contains all the dope on trailers and hitches, stabilizing jacks, oil coolers, auxiliary gas tanks, load-compensating springs, camper shells for pickups, CB radios and portable TVs, dual battery systems, electric converters and inverters, Sears' utility trailer chassis (heavy-duty and tilt-bed models), and heaps of camping equipment.

All of Sears' catalogs are available for the asking at the catalog counter of the nearest Sears store—if you're lucky. They are all popular items and are therefore frequently out of stock, in which case the proper procedure is to ask for the address of the nearest catalog-ordering center and send away for what you need. Five free catalogs.

Linda Seebach
306 North Plum Street
Northfield
Minnesota 55057

Very complete selection of Studebaker shop manuals, owners' manuals, parts catalogues, service bulletins, and price books. Also Studebaker and Avanti parts catalogues. Studebaker letterheads, 1937 design, are $2.50 per 100 sheets plus $1.00 postage. Also deals in Studebaker-Avanti parts ordered through South Bend. Write for lists of items available. Request price information on parts.

Seiberling Tire & Rubber Co.
345 15th Street NW
Barberton, Ohio 44203

Radial, belted, and bias-ply tires for most applications. Seiberling offers a radial, steel-belted truck tire, a wide-whitewall tire for classic and special-interest cars, 60-series nylon tires with raised white lettering, trailer wheel tires, and flotation tires, along with the standard lines. Free information.

Seibert Restoration
Greenville, Ohio 45331

Packard NOS parts and restoration services. Also some parts for other early cars. Will buy and sell cars on consignment. Send a stamped, self-addressed envelope with query.

Semperit of America, Inc.
156 Ludlow Avenue
Northvale
New Jersey 07647

Radial and conventional tires in most popular patterns and sizes. Publishes literature on technical tire data and applications. Free literature.

S.E.S.
Highway 212
Stillwater
Minnesota 55082

The S.E.S. fuel injection system is a low-pressure, constant-flow, bolt-on unit which sells for only $89.50. Even with necessary adapters for the VW, Datsun, Toyota, Vega or Pinto, the price is still under $100.00. Although the S.E.S. fuel injection unit differs from a carburetor in that it works on a demand principle, it is nevertheless a very simple unit requiring minimal maintenance. Performance gains are claimed to be more than worthwhile. Free literature.

Shankle Automotive Engineering
15451-F Cabrito Road
Van Nuys, California 91406

Racing engines of Ford or Alfa Romeo manufacture. Complete preparation and overhaul of Alfa engines. Parts and preparation for Ford Cortina, Lotus T/C Ford and 2-liter Ford Pinto engines. Complete race-ready, dry-sump Cortina or uprated engines available at $1,585.00. Engine components, headers, oil pans, brake pads and linings, and engine coolers for Baby Grand Pintos. Machine shop services available. Free literature.

Baby Grand Pinto from Shankle Automotive Engineering

Shaw's Speed Shop
98 North York Road
Willow Grove
Pennsylvania 19090

Retail and wholesale dealers for many popular high-performance accessories including B&M transmissions, Detroit Locker, Edelbrock, Holley, Hooker, Hurst, Iskenderian, Jahns Pistons, Judson, Koni, Mr. Gasket, Segal, Stewart-Warner, Vertex Magnetos, and many others. Free information.

Shelby International
Box 640
Gardena, California 90248

Carroll Shelby, who is no longer associated with supplying parts for the Cobra (see separate listing for Cobra Performance, Ltd.) and Shelby GT (contact Ford Products Information Center, 12263 Market Street, Livonia, Michigan 48150 for parts information), now manufactures alloy wheels and Shelby 60-series tires. Shelby wheels come in models for the Honda and Mini-Cooper, Datsun 240Z, compact cars, full-size cars (sizes up to 15″x11″), and light trucks. Other company products include sports car and VW headers, front end lift kits for domestic cars, rear leaf spring kits, shock extensions, traction bars, rear coil spring lift kits, adjustable pinion snubbers, and engine safety chains. Free literature.

Jay Sherwin
395 Dumbarton Boulevard
Cleveland, Ohio 44143

Mr. Sherwin, who is the Secretary-Treasurer of the Willys-Overland Jeepster Club, has literature on these makes for sale. Send a stamped, self-addressed envelope with queries.

Sidles Manufacturing Co. Inc.
7300 South General Bruce Dr.
P.O. Box 3537
Temple, Texas 76501

Those aluminum louvered sun shades which are often seen custom-fitted to the windows of domestic cars and recreational vehicles, are fabricated by Sidles from a special material known as Kaiser ShadeScreen. The screens can either be stationary or rolled down with the windows, depending upon the model. Sidles' brochure explains in detail the various types of shades available and installation procedures. Free catalog and price quote on windows desired. Specify make, model and year of car.

Sigma Engineering Company
11320 Burbank Boulevard
North Hollywood
California 91601

Racers suffering from continual buzzing noises in their ears will want to investigate the sonic "Ear-Valv" which costs $4.95 a set and is claimed to be a major advance over the ordinary ear plug. Free literature.

Sikora Brothers, Inc.
1324 Hird Avenue
Cleveland, Ohio 44107

Complete frames and chassis for rear-engine dragsters, Funny Cars and Altereds. Basic frame for rear-engine dragster is made from 4130 chrome moly and includes front axle, radius rods, tie rods, spindles, front wheels and tires, steering, steering wheel, brake handle, master cylinder, motor plate and mounts, clutch linkage, firewall, rear end housing (Ford or Chrysler), axles and brakes, and pushbar. Price is $2,500.00. Many extras include drag chute ($225.00), two Canard wings ($125.00), one large top wing ($200.00), body with seat ($600.00), Lenco two speed trans ($850.00), and reverser for transmission ($450.00). Free information.

Silhill Products
Department A. E.3
226 Mary Street
Birmingham B12 9RJ
England

Specializes in small accessories for British cars. One of the newest products is the Bowes Steam Injection unit which is claimed to offer better mileage and a lower fuel octane requirement. It works by passing water through the hot exhaust gases in a car's manifold and using steam to mix with gas and air. Price is approximately $35.00. Other products include gear change conversions for Cortinas and Minis, quartz halogen driving lights, interior rally lights, padded and shaped seat covers which improve lateral support, accessory rear defroster screens, a variety of air horns, alloy wheels, custom steering wheels, roof racks, trailer lighting sets, car compasses and thermometers, a dual carb synchronizer, timing lights, other tune-up tools, dashboard instruments, special engine and lubrication tools, car radios, an electric aerial, battery chargers, burglar alarms, a 12-volt battery-operated electric drill, waterproof covers for coils and distributors, a fly-off handbrake kit for BMC cars, and some trailer accessories. Free catalog.

Silver Seal Products
1060 Southfield
Lincoln Park, Michigan 48146

Valve spring inserts and adjusters for American and imported cars. Free catalog to jobbers only.

Silvo Hardware Co.
107-109 Walnut Street
Philadelphia
Pennsylvania 19106

Power and hand tools for all uses. Silvo carries Campbell-Hausfeld portable air compressors, Indestro and Crescent hand tools, Channellock pliers, Fox Valley test instruments, Plews lubrication equipment, Mitutoyo precision measuring instruments and various brands of power tools. Catalog, $.50.

H.D. Simmons
Route No. 1
Rayland, Ohio 43943

Vintage Chevrolet parts, NOS and repro, for cars 1916-57. Also sheet metal for most cars 1916-57. NOS Eagle radiator caps, $40.00 each; 1931 and '32 owner's manuals, $7.00 each; 1932 replacement free wheeling gear unit, $25.00; 1931-32 repro wiring harness, $35.00. Also some fiberglass repro parts. Send a stamped self-addressed envelope for parts and price lists.

Simpson Safety Equipment
22638 South Normandie Avenue
Torrance, California 90502

Specializes in competition lap belts and shoulder harnesses in many styles. Also lists drag chutes, fire-resistant racer's clothing, Lenco transmission safety blankets, and on-board fire extinguishing systems. The Simpson S-5000 Nomex Suit is available at $343.20 in a choice of colors. Chutes are $108.00 and up. Catalog $1.00.

Singer Owners Club
(Singer)
c/o D. Freeth
31, Rivershill
Watton-at-Stone
Hertfordshire
England

Club holds regular events throughout the year, from Singer National Day to sprints and production car trials. The bi-monthly magazine *Singer Owner,* contains a parts advertisements section. There are spares registrars in various categories, as well as a Club membership registrar. Yearly dues: about $7.00.

Singer Owners Club
of America
(Singer)
1578 Terilyn
San Jose, California 95122

Has annual meeting on the West Coast every spring and hopes to have an East Coast meeting in the near future. Publishes bi-monthly newsletter, *The Singer's Voice,* with technical data and parts information. Has Club machinist, making some repro parts, and expects to have Club badges available. The Club president, Corey Welty, sells Singer parts at cost to members and offers a few tips to prospective owners. Keep the cam change tension adjusted properly, says Mr. Welty, or the chain will cut the oil line leading to the cam, the cam will be ruined in about ten minutes and you will be $250.00 poorer. Also go easy on the rear axles since they are very tender and new ones are non-existent. Before buying a Singer inspect the wood portions of the body, as they are difficult to remanufacture unless you happen to be a cabinet maker. Yearly dues: $9.50 currently. Dues may vary from year to year depending upon Club projects.

Sioux Tools Inc.
Sioux City, Iowa 51102

The Sioux line of industrial power equipment includes air impact wrenches, air hammers and drivers, air drills, portable air grinders and sanders, electric grinders and sanders, bench grinders, portable polishers, electric drills and drivers, orbital disc sanders, valve face grinding machines, valve seat grinding sets, valve stem guide reamers, tapered pilots, flexible shaft units and accessories, impact wrench sockets, impact hammer and driving tools, drill and polisher accessories, and wire wheel brushes. Free catalog to jobbers and service garages.

Sissell's
10829 Slack Road
South El Monte
California 91733

Specializing in 6-cylinder performance equipment; offerings include cams for Chev and Ford, air flowed cylinder heads, racing timing gear sets, aluminum/bronze distributor gears, forged pistons and aluminum rods, thin beaded-steel Chev head gaskets, Chev quad intake manifolds, Ford and Chev headers and header hardware, and Weber carbs and manifolds for most 6-cylinder engines. A complete 45 DCOE Weber side draft package is $425.00. Air flowed heads for Ford, Chev, or GMC range in price from $325.00 to $375.00.

	Heads in the "Lions Share" series are $175.00 for popular V-8s, and $125.00 for a 6-cylinder engine. Company's air flow service has now been expanded to include Chrysler Hemis, large and small block Chev V-8s, Boss Fords, VW, and other engines. Free information.
John Sisto 3531 South Elmwood Avenue Berwyn, Illinois 60402	Sells old-car prints, and clippings from magazines and newspapers dating as far back as 1896. Free literature.
Siva Motor Car Co., Ltd. P.O. Box 41 Aylesbury Buckinghamshire England	Among the most interesting and futuristic fiberglass bodies available for the VW chassis is the Siva Saluki. It is a coupe with gull-wing doors and a manual headlamp retraction mechanism. The body color is molded in, and there is a choice of six shades. Optional extras include seats, dash, carpets, wheels, and Kleber VT 10, GTS tires. The export price is $848.00 for the basic kit. This is a considerable discount on the British price which includes VAT. Another interesting 'glass kit car is the multi-purpose Llama Country Car designed for Chrysler Imp (British Chrysler) components. This vehicle, on the general style of VW's "The Thing," has steel bumpers, a nylon coated windscreen, Cibie Headlamps, and a heater. Rear seats, and very useful front and rear fiberglass enclosures (panel truck-style with the removable front top designed like a Porsche Targa) are optional. Radial tires are also available. Export price for the basic body kit in four optional colors is $1,680.00. Free literature.
S-K Tools Division of Dresser Industries, Inc. 3535 West 47th Street Chicago, Illinois 60632	S-K metric and SAE wrench sets, and other common hand tools, are sold at many accessory stores and parts houses. Free literature.
Sky Top Products Co. 215 Dogwood Lane Mahwah, New Jersey 07430	Manufactures the following parts: 1929-31 Chevrolet brackets, $34.95; 1929-31 Chevrolet bumpers, $59.95; 1931-34 Chevrolet single bar front bumpers, $59.95; 1931-34 Chevrolet rear bumperette (2) $59.95. Plans to expand line to include later model bumpers. Write for further information.
Slep Electronics Co. 301 Highway Ellenton, Florida 33533	Makers of transistorized ignition systems available in both negative and positive ground. Prices with coil run from $39.95 to $59.95 depending upon output. Free information.
Small Car Essentials P.O. Box 412 Buffalo, New York 14240	VW accessories. Hand starter for $3.98. Rear-axle stabilizing spring for 1968 and earlier Beetles and Buses sells for $19.95. Adjustable main jet for all VW Solex carbs at $3.75 for earlier carbs, $4.25 for PICT 30-2 and later models. Master float valve claimed to increase performance of all carbs, $3.50. Also adapters to fit American wheels on VW, increasing track width, and VW fiberglass spoiler. Literature, $1.00.
Smith and Deakin Plastics 292 Tolladine Road Worcester England	Need a trunk lid for your DAF 55? Or a hood for a Wolsley Hornet? Smith and Deakin can oblige. They have fiberglass parts for a great many common makes as well

as some exotics. Makes covered include Alfa Guilletta, many Austin models, Austin-Healeys, Spridgets, British Fords, Hillmans, Jag sedans and "E" types, MG A/B/Cs, Minis, Porsche 356, Rovers, Sunbeam Alpines, Triumphs, Rileys, and others. Free parts and price lists.

Steve Smith Autosports
Box 11631
Santa Ana
California 92711

Steve Smith is the author of *The Stock Car Racing Chassis; Design, Theory, Construction* and *The Trans Am and Corvette Chassis,* as well as *The Complete Stock Car Chassis Guide.* Each book is available at $5.00. For those who want to take the advice in these books, Mr. Smith has available tire pressure gauges, durometers (tire rubber hardness testers) for $46.50, racing bucket seats, stop watches, brake proportioning valves ($27.95), and every club racer's dream of a Christmas gift: a tire pyrometer for $94.95. Free literature.

Snap-On Tools Corporation
Kenosha, Wisconsin 53140

Very complete line of professional-quality tools including SAE, metric and Whitworth wrenches, air conditioning service tools, complete mechanics' sets, pullers of all types, tire and wheel tools, hydraulic presses, bench grinders, special service tools, engine diagnosis and test equipment, and air-powered tools. Snap-On has franchised distributors in many areas of the country. Catalog, $1.00.

Snyder's Antique Auto Parts
12925 Woodworth Road
New Springfield
Ohio 44443

New and used parts for Model T and Model A. Has most mechanical parts, tires, original accessories, literature and some sheet metal and wood parts. Also upholstery and top kits for Model A. Some T items offered are: Scandinavia brand emergency brake linings ($3.25 a pair); brass hub caps (4 for $14.95); gas stick for direct measurement of fuel in tank ($.50); complete motor and transmission gasket set ($8.95); exhaust manifolds ($19.95); two piece brass repro timer, as used on the open valve engines ($63.25); transmission oil screen ($6.95); and repro starter switch ($9.95). Also in stock are some fine brass horns, at prices from $29.95 to $49.50, and wolf whistles for just $3.45. For the Model A: wheel bearings ($6.95 apiece); brake lining riveting tools ($3.50); steering box gasket set ($1.69); front springs ($19.95 apiece); mufflers ($10.95); exchange reground cams ($22.50); Tillotson carb rebuilding kit ($3.25); running board splash shields ($39.95 a pair); speedometer decals ($.75); and floor carpet kits (available for most models at $28.00 for front carpet only and $48.00 for front and rear). Catalog, $1.00.

Society of Automotive Historians
5 Queen Ann Drive
Newark, Delaware 19711

The Society is dedicated particularly to documenting facts on lesser known makes of vehicles, and doing research on the broad aspects of the effects of the automobile on society. There is one formal annual meeting which coincides with the A.A.C.A. Hershey Meet. The *SAH Newsletter* is published eight times a year, while the Society's technical publication, apparently still in the planning stages, is tentatively entitled *Journal of Automotive History.* To become an active member of the Society, an individual must have a historical article published in an SAH publication, or in another periodical or club publication which the Society finds acceptable. Those who do not meet this criterion can become associate members without voting rights. Yearly dues: $10.00.

Solar Automotive
124B Fulton Street
Princeton, Wisconsin 54968

The unique product provided by this company is a totally remanufactured and modified Corvair, named the Cavalier. Starting with a 1965-69 two door hardtop or convertible (supplied by the company or the customer), the car is totally stripped, sandblasted, chemically stripped of paint, welded to replace rusted areas with new metal, and the sandblasted areas are primed with zinc chromate. Then the front suspension is disassembled and completely gone over, and new tie rod ends and ball joints are installed. Fast steering arms and a hydraulic steering damper are fitted, along with new shocks. Every rubber component is replaced in both front and rear suspensions. Most braking system parts are replaced and a power brake booster is installed. Among engine options are a 300-horse Rajay turbocharged screamer, a 240 hp version with dual Weber carbs, a 200 hp engine with a 4-barrel Holley, and an engine with four Rochester carbs which develops 180 hp. All engines are Magnafluxed at critical points and rebuilt with many new parts installed. Transmissions are also disassembled and rebuilt. Sound deadening material is inserted in the body walls of the car, in the roof, under the cut pile carpeting and in the engine compartment area. Vinyl and cloth fully reclining bucket seats are installed, and the dash is fitted with oil pressure and temperature gauges plus an ammeter. Wheels fitted are 13″x6″ or 14″x6″ mags with Goodrich ER60-13 radials. Prices depend upon options selected. A very thorough order sheet and price list is sent to prospective customers, who may then specify exactly which options and services are required. Free literature.

Solid State Products Inc.
5516 Lyndale Avenue South
Minneapolis, Minnesota 55419

Manufactures a non-CD ignition system which is claimed to have all the advantages, such as long point life, of CD systems and none of the disadvantages. Free literature.

Solitron Devices, Inc.
256 Oak Tree Road
Tappan, New York 10983

Makers of performance and replacement ignition and charging system components. Products include a solid-state ignition system with dwell extender circuit, heavy-duty 12-volt coil, power inverter to operate 12-volt electronic accessories on 110-volt house current, replacement voltage regulators for alternator-equipped cars, 6-12 volt converters for using 12-volt accessories in a 6-volt system, and trio bridge exciter diodes to replace Delco parts in isolated field alternators. Free literature.

Southern African Veteran & Vintage Association (Vintage and Veteran Cars)
c/o Mrs. E.L. Nettleton
Box 7912
Johannesburg South Africa

The Association covers all vintage and veteran clubs in South Africa and Rhodesia, plus the V20 Club in Malawi. Addresses of member clubs can be supplied upon request. The Association publishes a magazine called *SAVVA Automobilist* quarterly for affiliates. Yearly dues: not applicable.

Southland
Box 3591
Baytown, Texas 77520

Makes Delta and Tiger CD ignition systems at prices from $29.95 in kit form up to $59.95. Free literature.

South Penn Restoration Shop
122 Ramsey Avenue
Chambersburg
Pennsylvania 17201

Handles body parts and top bows for vintage cars. Also offers restoration services. Free information and price list.

Sox and Martin, Inc.
P.O. Box P-426
Tucker Street Extension
Burlington,
North Carolina 27215

Drag race cars. Complete Plymouth and Dodge. Distributor for Chrysler performance parts. Legal NHRA engine blueprinting at $1,250.00 or $1,000.00 for short blocks. Blueprint block only includes hot tank, fit pistons, bore finish, cut block to minimum deck height, $350.00. 426 Hemi complete engine includes oil pan (ram manifold type), $4,450.00. 383-440 super stock, $2,900.00; 273-340 Chrysler super stock $2,900.00. Prices are for complete engines with all new parts. Components available are axle shafts, bearings, cams, carbs and manifolds, clutches and flywheels, con rods, oil pumps, windage trays, de-clutching fans, cranks, cylinder blocks, heads, valve seats, gaskets, distributors and other ignition parts, engine governors,

1973 Pro Stock Duster by Sox and Martin, Inc.

gear and pinion sets, hood scoops, pistons and rings, rear suspension components, auto transmission parts, 4-speed manual transmission and parts, valvetrain components, Fram filters, TRW pistons, Schiefer driveline components, Lakewood traction bars, safety bell housings, safety blankets for auto transmissions, roll bars, Edelbrock manifolds, Hurst shifters, Iskenderian and Racer Brown cams, A & A Fiberglass body parts, Smith Bros. pushrods, Stewart-Warner instruments, B & M Transmissions, Hooker Headers, Forgedtrue Pistons, Solar seats, Firestone racing tires, Carter/Holley carbs, Reid's race car trailers, Milodon oil systems, Sox & Martin aluminum oil pans, pinion bumpers, aluminum motor mounts, powdered rosin for drag racing, liquid rosin, pistons, tach drive cables, brake cylinder mounts, drive shaft loops, decals, patches, jackets and T-shirts. Catalog, $1.00.

Sparkomatic Corporation
Milford, Pennsylvania 18337

Sound equipment and speed shifters. Speed shift kits are available for most American cars (3 different models) and for the VW. Another floor shift model is made for GM and Chrysler cars with automatic transmission. Accessories include boots, consoles, chrome shift handles and knobs. Sound equipment available includes quad 4-channel adapters, many models of stereo speakers in all price ranges, speaker components, fader controls, tape deck floor mounts, speaker wire and cartridge cases. Sparkomatic also makes mechanics' creepers. Free literature.

The Sparkomatic M-5 "Mr. Shift" shifter

Spearco Performance Products, Inc.
2054 Broadway
Santa Monica
California 90404

Accessories for the Pinto, Vega, Courier and LUV. Pinto parts include finned aluminum valve covers, timing belt covers and air cleaners; complete induction kits with a 4-barrel intake manifold and Holley carb ($197.55); camshafts and valve train components; adjustable cam sprockets ($64.00); competition con rods for 2-liter Pinto ($132.00); forged aluminum pistons; Mallory dual point distributors; sedan and wagon striping kits; NASCAR hood pin sets; center consoles with room for instruments and

Vega dress-up kit and wheels from Spearco Performance Products, Inc.

sound equipment ($67.00); VDO gauges; alloy wheels; rear grilles; rally suspension kits with front and rear stabilizer bars, heavy-duty front springs and Ariston shocks ($283.60); rear traction control kits; turbocharger kits for Pinto 2-liter ($585.00 for standard model and $620.00 for competition model); headers; and a glasspack exhaust system. Vega goodies include striping kits, consoles,

Mini pickup wooden side rails from Spearco Performance Products, Inc.

polished aluminum valve covers, front bumper guards and spoilers, alloy wheels, front and rear stabilizer bars, rear traction bars, NASCAR hood pin sets, Ariston shocks, headers, side pipes, and complete induction systems. For the Courier and LUV there are hood stripes and side striping kits, tonneau covers, side pipe kits, rear stabilizer bars, interior carpeting kits, alloy wheels, and junior stake kits to extend the bed capacity with oak hardwood siding. Catalog, $1.00.

Special-Interest Autos
Box 196
Bennington, Vermont 05201

Although this magazine is not primarily devoted to car or parts advertisements (that function is fulfilled by its sister magazine *Hemmings Motor News*), I can't resist listing it in these pages. For any lover of those formerly neglected autos of the 1940-1960 era, *Special-Interest Autos* is required reading. Yearly subscription: $6.00; $5.00 to those who also subscribe to *Hemmings.*

Special Interest Cars
Parts Depot
12287 Westminster Avenue
Box 6500
Santa Ana, California 92703

Specialty is all parts for 1955-57 T-Birds, also some parts for older Edsels, Lincoln and Merc. *Parts Digest* listing parts, wiring diagrams and data plate information, $3.95.

Specialized Auto Parts, Inc.
301-L Adams Street
Houston, Texas 77011

Hard parts for early Fords and Chevrolets, some accessories. For Ford Model Ts, along with more mundane items Specialized Auto Parts carries tool bags with the Ford script patch for $3.25, solid brass oilers for $.70 each, leather crank holders for $3.85, exhaust whistle cut-outs for $28.20, radiator stone guards priced at $79.95, spare tire carriers for the 1930-31 coupe and roadster, and a variety of repair manuals, instruction books and lubrication charts. There are also repair manuals and collected service bulletins for the Model A, along with script tire covers at $10.50, rebuilt short blocks at an exchange price of $269.50, script rugs,

Ford Script Rug from Specialized Auto Parts, Inc.

decals and body plates, rumble seats, and top and body wood kits. For early Ford V-8s there is a large selection of hub caps, chrome-plated replacement grilles, blue porcelain oval script radiator emblems, running boards, cast-aluminum downdraft manifolds, and hard parts far too numerous to list. There are also some early Lincoln parts and a variety of reproductions of early Ford brochures, K.R. Wilson Ford service tool catalogs and Columbia overdrive literature.

For Chevrolets vintage 1916-48, the Specialized Auto Parts catalog is in mimeographed form and is not illustrated, yet it does list a fair selection of replacement parts at good prices.
Shipment within 24 hours is promised on all orders.
Ford catalog $1.00, Chevrolet catalog $1.00.

Specialty Coatings and Chemicals Inc.
7314 Varna Avenue
North Hollywood
California 91605

Makes vinyl color coating, cleaners and dressings, leather sealer, engine paint, carpet colorant, and motor glaze. Free literature.

Spectrum
P.O. Box 621
Auburn, Washington 98002

Authentic colors for antique and classic cars formulated. For $5.00 will research the color of any car and can supply all obsolete automotive colors in modern finishes. Will also do custom woodgraining services, quoting prices on inspection of parts to be finished. Sample metal panel sprayouts are $8.00 per 3″x5″ size panel. Other products are wheel seal for wood wheels and Dupont Refinish Manual for $2.50. Free information and color research form.

Speed Masters, Inc.
R.R. 3
Barrington, Illinois 60010

All-aluminum 327 Chev and 426 Hemi cylinder heads. Also aluminum trans case and side cover for Mopar 4-speed boxes. Warehouse distributor for various performance lines. Free literature.

Speed-O-Motive
9624 Atlantic Boulevard
South Gate, California 90280

Speed equipment for domestic cars. In stock are oversized pistons, performance camshafts, Hayden oil coolers, Cloyes timing gear sets, racing crankshafts, Mallory distributors, extra volume oil pumps, Thermo-Chem oil coolers, Jahns pistons for imported cars, Offy and Edelbrock manifolds, low-restriction air cleaners, competition safety belts, cool cans, Gabriel shocks, Cragar headers, steel embossed head gaskets, clutch components for street and strip, McLeod flywheels, Accel ignition components, and Sun tachometers. Catalog, $1.00.

Speed Products Engineering
3307 West Warner Avenue
Santa Ana, California 92704

Competition chassis components and hardware. SPE products include clutch safety housing, drive line couplers, coupler covers, main shafts, clutch assembly tools, aluminum engine plates ($50.00), disc brake kits ($85.00), Airheart calipers and master cylinders, aircraft quality steel brake lines, steering boxes, rack and pinion steering units, Funny Car "butterfly" steering wheels ($14.00-$19.50), bellcranks, flip-top fuel tank caps, rear end filler units, aluminum

A 90° starting system (30 lbs.) for rear-engined race cars from Speed Products Engineering

throttle pedals ($6.75), remote oil filter blocks, P&S spindles, weight brackets, clamp motor mounts and torsion bar assemblies ($60.00). Dragster rear, front and side wings; air foils; low pressure tire gauges; dragster front wire wheels; front wheel discs; Funny Car hubs; wheel spacers; frame rail and roll bar kits; chassis brackets; and Dzus fasteners are stocked. Free literature.

Speedway Mags
P.O. Box 1339
Ontario, California 91762

Mag wheels for domestic and foreign cars in sizes from 13″x5½″ to 15″x10″. Also makes wheels with ⅞″ negative offset for limited fender clearance applications on VW and Porsche. Free literature.

Speedwin Automotive Engineering
945 Motor Parkway
Hauppauge
Long Island, New York 11787

Machine shop and racing engine preparation services including blueprinting, engine balancing and dyno tuning. Stage I dyno tuning; which involves dyno read out, changing plugs and points, setting carburetor to specs with an exhaust gas analyzer, and performing a 20 point safety and maintenance check; is $59.95. Stage II and Stage III dyno tuning are also offered. Speedwin sells performance components for Vegas, blueprinted head assemblies, and speed equipment from the following manufacturers: Racer Brown, Crankshaft Co., Isky, Vertex, Crower, Stahl Headers, Mallory, Keystone, Engle Cams, Simpson, Milodon, Jahns, Venolia, Moon, Crane Cams, Supertanium Hardware, Doug's Headers, Edelbrock, Cyclone, Offenhauser, Holley, Forgedtrue, and Cragar. Free literature.

Sperex Corporation
16131 South Maple Avenue
Gardena, California 90248

VHT aerosol products include rust preventatives, penetrating oil, carb cleaner, mag wheel cleaner, degreasers, ignition sealants, wheel sealers, chrome protectors, tire glaze coating to prevent cracking, liquid wax, anti-seize lubricant, engine enamels, vinyl spray coating, mag wheel coating, tire traction compounds for drag racing, window tint, silicone spray, molysulfide dry lubricant, wrinkle-finish paint, gasket cement, fan belt dressing, wheel tint, spark plug cleaner, spray de-icer, starting fluid, and hood and deck paint. VHT Sperex is a heat resistant paint designed for the protection of exhaust systems. Traction compounds are also sold in bulk sizes, and include dragstrip coating available in a 54-gallon drum. Free literature.

Sport Land
3505 North 48th Street
Box 4511
Lincoln, Nebraska 68504

Aside from making kayaks and sailboats, Sport Land also has an intriguing dune buggy, and kits for a variety of fun cars. The C.R.V., a kind of gull-winged dune buggy (also available in a soft topped version) is made from Cycolac ABS and fits an uncut VW chassis. The body complete with dash, seat, and console is $799.50. The complete hardtop with gull-wing doors is $199.99. A superstructure kit for mid-engine mounting of VW or V-8 engines is $399.99. Other options are available. Sport Land's most unique vehicle is a three-wheeler with 5 or 10 hp engine and a torque converter. It costs $249.00 ready to ride or $149.00 in basic kit form without an engine. Another offering for family fun is the Mini-ATV with six wheels and engines from 2½ to 10 hp. The basic kit is $199.99, while the ready to ride model with 2½ hp engine goes for $299.99. In the big leagues again, the company sells fiberglass bodies patterned after the AC Cobra ($399.00) and the Corvette coupe ($599.00). Free literature. Plans are also available for the Mini-ATV and three-wheeler at $4.00 apiece.

Sports Accessories International, Inc.
2607 Hennepin Avenue South
Minneapolis, Minnesota 55408

Patches, decals, bumper-stickers and such-like things. Playboy bunny decals and patches; international flag emblems; embossed plaques saying "Protected by the Egyptian Army" and lesser witticisms; tape stripes of all types; emblem embossed cigarette lighters; chrome, metalflake or candy apple chopper helmets; surfer crosses on chains; jacket patches of sundry design; Jumbo name-brand decals; and bumper stickers saying "Don't Honk, I'm Peddling As Fast As I Can" and "I'm Not A Dirty Old Man, Just A Sexy Senior Citizen." If you're looking for a way to cover up the rust spots on your clapped-out Henry J, and keep the body panels in close proximity, jumbo stickers may be the answer. Small catalog $1.00.

Sports Innovations, Inc.
5301 Edina Industrial Boulevard
Minneapolis, Minnesota 55435

Makes a hub winch which mounts to a car wheel and uses the wheel's own turning power to pull car out of sand or snow. Price for complete kit, which is available with adapters to fit most American cars and 4WD vehicles, is $89.95 for 6,000-pound rated model and $94.95 for 8,000-pound model. Free literature.

Sportsmobile
1013 Main Street
Andrews, Indiana 46702

VW van conversions for the camping family. The Sportsmobile features an elevating roof to sleep two in the attic, a built in kitchen and dinette, and other comforts for family campers. Total sleeping capacity is five. Free literature.

The Sportsmobile based on a VW bus

SS Automobiles
1735 South 106th Street
Milwaukee, Wisconsin 53214

Here's a riddle: What has the classic good looks of an SS Mercedes, 4-wheel independent suspension, a 454 Corvette engine, standard air conditioning, AM/FM 4-speaker stereo system, power steering, either a Turbo-Hydro or 4-speed manual transmission, and Borrani type wire wheels? Of course, it's the Excaliber, available in a four-passenger Phaeton or two-passenger Roadster model (prices are $14,000.00 and $13,500.00 respectively). The bumpers, exhaust system and trim are hand crafted from stainless steel or aluminum and the fiberglass body is finished with 14 coats of lacquer. As you sit behind the polished wood steering wheel on reclinable contoured bucket seats made of fine English leather, you can press your foot down on the loud pedal and hit 60 in 6 seconds flat. The top speed is 130. Available accessories are a hardtop for all-weather comfort ($650.00), tonneau ($125.00), cruise control ($150.00), air horns and driving lights ($150.00), sidemount tire covers ($75.00), and tape player ($150.00). Daddy, buy me one of those. Free literature to serious customers.

Russell E. Stadt
(Marmon and Roosevelt)
5364 Stuart Avenue, SE
Grand Rapids, Michigan 49508

Mr. Stadt is the head of the Marmon Owners Club and former editor of *The Marmon News.* Unfortunately, due to Mr. Stadt's business interests, the Marmon Club is currently on inactive status and *The Marmon News* is no longer being published.

Marmon owners will be glad to know that Mr. Stadt is still maintaining a registry of Marmons and Roosevelts (about 300 Marmons currently listed) and has an extensive literature collection. Marmon owners seeking advice on identification, restoration, etc. will find Mr. Stadt responsive to their queries.

Mr. Stadt writes that Marmon parts are in short supply. Aside from a few Marmon 16 trim items, no parts are being remanufactured at this time. Some of the remaining factory stock of Marmon parts has been acquired and sold through the Club, but little remains. There is some possibility that more parts will be made available in the future, however.

Stahl and Associates
7-B North Diamond Street
York, Pennsylvania 17404

Makers of a complete line of performance accessories. Items include oil pump primers for Delco distributors ($8.95); fuel pump push rods for Chev V-8 ($5.95); timing chain and gear sets, valley oil baffles, aluminum and magnesium water pumps, crankshafts, adjustable TDC pointers, degreed harmonic balancers and aluminum crank and alternator pulleys, all for small and big block Chev V-8; accessory clutch drives (limiting water pump and alternator to 2,500 rpm) for small and big block Chevy and Mopar; extra-capacity oil pans for Chev and Mopar; complete 4-speed transmissions for GM, Ford, and AMC; transmission gearsets and parts; heavy-duty U-joints for Chev, Pontiac, and Olds; engine pre-heat systems for race cars; portable air compressors; precision engine assembly tools; axles for Chev, Pontiac and Olds; cool cans; fuel system components; tachometers; light cheater front tires for drag racing; mag wheel pilots; aluminum and titanium hardware; hood scoops; shock absorbers built by Koni to Stahl specifications; and a variety of decals, T-shirts, etc. See separate listing for Stahl Headers. The header company is not associated with Stahl and Associates although both have the same president. Catalog, $1.00.

Negotiable Securities. The true classic cars, produced between two World Wars and living defiantly in the face of a worldwide depression, needed no exterior flash to distinguish them from the common horde. They were as dignified and stately as J.P. Morgan's bank and as ruthless in their insistence that only the finest would do. Today they are cherished as the finest cars ever constructed, and their value appreciates year after year.

1. 1916 Crane-Simplex. One of the first true classics. The Crane-Simplex featured bank vault construction and exemplary engineering.

2. 1930 Du Pont. The Du Pont, as aristocratic as its name would indicate, was a chassis that became the basis for impeccable town cars as well as boat-tailed speedsters.

3. 1930 Pierce-Arrow Convertible Coupe. Often used as a showcase for the best American coachwork the Pierce-Arrow was an American Rolls-Royce, second to none.

1.
2.
3.

4. 1932 Packard Twin Six. The Packard 12-cylinder engine was famous for flexibility and silent power. Although sedans are not as valuable as open cars, any 12-cylinder Packard is included in the short list of irreproachable classics.

5. 1932 Marmon 16. The big Marmons were deceptive. Howard Marmon was an innovative engineer who insisted that his big cars handle and perform as well as any sportsters of their era. In high gear, at 15 mph, the Marmon would accelerate as swiftly and silently as an electric car with JATO assists.

6. 1937 Cord 812. The coffin-nose Cords were classics of the late depression era. Styled by Gordon Beuhrig and conceived by a master salesman, E.L. Cord, they were more delicate, and more makeshift, than earlier classics. But Cords were speedy and stylish. They had that indefinable pedigree that distinguishes true classics from lesser cars.

4.

5.

6.

Stahl Headers
325 North Queen Street
York, Pennsylvania 17403

Headers for Vega V-8, Camaro, Chevelle, Corvette and Stingray, Chevy II, Anglia, Grand National Chevelle, Mopar Wedge, Street Hemi, and other modified vehicles. Prices range from about $175.00 upwards. Free literature.

Standard Automotive
2204 Ohio
Quincy, Illinois 62301

Parts and literature for Model T and Model A. Some Model T items listed are: brake shoes (set of two, used), $2.95; hubcaps for wood wheels, available in brass, nickel, or chrome, $14.95 a set of four; aluminum pistons with pins in sizes from .020 to .060 oversize, $7.19; set of eight intake or exhaust valves, $10.95; hardwood steering wheel with brass spider, $27.95. For Model A: 23-piece nickel lug nut set for early 1928 models (includes spare tire lock nut), $19.95; complete set woven brake linings with rivets, $7.95; knock-off type wheel puller, $.79; exhaust system assembly, $12.19 including shipping; engine gasket set with copper covered head gasket, $5.95; new water pump, $12.95; Tillotson carb rebuild kit, $4.39; 20-20 ammeter with script, $2.39; front floorboard set, $10.95; and rumble seat mat in original splatter design, $5.95. Also offers many Ford history books and restoration/repair manuals. Catalog, $.10.

Standard Motor Products, Inc.
37-18 Northern Boulevard
Long Island City
New York 11101

Makers of Blue Streak ignition parts and charging system components, Jiffy carb rebuild kits, and automotive wire and cable. Many components are designed to fit imported cars and older domestic models such as DeSoto and Kaiser-Frazer. Consult catalogs at automotive parts house.

Standard Register
(Standard, Avon, and S.S.)
c/o J.R. Davy
Triumph Motor Co.
Fletchamstead
Coventry
Warwickshire CV4 9DB
England

This is a worldwide registry of Standard cars and associated makes. Although the Register's prime purpose is to record surviving examples, one or more field events are promoted each year and a newsletter, *Stanalgia,* is published thrice yearly. Members of the Register can also help with spare parts location provided a stamped, self-addressed envelope is sent with all communications. There are no dues, however the newsletter subscription price is approximately $2.40 a year. A Standard badge is also available for a fee.

Stan's Headers
5811 East Imperial Highway
South Gate, California 90280

Headers for VW and Porsche, off-road vehicles including International Harvester trucks, Corvair, Datsun 240Z, BMW 4-cylinder, and Opel GT & Kadett. Also has intake manifolds to adapt SU carbs to Corvair engines. Free literature.

Stant Manufacturing Co., Inc.
Connersville, Indiana 47331

Manufactures locking gas caps for emission control systems, and radiator pressure caps, as well as oil filler breather caps, thermostats, pressure system testers, and pressure cap testers. Free literature.

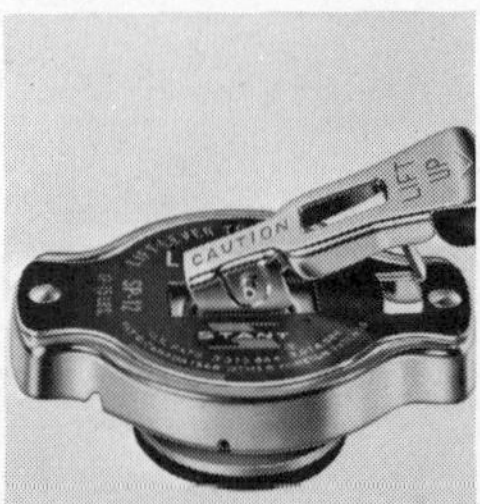

Stant Manufacturing Co., Inc. safety lock type radiator pressure cap

Star Machine & Tool Co.
201 6th Street SE
Minneapolis, Minnesota 55414

The Star line of tools and shop supplies include disc brake lathes, brake relining machines, brake drum lathes, brake shoe grinders, truck and shop cranes, and replacment parts for all machines. Free literature to professional mechanics.

Star, Starling, Stuart & Briton Car Register (Star, Starling Stuart & Briton)
c/o D.E.A. Evans
9 Compton Drive
Oakham
Dudley
Worcestershire DY2 7ES
England

Register covers all of the bicycles, tricycles, motorcycles, motor-tricycles and motorized forecarriages (as well as cars, of course), plus commercial vehicles and aeronautical equipment produced by the Star Cycle, Star Engineering, Star Motor and Briton Motor Companies of Wolverhampton, England. The years of production were 1886-1932. Listed in the Register are 126 Star cars, 8 Briton cars, 2 Stuart cars and 4 Star commercial vehicles, in various parts of the world. Along with published lists of existing cars, spec sheets, and historical articles published on a regular basis, the Register's guiding members will provide technical and historical advice, along with assisting in the location and manufacture of spare parts. Membership is limited to current owners of Star or related vehicles, or to those previously employed by one of the Star companies at Wolverhampton. Yearly dues: none.

Starting Line
138 Spring Street
Saratoga Springs
New York 12866

Accessories for Porsches including Colgan and Sportissimo "bras" which protect the front end from gravel and insects (various models for 356, 911/912 and 914), Sportissimo car covers, floor mats and extractor exhausts for all models, 5½" mag wheels, VDO instruments and senders, AMCO front and rear bumper guards, ski racks for 911 and luggage racks for 911 and 914, outside mirrors, an attractive 914 center console complete with glove box, cushioned arm rest, rocker switches and cut-outs for three instruments for $56.05, a 914 center seat as an alternative to the console for $16.95, a variety of front and rear sway bars for all models, 914 chrome wheels at $27.95 for the 4½" model and $29.95 for the 5½" variety, and hood/trunk retaining straps with plated steel fittings at $6.95. Also a number of standard goodies such as Carello and Hella quartz lights, Porsche-crested mugs, watches and key fobs, and tape stripes which say "Porsche" in large letters. Catalog free.

Ben Staub
2040 Little York Road
Dayton, Ohio 45414

Makes accessory trunks with cowhide straps and vinyl covers to fit Model A Ford and many other cars of the era. Trunk is available with either curved or straight back and in two sizes, 34"x13"x19" and 33"x16"x19". Other sizes and styles made on special order. Also has all sorts of trunk hardware on hand. Free literature.

Steam Automobile Club of America, Inc. (Steam Automobiles)
333 North Michigan Avenue
Room 3214
Chicago, Illinois 60601

Holds steam car meets in various parts of the U.S. each year. Sends out announcements of new steam car developments. Publishes quarterly magazine *The Steam Automobile.* Yearly dues: $10.00.

Lynn Steele 21144 Robinwood Farmington, Michigan 48024	New parts for early Cadillacs, La Salles, Buicks, Pierce-Arrow, Packard, and a few parts for Lincoln, Stutz and Auburn. Items reproduced include small body and rubber parts, running board matting and rubber, some cosmetic items, and many standard mechanical parts. Cadillac V-16 distributor cap cover is $45.00. Radiator hoses for V-12 and V-16 through 1937 are $35.00 a set. Luggage rack trim strips for 1930-31 V-16 are $95.00 a set. La Salle pedal pads are $12.50 a pair. Send a stamped, self-addressed envelope for parts sheets.
Roscoe Stelford RR 1, Box 146 Hampshire, Illinois 60140	NOS parts for Packard, Studebaker and Avanti. Some parts and prices are: Delco solenoid repair kit for 1955-56 Packard, $3.50; rear fenders for 1951-54 Patrician 4 door, $89.05; V-8 Packard/Studebaker camshaft, $20.00, and crankshaft, $120.00; 1939-47 series 120 cylinder head gaskets for small 8-cylinder, $6.50; clutch and brake pad sets, $6.25; wheel cylinder repair kits for 1935-56 Packard, $1.80; and rebuilt fuel pumps for 1951-54 8-cylinder, $12.50. Also has some body parts including rocker panels, rear fender panels, and dog legs for 1948-58 Packards and Clippers. Technical specification sheets on Packards from 1899 to 1956 are $.35 each. A 27-page listing of Packard passenger car production from 1899 to 1956, with technical specifications and production figures for each model is $5.50. Free literature.
Step Up Sales 800 San Antonio Road Palo Alto, California 94304	Self-retracting and bumper steps for 4WD vehicles and pickup trucks. Retracting steps come in small or king-size (12″x6″) styles. Bumper step also rolls out and retracts and it can be chromed as an option. Step Up Sales also makes outside and under-vehicle tire carriers and some accessories for VW Buses. Free literature.
Sterling Products Company Inc. 1689 Oakdale Avenue W. St. Paul, Minnesota 55118	Manufactures seat covers, fender protectors, head rests, automotive carpeting material, polyethylene car covers, tow ropes, Naugahyde car-top carriers, stereo tape cases, tissue dispensers, auto litter bins, window and console snack trays, utility mattresses for station wagons, stadium cushions, tote bags, racing-style jackets, crash helmets and goggles. Free information.
Stevens-Duryea Associates (Stevens-Duryea) c/o Warwick Eastwood 3565 Newhaven Road Pasadena, California 91107	If you are one of the lucky owners of the 81 Stevens-Duryea cars still in existence, your car is registered with Stevens-Duryea Associates already and you undoubtedly know that there are no membership requirements or dues. The group was formed so members could asist each other in keeping their cars on the road and participating in vintage car tours.
Stevens Engineering Co. 340 North Newport Boulevard Newport Beach California 92660	For the hard-core rally enthusiast Stevens offers electric counters, in single or dual models, which work from impulse units attached to the speedometer or front wheel of any car and indicate 100ths of a mileage both audibly and visually on 5-digit Veeder-root counters. The counters are either single-panel cabinet models ($41.00), dash-panel mounted ($24.00) or double-panel cabinct

The #641 Rally Timer from Stevens Engineering Co.

($73.00). Cabinet models are 6- or 12-volt while the dash-mounted model is 12-volt only. The speedometer impulse units are custom-made for particular speedos (although Stevens will convert one at a nominal charge) and range in price from $38.00 to $50.00. The wheel-mounted impulse unit costs $50.00 and is for use on cars which cannot be fitted with the speedometer variety. The counters are for use with Curta mechanical calculators, or one of the solid-state mini-calculators which have become so popular these days. The Stevens catalog describes their workings in detail.

Other rally items are stopwatch holders in sizes to fit 2″ or 2¼″ diameter watches for $2.50 and $2.75 respectively. An adjustable stopwatch holder mounted on a spring or slide clip for easy attachment to clipboards is $6.95. A 6- or 12-volt spring-clip-mounted clipboard light with four-foot cord and plug for a cigarette lighter socket is $5.25. Stevens Rally Indicators—sort of like circular slide rules designed to make time/mileage/speed calculations—are $8.50 for the 6″ diameter version and $14.00 for the deluxe 9″ model. Both are supplied with a leatherette slip case. Rally Readers with tops of translucent red plexiglass, illumination from below, and rollers to hold eleven or more 8½″x11″ rally instruction sheets taped end to end are $24.00. Small catalog free.

Stewart-Warner Corporation
1826 Diversey Parkway
Chicago, Illinois 60614

Makers of dash instruments, flexible shafts and drive equipment, sending units and electric fuel pumps. Catalog, $1.00. Other literature can be consulted at accessory dealers or speed shops.

Stilko
7445 Convoy Court
San Diego, California 92111

Makes "Lifetime" oil filter which uses the element politely known as "TP," and more familiarly known as toilet paper. Free literature.

Stitts
2771 U.S. Highway No. 1
Trenton, New Jersey 08638

Top and upholstery materials. Has mohairs, broadcloths, velours, bedfords, headlining cloth, and Model A and T fabrics. Will match samples. Free information.

The Stockland Co.
1331 East Street
Gertrude Place
Santa Ana, California 92705

Fiberglass shells and tonneau covers for pickup trucks. A standard bed or short bed pickup canopy has a base price of $400.00, with tinted windows, jalousie windows, and sliding side windows available as extras. A canopy is also available for the El Camino. Pickup utility boxes are $120.00, with optional sliding tray and rails $15.00 additional. Free literature.

Strange Engineering Co. Inc.
739 Howard Street
Evanston, Illinois 60202

Chassis parts for drag racing, Pro Stocks, funny cars and top fuel cars. Custom housings for any American made rear end. Specialty is Dana Series 60 housings, with all internal parts and many gear ratios in stock. Other products include disc brakes, using Kelsey-Hayes calipers and master cylinders, front spindles and torsion bars for funny cars, and aluminum spindles and coil-over-shock units for Pro Stock cars. Free price list.

Strippers, Inc.
Automotive Division
R.R. 2, Box 86
Cambria, Wisconsin 53923

Makers of equipment for large-scale paint stripping. Cost of basic set-up is probably beynd reach of individual, but should be of interest to clubs and those who can use the equipment commercially. Free information.

Bill Stroppe and Associates
2180 Temple Avenue
Long Beach, California 90804

Stroppe's Baja Bronco kit includes a modified Ford C-4 automatic transmission, Gates Commando tires, wide steel wheels, dual shock absorbers front and rear, and a shock mount kit, rear fender flares, roll bar, front bumper braces, trailer hitch, rubberized steering wheel, spare tire cover, chromed lug nuts, and name plate. The kit price is $1,295.00. Other Bronco accessories include power steering ($370.00); Detroit Locker rear end units; modified C-4 transmission kits; 4-speed manual transmissions with Hurst shifters ($675.00 with $75.00 tail shaft housing core charge); engine performance kits (prices range from $224.85 to $369.30); rear fender flares; headers ($116.00); dual exhaust kits with Glasspack mufflers; air and oil filters; transmission oil coolers; front and rear air bags to fit inside coil springs; heavy-duty shocks; front and rear shock mounts

Parnelli Jones in the "Big Oly" Bronco prepared by Bill Stroppe and Associates

for dual shocks; Cibie lights; front bumper braces; tow bars and trailer hitches; roll bars and roll cages; Bostrom suspension seats ($109.95); console front seats; competition harnesses and safety belts; Auto Meter tachometers; tire covers; waterproof distributor and coil caps; Flex-A-Lite fans; hood lock kits ($5.95); alternator power taps; 12-volt mini air compressors; electric Superwinches; fiberglass Bronco body parts; McHal helmets; and hydraulic jacks. Stroppe also manufactures complete Baja Broncos with red, white, and blue paint jobs and many heavy-duty components. Vehicles are available on special order through local Ford dealers. For the Ford Courier offerings include fiberglass pick-up box covers, alloy wheels, rear step-bumpers, tonneau covers and bows, side stripes, interior carpeting, and pick-up bed liners constructed of marine plywood carpeted in Ozite, with well covers in padded black vinyl. Price for complete bed liner is $139.95. Catalog, $1.00.

ST Spares
2 Summerhill Close
Haywards Heath
Sussex
England

Mostly used parts for Sunbeam Talbots. Manifolds, carbs, voltage regulators, radiators, heaters, steering boxes, wheels, and some small body parts. No engine blocks, doors, or fenders. Will try to locate parts on request. Send international reply coupon with queries.

Stude Auto Parts
Route 8, Box 191
Durham, North Carolina 27704

NOS parts for Studebaker and Avanti. Tom Harton, who runs the business, has come to be known as "Avanti Tom." Along with NOS parts, Tom has more than 140 Studebaker parts cars from the 1950's and early 1960's. An Avanti parts catalog and workshop manual are available at cost. Free information. Write for price quotes on parts you need.

The Studebaker Driver's Club, Inc. (Studebaker)
P.O. Box 3044
South Bend, Indiana 46619

Almost 4,000 members of this Club enjoy benefits which include a monthly magazine, *Turning Wheels,* with technical advice and a classified advertisement section for parts sources, a national meet plus interstate and local events, a sales registry to help determine car value in case of accident or damage, and a big selection of jewelry, badges and decals. Yearly dues; $6.00 for all members of household. Outside of North America, add $2.00 for postage.

Studebaker Owners' Club of America (Studebaker & Related Marques)
P.O. Box 5294
Pasadena, California 91107

Devoted not only to various Studebaker models over the years, but also to affiliated or related marques such as Garford, EMF 30, Flanders 20, Erskine, Rockne, Pierce-Arrow, Packard, Avanti and Excalibur. Local chapters have monthly meetings and participate in a variety of other activities, while there is one big Western States Meet each year. Club publication is the bi-monthly *Style and Stamina* with a classified section free to members. Yearly dues: $6.00, or $5.00 without voting privileges. Life membership is $100.00 for U.S. and Canada. Wives of active or life members can join for an additional $2.00.

Studs for Bugs
2822 State Street
Hamden, Connecticut 06517

Makes studs to adapt VW wheel lugs to work in the same manner as American lug nuts work. Free literature.

Subaru of America Inc.
7040 Central Highway
Pennsauken, New Jersey 08109

Subaru distributor.

Summers Brothers
909 West Mission Boulevard
Ontario, California 91762

Racing engine and chassis components available include cam gear drives for Chev and Chrysler, heavy-duty axles for GM cars and dragsters, 4-bolt steel billet main caps, 12-bolt Chev axle/spool combos, full floating hub assemblies for early Ford and Olds/Pontiac, and Ontario locker spools designed to completely replace rear end carrier assemblies and limited slip differentials. Ontario lockers are priced at $171.88 to $179.69, depending upon the model. Four-bolt main caps are $70.31 for small block Chev and $78.13 for large block Chev and Chrysler. Free literature.

Summer Brothers' 12-bolt Chev axle/spool

Summit Auto Center
755 North Main Street
Akron, Ohio 44310

Performance parts for most American cars. Items carried include headers, mag wheels, racing cam shafts and high performance valve train components, dash instruments, traction bars, Lakewood safety blankets for auto transmissions, Hurst shifters, oil and transmission coolers, Moroso deep sump oil pans and oil pump extensions, lightweight water pumps for small block Chevrolets, quick-change cam timers, slick shift sliders to eliminate synchronizer drag on Borg-Warner and Muncie transmissions, fuel block Y-kits, Gabriel shocks, Velvetouch metallic brake linings and disc brake pads, side mount exhaust systems by Thrush, Hurricane flexible fans, Grant steering wheels, Judson electronic magnetos, TRW pistons, Weber clutches, and a complete line of other performance accessories from various manufacturers. Also carries hot-rodding manuals published by H.P. Books. Free information.

Sunbeam Talbot Alpine Register (Sunbeam)
c/o R.N. Hardy
18 Gilmore Crescent
Ashford
Middlesex
England

Current club activities comprise driving tests, film shows, monthly social meetings, and an annual concours. The register has recently become affiliated with the R.A.C. and may soon hold competitive events. The *Sunbeam Talbot Alpine Register Newsletter* is published quarterly, and the Register has a fair library of technical information and a stock of spare parts. The cars of interest to members are Alpines from 1943-57 and Sunbeam Sedans back to 1936. Among spare parts sources recommended are: Grimes-Hadleigh Garages, Ltd. Marlpit Lane, Coulsdon, Surrey

CR3 2YE, England, and Charlie E. Moar, 3 Palace Craig Street, Shawhead, Coatbridge, Lanarkshire ML5 4SG, Scotland. Yearly dues: $6.00.

Sun Electric Corporation
6323 Avondale Avenue
Chicago, Illinois 60631

Along with the well-established line of Sun tachometers, the company also makes automotive test equipment such as large engine performance testing stations for professional use, bench distributor testers, air conditioning test equipment, generator and alternator bench testers, oscilloscopes, transistor regulator testers and ignition simulators. Of more general interest to the home mechanic are Sun timing lights, compression testers and fuel pump testers. Free information.

Sunnen Products Company
7910 Manchester Avenue
St. Louis, Missouri 63143

Engine rebuilding equipment for professional mechanics. Sunnen products include automatic cylinder resizing machines, precision honing machines for rod reconditioning, heavy-duty cap and rod grinders, pin presses, and a variety of precision measuring instruments. Two pamphlets printed by the Company, on reconditioning rods and precision pin fitting, are particularly informative. Free literature.

Superchargers and Kits, Inc.
2427 Riverside Drive
Los Angeles, California 90039

Exclusive distributor for Paxton Superchargers and installation kits. Prices for basic unit are $295.00 for street model and $355.00 for competition model. Add $100.00 for variable speed version of either model. Accessories include pressure gauges, carb bonnets and fittings, carb enclosures, and hoses to fit. Free parts and price list.

Superior Performance Products
P.O. Box 7603
Van Nuys, California 91409

Wheels, chassis components, cosmetic accessories, RV accessories, towing systems, seatbelts and exhaust components. Superior products are sold by speed shops and parts suppliers across the country. Along with a general catalog, there are separate catalogs for alloy wheels and RV accessories. Wheels are available for domestic and import cars, and for special competition applications. Sizes range from 13″x5½″ to 15″x10″ and include both chrome and aluminum versions. The RV accessories catalog lists bumper and frame hitches, trailer couplers, trailer electrical connectors, auxiliary lights, safety skids, wheel chocks, utility tie-downs, camper shell anchors, trailer roll-up jacks, trans coolers, front spare tire carriers, bumper-mounted cycle carriers, and hoisting and jacking tools. General catalog listings include springs to fit over shock absorbers (some models vinyl-coated); single leaf helper springs; heavy-duty coil springs; lift kits; spring boosters; car ramps; bicycle carriers; walnut steering wheels; steering wheel covers; VW rear suspension control bars; VW shift kits; headers for VW and Porsche; VW intake manifolds; ball joint repair kits; VW bumper guards; VW overload springs; station wagon air deflectors; splash guards; tow straps; radiator bug screens made of fiberglass; universal rear window sun blinds; Bermuda bells;

burglar alarm systems; truck step-ups; exhaust extensions in many styles and diameters; license plate frames; and seat belts and harnesses. Free information. Consult catalogs at Superior dealers.

Super Plus, Inc.
Bank of America Center
Suite 1120
315 Montgomery Street
San Francisco, California 94104

Manufactures fiberglass hood unit to convert any Volkswagen Beetle or Super Beetle into a mini-replica of a 1940 Ford. Product is available only through authorized VW dealers. Free literature.

Super Speed Equipment Co.
1550 Clark Street
Arcadia, California 91006

Makers of "Superod" forged aluminum rods for competition engines. Rods are kept in stock for popular Chev, Ford and Chrysler engines and are available on special order for many other American engines. Prices for set of eight rods are $223.50 for 283/327 Chev, 302/350 Chev, 289/302 Ford; $261.00 for 396/427 Chev, 392 and 426 Chrysler Hemi. Catalog, $.50.

Surplus City
11796 Sheldon Street
Sun Valley, California 91352

Original military canvas products such as tops, doors, side curtains, seat covers, and cargo covers for military Jeeps, Mighty Mites, Dodge M37s, and Willys M17 ambulances. Also has NOS military Jeep parts and accessories such as GI gas can carriers, rifle racks, rear seat tool and storage boxes ($28.50), pintle hooks (used, $15.00) and military technical manuals for vehicles and weapons. Free literature. Mighty Mite M422 and M422A1 catalog, $1.00.

Swanson Motor Racing, Inc.
713 West 16th Street
Costa Mesa, California 92627

Sells racing hardware and accessories along with complete Royale Formula cars and the Brabham BT40B Formula B car. The Royale RP16 Formula Ford is $6,250.00 in race-ready form. The RP18 Super Vee is $5,450.00 less engine and tires. Racing accessories sold include B & B clutches, Phoenix on-board fire extinguishing systems, Hawk instruments, Heuer timers, Aeroquip hose, Marchal lights, Minilite and Eagle wheels, shocks made by Armstrong, Spax and Koni, Weber carbs and parts, Perfect Circle piston rings, Lucas fuel injection and ignition equipment and VHT engine paint. Other items include International Racing Designs trailers, Bell helmets, Nomex and Fypro fire resistant clothing and Ferodo brake pads. The company's cylinder head work is done by Al Gunter who will do complete cylinder head porting and flowing, make custom valves and magnesium and aluminum valve collars and keepers, and do Heli-Arc welding on just about any metal. Free literature.

Swedish-American Motorsport
1635 Ohms Way, Suite E
Costa Mesa, California 92627

Competition and rally equipment for 4-cylinder Saabs. A Stage 1 tuning kit, with intake manifold, 28/36 Weber carb, and chrome air filter is $180.00. Cams with various durations are $80.00 exchange or $100.00 outright. Other items include competition valvetrain components, brake pads, front and rear sway bar kits ($85.00 for both), a cross ram intake manifold for two DCOE Weber carbs, piston ring sets, fuel and water pumps, clutch components, Bilstein gas shocks,

GT wheels, Recaro seats, driving lights and special paint. Company will also do complete preparation of race and rally Saabs. Free catalog.

Sydmur Electronic Specialties
1268 East 12th Street
Brooklyn, New York 11230

CD Ignition Systems in three sizes for cars and most other motor vehicles. Free literature.

Systematics, Inc.
547 Wheeler Street
St. Paul, Minnesota 55104

Manufactures the SparkPak discharge ignition unit, and the AutoStart electronic temperature control system which automatically stops and starts an engine to keep the interior of the car warm. Free literature.

Tabline
One-A Orchard Lane
Berkeley, California 94704

Imports Italian Dellorto carburetors and can supply all replacement parts. Free information.

Taylor Enterprises
7642 Clairemont
Mesa Boulevard
San Diego, California 92111

Upholstery specialties including mini-truck upholstery kits (standard carpet kit, $40.00; seat cover kit, $60.00; kick panel and door panel kit, $45.00; and sun visor kit, $12.00), sports touring and racing seats, custom van interior kits, and tire covers. The Taylor seat with a chrome-moly tube frame and interlocking woven nylon mesh suspension ($225.00) is specially designed for off-road racing vehicles. Taylor's hi-back bucket seat, available with a high swivel mount, is suitable for installation in vans. The seat price is $60.00 and the swivel mount is $22.50. Other van accessories made by Taylor are roof racks, access ladders, safety steps, roof vents, door extenders (provide clearance for wide tires on sliding door models), round portholes, and U.S. Indy mag wheels. Minicar offerings include custom consoles, interior dress-up kits, and upholstery kits for Pinto and Vega. Catalog, $1.00.

Suspended seat for off-road vehicles and race cars by Taylor Enterprises

James E. Taylor
306 Waverly
Bartlesville, Oklahoma 74003

Maker of Taylor TSD rally calculator selling for $7.50. Also rebuilds SU carbs. Free literature

Team Hartwell
43 Holdenhurst Road
Bournemouth
England

Team Hartwell are the primary Chrysler tuning specialists in Britain. They offer suspension and engine conversions for the Hillman and Sunbeam Imp, the Hillman Avenger series, the Hillman Hunter and Sunbeam Vogue, the Sunbeam Rapier and Alpine, the Humber Sceptre, and the Hillman Minx Saloon and Estate. An extensive price list with complete conversion information is available free upon request.

Techintread Corporation
P.O. Box 976
Winona, Minnesota 55987

Radial retread tires in both compact and American sizes. Retreads are guaranteed through the first half of tread life or two years. During this time tires which fail will be replaced free of charge. Tires which fail during the second half of tread life will be given credit based upon the percentage of tread remaining. Free literature.

The Texberry Co.
P.O. Box 33367
Houston, Texas 77033

Makes custom glassware with illustration of a particular antique or classic car (make, model and year as specified) and owner's name. $17.95 for a set of four tumblers. Free literature.

Virgil Thacker
Lincoln, Kansas 67455

Mr. Thacker has over 500 tons of pre-1930 parts for different cars. Most parts are used. As you might expect, there are far too many parts to catalog, but specific inquiries are always answered. Send a stamped, self-addressed envelope with all queries.

Thermo-Chem Corporation
P.O. Box 45504
Tulsa, Oklahoma 74145

Makers of engine and transmission oil coolers, oil cooler adapters, and trailer sway control units. Free literature.

Doug Thorley Headers
7403 Telegraph Road
Los Angeles, California 90040

Doug Thorley headers come in economy and performance models, and many are available with smog air pump fittings. Standard headers are $95.00, with smog device an additional $25.00. Other products include headers for VW and popular imported cars, truck headers, header mufflers, tail pipes, side pipes, and exhaust system hardware. Catalog, $1.00.

Hank Thorp, Inc.
P.O. Box 201
Edison, New Jersey 08817

Minilite magnesium wheels are available for sports cars and foreign sedans as well as for many racing applications. Standard magnesium wheels run in size from 10″ x 4.5″ to 15″x7.5″ and are priced from $61.50 to $129.50 per wheel. Trans-Am magnesium wheels in 13″ and 15″ sizes are priced from $133.00 to $202.00 per wheel. For those who find these genuine mag wheels too rich for their blood, Minilite Sport Wheels are priced at $180.00 a set of four in size 13″x5″, to $260.00 a set for size 14″x7″. Free information.

Thunderbird Classic Parts
c/0 Carl Maroney
2106 Colice
Huntsville, Albama 35801

New, genuine Ford parts for 1955-57 Thunderbirds. Over 600 different new parts in stock and others obtainable. Large stamped, self-addressed envelope with query.

Timmis Motor Co.
4351 Blenkinsop Road
Victoria

Manufactures fiberglass 1934 Ford roadster replicas. Will supply body only or complete car with V-8 engine, 16″ wire wheels and full upholstery with rumble seat. Cars are

British Columbia Canada	custom built to order. Also supplies some spare parts for Fords. Send a stamped, self-addressed envelope with query.
Tom's Auto Glass Co. 1401 25th Street Bakersfield, California 93301	Supplies sliding-glass window kits to replace the fixed rear side panes in Toyota Land Cruisers. A kit with hardware and instructions but no glass is $37.95. Kits with pre-cut glass for later model Land Cruisers are $67.95. Tom's says that shipping is no problem. Free literature.
Torque Converters, Inc. 711 Ioka Street Memphis, Tennessee 38126	Rebuilt torque converters for all American and foreign cars. Also industrial converters rebuilt. Racing torque converters and auto transmission parts available. Inquire through your local speed shop or write for information.
Total Performance Products, Inc. 1000 West Oak Street Burbank, California 91506	Flexible aluminum fans in models for large and small cars. Foreign car applications include the 24OZ, Mazda 1800, Rover, Renault Dauphine, Sunbeam Tiger, most Toyotas including the Land Cruiser, Triumph TR3 and 4, and Volvo. Price is approximately $19.00. Other cooling system products include spacers for fan clutches, transmission coolers, VW oil coolers, and power steering cooling units. Free information.
Toulmin Motors, Ltd. 181 London Road Isleworth Middlesex England	New parts for T-series MGs (TA onward) and for the MG A/B. Mechanical parts for T-series cars include a competition full-flow exhaust system (XPAG) for about $85.00 and a front anti-roll bar for $14.00. Carpeting, convertible tops, sidescreens and tonneau covers are also listed. Some fiberglass body parts are made for T-series MGs along with a number of 'glass components for the MG A/B. For the later cars, wire wheels are $24.00 apiece and an alloy finned rocker cover goes for $72.00. Close ratio and standard gearbox parts, exchange starter motors, exhaust system components, seats available on an exchange basis, front suspension parts, and cosmetic accessories are among the other items offered. Free price list.
Toyota Motor Distributors Inc. 2055 West 190th Street P.O. Box 2991 Torrance, California 90501	U.S. distributor; service manuals.
Toyo Tire Co. 3136 East Victoria Street Compton, California 90221	Toyo's line-up includes steel belted radials, radial snow tires, wide tread compact car tires, steel radials for pickups and vans, 8-ply rated camper and off-road vehicle tires, and ordinary bias ply tires for import and domestic cars. Free literature.
The Toy Store 9058 Culver Boulevard Culver City, California 90230	Accessories and performance equipment for Toyota cars and mini-pickups. Suspension kits for the Corolla KE20 or TE2 series, consisting of new front springs, lowering blocks for the rear springs, and longer U-bolts; are $49.95. Kits with four springs, for the Celica and Carina, are $85.00. An accessory Panhard Rod for the Toyota 1100,

Denim seat covers from The Toy Store

1200 and 1600 is $19.95. A similar anti-sway device for the Hilux pickup is $29.95. Engine performance accessories include a choice of three cam grinds, forged pistons, Offy manifolds, Weber carbs and manifolds, complete modified cylinder heads and engine blocks, engine oil coolers, and headers. Hard parts available include tune-up kits, clutches and brake pads. The Toy Store also carries front spoilers for most Toyotas, 5-speed conversion kits ($125.00 or $245.00 with close ratio gears), service manuals, and a variety of cosmetic accessories such as denim seat covers and racing side stripes. Free literature.

Trade-Winds Engineering
Box 239, 81-20 25th Avenue
Jackson Heights
New York 11370

Mostly a distributor for racing parts and accessories. Hepolite, Venolia and TRW pistons; Hasting's Moly and Deves piston rings; Vandervell and TRW Clevite bearings; Isky, Racer Brown, BMC Competition and Crower Cams; Holby and Lucas oil pumps; Mocal and Serck oil coolers; Victor gasket sets; nitrided cranks; Loctite; Borg & Beck clutches; Trans-Dapt scatter shields; trans parts for Mini Cooper, Sprite, Triumph and MGB; Webster gears; Formula A, B and Ford metalastic rubber driveshaft doughnuts; Ampep and NMB rod ends; Koni shocks; BMC competition axles for Sprites and Midgets; sway bars; Ferodo, Raybestos, Lakewood and Velvetouch brake pads; Aeroquip brake lines; Hooker and Cyclone headers; ANSA and Stebro free-flow exhaust systems; Teledyne and Varley batteries; roll bars; racing harness systems; Bell helmets; Nomex and Fypro flame resistant clothing; Phoenix on-board fire extinguisher systems; spooks and spoilers for most cars; VDO and Stewart Warner instruments; Uni-Syn carb synchronizing device; Drager tire gauges; Racemark steering wheels; Heuer watches; bucket seats; car covers; lap boards; fiberglass body parts for many European cars; BWA, Cosmic, Appliance, Formula Ford and Minilite wheels; Semperit, Vredestein, Goodyear, B.F. Goodrich and Firestone tires. Also carry AMCO accessories; Ansen, Cragar and U.S. Indy wheels; Cee-Dee Ignition systems, Interpart speed equip.; products by Spearco, Autodynamics, Pirelli, Shelby and Wink. Free catalog.

Trans-Go
2627 Merced Avenue
El Monte, California 91733

Reprogramming kits for popular automatic transmissions. Two types of kits available are Competition for the fastest shifting possible and Tow-or-Go kits for heavy-duty use. Kits are available for Turbo-Hydro 350 and 400, Ford C-4 and C-6, Ford FM/3, Torqueflite and Powerglide. Also available are individual transmission components. Reprogramming kit prices range from $29.95 to $39.95. Complete installation instructions are supplied and it is not necessary to remove the transmission for installation. Catalog, $1.00.

Walter O. Trautwein
725 Old Kensico Road
Thornwood, New York 10594

Repro parts for 1932-36 Fords only. 1932-6 Roadster-Phaeton windshield frames are $85.00 each; 1932 stainless steel, machine turned dash panel, $25.00; 1932-36 ignition switch plates, $2.00 each; 1932-36 Ford Greyhounds, $25.00; 1932-36 Ford script radiator hose with red stripe, four hoses and eight clamps, $9.00 a set. Many more items in the works. Write for further information.

Travel Safe
P.O. Box 484
Orinda, California 94563

Adjustable equalizing hitches and sway control units. Manufactures the well-known Derr Sway Control ($47.50) designed for use with Class III hitches. Free literature.

Treuhaft Automotive Specialties, Inc.
2161 South Dupont Drive
Anaheim, California 92806

VW and off-road racing accessories. Among the offerings are power pulleys; counterweighted cranks; SPG roller bearing cranks; crankshaft gear pullers; pulley seal cutters; Crown dowel jigs; heavy-duty clutch plates and lightened flywheels; Kolbenschmidt and Mahle big bore kits; Deves piston rings; Weber and Solex intake manifolds; Plenum manifolds for single port and dual port heads; carb linkage assemblies; electric fuel pumps; air cleaners; complete dual carb systems with Solex carbs, manifolds, linkage and air cleaners ($179.95); Weber and Holley carbs; Treuhaft cams and valve gear; Bosch ignition components; VW deep sumps and windage trays; oil cooler and filter adapter kits; Bug, Bus, Ghia and Porsche 914 headers; Koni shocks; front and rear sway bars; universal bicycle racks; Crown heavy-duty drivetrain components; nerf bars; VW shifters; VW dual port cylinder heads; custom steering wheels; Bug and Bus fiberglass body components; Nomex clothing; Bell helmets; and racing safety belts and harnesses. Company also has special VW tools and precision measuring instruments including head and case cutters, valve guide boss cutters, boring plates, Neway seat cutter kits, case boring bar outfits, and Mitutoyo micrometers and thickness gauges. Dune buggy components available are front and rear bumpers, headlights, windshield frames, wiring harnesses, skid plates, roll bars, mechanical and hydraulic steering brakes, hydraulic clutch kits, and bucket seats. Company also sells complete Zink Formula Vee cars and car kits. The Formula Vee kit, with most necessary items other than an engine/transaxle and steering box, sells for $1,555.00 Catalog, $2.00.

Trik Race Car Products 6 River Park Drive Bricktown, New Jersey 08723	High performance engine components for 340 cu. in. Chrysler engines only. Also some chassis bits and pieces. Go-power items are aggressive Delco distributors, a degreed harmonic balancer, aluminum crankshaft and alternator pulleys, head gaskets, flat top or high domed racing pistons, a quick change cam timer (this item is designed to fit all small block Chrysler V-8s), a cam gear drive, valve train assemblies, a complete maximum performance oil system with deep sump, solid steel motor mounts, an aluminum gas cooler, fuel system Y-block kit, engine pre-heat kit to allow a race car engine to be brought up to running temperature before starting, and hi-performance cams. Chassis components for Darts, Demons, Dusters, 'Cudas and Challengers are high lift torsion bars, drag racing rear springs, an offset rear spring hanger and perch kit, and an adjustable pinion snubber. Catalog, $1.00.
Tri-Mil Industries 2740 Compton Avenue Los Angeles, California 90011	Headers for VW, all Porsches, Porsche engines installed in VWs, Toyota including Land Cruiser, Spitfire, Spridget, MGB, Opel, Ford Pinto, Vega, BMW 1600 and 2002, Datsun including 2000-model. Also zoom tubes and side pipes. Intake manifolds for single port VW engines, for dual port heads taking Zenith or most American dual barrel carbs, and 180-degree crossfire manifolds for Weber or Solex carbs. Other products include engine stands, tow bars, tapered stingers, dune buggy exhaust systems, and VW one-piece nerf bar bumpers. Free literature.
Trio Tire Service Inc. 280 White Horse Pike Clementon, New Jersey 08021	Manufactures retread tires for the trade. Free literature.
Tri-State Racing Converters 10007 Springfield Pike Cincinnati, Ohio 45215	Rebuilt torque converters for all foreign and American cars. Racing torque converters for Turbo-Hydro, Torqueflight, Cruise-A-Matic C-4 and Powerglide transmissions. Also distributes a complete line of trans parts, new and used. Free literature.
Triumph Owners Club & Triumph Register (Triumph, Pre-1940) c/o Barry K. Ambrose 51 Cow Lane Fulbourn Cambridge CB1 5HB England	Club publishes a regular newsletter, maintains a technical library, keeps tabs on sources for spare parts, and holds an annual rally at Woburn Abbey in Bedfordshire. Yearly dues: $3.50.
Trojan Ltd. Vintage Car Division Kingsley House Trojan Way Croydon CRO 4XL England	A good source of Bentley parts, especially those for the "real," pre-Rolls Bentley. Will also do complete restorations on any antique or classic, and manufacture parts to order from customer's specifications or drawings. Has parts for some other classic British cars in stock. Send international reply coupon with queries.
Al Trommers 61 Jane Street New York, New York 10014	Mr. Trommers' specialty is supplying hub caps and wheel covers for any early car, along with any recent special-interest car. Thousands of hub caps, including caps for

wooden and wire wheels, are in stock. Send a stamped, self-addressed envelope with queries. If the hub cap you need is not in stock, Mr. Trommers will make an effort to locate it.

Truck Bumpers, Inc.
P.O. Box 341
Sunnyvale, California 94086

Makes the Model 103 Toolbox bumper which has universal mounting brackets for all U.S. pickup trucks. The bumper has over 3,500 cu. in. of storage space, with enough room for a Hi-Lift jack and a selection of tools. It has 4″ steel channel bracing and locks with a single hasp system. Price is $125.00. Free literature.

True Pivot
5015 North Gates
Fresno, California 93705

Manufactures sway-controlled equalizing trailer hitches in four models, depending on the size of the trailer. Prices range from $109.95 to $135.95. Free literature.

Ez Truman
1330 Market Street
Youngstown, Ohio 44507

Sells sandblasting equipment and air compressors. Prices are as low as $89.50 for mini-blaster and $263.00 for air compressors. Free literature and information on sandblasting process.

TRW
8001 East Pleasant
Valley Road
Cleveland, Ohio 44131

Performance engine parts for American cars and VW. The extensive TRW catalogs list pistons, rings, valves, pushrods, valve springs, cams, lifters, bearings and valve locks for many models. The TRW performance parts catalog is $1.00. An excellent publication entitled *The Racing World & TRW* is a combined catalog and informative explanation of engine blueprinting, the construction of high performance parts, machine shop operations, and various further topics of interest to enthusiasts. The cost of this publication is $1.50.

Tucker Auto Club
(Tucker)
c/o Richard Jones
315 Arora Boulevard
Orange Park, Florida 32073

Yes, there is a Tucker Club which has just started recently. Publications are a monthly newsletter with free want advertisements for members, and *Tucker Topics,* a quarterly magazine. No events yet other than an annual meeting, but some are planned for the future. Technical advice, parts location, and library services available.
Yearly dues: $6.00

Turbo Action
Box 5581
Jacksonville, Florida 32207

Racing auto transmissions and transmission parts. Company has heavy-duty, street & strip, and competition versions of the Turbo-Hydro 350, Turbo-Hydro 400, Torqueflite 727 and 904, and Ford C-4 and C-6 transmissions. Ford C-6 competition version is $295.00 with $150.00 core charge. Also available are shift kits, valve bodies, special bands and clutches, trans filters, seals, overhaul sets, and adjustable modulators. Catalog, $1.00.

TVR Cars of America Ltd.
572 Merrick Road
Lynbrook, New York 11563

TVR distributor.

T.V.R.C.C.
(TVR)
c/o P.M. Watkiss
4 Ninnings Lane

A small but enthusiastic group which holds an annual get-together and publishes the magazine *Sprint* approximately every two months. There is also an annual

Concept Cars. Once in a great while there is a rare genius who sits down at the drawing board and comes up with a totally fresh concept of the passenger car. More often, concept cars are the result of public relations genius rather than engineering ability, or their designers go round and round the merry-go-round, snatching frantically at ideas as though they were brass rings.

1. 1933 Dymaxion. Buckminster Fuller's idea of a motor car consisted of a stressed-skin fuselage and three wheels. Both fast and economical, the Dymaxion was almost produced by Ford, until some high Ford official rolled one over and was fatally injured.

2. 1935 Stout Scarab. Bill Stout's design, produced at the Stout Engineering Laboratories in Dearborn, was a radically-engineered production package as well as a notable advance in aerodynamics and space utilization. Circumstance, and some initial bugs which may well have been worked out, prevented series production.

3. Stout Scarab Interior. The Pullman Car interior was another feature of Stout's design.

4. 1938 Phantom Corsair. Built for Rust Heinz, heir to the 57 varieties fortune, the Phantom Corsair was constructed on a Cord 810 chassis by the fine custom coachbuilders, Bohman and Schwartz. It was a hit at the 1939 New York World's Fair and displayed a number of advanced features. The car was later remodeled and purchased by comedian Herb Shriner. It is now at Harrah's Automobile collection.

1. *2.* *3.* *4.*

5. *1948 Tucker.* Preston Tucker's rear-engine 6-seater sports sedan was not a dream car. It was designed for mass production and had many advanced safety features. A lack of financing, combined with production problems, ended the manufacture of this controversial vehicle almost before it began. Today the Tucker is a rare and costly collector's car.

6. *1948 Tasco.* A design from The American Sports Car Company, the Tasco had airplane-strut wheels and a battering ram front end. Surprisingly, the coachwork was by the distinguished American firm of Derham, better known for Cadillac and Packard limousines.

7. *AnyCar II.* Trust Manufacturer's Hanover to commission a junkyard special, combining parts from 50 cars dating from the 1930s to the '70s. Hmm . . . not all that bad, is it?

5.

6.

7.

Rabley Heath
Welwyn
Hertfordshire
England

roster and some technical publications. Information on spare parts is available. Yearly dues: $9.50 U.S.

20 Ghost Club
(Rolls-Royce)
c/o W.F. Watson
Aldwick Hundred
Aldwick, Bognor Regis
Sussex
England

Regular Club activities comprise driving tests, concours, tours, and visits to stately homes. Principal Club publication is *The Record.* All members must own a Rolls-Royce, preferably an older model. Yearly dues: $12.00.

Ultra Seal International
1104 Wilcox Avenue
Los Angeles, California 90038

Makers of Ultra Seal tire puncture preventative. Sizes are 8 ounce, 16 ounce, and one gallon. Free literature.

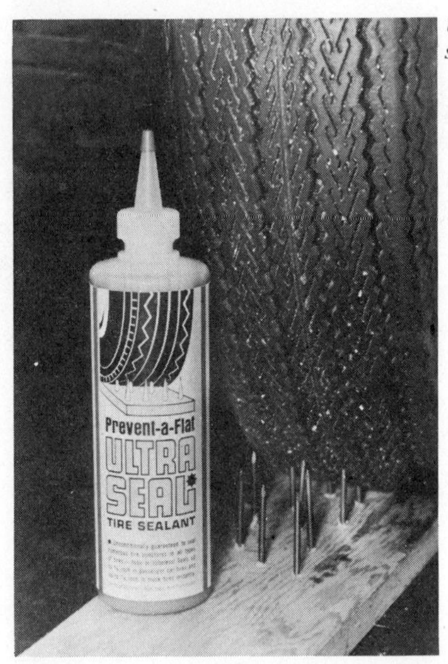

Ultra Seal tire sealant

Union Carbide Corporation
270 Park Avenue
New York, New York 10017

Makers of Prestone anti-freeze and summer coolant. A wall chart showing cooling system parts, along with a brochure giving product information and cooling system care tips is available. Free literature.

Union Electrical
7311 Cottage Avenue
North Bergen
New Jersey 07047

Replacement ignition components for late-model domestic and foreign cars. Catalog lists ignition parts for such off-beat makes as Allard, Alvis, Armstrong-Siddeley, Borgward, Bristol, DKW, Dyna Panhard, Ford Taunus, Goliath, Lagonda, Metropolitan, Riley, Singer, Standard and Wolseley. Also has PCV valves, coils, regulators, and generator and starter brush sets for many overseas makes. Consult catalog at wholesale parts house.

United Karmann Ghia
Owners of America
(Karmann Ghia)
c/o Frank Camper
2341 Court R
Ensely, Albama 35218

Mr. Camper states that this is not a club but rather an association of people united by common interests. The non-club publication is entitled *Redline.* There are no dues other than postage. Those who write to Mr. Camper will be placed on a permanent mailing list.

United Tool Processes Corporation
P.O. Box 914, 72 Park Street
New Canaan
Connecticut 06840

Engine rebuilding equipment available includes valve guide drivers, valve train blueprinter, valve stem height gauge, valve guide coring tool, and complete valve tool sets. Free information.

Universal Tire Co.
14622 Southlawn Lane
Rockville, Maryland 20850

Distributes many major brands of tires including tires for antique cars and motorcycles. Also sells by mail order American and Superior wheels, Stanley and Cibie lights, Bowman Astrosonix eight-track tape decks and radios, Koni shock absorbers, and NGK spark plugs. Free literature. Comprehensive tire guide for $.99.

Unlimited Fiberglass
1845 West Commonwealth
Fullerton, California 92633

Fiberglass parts available include spoilers for Pinto, Vega, Porsche 914, Mustang, Capri, VW, Camaro, Datsun 510, 240Z, and Ford/Chev/Dodge vans. Also custom scoops for street machines and Pro Stock cars. If you intend to build a Pro Stock Pinto, 1967-70 Camaro, Chevy II, Datsun 510, Maverick or Mustang, Unlimited Fiberglass can supply fenders, hoods, deck lids, and other essentials. Fiberglass replicas of 1948-52 Anglias, Corvette rear fender flares, Bronco rear flares, 1955-57 Chev front ends, 1917-22 "T" buckets, and racing seats complete the line up. If you want something exotic, the company maintains complete tooling facilities for the manufacture of reinforced polyester molds and can make you anything from a fiberglass Cadillac Tulip roadster to a seat for your portable john. Free information.

Upson Tools, Inc.
Box 4750
Rochester, New York 14612

Makes screwdrivers, nutdrivers, scratch awls, and four-in-one screwdriving tool. Tools also come in kits especially designed for mobile home and RV owners. Free literature.

Urus Performance Products
Box 151
Lake Bluff, Illinois 60044

Pinto and Vega performance thingamajigs. Urus offers speed shifters, stainless steel splashguards, bumper guards, burglar alarm systems, full length center consoles ($50.95), Vega walnut veneer door panel kits, dash instrument panels, VDO gauges, traction bars, Vega competition lower control arms and driveshaft loops, Vega V-8 conversion kits, Offy manifolds, headers, freeflow exhaust systems, Vega Air Lifts, Koni shocks, Vega front and rear sway bar kits, Pinto competition suspension packages ($62.50), Fenton alloy wheels, front and rear spoilers, Cibie lights, interior carpeting, Pinto hot pants, hatchback camper tents, wire and mag style wheel covers, and Turbocharger kits for the Vega, Pinto, and Capri. Catalog, $1.00.

Usarica
Box 216
Canoga Park, California 91305

Carries a variety of foreign car goodies including driving lights, club badges, crested jewelry, robes with marque patches, insignia mugs and key cases, Maserati air horns, Bell helmets, and crested desk pen sets. Free catalog sent from time to time in newsletter style.

U.S. Sunroof Corporation
360 Stewart Avenue, Unit F
Addison, Illinois 60101

Makers of pop-top sunroofs constructed of tinted plexiglass, in size 18″x35″, for universal installation. The price is $60.00. Other dress-up accessories are Continental style grilles and trunk lids, oval "opera" windows, landau bars, and Lincoln Mark IV hood ornaments. To dress-up your Ford or Toronado there are kits which include Continental style grille caps, deck lid kits, and "opera" windows. Ford kit is $230.00. Toronado package is $250.00 without windows. Free literature.

Val-Chem/Competition Engineering
P.O. Box 153
North Madison, Ohio 44057

Acid-dipping, lightweight glass, fiberglass components, construction of tube chassis and roll cages, aluminum and steel sheet metal work, factory body shells in stock. Owner Mike Valerio runs his own Pro Stock Camaro and offers complete race car building—"Whatever the customer specifies for any class they wish to run." Catalog unavailable at time this was written.

Valley Obsolete
11604 Vanowen
North Hollywood
California 91605

The largest selection of NOS Ford items on West Coast, claims owner Bill Norton. Parts are for 1909-43 Fords, and also some 1955-57 Thunderbird parts. Has complete line of repro early Ford parts. Send a stamped, self-addressed envelope with query.

Van Norman Machine Co.
3640 Main Street
Springfield
Massachusetts 01107

Power automotive tools for professionals. Equipment includes brake drum lathes, valve regrinders, boring machinery, crankshaft grinders, valve refacers, hydraulic presses, parts cleaning equipment, and pressure testing and circulating machinery. Free information.

Van Owners Club of America (All Vans)
R.R. 1, Box 6
Berme Road
Kerhonkson, New York 12446

Publishes *Beautiful Boxes*—a bi-monthly newsletter—and provides technical information and some library services to members. Also obtains discounts for members on van accessories. (As the Club's president, I refrain from further comment.) Yearly dues are $6.00.

VDO
116 Victor
Detroit, Michigan 48203

6109 Lankershim Boulevard
North Hollywood
California 91606

Two lines of instruments, the Cockpit and Jet Cockpit, are distinguished from each other mainly by their design—the latter having an aircraft look about them. All VDO instruments are round and have dark faces with light dial markings which stand out clearly and tastefully. They are designed to work only with VDO sending units and adapters.

In Cockpit styles there are three tachometers. Two have shift pointers and rev limits of 6,000 and 8,000 respectively. The third is an economy model for 4-cylinder, 4-cycle applications only. It has a 7,000 rpm limit and sells for $39.50. There are both electrically and mechanically actuated pressure and temperature gauges, a voltmeter, an ammeter, a vacuum gauge, an electric clock, an engine hour meter which gives the total time an engine has been in operation, an electric fuel gauge, and speedometers with 120 or 160 mph limits. Those wanting a speedometer to fit a custom vehicle can write VDO for a "ratio test form."

In Jet Cockpit style there are 6,000 and 8,000 rpm tachs; electric pressure, fuel and temperature gauges; a voltmeter;

ammeter; clock; and 120 mph speedo. VDO electric instruments are available in both 6- and 12-volts.

For VWs there are numerous instruments which match the originals (also supplied by VDO) and they fit in cut-out panels which neatly replace those on the standard pre-1973 VW dash.

Classic Porsche fanciers can buy electric pressure and oil temperature gauges, along with an ammeter, which have black dials and green numerals to match the standard instruments on all 356-series.

A line of custom transistorized tachometers match the original style instruments in BMW 1600/2002, Audi 100-series, Mercedes gas or diesel-engined cars, and VW Type IIIs.

VDO's MiniCockpit design is a module containing electric temperature and pressure gauges plus a voltmeter. It is mounted on its own pedestal and can be affixed above or below the dash.

VDO's "Mini-Cockpit" panel

The ultimate in automobile clocks is probably VDO's quartz electronic model for 12-volt systems only and priced at $75.95.

Another unique instrument is a turbocharger gauge, which monitors manifold vacuum, at $14.75.

There are numerous brackets, mount panels (1, 2, or 3 holes) and mounting cups to be used in installing VDO instruments, and there is also a complete line of senders and wiring kits to adapt them to both foreign and domestic cars. The catalog gives applications in detail.

Dedicated rallyists will also want to look at VDO's "T" gear drive, in various thread sizes, to allow custom installation of a second speedometer or rally instruments. Catalog $1.00. For freebies you can get a small brochure on VDO's auto instruments, snowmobile gauges, marine instrumentation, or motorcycle/mini-bike gauges.

Richard Veen
Postbus 6282
Amsterdam, Holland

Auto literature. Most items are postwar, are of less than book length, and include many American makes. Free lists.

Velvetex Industrial Corporation
P.O. Box 1019
Ft. Lauderdale, Florida 33302

If you want your car to attract the fuzz, the best way is to cover it with a special epoxy and shoot nylon fibers on electro-statically. This can be done just to car tops or to entire cars for a real custom look. Company has dealers in most areas of the country who will flock-up your car for a price. Free literature.

Veteran & Vintage Car Club of Luxembourg (Vintage and Veteran Cars)
c/o Joseph Wantz
41 rue de la Paix
Petange
Luxembourg

Sponsors the Tour de Luxembourg pour Voitures Anciennes and the Tour du lac de la Haute Sure, which are both rallies for cars constructed before 1940. There is a monthly Club newsletter which includes information on spare parts sources. The 50 Luxembourgeois who are members of the Club own a total of 150 cars constructed before 1940. Yearly dues: 750 lux francs a year for active members; 1000 lux francs for associate members. Ask your bank how much that is in dollars.

Veteran Car Club de Belgique (Vintage and Veteran Cars)
147, Chaussée de Haecht
1030 Bruxelles
Belgique

Limited to owners of vehicles produced prior to 1930, this Club holds monthly meetings and an annual competitive event. The Club gazette is published quarterly, and technical advice plus library services can be supplied. Yearly dues: about $15.00.

Veteran Car Club do Brazil (Vintage and Veteran Cars)
c/o Oggi Pozzoli
Rua Santo Antonio 611
Terreo
Sao Paulo
Brazil

Regular Club activities consist of monthly meetings, four outings a year, and a concours in May. The Club publishes a quarterly magazine *O Carbureto,* and can supply information on local sources for parts and service. Yearly dues: approximately $6.00.

Veteran Motor Car Club of America (Antique Cars)
105 Elm Street
Andover, Massachusetts 01810

VMCCA has regions and local chapters and covers all antique cars, although ownership is not a prerequisite to joining. There are more than 4,000 Club members throughout the world. The VMCCA sponsors meets nationally, and publishes a bi-monthly glossy magazine, with a classified section, called *Bulb Horn.* Yearly dues: $10.00 U.S., $12.00 foreign. Membership in the national organization is a prerequisite to joining a region or chapter. Family memberships for the spouse or child of an active member are $2.00 a person. Life memberships are also available subject to the approval of the VMCCA Board of Governors.

The 'Vette Shop, Inc.
22183 Telegraph Road
Southfield, Michigan 48075

Also known as Don Bailey's Corvette Shop, the company has a large line of custom accessories plus a few performance parts. Complete header systems go for $264.00 and up. Holley carbs are about $65.00 for the 650 C.F.M. model and $80.00 for the 800 C.F.M. model. A super tilt custom front end for 1968-73 Vettes is $650.00. Miura-type rear window louvers to fit 1968-73 Corvette coupes are $125.00 with hardware. Very neat Corvette racing mirrors with a black plastic ABS body sell for $17.00 a pair. Other items in the Don Bailey bag of good things are Hurst shifters, Delco shocks, three types of spoilers for late model Corvettes, custom tail light lenses, wood paneling for dash and console,

	European-style headlight covers, 1968-73 rear fender flares, L-88 hood scoops, trailer hitches, hardtop hoists, an inside rear view mirror with a built-in map light, tune-up and lubrication tools, luggage racks and ski racks by AMCO and Mohn, three types of stereo speakers, Lucas and G.E. aircraft lights, burglar prevention devices, and many fiberglass body parts. Catalog, $1.00.
VFN Fiberglass 501 Interstate Road Addison, Illinois 60101	Makes a complete line of fiberglass hood scoops, as well as 'glass hoods, fenders and doors for some American cars and VW. A Vega front spoiler with air ducts for disc brakes sells for $36.40. Vega doors are $105.00. Hoods are available for the 1970 AMX, 1968 Dodge Dart and 1972 El Camino. VW front and rear flared fenders are $36.40 and $29.95 respectively. Free literature.
View-Craft 18333 Main Street Carson, California 90248	Camper shells for standard and mini pickups. Models available for Mazda, Courier and LUV pickups. Options include extra windows and full cargo doors. Prices range from $289.00 for the least expensive mini model up to $484.00. Free literature.
Vintage and Classic Car Club (Vintage and Veteran Cars) P.O. Box 124 Ballarat East Victoria 3350 Australia	Along with monthly meetings and rallies, the Club publishes a newsletter each month and aids members in restorations. Yearly dues: $5.00.
Vintage Austin Register (Pre-1930 Austin) c/o J. C. Stringer 17 Grove Park Avenue Sittingbourne Kent England	Holds monthly meetings in London and publishes *The Vintage Austin Magazine* quarterly. Offers technical advice, parts location, and some repro parts. The Vintage Austin Register has branches in New Zealand and Australia. Yearly dues: $3.60.
Vintage Automobile Club of Montreal (Vintage Cars) P.O. Box 246, N.D.G. Station Montreal 260 Quebec Canada	Sponsors both social and competitive events, and publishes a glossy magazine *Le Chauffeur.* Yearly dues: $10.00.
Vintage Auto Parts 24300 Woodinville-Snohomish Highway Woodinville Washington 98072	Mr. Jarvis advises that VAP has a 10,000 square foot warehouse loaded with antique and special-interest car parts plus a filled storage and wrecking yard. Parts are for all cars from 1915 to the present. Specialties are pre-WWII pistons, rings, valves, front end suspension parts, tie rod ends and draglinks, and king bolt sets. It is probable that this is the largest inventory of early car parts in the U.S. Send a stamped; self-addressed envelope with query.
Vintage Auto Shop 430 Mill Street Cincinnati, Ohio 45215	Complete restorations on any vintage car at a basic rate of $10.00 an hour. Most present work is concerned with Rolls-Royces. Write for further information.

Vintage Car Club of Canada (Vintage and Veteran Cars)
P.O. Box 3070
Vancouver
British Columbia
Canada

Club has five chapters, all in British Columbia, with a total membership of 425. Principal events are: May Tour—a two-day tour usually held the last week in May; Easter Parade—on Easter Sunday; Boxing Day Run—15 mile run around Stanley Park on December 26th; and Swap Meet—usually the weekend before Easter. Club magazine is *The Vintage Car.* Yearly dues: $12.50.

Vintage Car Club of Rhodesia (Vintage Cars)
c/o A. H. Phillips
P.O. Box 465
Salisbury
Rhodesia

This Club is rather exclusive, as membership is by invitation only. Activities include monthly social events and a quarterly magazine, *B 431.* Club members are interested in building up their collection of metal car badges, and might like to hear from American hobbyists. Yearly dues: $4.00; entry fee, $10.00.

Vintage Motor Club (1919-1930 Cars)
Rosedale
24 Olive Street
Denistone East
Sydney
New South Wales
Australia

Sponsors numerous competitive and social events, along with publishing a Club bulletin. There is a small library for members' use. Yearly dues: $6.00. Members must possess a 1919-30 car.

Vintage Porsche Register (Porsche, 1953 and Previous)
c/o Victor Skirmants
27244 Ryan
Warren, Michigan 48092

The Vintage Porsche Register is a listing of 1953 and older Porsches in the U.S. There are presently seventy-five cars listed. The Register is available free of charge to vintage Porsche owners. For parts sources and technical advice in restoring a classic Porsche, Mr. Skirmants suggests that Jim Barrington of 110 Wisteria Way, Mill Valley, California 94941 may be able to help.

Vintage Racing Cars, Ltd.
Derby Road Garage
Northampton
England

Specializes in parts and service for vintage British racing cars. Also carries a stock of Alvis spares. Company recently took over AutoVac and now can supply parts and service on any AutoVac fuel pump. Free information.

Vintage Restorations
4 Whybourne Crest
Tunbridge Wells
Kent
England

Restores or repairs dashboards and instruments on veteran and vintage cars. Has some restored instruments for sale to fit cars from 1904 to the present. Send international reply coupon for estimate or query.

Instrument restorations from John E. Marks of Vintage Restorations

Vintage Specialists Box 225 Freeport, New York 11520	Vintage and sports car parts for MG (1929 to the present), Jaguar and Austin-Healey. MG workshop manual; $9.95; TC axle, $135.00; rack & pinion for TD/F, $90.00; valve cover with "MG" on top, $38.00; cylinder head, $88.00; exchange gear box, $220.00; rebuilt short block, $350.00 or $115.00 exchange; tach, $65.00. Most mechanical parts, many body parts, wire wheels, and some accessories. Also deals in vintage MGs, restored and original, and has shop facilities for mechanical restoration. Parts sold are NOS, new and used. Has some parts for Bugatti and other vintage sports cars. Catalog, $.25. Special MG A, Austin-Healey and Jaguar catalog, $.25.
Vintage Sports-Car Club **(Pre-1931 Cars)** P.M.A. Hull V.S.C.C. Office 121 Russell Road Newbury Berkshire England	Although primarily devoted to running competition events for British vintage car owners, the Club also has overseas members who enjoy receiving the quarterly magazine, *The Bulletin,* and monthly newsletter published by the V.S.C.C. The Club has a spares registrar and book and film libraries. The only parts manufactured under V.S.C.C. auspices are beaded edge wheel rims sized 895 x135, 820x120 and 710x90. Yearly dues: Approximately $7.50.
Vintage Sports Car Club **of America, Inc.** 170 Wetherill Road Garden City, New York 11530	Principal activities are six or eight events a year, primarily races and hill climbs. Quarterly bulletin is *Vintage Sports Car.* Also technical information services. Yearly dues: $15.00; initiation fee $7.50.
The Vintage Sports Car **Club of Australia** **(Vintage and Veteran Cars)** 247 Waverly Road East Malvern, 3145 Melbourne Australia	Club events include hill climbs, trials, sprints, and gymkhanas. There is a monthly *V.S.C.C. Newsletter,* and a bi-monthly Club bulletin. The V.S.C.C. also maintains a small library for use by members. Yearly dues: $13.00.
Vintage Sports Car Club **of South Australia** **(Vintage Sports Cars)** Box 90, Rundle Street P.O. Adelaide South Australia 5000	Club runs a number of social/competitive events which include trials, rallies, and a weekend concours. The Bateman Shield is awarded to the member who has the best performance in Club events each year, while the Restoration Trophy is awarded for the best car restoration. *The Vintage Bulletin* is the Club's monthly publication and includes a parts and cars advertisement section. A library is maintained for members. Full membership available only to past or present owners of vintage or late-model thoroughbred sports cars. Full membership, $10.00 a year; country and overseas membership $2.00.
Vintage Thunderbird Club **of America** **(1958-60 Thunderbirds)** c/o Larry J. Seyfarth 26056 Deerfield Dearborn Heights Michigan 48127	Squarebird lovers feel that the 1958-60 T-Birds are more stylish and distinctive than their earlier or later brethren. Although there has been a move to admit 1961-66 Birds into the ranks of the elite, no word has been received as to the outcome as yet. The Squarebirders publish a bi-monthly journal, *Squarebird Scoop* in which the doings of local chapters are reported and classified advertising is accepted free of charge. Mr. Seyfarth, the Club president, states

that he has the most complete file of parts information available anywhere for 1958-60 T-Birds and will be glad to advise anyone who sends a stamped, self-addressed envelope. He states that most mechanical parts are still available from Ford, but soft trim and rubber mouldings are very scarce. Some exterior chrome trim is not available from Ford. Padded dash covers can still be obtained in black and blue; for other colors dye must be used. A California member of the club, Elmer Knitter, is supplying his fellow members with many used parts from that state. Yearly dues: $5.00.

Vintage Tyre Supplies
Jackman Mews
North Circular Road
Neasden, London N.W.10
England

Can supply Dunlop tires for most any antique or classic car. Although the cost of shipping tires overseas might be prohibitive for American enthusiasts, this company can supply tires for vintage cars being imported from England. Free literature.

Volks Tool Supply
P.O. Box 660
Houston, Texas 77001

A fine selection of tools for anyone with a pet Bug or Bus. Eight sockets sized 9-19 mm are $3.69. Large sockets in 24, 30, 36, 41 and 46 mm sizes are also available. A 6-piece German Hazet set of metric box-ends is $11.40 and a 7-piece open-end set is $15.75.

A cylinder head saver kit for retapping stripped spark plug holes is $12.98, and thread inserts in two styles are $.75 each. There is also a tap and installer for case studs.

Kukko brand German pullers are sold for the crankshaft gear ($10.95), generator bearing ($5.95) and V-belt Pulley ($7.90). The generator bearing puller can be used on small gears and battery terminals. There is also an oil pump puller ($5.20) and hub puller for 4-bolt models ($5.79).

Among the wrenches designed to make the VW mechanic's life easier are a gearbox carrier wrench, carburetor flange wrench for Type Is and IIs pre-1970 and post-1970, wheel bearing adjusting wrenches in sizes 24 mm, 27 mm and 32 mm, clutch adjusting "star" wrenches, a valve-adjusting wrench which is hollow to allow a screwdriver to be inserted through it, Hazet Solex carb jet and fuel tap wrenches, a swivel-head wrench for oil pressure switches, an oil cooler wrench, oil pump wrench, brake bleeder wrench, rear axle cover wrench, transmission filler socket, 36 mm box-end rear axle nut striking wrench, hex-head joint flange socket wrench, fuel pump wrench, and a whopping big 46 mm open end wrench for Type III muffler fixing screws.

Also a tie rod end press ($7.25 for Bugs, $9.39 Buses), disc brake puller ($8.95), 3-piece oil seal installer ($6.95), dial indicator ($13.49) and indicator holder ($7.29), vernier calipers ($14.95), clutch pilot tool ($7.05), 50 to 100 mm piston ring expander ($3.79) and piston ring compressors in four sizes.

A valve seat cutting kit, with cutting heads, pilots and wrenches, sells for $49.80, with individual heads available separately. A valve guide kit in 7 or 8 mm sizes is $10.19, while there are two price levels for valve guide reamers.

Valve spring compressors, lock-ring pliers, stud pullers, a torsion bar socket and torsion arm drift pin, piston pin drifts, and a quick-change push rod tube are some other items in stock. Those who do their own tune-ups will also want to check out a static timing light ($3.58) and 4-cylinder tach/dwell meter ($15.95.)

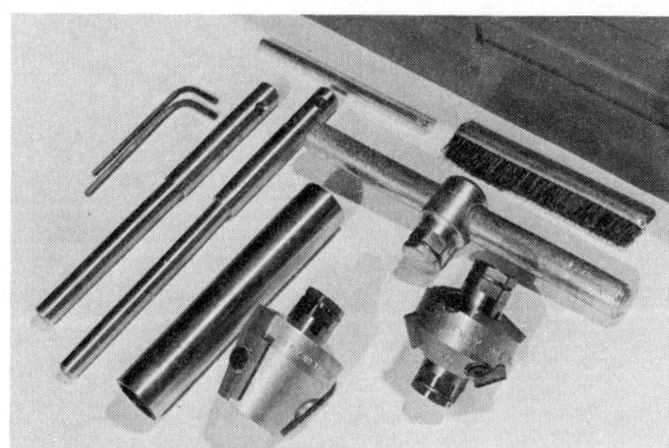

Precision valve seat cutting kit by Volks Tool Supply

Owner Nelson Antosh plans to expand his inventory in the future and issue an even larger catalog. Meanwhile the current catalog, which lists 93 items and specifies the assemblies they are designed to fit, is an education in itself. Catalog $.50.

Volkswagen of America, Inc.
Englewood Cliffs
New Jersey 07632

U.S. distributor; service manuals.

Volkswagen Owner's Club (VW)
c/o Paul Harris
1a Manor Road
Toddington
Dunstable
Bedfordshire
England

Divided into five British regions, all of which hold monthly meetings, this Club also organizes various rallies and trials. There is an excellent monthly magazine *Beetling,* plus newsletters from each center. Yearly dues: $4.80.

Volvo Owner's Club (Volvo)
c/o Peter Ruddock
The Manor House
Helperby
Yorkshire
England

Holds rallies and "Best Kept Volvo" competitions each year, as well as assisting with the sponsorship of a Volvo in the R.A.C. Rally. The Club's quarterly magazine is entitled *Volvo Driver*. Other services are technical advice and repair manuals available on loan. There are more than 1,000 members in this rapidly expanding Club, and it is not necessary to be a Volvo owner to join. Yearly dues: $4.80.

Volvo Western Distributing Co., Inc.
1955 190th Street
Torrance, California 90501

Service manuals.

VW Enthusiast Association
P.O. Box 3571
Wilmington
North Carolina 28401

Operated by Kaslaw Enterprises and designed as a buyers' service to Volkswagen owners east of the Mississippi. A full line of brand name accessories and repair parts is available. A monthly newsletter *VEA Members Talk* contains how-to-order information and a listing of new products available. Every four months a roster of members and a list of non-dealer garages specializing in VW repair is published. One time membership fee, $2.00.

Waibel Competition
Route 5, Box 683
East Main
Lakeland, Florida 33801

Competition engines and short block assemblies, machine work. Complete 265 or 283 Chev short block assemblies: base price $975.00 For 1957-64 Chev and 1956-62 Corvette rear axles are $125.00, steel strap to prevent rear end breakage on Chev, Corvette and Chevy II, $9.95. Dealers for B & M, Forged True, TRW, Lunati Cams, Crane Cams, Accel Ignition, Mr. Gasket. Competition machine work, engine balancing, and magnafluxing. Catalog, $.50.

Burton Waldron
Box C
Nottawa, Michigan 49075

Specialty is exhaust systems for cars 1925-55. Also transmission rebuilding and general parts for older cars. Send a stamped, self-addressed envelope with query.

B. Walker
17 Dainton Close
Upper Park Road
Bromley
Kent
England

Specializes in 1929-37 MG Midget, Magna, and Magnette models. Has both new and used mechanical parts and some body parts. A set of four cycle fenders for J2/F2 models is £33 (approximately $80.00). J2/F2/L2 "mottled" aluminum dashboards sell for £14.75 (approximately $35.00). Some other items available include J2/PA/PB original workshop manuals; chromed octagonal radiator caps; octagonal "apron hold-down bolts" with enameled MG crest; front and rear axles; steering boxes; bellhousings; brake sets; honeycomb radiators; carburetors; fuel pumps; J2 and P-series doors; and rear tail lights. Send international reply coupon with queries.

Walker Manufacturing Co.
1201 Michigan Boulevard
Racine, Wisconsin 53402

Replacement exhaust systems for U.S. cars and trucks. Also exhaust components for Capri, Colt, Cricket, Opel, Austin, Austin-Healey, Datsun, Fiat 850, Nash Metropolitan, MG (1956-present), Morris, Renault, Toyota, Triumph, VW and Volvo. Consult catalog at wholesale parts house.

Ian Walker Service, Ltd.
Department AE
236 Woodhouse Road
London N.12
England

Ian Walker, a name to reckon with on the British rally and racing scene, specializes in engine conversions for British Fords, Minis, Spridgets, and Lotus Twin Cams. Engines are available in various stages of tune for road, rally and racing. Individual engine performance components and exhaust systems are separately available. Reconditioned performance engines and short block assemblies can be had. Precision machine shop services available include cylinder reboring, crank regrinding, dynamic and static balancing, cam reprofiling, line boring, and other services. Formula car preparation and the sale of suitable engines is another Walker specialty. Free literature.

Wallfrin Industries, Inc.
1535 Hart Place
Brooklyn, New York 11224

Goodies, tools, cosmetic items, chemicals and quartz iodine lights. Products include auto top carriers in many models, including one for Volkswagen, and special carriers for surfboards and skis; auto top carrier accessories including octopus tie downs; door guards; tape striping kits; wood grain vinyl interior kits; auto paint; amber lenses and red, blue, green, purple or amber bulb dyes; tire paint; coolant overflow kits; decals and emblems; driving lamps; burglar alarm kits; AM or FM car radios; mono to stereo converters; 6- to 12-volt boosters; stereo speakers in various models; stereo fader control kits; stereo slide-out with lock and universal plug; rubber spring supporters; muffler hose and upholstery repair tape; tire gauges; chrome wheel dust caps and lug nuts; compasses and auto thermometers; auto auto clothing hangers; steering wheel covers—including a hi-pile Acrilan model; rear deck mats in "jungletone," "shaggy," or "stars and stripes"; battery, coolant and voltage testers; battery service tools; spark plug and ignition tools; oil change and filter tools; brake service tools; many gas can models; and tow rope. Order through your wholesaler.

Roger Ward Enterprises
1115 Chestnut Street
Camden, New Jersey 08103

Nylon and Polyester tires in most popular sizes. Free literature.

George Warner
P.O. Box 825
Port Hueneme
California 93041

Owners' manuals, service manuals, and wiring diagrams for Packard, Chevrolet, and Buick. Free lists.

Warn Industries
18601 Pacific Highway South
Seattle, Washington 98188

Off-road and 4WD accessories including free-wheeling hubs and winches. Warn's new Positrac limited slip differential unit to fit 2 and 4WD pickups and utility vehicles, comes with installation instructions. Free-wheeling hubs are available in both manual and automatic locking models for most 4WD vehicles. The Warn line-up of winches includes an electric Miniwinch ($189.00), larger electric winches, and PTO models. Other products made by Warn include a small utility hoist with 1,500 pound lifting capacity for pickup trucks ($395.00), catalytic heaters, mechanical and electronic back-up alarms, portable gasoline winches with a 1 hp 2-cycle engine, and automatic gravity actuated back-up alarms. Free literature.

Warn Model 800G portable gasoline winch

Warren Enterprises
Box 563
Skokie, Illinois 60076

Sells 150,000 candlepower sealed beam units for 4-light headlight systems. Price is $11.95 a pair. Lights are not approved in all states. Free literature.

The Motorized Carriage. Way back when 60 mph was a speed record and Mother and Dad sped around Central Park on Sunday, scaring all the horses, any neighborhood kid could tell you that the bank president owned a Duryea, and the no-good racketeer down the block rode around with his blond girlfriend in an Apperson Jackrabbit. "Gee, Mister, I bet it cost a thousand dollars?"

1. 1902 "Curved Dash" Oldsmobile. The first American car in mass production. The "merry Oldsmobile" featured a 7 hp engine, tiller steering, and 28″ wooden wheels.

2. 1904 Orient. The Orient "Buckboard" was as primitive as the name implied, and one of the first economy cars on the market.

3. 1905 Franklin. This was the early precursor of a distinguished line of American autos which featured air-cooled engines and above-average engineering. The H.H. Franklin Co. continued producing cars until the Depression finally took its toll.

1.

2.

3.

4. 1906 Cadillac "Tulip" Roadster. The "Tulip" roadster, with a rear engine and less horsepower than a 2CV Citroen has today, sold for all of $800, complete with leather top.

5. 1906 REO. Ransom E. Olds was a founder of the American motorcar industry, and today his name is perpetuated by the Oldsmobile. But Ransom had financial problems which caused him to leave the budding Olds Corp. and begin manufacturing cars with the REO nameplate.

6. 1908 Oakland. In the year General Motors was formed, one of the mainstays of their line was the reliable 4-cylinder Oakland, later to become the Pontiac.

4.

5.

6.

7. 1909 Sears. Yes, there was a Sears automobile, and it sold quite well in those far-gone days.

8. 1909 Stanley Runabout. The Stanley brothers, F.E. and F.O., produced a steamer that was quite competitive with the gasoline-engined cars of its day. Stanley Steamers, with Fred Marriott at the helm, held the world's speed record for a time.

9. 1906 White. The White was also a steamer, and White cars and trucks had a fine reputation in their day.

7.

8.

9.

10. 1907 Apperson Jackrabbit. Apperson was a successful manufacturer of both racing cars and touring limousines. This example is from Henry Austin Clark's Long Island Automotive Museum.

11. 1909 Hupmobile. The Hupmobile was a medium-priced touring car, aimed squarely at the intermediate family-car market. This Mercerlike roadster is a rarity.

12. 1913 White Touring. White steamers continued in production for a good many years and rivaled Stanley and Doble in the excellence of their engineering. Today, they still fetch a premium price.

WASO Ltd. Whiteway Road Queenborough Sheerness Kent ME1 5EQ England	Burglar alarm systems, locking gas caps, emergency brake locks, roof racks and steering locks designed to fit most British and continental cars. Free information.
Waterman Racing Engines 1939 West Artesia Boulevard Gardena, California 90247	Sells complete Chrysler Hemi engines, short blocks, blueprinted racing blocks, cranks and crankshaft assemblies, stroker pistons, aluminum rods and main caps, oil pans, complete high-pressure oil systems, head assemblies, valve train gear, rocker stand assemblies, solid copper head gaskets, valley covers, and superchargers. Some components available for small and large block Chevy engines as well as for the 392, 417 and 426 Chrysler engines. A complete ready to run 484 cu. in. blown fuel Hemi engine is $6,700.00. Stroker 426 short blocks are $3,294.54. Race-ready 426 blocks with aluminum main caps go for $720.00, and complete 426 blown fuel heads are $925.00. Free information.
Watervliet Plating Co. 911 11th Street Watervliet, New York 12189	Custom plating in nickel or chrome for any car or part. Write for estimate or ship parts and company will call with estimate.
Watervliet Tool Co. 413 North Pearl Albany, New York 12201	Lifting equipment for the professional or home mechanic. Hydraulic floor jacks range from a portable mini model with 1¼ ton capacity to big 20-ton models for garage use. Also makes transmission jacks, jack safety stands in low and high models, air lifts, hydraulic wheel dollies, workshop presses, shop and truck cranes, hydraulic bumper jacks and small standard hydraulic jacks. Free literature.
Edward E. Watson, Jr. 5511 Remmell Avenue Baltimore, Maryland 21206	Supplies car covers and brass covering kits for all cars. Carbide tank covers are $1.75 for the round variety and $2.50 for the square kind. Other covers are for radiators, headlamps, side and tail lamps, bulb horns, windshields, speedometers, and other components. All covers are made to order. Send a stamped, self-addressed envelope with query.
H.H. Watson Co., Inc. Morris Lane East Providence Rhode Island 02914	Complete sandblasting equipment, including air compressors, for home and commercial use. Also sells industrial equipment such as steam cleaners, high-pressure washers, and hoists. Free literature.
WD-40 Company 5390 Napa Street San Diego, California 92110	Makers of WD-40 anti-corrosion lubricant for automotive and marine applications. Free literature.
Weaver Bros. 14258 Aetna Street Van Nuys, California 91401	Dry sump pumps for all Chev and Ford V-8 engines. Standard pump is 3-stage, with additional stages available. Pump can be adapted to other engines. Also sells aluminum gear belt pulleys in various sizes, and water pump and injector pump drive kits for small and large block Chevrolet engines. Free literature.

Web Accessories
P.O. Box 191
Old Bethpage
New York 11804

Racing windscreens and fiberglass body parts. Racing screens are $16.95 apiece or $29.95 the set. Fiberglass parts are for the MGA-B-C and TR-series Triumphs. Fenders have been discontinued, but rocker panels, MGA front aprons, and TR transmission covers are still available. For VWs a unique product is a fiberglass rear panel to make later Bugs look like split-windows. The panel is $19.95 and plexiglass panes to fit are $7.95 the set. There are also wide fender flares for 1955-71 Bugs ($59.95) which will cover 10½″ wide wheels. NASA hood scoops with flush air intake are available in three sizes priced from $5.95 to $13.95. Free literature.

Weber Speed Equipment
310 South Center Street
Santa Ana 37
California 92703

Performance clutches and flywheels for domestic cars plus 240Z, Datsun 510 and pickup, Vega, Pinto, Gremlin, Corvair, and VW. A Corvair aluminum flywheel/disc/pressure plate assembly is $257.00. A steel flywheel and pressure plate assembly for the Datsun 510 and pickup is $235.18. Catalog, $1.00.

T. L. Weems
Box 34665
Dallas, Texas 75234

Sells automotive literature including sales brochures, owner's manuals, shop manuals and magazines. Send a stamped, self-addressed envelope with queries.

Wells
Fond Du Lac, Wisconsin 54935

Hard parts available for most domestic cars and many foreign makes include carb rebuild kits, ignition components, PCV valves, vacuum modulators, solenoid repair kits, starter relays, ignition lock cylinders, light switches, terminal blocks, trailer connectors, voltage reducers, regulators, and other electrical components. Consult catalog at wholesale parts house.

Wells Cargo, Inc.
1503 West McNaughton Street
Elkhart, Indiana 46514

Custom-built, all-enclosed trailers for transporting antique and classic cars and racing cars. A typical 14′ tandem-axle trailer with swing-down rear door, ramps on door, winch, and pulleys to raise and lower door, is

Transporters for all antique and classic vehicles from Wells Cargo, Inc.

$1,838.30. A more elaborate 18′ model with upper half of walls lined with pegboard, 110-volt lights and outlet, 12-volt dome lights, and roof vent is $2,525.30. Trailers have electric brakes, plywood inner walls and floor, and come with hitch ball and safety chains. Storage and sleeping facilities can be built in. Free literature.

William E. Welsh 1108 Oak Grove Avenue Steubenville, Ohio 43952	Parts for postwar Jaguars, XK-120 through XK-E. Mr. Welsh is reputed to have the largest private collection of Jaguar parts in the country. Free information.
Corey Welty 1578 Terilyn San Jose, California 95122	Mr. Welty deals in replacement parts for pre-Rootes Singers. Since Singer engines and transmissions were fitted to many H.R.G.s, he is also a parts source for that marque. There is no catalog, but a postcard should bring a prompt reply.
Westberg Manufacturing Co. 3400 Westach Way Sonoma, California 95476	Electric tachometers and dash instruments, plus tune-up equipment. Westberg makes four electric gauges (pressure, temperature, amps and fuel level) for $14.80. Dash panel is $5.90 and sending units are extra. Tune-up instruments include Enginaid electronic testers, vacuum testers and an automatic transmission test kit. Free information.
Western Communications 5061 Arrow Highway Montclair, California 91763	When driving out among the sand dunes, many areas require that cars mount a flag on top of a long pole. Western Communications has a 10′ long fiberglass shaft, with a flag and light, for $24.95. Other versions of the buggy whip come in various lengths, and some can also be used as a radio antenna. Free literature.
Western Coupling Corporation Burbank, California 91502 	Sells fuel delivery components including stainless steel wire braided hose, stainless steel and aluminum hose end fittings, and tube-to-pipe adapters. Also has small and big block Chev and Chrysler tunnel rams, and universal tunnel ram systems for two dual feed carburetors. Free literature.
Western Ohio Wheels 2326 East River Road Dayton, Ohio 45439 	Wire, aluminum and mag wheels. Distributor for American, GT, U.S. Indy, Minilite, Chassis Engineering, American Magnesium, Trans American, Dayton and Dunlop wheels. Minilite, Chassis Engineering and American Mag wheels are $75.00 each in 10″x6″ size up to $200 each in 15″x10″. U.S. Indy are $32.00 in size 12″x5½″ to $70.00 for 16″x9.75″. Trans American wheels in sizes 13″x5½″, 14″x6″ and 15″x6″ are $38.00. Dunlop wires are $35.00 in size 13″x4″ up to $48.00 for 15″x5½″. Rebuilding charges are $.60 a spoke or $.75 a spoke chromed. American wheels for Porsche, size 15″x7″ are $64.00. Dayton wire wheels in cross lace or radial lace pattern are available with adapters to fit almost any car. Standard sizes are 13″x5½″, 14″x6″, 14″x7″, 15″x6″, 15″x7″, 15″x8″. Special order wheels avail up to 14″ wide and any offset or reversed rims. Also fender flares for Mini-Minor at $20.00 for a set of four, VW wheel adapters, anti-sway bars, balance weights, mag locks, racing tire valves, spacers, wheel seal, clear coat, headers, spoilers, oil coolers, roll bars. Flyer, $.25.
Westside Jeeparts 831 Wadsworth Avenue Denver, Colorado 80215	Full line of parts and accessories for 4WD vehicles. Free information.
Wheel City 7000 Schaefer Dearborn, Michigan 48126	Among the brands you can choose from at this wheel supermarket are Appliance, E-T, Cragar, American, Ansen, Keystone, Clement and styled steel O.E.M. Racing tires

available include M&H, Goodyear, Firestone, Stahl and Bridgestone. On the shelves you will also find Appliance headers, Gabriel and Hurst shocks and Ansen traction bars. Free catalog to wholesalers. Others may inquire about prices.

Wheel Repair Service of New England
176 Grove Street
Paxton, Massachusetts 01612

Rebuilds Dunlop wheels, trues and tunes wheels, does wheel balancing, and can straighten domestic and foreign disc wheels. Also will completely rebuild antique wheels, quoting price after inspection of wheels. Complete restoration costs per wheel run $100.00 and up. Prices for Dunlop wheel rebuilding run from about $34.00 up to $70.00 for some chromed wheels. Write for further information.

Bill White
1295-A6 Springdale Drive
Louisville, Kentucky 40213

Authentic Ford, Mercury, Edsel, and Lincoln automobiliana. Send a stamped, self-addressed envelope with query.

Whiteley Auto Wreckers
R.D. #1
Carmichaels
Pennsylvania 15320

Advertises "largest stock of old car parts anywhere." Both NOS and used parts for cars 1905-73. Cadillac, Packard, Auburn or you name it. Also literature, old accessories. Send a stamped, self-addressed envelope with query.

R.J. Whitney
Emily, Minnesota 56447

Has more than 2,000 parts cars dating from the middle 1930s to the present, with a few older cars from the mid-1920s in stock. Mr. Whitney writes that he does not have many convertible parts on hand since Minnesota gets cold. However, chances are good that he has the components you are looking for. Send a stamped, self-addressed envelope with queries.

J.C. Whitney & Co.
1917-19 Archer Avenue
P.O. Box 8410
Chicago, Illinois 60680

"If you don't know about the J.C. Whitney Catalog and you are a car nut, you are going to regret all the years that you lived without holding one in your hand," wrote Jean Shepherd in a recent issue of *Car and Driver*. It seems as if Whitney has everything—and the price is usually right.

Just about any mechanical part for domestic cars and most foreign cars is catalogued by Whitney. Then there are all the chrome engine doodads you'll ever want, upholstery and materials, carpets and mats, convertible tops, pickup and van items, trailer hitches, RV accessories including toilets and fridges, 'glass scoops and fenders, rebuilt engines, all kinds of dash instruments, headers, competition chassis components, tune-up equipment, air-conditioning parts and tools, gaskets for early and late-model cars, tire and body tools, hand tools, lube equipment, mucho VW accessories in a special section, dune buggy items, Jeep and off-road vehicle parts and accessories, another section of early Ford items (T, A, and V-8), parts for early Chev and some other veteran cars, Corvair items, Japanese cars parts—and so on. The Whitney Catalog is only about 170 pages, but you can spend three days reading all the fine print crammed into thousands of little boxes.

304

Want a fiberglass Jeep? Whitney will sell you a body for $249.95, front fenders at $29.99 apiece, a hood for $34.99, and a grille at $37.95. Or how about 1907-11 Buick front floor mats at $20.25? Or maybe you need a generator for your Fiat Multipla? Or taillight lenses for a Morris Minor? Or new ball joints for a Borgward Isabella? There's a reason why many car enthusiasts check the Whitney catalog first whenever a part or accessory is needed.

Price is a part of the Whitney mystique. Their prices are consistently below the dealer's list on foreign and domestic hard parts, and almost always a little less than the competition on accessories. Everything is priced at $9.99, or $19.99, or $29.95, and it's a genuine bargain. Whitney parts have the reputation of being serviceable—though the magic spark plugs and suchlike items they list should be considered as strictly for laughs.

Once you buy from Whitney and get on the mailing list, catalogs come thick and fast. Then you can look in the front pages for the items too new to index, and check up on the latest goodies. How about extra wide whitewall tires at prices of $49.99 and up? Rear step bumpers for pickup trucks at $29.98? Vacuum windshield wiper motors for 1939-56 cars and trucks for as low as $12.98? Denim seat covers for $6.95 apiece? Upholstered bucket seats at $20.65? 1954-65 VW front axle beams for $42.95? A portable electric (12-volt and 110-volt) fridge for $69.95? A 2 amp battery charger selling at $4.98? Headers for the 240Z, with smog fittings, going for $107.95? 1955-66 VW and Karmann-Ghia front stabilizer bars for $6.98? Hydraulic floor jacks with 3000 pound capacity for $79.95? Crash helmets meeting all competition specifications for $19.95? Dyno tuning kits for popular foreign cars at $11.98 to $17.98? Chrome bicycle carriers at $9.98? Model A battery hold-downs for $1.89? Air shocks for domestic cars selling for $39.95 the pair? Car radios as low as $16.98. Alloy wheels size 14″x6¾″ for $29.95? Foam-covered steering wheels priced from $7.18 to $9.44?

There's a special Whitney catalog of motorcycle accessories, and another strictly for foreign cars, but they're both excerpts from the main catalog. There is also the mysterious catalog put out by Warshawsky & Co., from a nearby address in Chicago, which turns out to be exactly the same as the Whitney Catalog, although the front pages are slightly rearranged.

J.C. Whitney & Co., I love you. And I'd love you even more if you straightened out that last order I sent you and stopped mailing it in bits and pieces. But I realize that no one is perfect. Catalog, $1.00.

Paul B. Wiesman
48 Appleton Road
Auburn, Massachusetts 01501

Shop manuals, owner's manuals, parts books and sales literature for cars 1900-72. Also photocopies of rare manuals. Stock list on computer. Send a stamped, self-addressed envelope with query.

Wilco P.O. Box 1128 Rochester, New York 14603	Racing accessories and foreign car dress-up items. Distributes Nomex clothing, Bell helmets, street and competition roll bars, Halda rally timers, Heuer timers, Stevens and Taylor dial calculators, American Racing mags, Destino steering wheels, Lucas and Cibie lights, AMCO accessories, Stelling & Hellings air filters, Beattco convertible tops, K.L.G. tune-up instruments, electric Superwinch winches, Casler and Hooker headers, Automat car carpets, Smiths instruments, Fiamm airhorns, Rupert seat belts and harnesses, Bausch and Lomb sunglasses, and Wanner grease guns. Wilco has an interesting padded seat cover with lateral support arms which fits many sports cars and small foreign sedans and costs $24.95 a seat. Other products in the line-up are metric and Whitworth hand tools, metric torque wrenches, headlamp and spotlamp stoneguards, Abarth exhausts, Koni shocks, Semperit tires, and service manuals by Bentley, Chilton, and Clymer. Catalog, $1.00.
Wild Enterprises 545 Aldo Street No. 21 Santa Clara California 95050	Formula Vee competitors should be familiar with Wild flow-tested heads, which sell for $350.00 a set and are supplied in ready-to-bolt-on condition. Company also offers competition valve jobs, fly-cutting, valve guide replacement, and Formula Vee intake manifolds. Will do flow testing on customers' heads and manifolds. Free list of services and prices.
A.D. Wills Yew Tree Cottage Little Brady Dorset England	Specializes in engine gaskets for cars from 1908 to the present; mostly English cars but some American. Also has small mechanical parts such as valves, pistons, ignition parts, generators, starters, and magnetos. Kingpin sets and tie rod ends are always in stock. Mr. Wills has owners' manuals for some British cars from 1912 to the present. Send international reply coupon with queries.
The Wills Club **(Wills Sainte Claire)** Ken Caldwell, Director 705 South Clyde Avenue Kissimmee, Florida 32741	The 78 known examples of this marque which survive are listed in The Wills Club registry and most of their owners are quarterly recipients of the club newsletter *The Gray Goose*. Parts location is the main service to members, plus expert technical advice. It is not necessary to own a Wills Sainte Claire to be a Club member. Yearly dues: $3.00.
Willys Club of America **(Willys)** c/o Ron Ladley 1117 Sydney Street Apartment D-26 Philadelphia Pennsylvania 19150	Covers all Willys vehicles 1933-63. Club has annual meeting, supplies members with original Willys sales literature, publishes bi-monthly newsletter (monthly is planned). Membership open to Willys owners only. Yearly dues: $5.00.
Willys-Overland **Jeepster Club, Inc.** **(Willys and Jeepster)** 395 Dumbarton Boulevard Cleveland, Ohio 44143	There are three official Club meets a year, and members participate in various combined events. The Club issues a monthly newsletter and keeps a membership roster. In the way of services, all requests for aid are answered as a matter of policy. Yearly dues: $5.00 per family.

The Willys-Overland-Knight Registry (Willys-Overland, Knight)
P.O. Box 4191
Dallas, Texas 75208

Holds annual meet and corporate meeting. Maintains parts locator service and extensive library of reference material with copying service for members. Also has reproduction projects for hard-to-find parts. Publications are monthly newsletter with free advertising privileges; quarterly magazine, *Starter;* and annual roster of members including geographical roster. Yearly dues: $6.00, U.S. and Canada, $7.00 overseas.

W.F. Wilson
72 Riverside Drive
Binghamton, New York 13905

Franklin and Mercedes parts. Send a stamped, self-addressed envelope with query.

Winnco, Inc.
10329 Detroit Avenue
Cleveland, Ohio 44102

This company recently took over the business of the corporation formerly known as "The Winner's Circle". They sell Nomex clothing Bell helmets, Heuer and Halda timers, Lucas and Cibie lights, Astrali steering wheels, Talbot mirrors, Stewart Warner instruments, Judson magnetos, Cosmic road wheels, Semperit tires, Raybestos and Velvetouch brake linings, Koni shocks, Stebro exhaust systems, and a selection of SCCA competition items for Spridgets and MG A/Bs. Spridget competition exhaust headers are $102.00; SU carb sets go for $95.00 exchange, and Hepolite pistons range in price from $17.95 to $36.00 each, depending upon the model. An unusual Winnco-distributed product is the A.S.T. (Aircraft Safety Tab) clip which inserts between the head of a standard hex bolt or nut and the mounting surface, permitting easy safety wiring. Catalog, $1.00

Winters Transmission Service Inc.
2819 Carlisle Avenue
York, Pennsylvania 17404

Winters' specialty is racing transmissions for street or strip. They offer modified versions of the Turbo-Hydro, Torqueflite, Ford C-4 and C-6 and Powerglide transmissions. Also available are modified torque converters with high stall speeds, manual clutch versions of the Turbo-Hydro, Torqueflite, and C-6 transmissions and high performance drivetrain components. A full competition Turbo-Hydro 400 transmission is priced at $265.00. There is also a street and strip version ($227.57), a Turbo-Hydro for Blown Fuel dragsters ($357.61), and a Voyager version for motor homes and tow vehicles ($306.52). All prices are exchange and core charges run from $100.00 to $175.00. Transmission and drivetrain components, such as modified valve bodies and heavy-duty input and output shafts, also available. Shift kits and Hurst Dual-Gate shifters are available for most applications. Other products include competition clutch discs and pressure plates, transmission shields, and trans coolers.
Catalog, $1.00.

Wire King
Box 222
North Olmsted, Ohio 44070

Electrical wire, terminals, rubber sleeves, rubber bumpers, terminal crimping and swaging tools, grommets, non-metallic auto loom, universal line connectors, stainless steel conduit, lamp sockets, terminal/junction blocks, hot feed connections, wire loom clips, and wiring clips. Wiring diagrams for cars 1917-60 are $1.00 each. Wiring harnesses are not stocked but can be custom built following the pattern of an old harness. Catalog, $1.00.

B.S. Wisniewski, Inc.
201-245 West Maple Street
Milwaukee, Wisconsin 53204

Along with keeping many mechanical parts in stock for the Model T and Model A, Wisniewski can also supply parts for all makes of old cars. Among the items they keep warehoused are pistons and rings, valves and tappets, timing gears and chains, cranks, oil and water pumps, distributors, starters, generators and brushes, fans and pulleys, bearings and gaskets, front and rear seals, exhaust manifolds, clutch components, U-joints, some transmission gears, differential gears, axle shafts, shackle sets, leaf springs, kingpins and bolts, tie rod ends, bushings, grease fittings, some steering arms, sector shafts and gears, exhaust systems, shock absorbers, wheel bearings and races, hub caps, axle nuts, wheel rims. Also on the shelves are a great variety of gaskets, many styles of cigarette lighters, older spark plugs, replacement cables for mechanical brake systems, early car grilles, emblems and other ornaments, running board step plates, bumper guards, dash switches, distributor caps, ignition switches, point sets, door and window lift handles, brass fittings, side wings, steering wheels, bulbs, light lenses, and coils. Some fiberglass body parts are available for early Fords as well as more recent cars such as Studebaker Hawks, Willys, Henry J, Checker, Corvair, T-Bird, Mustang, Falcon, VW, and others. In the literature library there are a good many original owners manuals, workshop manuals, and parts lists for antique and special-interest cars. General antique and classic parts catalog, $1.10; Model A catalog, $.50.

Andrew Wittenborn
152 Mountain Road
Pleasantville
New York 10570

NOS and used 1935-55 Chrysler product parts, mostly mechanical. Also 1930-33 Franklin parts. Mr. Wittenborn will also take photos of antique cars, in either black and white or color, at reasonable prices. Send a stamped, self-addressed envelope with query.

WIX Corporation
P.O. Box 1967
1301 East Ozark Avenue
Gastonia
North Carolina 28052

Oil, air and gas filters for most domestic and American cars. Also makes auto transmission filters, vacuum modulators, filter adapter kits, oil filter wrenches, flexible oil lines and suction pumps for filling or draining differentials and transmissions. Catalog available only to jobbers.

M. Wolf
Box 275
Chatsworth, California 91311

Sells the well known Curta mechanical calculator used so often by rallyists. Calculator comes in two models at $125.00 and $165.00, depending upon digital capacity. Free literature.

Wolseley Register
(1895-1947 Wolseleys, excluding Hornet Specials)
c/o Robert S. Burrows
17 Hills Avenue
Cambridge CBI 4UY
England

The Wolseley Register sponsors an annual rally and publishes a frequent newsletter. Parts location and technical advice are offered through the newsletter. Yearly dues: $2.50.

Wolverine Gear and Parts
Osseo, Michigan 49266

Engine performance parts for most American engines. Carries camshafts, bearings, chrome moly push rods, solid tappets and hydraulic racing tappets, heavy duty aluminum valve spring retainers, high-tension valve springs, Teflon valve stem oil seals, heat-treated split valve locks, high volume oil pumps, screw-in rocker arm studs, locking rocker arm adjusters, head bolt washers, heavy duty timing chain and sprocket sets, and ring gear spacers. Also has valves for high performance Chevrolet engines and adjustable rocker arms for Chrysler Corporation cars. Free information.

Peter Wood
Westwood
Church Street
Twyford
Buckinghamshire
England

Mr. Wood specializes in mechanical and body parts for MGs, particularly MG A and MG A Twin Cam models. In stock are all mechanical and body parts, as well as many repro body parts in fiberglass, made from Mr. Wood's own molds. Steel and alloy body panels are produced as well. In addition, Mr. Wood stocks mechanical and some body parts for all T-MGs and parts for the MG B, MG C, MG Magnette, and other models. Having been in business since before 1930, Mr. Wood has accumulated a considerable number of spare parts for other British cars, 1920 to date. Send international reply coupon with queries.

The W.P.C. Club
(All Chrysler Products)
17916 Trenton Drive
Castro Valley
California 94546

This Club, named after Walter P. Chrysler, has an annual meeting, a car meet, and sponsors two classes in the Silverado Concours each year. The seven Club regions hold monthly meetings and sponsor tours. The Club maintains a roster of technical advisers to advise members on restorations. The *W.P.C. News,* published monthly, carries technical articles, historical information, and has a large swap mart section. Membership dues: $5.00 per year U.S.; and $6.00 foreign.

WREP Industries, Ltd.
2965 Landwehr Road
Northbrook, Illinois 60062

The *Hard Core Racers' Catalog* published by WREP lists all types of hardware, tools, and raw materials for the racer/mechanic. Items available include Moon fuel blocks, tubeless tire valves, air check valves, swing check valves, hood pin kits, remote oil filter mounts, leather hood straps, VHT wheel seal, in-line gas filters, fuel pressure gauges, high-grade metric and SAE fasteners, aircraft jamb nuts, Avdel Ball-Lok quick release pins, Avex blind rivets, Dzus fasteners, Heim rod ends, Rajah terminals, silicone ignition wire, Al Ray distributor terminals, Loctite products, Permatex and Gasgacinch gasket materials, Devcon F aluminum filled epoxy compound, Devcon Flexane urethane and primer, fiberglass repair kits and body filler, epoxy paint, Meguiar wax, Met-L-Chek flaw-testing material, welding supplies, roll bar kits for do-it-yourselfers, Nomex clothing and Bell helmets, Rupert safety restraints, Heli-Coil thread inserts, drill bits, Aeroquip teflon hose, "super-gem" hose ends, metric brake line adapters, British thread swivel hose ends, suspension plugs, tie-down belts, VW dry sump pumps and Varley batteries. A number of Formula Ford parts are kept in stock including Hewland gear wheels ($34.75 each), rubber doughnuts ($16.00), engine gaskets, bearings, pistons and rings, blueprinted Cortina GT crankshafts ($165.00), Gilmer belts and drives, F/F dry sump pumps and pans, Weber carb rebuild kits, and competition Echlin points. Also listed are a number of tools for the race mechanic including safety-wire pliers, Champion spark plug viewers and Moon tire durometers. Free literature.

Ed Wright
16 Carnavan Circle
Springfield
Massachusetts 01109

Many Ford parts, 1928-41 (mostly NOS). Also accessories such as clocks, motometers, mascots, hub-caps, wooden parts and wire wheels for other special-interest cars. Send query with a stamped, self-addressed envelope—mandatory.

The Wright Place
P.O. Box 3116
Chula Vista
California 92011

Specializes in heavy-duty chassis components for off-road VWs. Components available include spindles ($140.00), links ($52.00), tie rods ($45.00), link pins ($55.00), king pins ($20.00), rocker arm shafts, and steering quickeners (four different types, all $7.50). Free literature.

Wyatt Enterprises, Inc.
627 East Indian School Road
Phoenix, Arizona 85014

Makes the AlRay distributor terminal for high performance cars. Free literature.

The XK Club
(XK-120, XK-140 and XK-150 Jaguars)
46 Toll Bar Road
Great Boughton
Chester
Cheshire CH3 5QX
England

Jaguar XK enthusiasts should be interested in this transatlantic group which publishes a bi-monthly newsletter and can locate British parts sources. It is not necessary to own a Jaguar to belong. Yearly dues: $8.00.

Ye Olde Classic Cars
(Jerred Co.)
7515-59th Street
Summit, Illinois 60501

Not many classic Type 35 Grand Prix Bugattis around any more, unless you're Bill Harrah or someone, but now there's the inevitable 'glass repro—and for the VW chassis! The Targlia Mk V kit includes radiator shell with medallion and mesh, cycle fenders, front louvre pan and louvre set, chrome 6- and 12-volt headlights, roll windlace cockpit edge trim, motometer for radiator shell, formica dash overlay that resembles mahogany, Brooklands style plexiglass windscreens, full-size plexiglass windshield, and pre-marked plywood for dash, seats and bulkheads. The body is shipped finished in white gelcoat. Cost is $795.00, while literature and plans are $5.00. For the same prices you can also have a Porsche Spyder 550/RSK replica—a very Spyder looking replica which combines the 550 front end with the RSK rear—or the Kubelsport, a Kubelwagen replicar which is more authentic looking than VW's current "The Thing." Although literature and plans for each car cost $5.00, a flyer giving the general specs is free. Jerred was the first in the field with their Bugatti replicar, and they warn about inferior imitations.

Yesteryear T's
1055 Dudley
Lakewood, Colorado 80215

Parts and accessories for Model T Fords. Free information.

Z Club of America, Inc. **(Datsun 240Z)** 124 Getty Avenue Clifton, New Jersey 07011	Sponsors activities such as regional rallies; has list of discount parts sources for Datsun 240Z; publishes newsletter entitled *Z Club Quarterly.* Members will also receive window decal, discount accessory catalog when available. Yearly dues: $10.00.
Zelenda Machine **and Tools Corporation** 66-02 Austin Street Forest Hills, New York 11374	Special tools for Volkswagen, Porsche and Audi. Although many tools are designed for the professional, others are of interest to the home mechanic. Sockets in large metric sizes and wrenches to fit VW wheel bearings are among the most generally useful items. Also has variety of engine service tools, precision instruments, and assorted pullers, bushing drivers, etc. Write for information or consult large catalog at wholesale parts supply house.
Zenith Wire Wheel Co. 155 Kennedy Avenue Campbell, California 95008	Hand-crafted, 72-spoke, triple-chrome-plated, cross- or radial-laced wire wheels. Available for most cars other than Cadillac Eldorado, Oldsmobile Toronado and Mercedes 300 SL. Sizes are 13″x5½″, 14″x6″, 14″x7″, 14″x8″, 15″x6″, 15″x7″, 15″x8″, and 15″x10″. A full set would consist of five wheels, four adapters, four knock-offs, and a lead hammer. Sets range in price from $600.00 to $675.00. Wheels size 15″x10″ are $700.00 a set of four. Wheels and components also available separately. Free information.
Zerrecon 1549 North 51st Street Milwaukee, Wisconsin 53208	Manufactures grommet set to mount Datsun 240Z steering housing more rigidly to the framework for better steering control. Cost is $15.00 a set. Free information.
Zink Manufacturing Corporation 5622 South Boulevard Charlotte North Carolina 28210	Makers of the Zink Formula Super Vee car, with Hewland transmission and VW 127v wet sump engine, selling for $6,250.00. The Zink Formula Vee is $4,295.00 in race-ready form, or $1,495.00 for the engineless kit. The Zink kit, which is quite complete, can be assembled with hand tools, pop rivet gun, and ¼″ drill in about 40 hours of spare time. A Vee engine, developing over 50 hp, is $1,350.00. A transport trailer with brakes, lists for $450.00. Options include seat belts, shoulder harness, submarine straps, Sebring mirrors, fire extinguishers, sump extension kits and leather rimmed steering wheels. Formula Vee components and machine shop services available separately. Free literature.
Zoom Route 5, Dovesville Highway Darlington South Carolina 29532	This division of Perfection American Corporation manufactures performance gears, clutches, and flywheels. Zoom makes ring gear and pinion sets, throwout bearing assemblies with nylon retainers, Spiraluminum clutch discs, steel-backed clutch discs, clutch cover assemblies, timing sets, U-joints, steel billet flywheels and gears, and parts for GM, Ford, and Chrysler 4-speed transmissions. Free literature.
John P. (Phil) Zurbuchen **Antique Cars and Parts** Route 1 Dodge City, Kansas 67801	Parts for Ford Model T, Model A, Model B, and early Ford V-8. Send a stamped, self-addressed envelope with query.

Index

B

B

D

D

F

G

I

J

L

M

N

S

S

T

T

U

V

V

Photo Credits

Pages 20-23. 1. 1911 Mercer. Photo copyright 1950, Henry Austin Clark, Jr., Long Island Automotive Museum, Southampton, Long Island, N.Y. 2. 1929 Du Pont Speedster. Photo copyright 1963, Henry Austin Clark, Jr., Long Island Automotive Museum, Southampton, Long Island, N.Y. 3. 1913 Mercer Raceabout, Series J. Photo courtesy of Harrah's Automobile Collection, Reno, Nevada; an attraction of Harrah's Hotels and Casinos, Reno and Lake Tahoe. 4. 1922 Templar. Photo courtesy of Thompson Museum, Cleveland, Ohio. Photo by the Robert E. Burke Studios. 5. 1933 Auburn. Photo courtesy of Harrah's Automobile Collection, Reno, Nevada; an attraction of Harrah's Hotels and Casinos, Reno and Lake Tahoe. 6. 1927 Stutz Black Hawk. Photo courtesy of Harrah's Automobile Collection, Reno, Nevada; an attraction of Harrah's Hotels and Casinos, Reno and Lake Tahoe. 7. 1935 Duesenberg SSJ. Photo copyright 1971, Henry Austin Clark, Jr., Long Island Automotive Museum, Southampton, Long Island, N.Y. 8. 1937 Cord Convertible Coupe. Photo courtesy of Harrah's Automobile Collection, Reno, Nevada; an attraction of Harrah's Hotels and Casinos, Reno and Lake Tahoe.

Pages 36-37. 1. VW on Skis. Photo courtesy of Small World, Volkswagen of America, Inc., Englewood Cliffs, N.J. 2. VW "Schwimmer". Photo courtesy of Small World, Volkswagen of America, Inc., Englewood Cliffs, N.J. 3. VW Planter. Photo courtesy of Small World, Volkswagen of America, Inc., Englewood Cliffs, N.J. 4. Wooden You Like a VW? Photo courtesy of Small World, Volkswagen of America, Inc., Englewood Cliffs, N.J. 5. Are You Privy? Photo courtesy of Small World, Volkswagen of America, Inc., Englewood Cliffs, N.J.

Pages 48-49. 1. Rolls-Royce Sedanaca de Ville by H.J. Mulliner. Long Island Automotive Museum, Southampton, Long Island, N.Y. 2. 1948 Rolls-Royce Sedanaca de Ville by Saoutchick. Long Island Automotive Museum, Southampton, Long Island, N.Y. 3. Rolls-Royce Sport Touring. Long Island Automotive Museum, Southampton, Long Island, N.Y. 4. Rolls-Royce Limousine by Hooper. Long Island Automotive Museum, Southampton, Long Island, N.Y. 5. Rolls-Royce Silver Wraith by Hooper. Long Island Automotive Museum, Southampton, Long Island, N.Y. 6. Rolls-Royce Corniche Convertible. Photo courtesy of Rolls-Royce, Inc.

Pages 62-63. 1. Ferrari 166 "Inter" by Touring. Long Island Automotive Museum, Southampton, Long Island, N.Y. 2. 1953 Alfa-Romeo by Castagna. Long Island Automotive Museum, Southampton, Long Island, N.Y. 3. 1953 Alfa-Romeo by Ghia. Long Island Automotive Museum, Southampton, Long Island, N.Y. 4. 1953 Alfa-Romeo by Vignale. Long Island Automotive Museum, Southampton, Long Island, N.Y. 5. 1961 Ferrari California. Photo copyright 1966, Henry Austin Clark, Jr., Long Island Automotive Museum, Southampton, Long Island, N.Y.

Pages 76-77. 1. 1928 Mercedes SSK. Photo courtesy of Mercedes-Benz, Inc. 2. 1928 Mercedes SSK. Photo courtesy of Mercedes-Benz, Inc. 3. 1938 Mercedes 540K. Photo courtesy of the Henry Ford Museum, Detroit, Michigan. 4. 1954 2.5 Liter Grand Prix Mercedes. Photo courtesy of Mercedes-Benz, Inc. 5. 1955 Mercedes-Benz Monoposto. Photo courtesy of Mercedes-Benz, Inc. 6. 1955 Mercedes-Benz 300-SLR. Photo courtesy of Mercedes-Benz, Inc.

Pages 114-117. 1. 1933 Pierce Silver Arrow. Photo courtesy of Hurrah's Automobile Collection, Reno, Nevada; an attraction of Harrah's Hotels and Casinos, Reno and Lake Tahoe. 2. 1938 GM "Y-Job". Photo courtesy of General Motors, Detroit, Michigan. 3. 1950 GM Le Sabre. Photo courtesy of General Motors, Detroit, Michigan. 4. 1950 GM XP-300. Photo courtesy of General Motors, Detroit, Michigan. 5. 1955 Corvette Nomad. Photo courtesy of General Motors, Detroit, Michigan. 6. 1956 Chevrolet Impala Dream Car. Photo courtesy of General Motors, Detroit, Michigan. 7. 1954 GM Firebird I. Photo courtesy of General Motors, Detroit, Michigan. 8. 1956 Firebird II. Photo courtesy of General Motors, Detroit, Michigan. 9. GM Firebird III. Photo courtesy of General Motors, Detroit, Michigan. 10. 1973 Chevrolet XP 898. Photo courtesy of General Motors, Detroit, Michigan. 11. Chevrolet Astro I. Photo courtesy of General Motors, Detroit, Michigan. 12. GM Runabout. Photo courtesy of General Motors, Detroit, Michigan.

Pages 136-137. 1. 1926 Bugatti Type 35 Grand Prix. Photo copyright 1963, Henry Austin Clark, Jr., Long Island Automotive Museum, Southampton, Long Island, N.Y. 2. 1936 Bugatti Type 57 "Atlantique" Electron Coupe. Photo copyright 1971, Henry Austin Clark, Jr., Long Island Automotive Museum, Southampton, Long Island, N.Y.

Pages 192-195. 1. 1947 Kaiser. Photo courtesy of Harrah's Automobile Collection, Reno, Nevada; an attraction of Harrah's Hotels and Casinos, Reno and Lake Tahoe. 2. 1949 Ford Sedan. Photo courtesy of Ford Motor Company, Detroit, Michigan. 3. 1953 Chevrolet Corvette. Photo courtesy of General Motors, Detroit, Michigan. 4. 1950 Oldsmobile 88. Photo courtesy of General Motors, Detroit, Michigan. 5. 1955 Chevrolet Bel Air. Photo courtesy of General Motors, Detroit Michigan. 6. 1955 T-Bird. Photo courtesy of Ford Motor Company, Detroit, Michigan. 7. 1960 Nash Metropolitan. Photo copyright 1973, Henry Austin Clark Jr., Long Island Automotive Museum, Southampton, Long Island, N.Y. 8. 1956 Chrysler 300B. Photo courtesy of Chrysler Historical Collection, Chrysler Motor Corp., Detroit, Michigan.

Pages 218-219. 1. Ford's First Car. Photo courtesy of Ford Motor Company, Detroit, Michigan. 2. Model T Ford. Photo courtesy of Ford Motor Company, Detroit, Michigan. 3. Model A Ford. Photo courtesy of Ford Motor Company, Detroit, Michigan.

Pages 232-233. 1. 1949 MG TC. Photo copyright 1966, Henry Austin Clark, Jr., Long Island Automotive Museum, Southampton, Long Island, N.Y. 2. 1952 Allard J2X. Long Island Automotive Museum, Southampton, Long Island, N.Y. 3. 1954 H.R.G. Photo copyright 1967, Henry Austin Clark, Jr., Long Island Automotive Museum, Southampton, Long Island, N.Y. 4. 1952 Jaguar XK-120 Convertible. Long Island Automotive Museum, Southampton, Long Island, N.Y. 5. 1958 Austin-Healey. Long Island Automotive Museum, Southampton, Long Island, N.Y. 6. 1957 Jaguar XK-SS. Long Island Automotive Museum, Southampton, Long Island, New York.

Pages 264-265. 1. 1916 Crane-Simplex. Photo courtesy of Harrah's Automobile Collection, Reno, Nevada; an attraction of Harrah's Hotels and Casinos, Reno and Lake Tahoe. 2. 1930 Du Pont. Photo courtesy of Harrah's Automobile Collection, Reno, Nevada; an attraction of Harrah's Hotels and Casinos, Reno and Lake Tahoe. 3. 1930 Pierce-Arrow Convertible Coupe. Long Island Automotive Museum, Southampton, Long Island, N.Y. 4. 1932 Packard Twin Six. Long Island Automotive Museum, Southampton, Long Island, N.Y. 5. 1932 Marmon 16. Long Island Automotive Museum, Southampton, Long Island, N.Y. 6. 1937 Cord 812. Photo copyright 1965, Henry Austin Clark, Jr., Long Island Automotive Museum, Southampton, Long Island, N.Y.

Pages 282-283. 1. 1933 Dymaxion. Drawing courtesy of *Special-Interest Autos,* Box 196, Bennington, Vermont 05201. 2. 1935 Stout Scarab. Long Island Automotive Museum, Southampton, Long Island, N.Y. 3. Stout Scarab Interior. Long Island Automotive Museum. 4. 1938 Phantom Corsair. Photo courtesy of *Special-Interest Autos,* Box 196, Bennington, Vermont 05201. 5. 1948 Tucker. Photo courtesy of Harrah's Automobile Collection, Reno, Nevada. 6. 1948 Tasco. Long Island Automotive Museum, Southampton, Long Island, N.Y. 7. Any Car II. Photo courtesy of Manufacturers Hanover Trust Co., New York.

Pages 296-299. 1. 1902 "Curved Dash" Oldsmobile. Photo courtesy of General Motors, Detroit, Michigan. 2. 1904 Orient. Photo courtesy of the Thompson Museum, Cleveland, Ohio. 3. 1905 Franklin. Photo courtesy of the Thompson Museum. 4. 1906 Cadillac "Tulip" Roadster. Photo courtesy of Cadillac Motor Car Division of General Motors, Detroit, Michigan. 5. 1906 REO. Photo courtesy of the Thompson Museum. 6. 1908 Oakland. Photo courtesy of General Motors Corp. 7. 1909 Sears. Photo courtesy of the Thompson Museum. 8. 1909 Stanley Runabout. Photo courtesy of Harrah's Automobile Collection. 9. 1906 White. Photo courtesy of the Thompson Museum. 10. 1907 Apperson Jackrabbit. Long Island Automotive Museum. 11. 1909 Hupmobile. Photo courtesy of the Thompson Museum, Cleveland, Ohio. 12. 1913 White Touring. Photo courtesy of the Thompson Museum, Cleveland, Ohio.